The Creative Instigator's Handbook

The Creative Instigator's Handbook

A DIY GUIDE TO MAKING SOCIAL CHANGE THROUGH ART

Leanne Prain

ARSENAL PULP PRESS
VANCOUVER

THE CREATIVE INSTIGATOR'S HANDBOOK

ARSENAL PULP PRESS
Suite 202 – 211 East Georgia St.
Vancouver, BC V6A 1Z6
Canada
arsenalpulp.com

The publisher gratefully acknowledges the support of the Canada Council for the Arts and the British Columbia Arts Council for its publishing program, and the Government of Canada, and the Government of British Columbia (through the Book Publishing Tax Credit Program), for its publishing activities.

Arsenal Pulp Press acknowledges the xʷməθkʷəy̓əm (Musqueam), Sḵwx̱wú7mesh (Squamish), and səl̓ilwətaʔɬ (Tsleil-Waututh) Nations, custodians of the traditional, ancestral, and unceded territories where our office is located. We pay respect to their histories, traditions, and continuous living cultures and commit to accountability, respectful relations, and friendship.

Cover and text design by Jazmin Welch
Edited by Catharine Chen
Proofread by Alison Strobel
Indexed by Catharine Chen

Front cover photographs (top to bottom): The Spirit of the Animals Is in the Wheels, 2016, Detroit, Michigan. Photo: Doug Coombe; Significant Seams, The Quarantine Quilt Project, 2021. Photo: Jim Wileman; Tyree Guyton, *Dotty Wotty House*, The Heidelberg Project, Detroit, Michigan. Photo: The Heidelberg Project Archives; Candy Chang, *Before I Die*, 2011, New Orleans, Louisiana. Photo: Kristina Kassem.
Back cover photographs (top to bottom, left to right): Candy Chang, *Before I Die*, Bangkok, Thailand. Photo: Buddhika Network and Thai Palliative Care Society; Tyree Guyton, *Meet Me Halfway*, The Heidelberg Project, Detroit, Michigan. Photo: The Heidelberg Project Archives; Terrence Kelleman, The BE MIGHTY Project, New York, New York. Photo: Terrence Kelleman; Aram Han Sifuentes, Protest Banner Lending Library, 2019. Photo: OffThaRecord x Steer. Home Is Here: March for DACA & TPS.
Photographs appear with the permission of contributors.

Printed and bound in Canada

Library and Archives Canada Cataloguing in Publication:
Title: The creative instigator's handbook : a DIY guide to making social change through art / Leanne Prain.
Names: Prain, Leanne, author.
Identifiers: Canadiana (print) 20210334088 | Canadiana (ebook) 20210334096 | ISBN 9781551528755 (softcover) | ISBN 9781551528762 (HTML)
Subjects: LCSH: Political art. | LCSH: Arts—Political aspects. | LCSH: Arts and society. | LCSH: Artists—Political activity. | LCSH: Artists and community. | LCSH: Social action.
Classification: LCC NX180.A77 P73 2022 | DDC 700.1/03—dc23

For Alex and Ethan:

MAKE IT WONDROUS.

CONTENTS

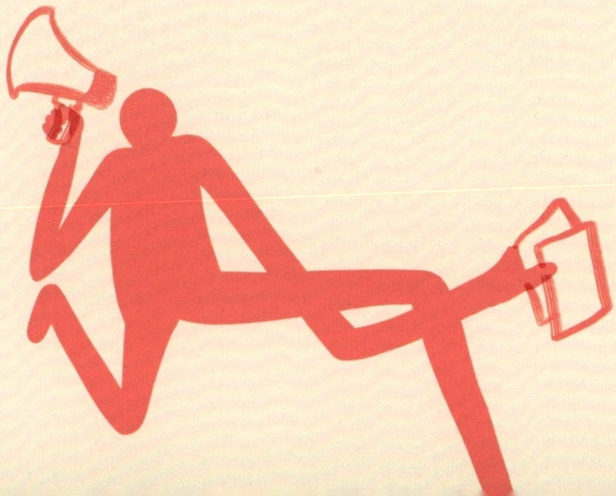

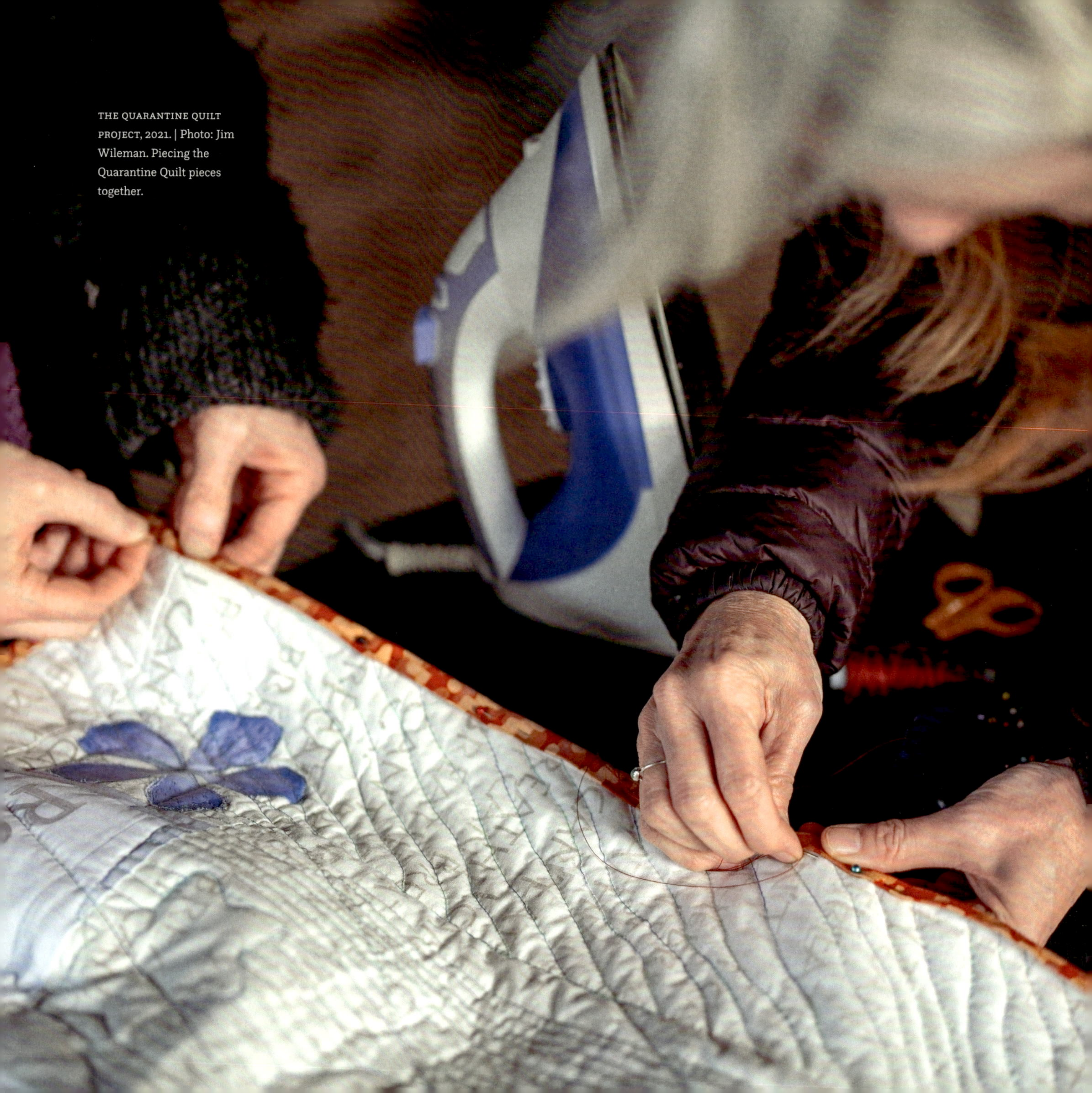

THE QUARANTINE QUILT PROJECT, 2021. | Photo: Jim Wileman. Piecing the Quarantine Quilt pieces together.

PREFACE

As a young child, I would often visit the public library where my grandmother worked. In the middle of the room was a giant red wooden sandbox filled haphazardly with picture books. Although I wasn't old enough to read, there was a magic in being able to fish out any book that I desired. Of the many books that I discovered in that sandbox, there was one with pen-and-ink illustrations that I still recall vividly forty years later.

The story was about three latchkey kids who are left home alone without adult supervision. They live in a beige house and eat bland food, and there is nothing to entertain them. One day, they discover a treasure trove of paint samples in the garage. They decide to paint the exterior of their parents' house. Suddenly the family's ordinary three-story home and bland picket fence is covered in a wild variety of paint colors: brilliant shades of orange and lemon yellow, red and purple, royal blue, and kelly green. They even go so far as to paint the family dog with spots—although that may be an embellishment of my memory.

Understandably, when our protagonists' parents return, they are upset at the children. But one by one, the neighbors come over to shower the family with compliments. By the end of this happy story, the whole block has received a colorful makeover and, of course, spirits have been lifted in the process. The children were right after all. One simple act of defiance became something bigger: the foundation for a more connected neighborhood.

I wish I could remember the title of the book. I've tried to find it since, to no avail. Still, it left an impression on me that I'll never shake: our creativity is a force to be reckoned with, and the simple act of doing something a little different can make meaning and bring people together. While in reality, just painting a house like a rainbow is not going to result in a happy neighborhood, creative work is our best fighting chance in a world of complex challenges.

Every time I scroll through my social media feeds, I see a stream of colossal art projects from all around the world. These projects may seem ubiquitous, but they aren't. It takes only a millisecond to press down your finger and "heart" such a project, but don't forget that it can take days, months, or years of time, passion, and dedication to create one. It takes actual people, in real life, with their creative intentions, to make work that changes us emotionally, socially, and intellectually.

It has been said that we are living in the most innovative age in human history, the digital renaissance. From recording podcasts in our cars to sharing adventures with a GoPro point-of-view camera, we have incredible digital tools at our fingertips to use and abuse whenever we want. And yet, despite the richness of these tools that are readily available to many of us, there is a continued resurgence of making things by hand. I think this is why the handmaking techniques of our ancestors continue to be practiced and shared in our communities, in the midst of our technology-rich lives. It is meaningful—emotionally and spiritually—to do something that is linked to our past and that can affect the present. From the person who knits in their car at the office park to the hipster blacksmiths of Williamsburg to Toronto's artist-run spaces, there is no shortage of creative capacity in our society. Whether digital or woven, wheatpasted or conceptual, when we choose to make something a little bit outside the norm, we have the opportunity to engage in acts that allow us to seek meaning, to reassure, to represent our true selves, and to connect with others.

Over my many years as an author, community arts organizer, and design professional, I've consistently observed the natural tensions that exist between art, activism, making, impact, participation, and social engagement. I conceived of the idea for this book in 2017, but it was written during the first year of the COVID-19 global pandemic, at a time when I was among the privileged who had the luxury of being shuttered at home, away from the everyday world that I had taken for granted. Writing a book during a pandemic was not in my plans, but strangely, the experience reinforced the themes that I had wanted to explore in my writing: creativity as a source of solace, connection, and activism. In this time of great tragedy, the remarkable began to occur: arts programming was celebrated online, protests occurred through digital art, and people made things together, whether it was baking bread, knitting for charity, creating protest art, attending virtual festivals, or singing sea shanties on TikTok. No matter how much the virus scared us or bent seemingly stable societal structures to reveal murky and uncomfortable truths, creative acts continue to be the salve that helps connect communities far and wide while offering hope and continuity in uncertain times.

I wrote this book for the many people I've met throughout the last decade who have something to say through their creative work, but may not be entirely sure how to say it. They might be making alone in their living rooms, unsure how to expand their practice, or they may be some of those rabble-rousers who need to find their community in order to make things happen. No matter where you are starting from, I hope you will consider these pages as a call to action: go and make that crazy, amazing idea real. The world needs you and your unruly imagination.

CHAPTER 1

CALLING ALL CREATIVE INSTIGATORS

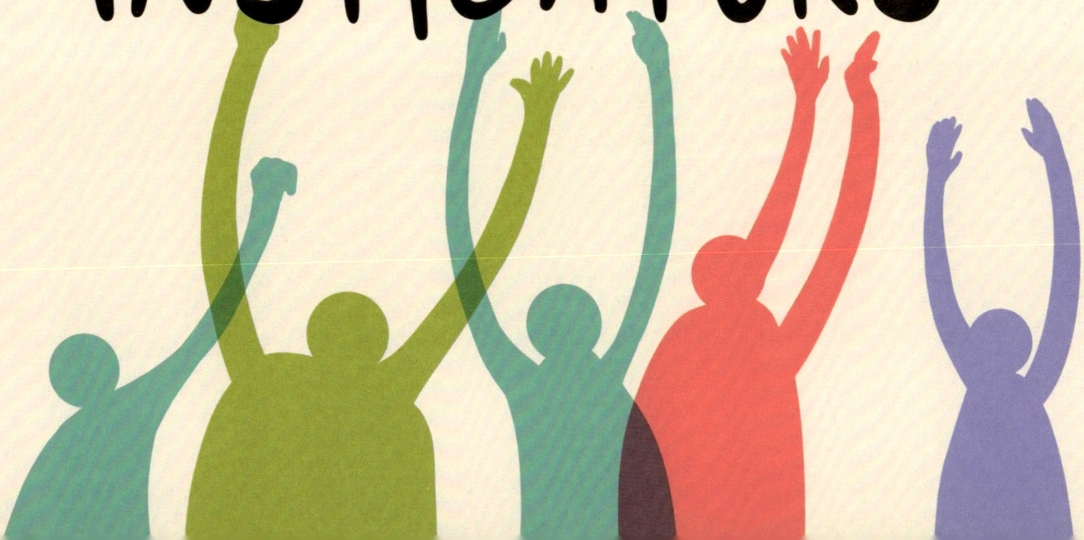

"2+2=8, create your own reality."

TYREE GUYTON

A creative instigator is someone who possesses an extraordinary skill: they've mastered the art of positive troublemaking. If you've picked up this book, I can assume two things: one, you are a creative person, and two, you have an interest in changing the world around you. I think you have what it takes to be a creative instigator.

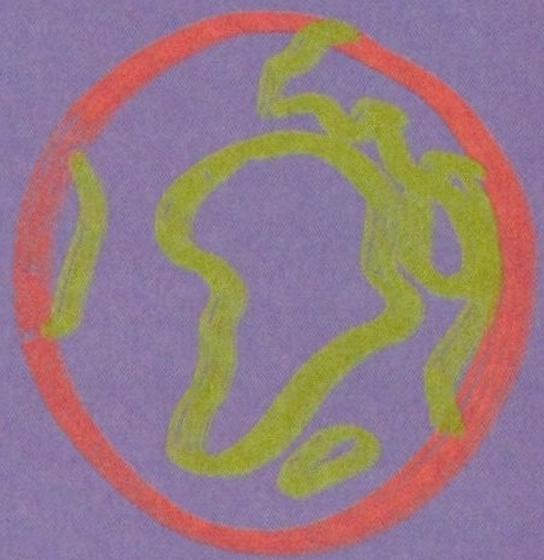

The artists, designers, activists, and other troublemakers discussed in this book all make a difference by using their creativity to connect people. Sometimes this work is participatory, inviting the public into an act of making art together, and sometimes this work is more of a collaborative effort—but common to all of those profiled is that they all strive to make an impact. The case studies in this book look at the genius, motivations, and methods of these rule-breakers, visionaries, and mad scientists. They don't always follow society's polite directions, and they are comfortable charting the unknown. I hope that their stories and advice inspire you to attempt some creative rabble-rousing of your own and to use your creativity to work with others in true, authentic connection.

Artistic troublemaking is not prescriptive. There isn't a tidy checklist of to-do items that will ensure you make an impact on the world around you. Instead, this book presents various ideas and approaches to consider. On your journey, there might be failures and moments of doubt, but I challenge you to go ahead, willingly embrace the ups and downs, and try that thing that you've been thinking about.

ART AND RESISTANCE

The year 2020 may have been the first time in human history when every person in the world was facing a common trauma—COVID-19. Each of us experienced an enormous change over a matter of weeks. The pandemic altered every aspect of human life. And it wasn't just disease that marked 2020 as a brutal year in human history; economic inequity, violence, racism, environmental destruction, fascism and nationalism, and fear-mongering and ignorance surfaced in the public consciousness. We witnessed how caring and reliable humans can be, but equally, how destructive and self-serving. The pandemic forced us to take a hard look at how our societies are built, who they benefit, and who they don't. We learned more about who we are—the good and the bad. Each and every one of us has work to do to repair society for the better.

I don't know about you, but for me, time feels more limited, and its passage significant. There are days when I ask myself, what change do I want to see during my limited time on this planet? How can I contribute to lasting change? How can I help make a society in which outrageous joy and truth-telling are part of everyone's lived experience?

Human beings have a need to come together, even when something as deadly as a virus is keeping us six feet apart. As the fight against disease, war, environmental crisis, fascism, and racism has taught us, there is strength in numbers. In times of crisis, the media looks for fixers in the form of economists, politicians, and lawmakers, but rarely does it look to artists, designers, and activists—those among us with the greatest capacity to be changemakers. Art is like the childhood game Telephone where one person interprets the story of another in their own way. Art weaves itself through human history, with one piece of work referencing what came before while also becoming something entirely new. It is a way of sharing experiences through the generations, across cultures. It exposes us to different narratives and helps communities seek to understand one another.

MAKING IS AN ACT OF HOPE

You don't need witchcraft, a sleeve of tattoos, or an MFA to be a creative person. You do, however, have to allow yourself to be vulnerable if you want to involve other people in your creativity. Being an artistic changemaker often means getting comfortable with being uncomfortable. Butterflies, nausea, a twinge of anxiety—everyone approaches the creative process differently, but for most of us, sharing your whole self involves the most dangerous of emotions: trust. Trust in yourself and trust in other people.

You don't need to paint a mural on a skyscraper (though if you are inclined, I'm not going to argue), but you should do something that stretches your creative limits and invites other people to participate.

BETSY GREER, You Are So Very Beautiful. | Photo: Cynthia Combs. Signs collected for the Baltimore drop by Mary England.

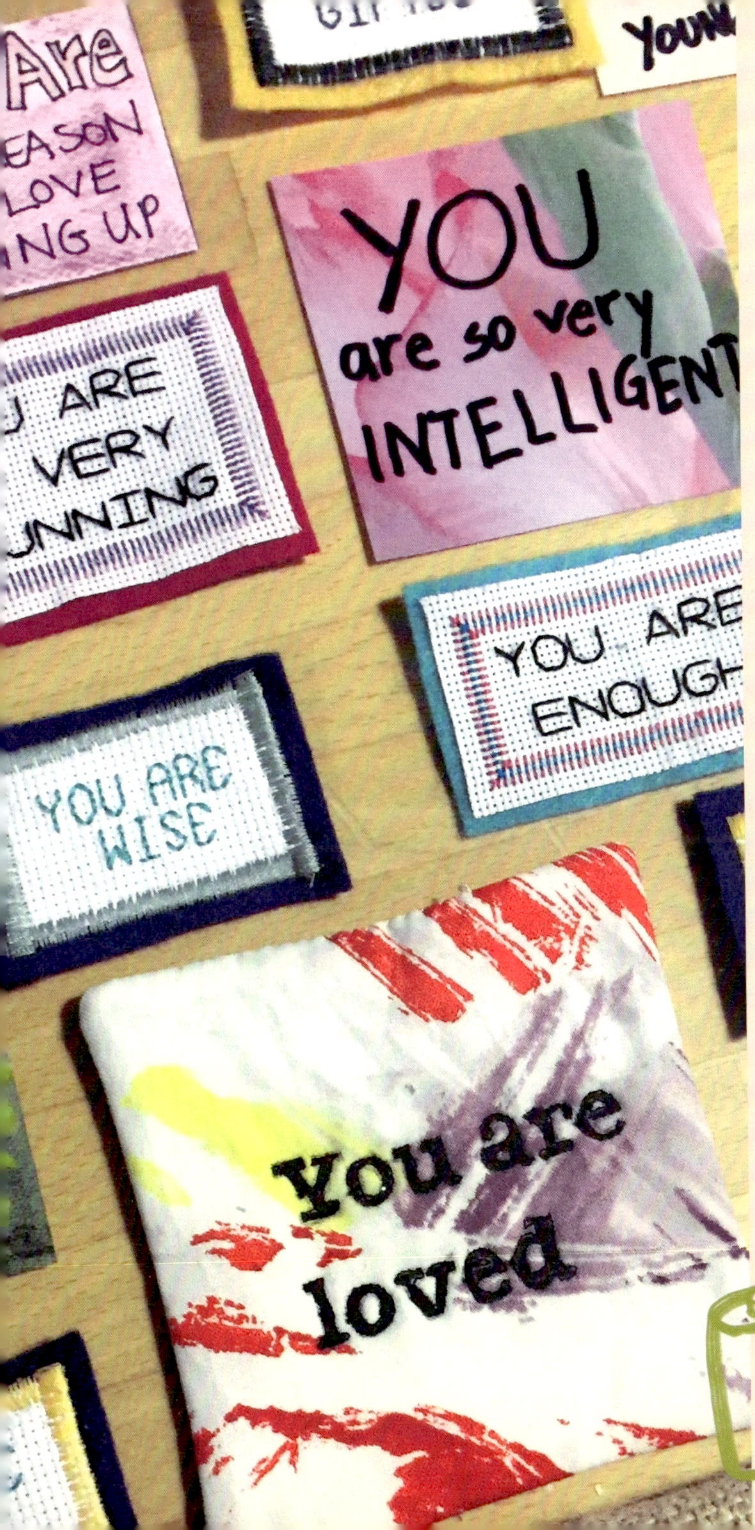

You Are So Very Beautiful

Want to participate in this project?

All it takes are four tiny things:

- **MAKE A SIGN** (no bigger than palm size, please) that contains an affirmation starting with "You are" on it. Many of them have been stitched, but feel free to get creative. People have also done things like painted rocks and made balloon roses!
- **TAG:** It's up to you if you tag it with your @social_media_handle, but please tag the back of the sign with #yasvb.
- **PLACE** the sign somewhere in your city. On a window ledge. On a bus seat. Under the edge of a flower pot. In a change machine slot. Anywhere it might be found by someone.
- **DOCUMENT!** If you have your phone or camera on you, please take a photo and either post it on social media with the hashtag #yasvb or email Betsy Greer (*betsy@craftivism.com*) the photo(s) so Betsy can share them!

To see examples of what others have done, check on the #yasvb hashtag on Instagram!

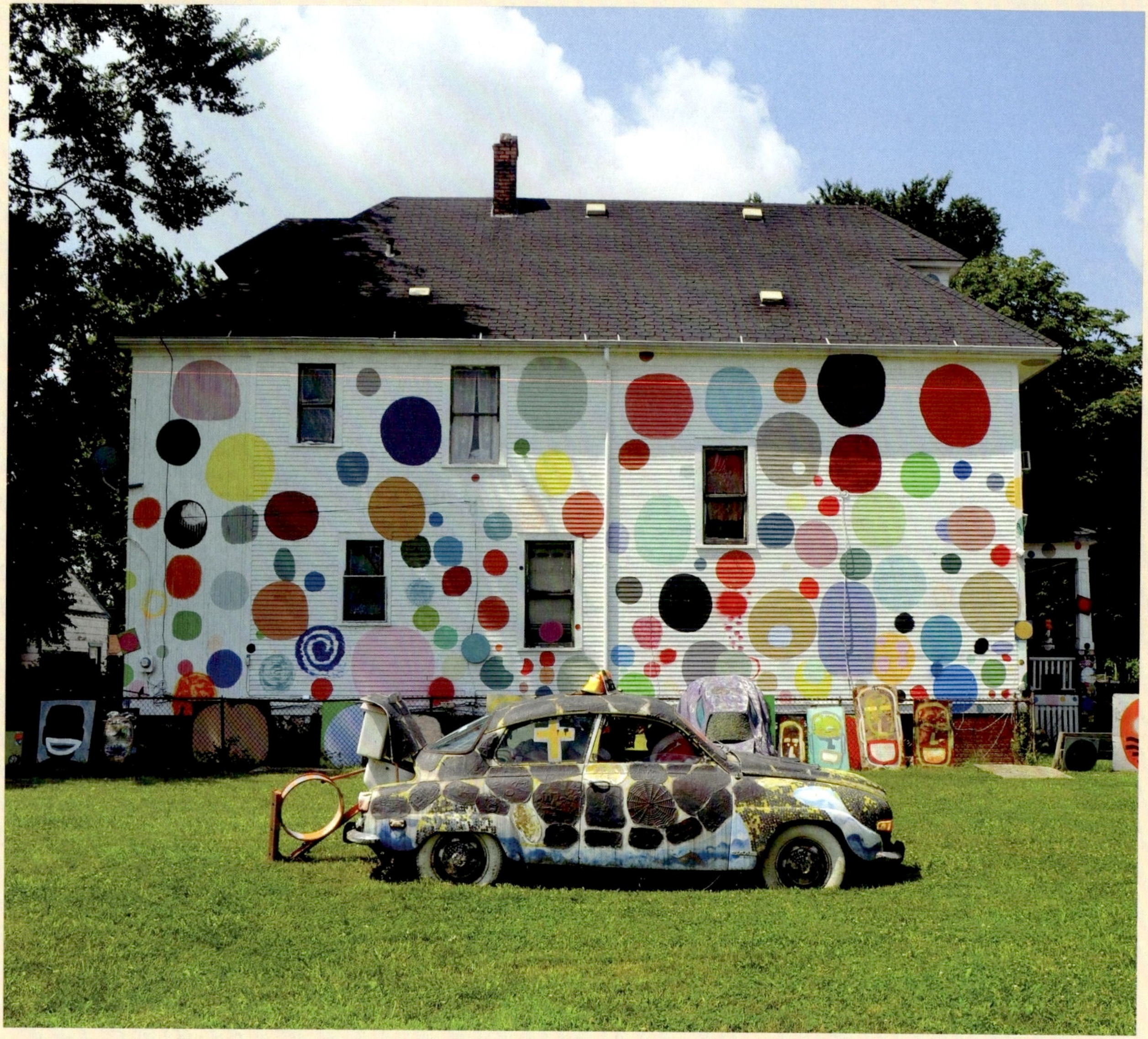

TYREE GUYTON, *Dotty Wotty House*, The Heidelberg Project, Detroit, Michigan. | Photo: The Heidelberg Project Archives

Creativity is everywhere. You might walk down a city street and watch a contemporary dance performance by aerial dancers leaning off the edge of a skyscraper. Pass through an alleyway and marvel at a mural telling the unknown history of the place where you stand. Sit in a community garden and find a wall of painted rocks. These human-made marvels are not impossible projects; people just like you started them. They realized a singular idea and worked with others toward a common goal.

Here's what a project started by a creative instigator could look like:

- A public performance in which you deliver only good news, like the New York Times Special Edition, a free newspaper of utopian news stories distributed throughout New York City by the Yes Men in 2008.
- The Get Down with the Lockdown, a Facebook group created by Christa Karlie and Steve Craik during the 2020 pandemic to highlight live music, visual arts, and the written word while bringing the "social back into social media while social distancing."
- A 300-foot-long "Black Lives Matter" mural painted by a group of fifty artists on Greenwood Avenue in Tulsa, Oklahoma, in advance of a Trump rally on Juneteenth 2020.
- A fence of knitted hearts on a commercial street to show love to those who have lost their businesses due to COVID-19, like It's Nobody's Business, a yarn bombing created by Deirdre Pinnock in Vancouver, BC.
- The You Are So Very Beautiful project launched by craftivist Betsy Greer in 2015, in which participants were invited to create a palm-sized work displaying an affirmation beginning with "You are ..." Each piece was tagged with the hashtag #yasvb before being placed somewhere out in the wild.

Often, when we encounter a complex, inspiring art project, it can seem intimidating. We might feel awe, bewilderment, even a bit of jealousy. How did they do it? It may seem impossible. Our inner monologue might sound something like this: "I could never do this because X," or "They were able to do that because of Y."

TRY THIS

Write It Down

Grab a pen and a notebook—you're going to want to write down your ideas as they develop. Keep the notebook next to your bed. Scribble down the last thing that you think about at the end of the day and any questions you have when you wake up. Doodle. Mind-map. Glue in images and found phrases. The blank page is the first place where we can dream aloud. Don't evaluate what you record; instead, focus on capturing your ideas. You'll be able to refine them later.

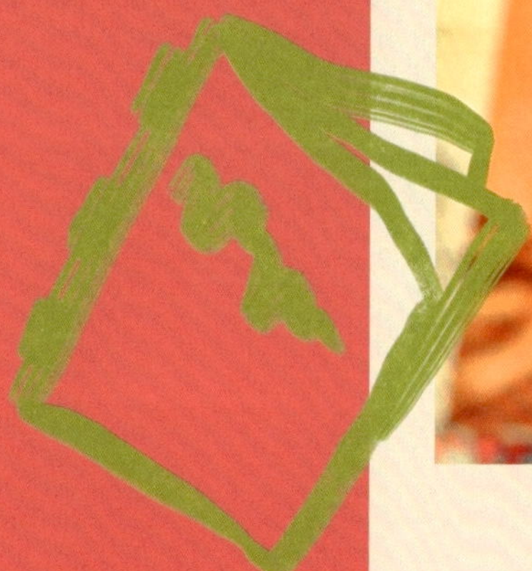

And it's true, not all of us have the same time, money, family support, fancy grants, or funding, but I believe that if you start something and see it through, you can find a way to make it real.

Artist Terrence Kelleman of the BE MIGHTY Project (see page 43), described the process of creative discovery this way: "A lot of this is feeling around in the dark—you have to figure it out. If you trust yourself and let go of the voices stopping you, it will be awesome."

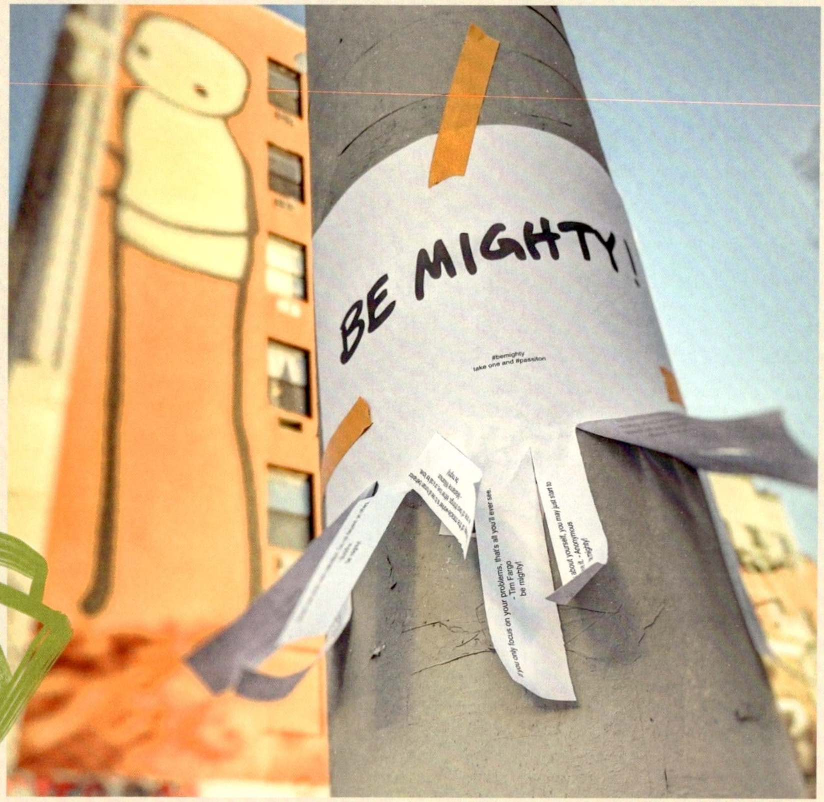

TERRENCE KELLEMAN, BE MIGHTY Project, New York, New York. | Photo: Terrence Kelleman

ART SNOBBERY ONLY HELPS ART SNOBS

When I was seventeen, I enrolled in a university art history program. During the academic year, I worked as an assistant at the university art gallery, helping out with installations and openings. Each summer between my studies, I would return to my hometown and work at a community arts council, running summer programs for kids and supporting public festivals.

The more I studied art history, reading essays about European art salons, the further away I felt from the art that I loved and interacted with in my day-to-day life. My academic readings didn't acknowledge the Indigenous art of the Pacific Northwest island where I grew up. My studies didn't celebrate the public art activities that I hosted at my job, for example, meeting hundreds of people who joined in community lantern festival workshops, all eager to make something by hand. My summer job didn't teach me why the gallery curator I worked for asked me to collect posters from the infamous UBC APEC '97 protests so we could maintain them in the university's art collection. The fact that these worlds—the gallery, the community arts council, and my formal studies—did not mix was strange to me.

The more that I formally studied art, the less accessible it seemed. Art on the page wasn't living and breathing, like the art-making that I knew—the art that got people excited, connected strangers, and changed how they interacted with one another.

I believe that art and design can belong to everyone. When art is categorized into high art versus pop culture, professional versus amateur, or outsider versus accomplished, we exclude some people and their voices. But when treated responsibly, creativity can be our common language. It enables us to exercise our dark humor and those sides of ourselves that we don't always allow to surface. It makes us meet our truths. It lets us show each other who we are without having to use words that we are scared to speak. I believe that creativity opens the door to making just about anything possible.

CASE STUDY

HOW TO MAKE EVERYTHING OUT OF ANYTHING

A CONVERSATION WITH

Thomas Dambo

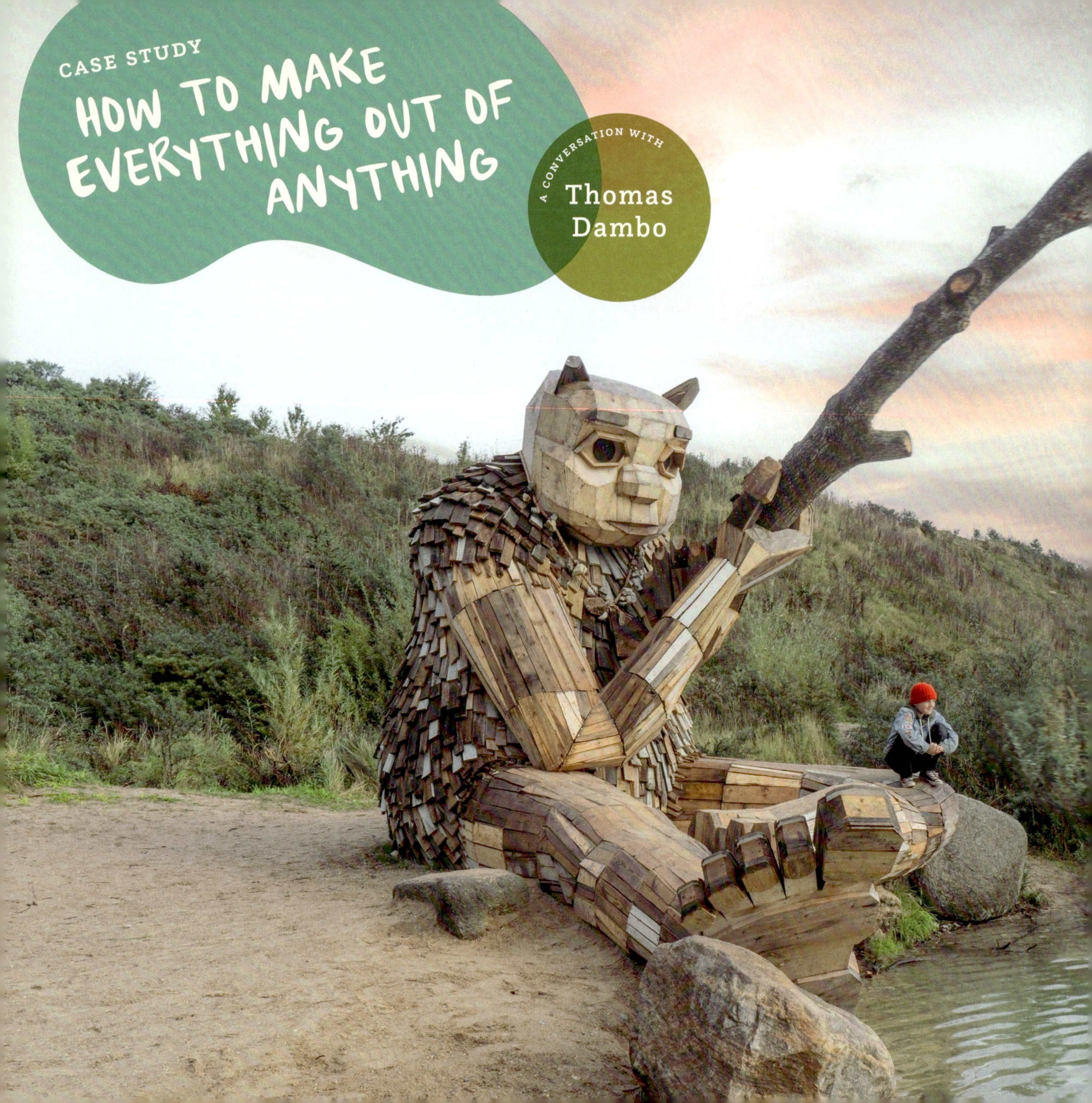

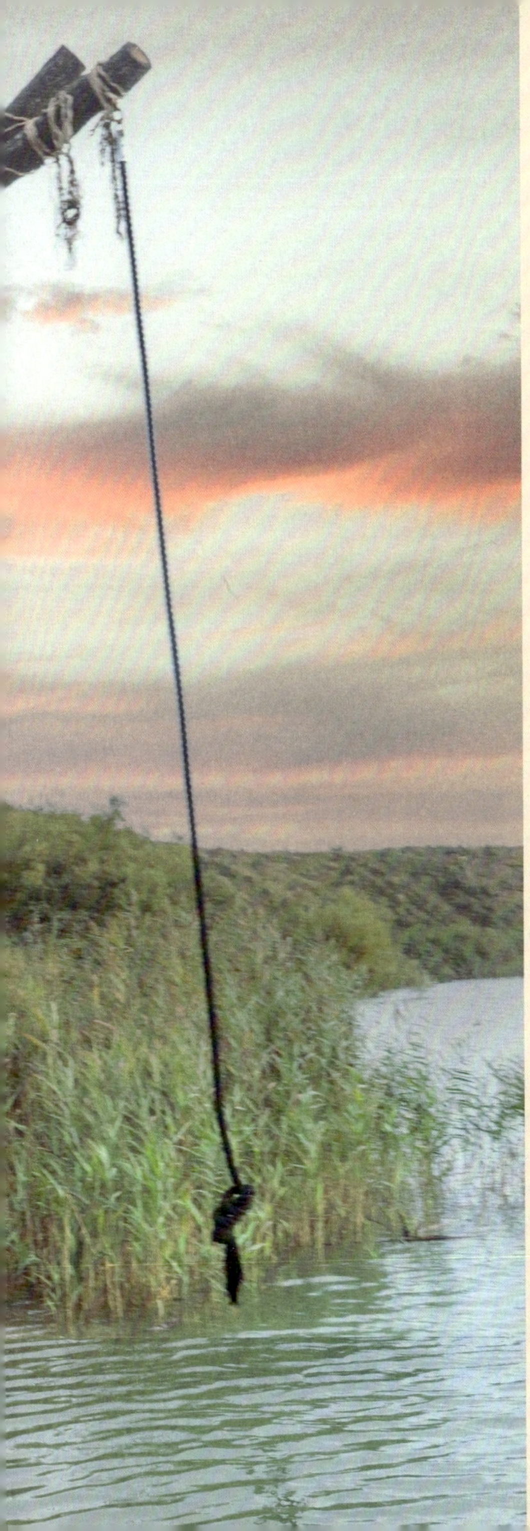

Danish artist Thomas Dambo is a recycling wunderkind; he upcycles materials, makes massive collections of birdhouses that adorn the sides of city buildings, and has built seventy-three enormous wooden trolls in locations throughout the world. We can learn from Thomas's whimsical creations and his optimism; his work demonstrates that we can inspire people to visualize a better world simply by reusing the materials around us.

LEANNE: How did you start working with recycled materials?

THOMAS: As a child, if I wanted to build something, I would just go into the trash and find whatever I needed. I would bike around the neighborhood to find things. This experience taught me that you can create a million different objects out of a broken thing. If you look at waste with the mindset of opportunity, nothing is waste.

LEANNE: How did the first troll come about?

THOMAS: I became aware that that I could find all the scrap wood I needed anywhere in the world. Mostly from shipping pallets, a type of "trash" material that I could always source.

By that time, I had made many community projects with volunteer help, and I was in the rare position of having people who wanted to help me. There are a lot of people who want to be a part of something big and crazy, but don't have the time or the daring to venture into it themselves. I had a moment of clarity: "If I can find an aesthetic that looks like it is from trash, but not too hard to build, the volunteers can help to do it."

I like that rough aesthetic of the trolls, because at large scale, you don't need to make it perfect. I tried to design the trolls in a way that the gaps and imperfections work with the sculpture, rather than against it.

THOMAS DAMBO, *Runde Rie*, Lynghøjsøerne, Roskilde. | Photo courtesy of Thomas Dambo. One of ten giant trolls in the wild across Denmark.

LEANNE: Each of your trolls has a story. You've made videos with songs and narratives for each sculpture. How does story play into your work?

THOMAS: Originally, I started out in hip-hop. I put out ten records and recorded more than a hundred songs. In writing rap, I took a storytelling approach to the lyrics. Now I tell stories because I want to show that we can create a better world with our trash and that we are producing too much trash now. I try to make that story interesting and funny. Stories about the environment can be really boring or sad. I figured that more people would listen if I put them into a fairy tale where the moral of the story is to take care of the world, rather than saying the North Pole is melting.

The story works on different levels for children and adults. Trolls come from the stories of folklore, back in the days when folklore was used to explain natural phenomena, like explaining why the moon changes and chases the sun. It's appealing to use a story. It puts perspective on our modern-day problems; we are just a little piece of time in history. My stories explain the future from the perspective of the trolls. Even though we humans have messed up the world so much, the trolls will still be here to tell the story a thousand years from now.

Last year [2020] we were supposed to go to Australia, Burning Man, and the Olympics, but everything got canceled due to the pandemic. Instead, I chose to do a project at home in Denmark. We built ten sculptures and hid them in different locations that people don't often go to. It was a big success.

LEANNE: You've said that it's important to play and to "do something a little stupid and party with trash." How do you remind people who are working with you to play and be a little bit silly?

THOMAS: The more you plan, the less you play. There is also the problem of working with trash: if you don't know which materials you will have, it's impossible to plan meticulously. You don't know if you'll end up with a

THOMAS DAMBO, *Hans Hulehånd*, Østre Dæmning, Odense. | Photo: Thomas Dambo. One of ten giant trolls in the wild across Denmark.

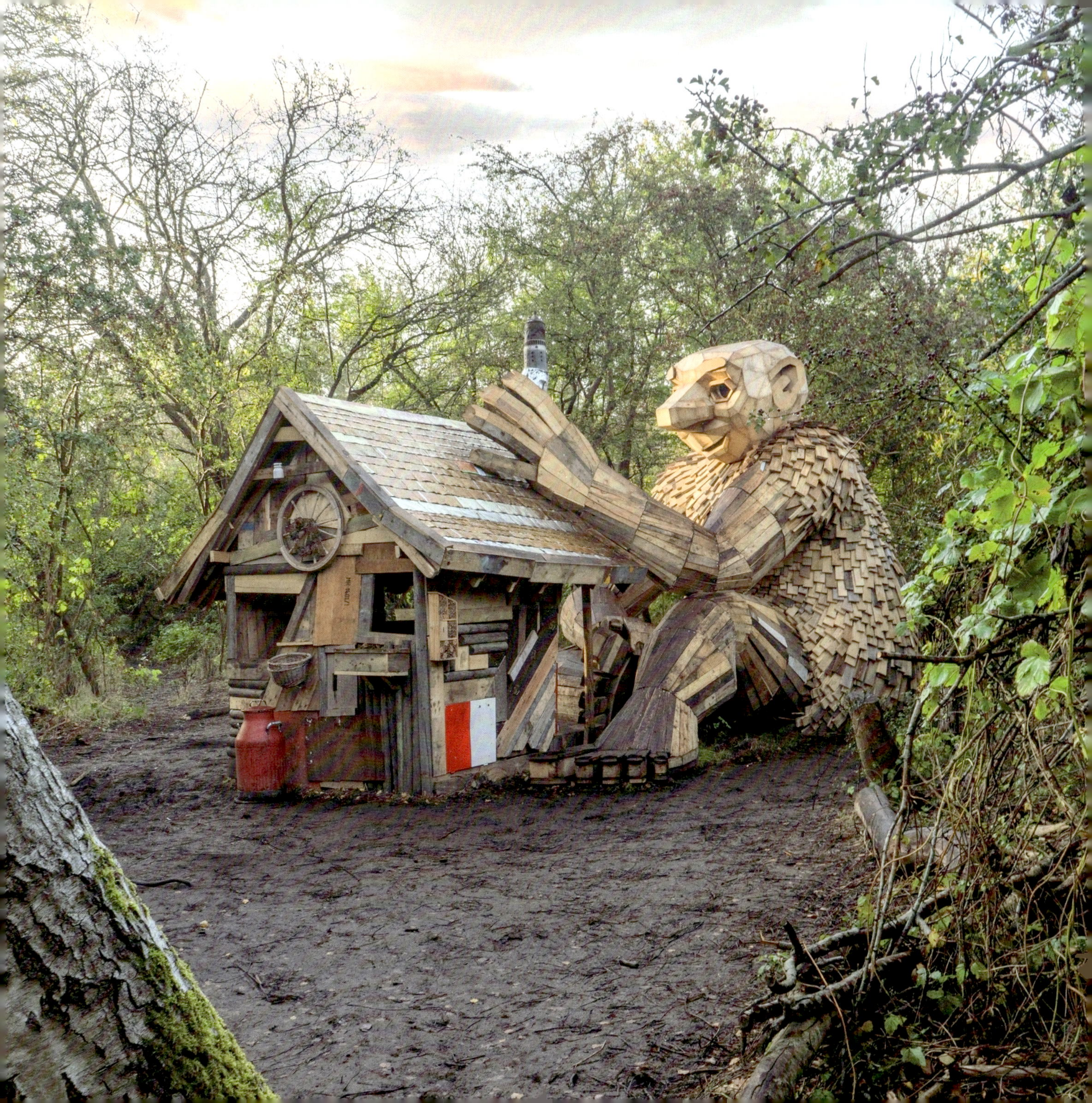

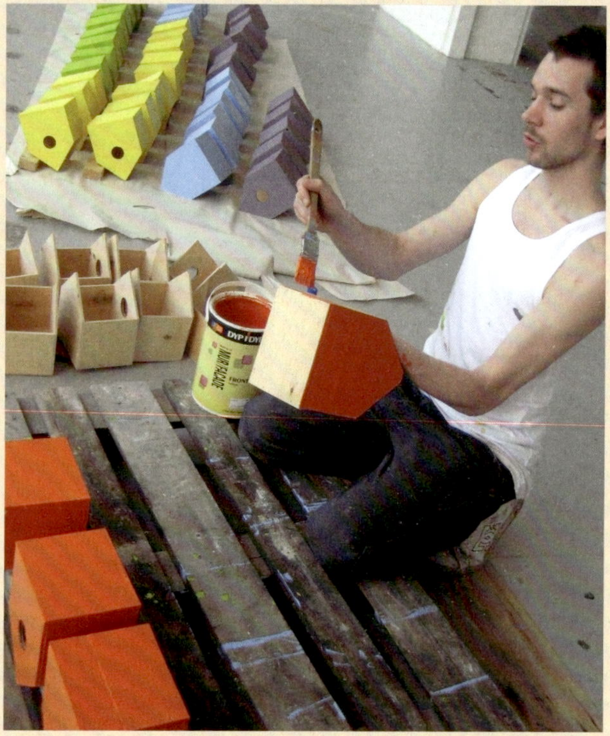

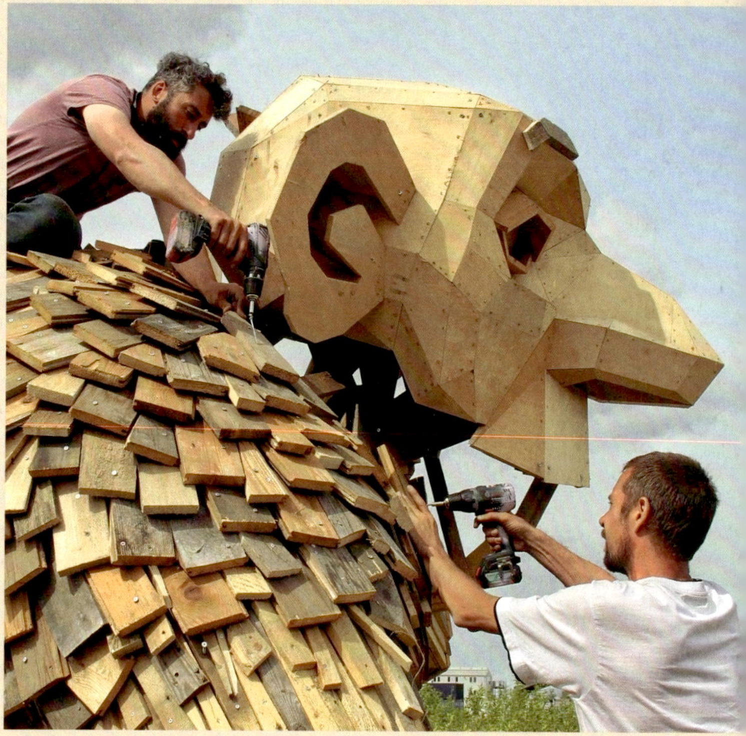

five- or eight-meter-long [sixteen- or twenty-six-foot-long] piece of wood, so you leave some of those things to chance. When you're building something like a troll, you don't have a set image that you have to live up to.

LEANNE: What advice would you give to an emerging artist?

THOMAS: In everything you do, you need to realize your own dreams.

THOMAS DAMBO *is an artist based in Copenhagen, Denmark. Together with his crew, Thomas makes beautiful and fun projects out of recycled materials found in city dumpsters. He hopes to inspire people to have fun and to think of trash as a resource.* ***thomasdambo.com | trollmap.com***

ABOVE LEFT: Photo courtesy of Thomas Dambo. Thomas painting a birdhouse as part of the Happy City Birds Project. All of the birdhouses are made from recycled materials and scrap wood. Most of the paint comes from a Danish paint company that donated a truckful of paint that was toned incorrectly.

ABOVE RIGHT: Photo courtesy of Thomas Dambo. Thomas Dambo at work.

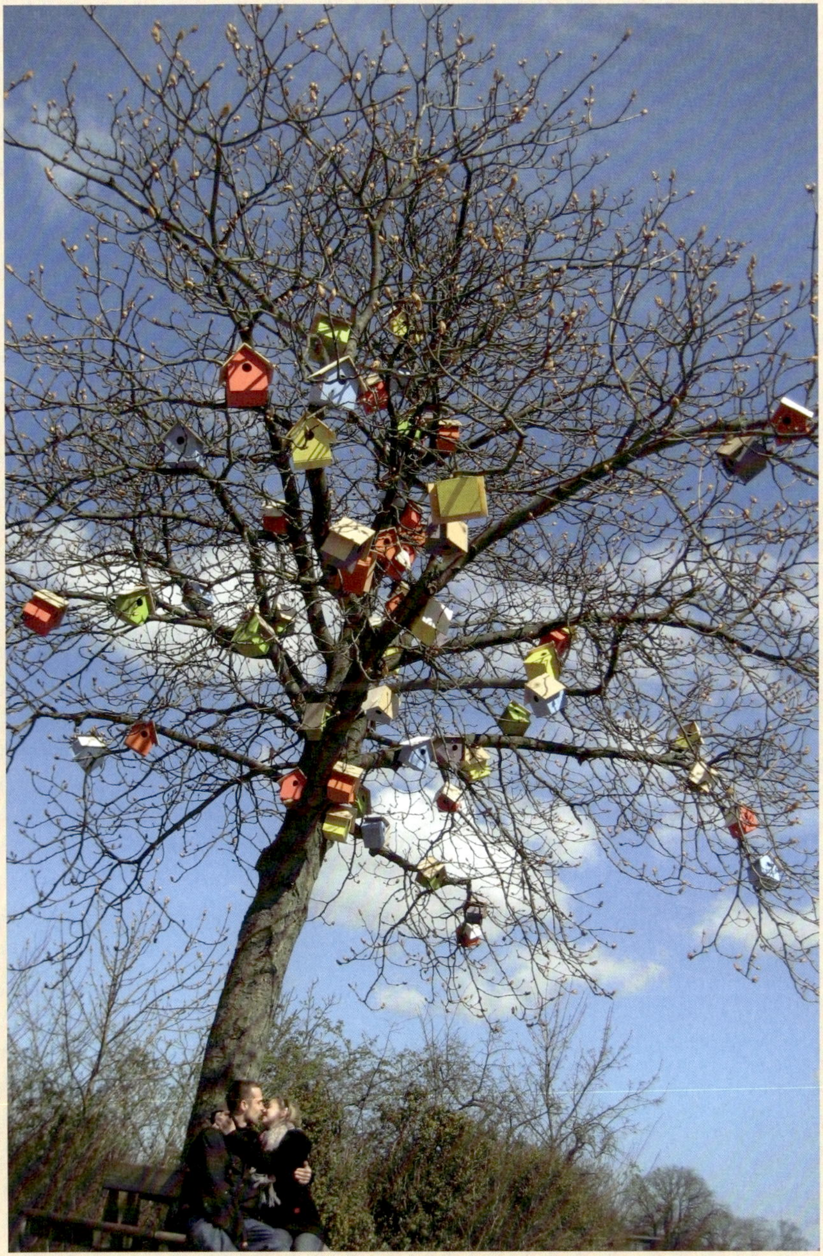

HAPPY CITY BIRDS PROJECT. | Photo courtesy of Thomas Dambo. Since 2006, Thomas has made and installed over 3,500 birdhouses, in different shapes and colors, all over the world.

AN UNRULY MANIFESTO

My manifesto for creative instigators is a haphazard one, but there are some common themes I've observed among the creative troublemakers who I interviewed for this book. Why not take some tips from them and experiment with their techniques?

JUXTAPOSE IDEAS	Mix and match different ideas until they become something new.
STRIVE TO SEE THE BIG PICTURE	Seek what must be illuminated beyond all else.
GET IT WRONG	Be open to failure and to messing things up. Know that you won't always get it right, but try it out, regardless.
BE INQUISITIVE	Question if there is a correct answer at all. You will often discover that every question has several possible answers ... or perhaps the question itself should be a different one.
MAKE OPPORTUNITIES TO CONNECT	Design and construct projects for participants, not passive observers.
SEEK CREATIVITY IN OTHERS	Our best strengths are most often discovered when we support others and help them to find their skills. Look for what people don't see in themselves and celebrate it.

BE PATIENT Meaningful work can take much longer you might think it will. Recognize that sometimes waiting is part of the process.

SHOW PERSISTENCE A creative instigator knows that sometimes a gentle but firm nudge is needed to make things happen. They must be willing to foster a plan B—or even a plan C—as required.

FOLLOW YOUR CREATIVE IMPULSES

In the following chapters of this book, I'll take you through the different stages of the creative process. You will learn about getting in touch with your best creative self, how to find an army of like-minded collaborators, how to ideate and prototype your project, and how to research your subject matter. You'll learn how to execute your project and test the waters, as well as how to make your ideas scalable and how, if you wish, to preserve them for the future.

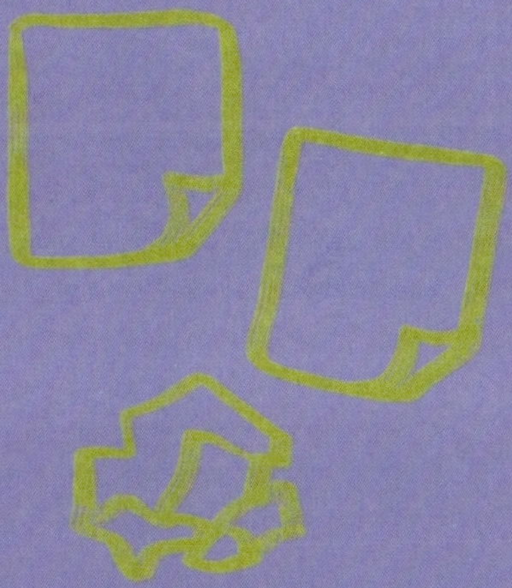

Your first project as a creative instigator could change your life, but it probably won't. I don't promise you a perfect plan, a road map, or a parachute, but I do hope this book gives the right vantage point to jump out of the plane and make a spectacular landing. Here's to dreaming outrageously, envisioning a better future, and trying out your wildest ideas. At times, our dreams are held together with Scotch tape and glue, and they may begin with just a small squiggle on an index card ... but if you continue to work on them, I genuinely believe that you can make anything happen.

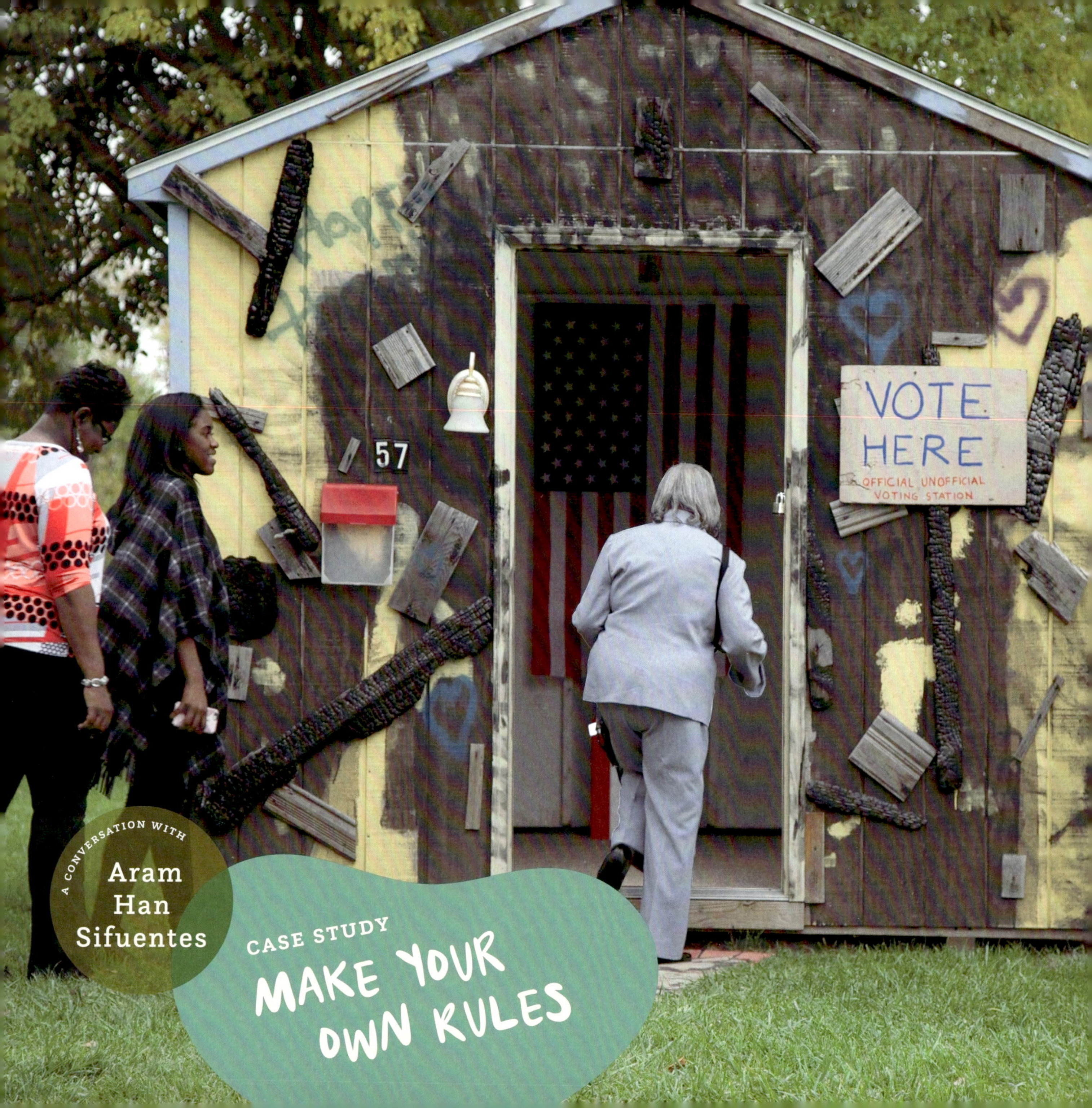

A CONVERSATION WITH

Aram Han Sifuentes

CASE STUDY

MAKE YOUR OWN RULES

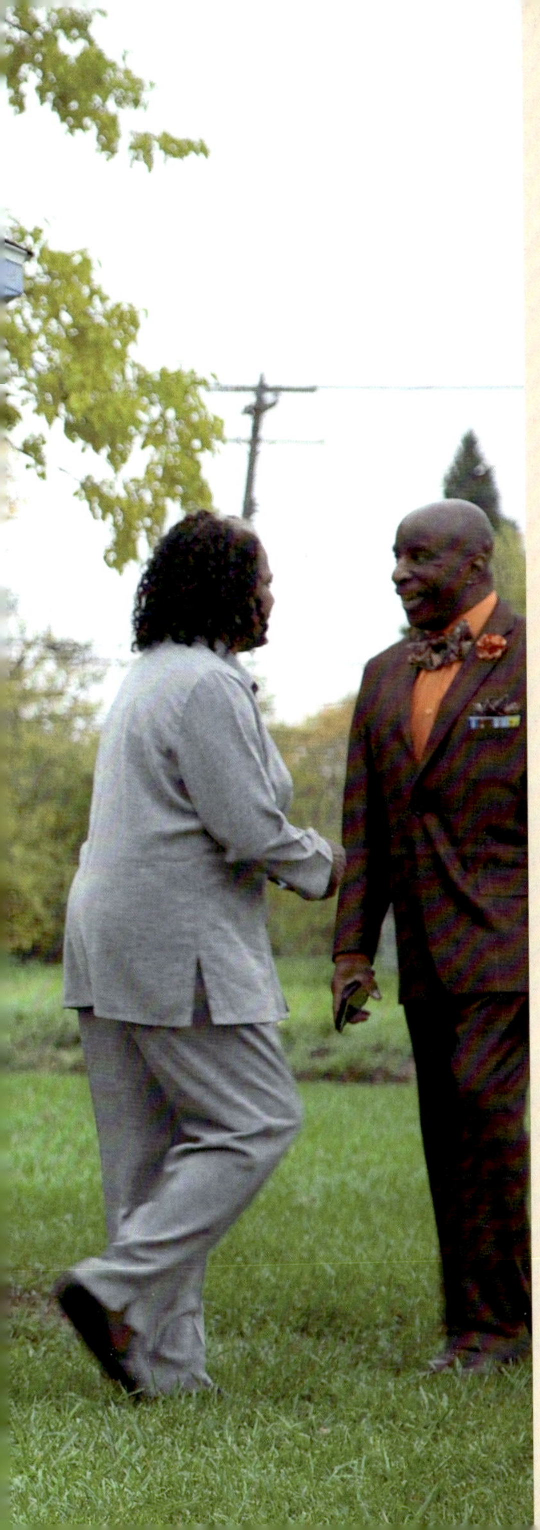

Aram Han Sifuentes is a socially engaged fiber and social practice artist, a performance artist, an arts educator, and a professor based in Chicago, Illinois. Her Protest Banner Lending Library allows anyone to borrow a protest banner for their needs, and the Official Unofficial Voting Station re-creates the experience of voting for those who do not have access. Both are examples of how artists can use their skills to rally against systemic oppression while providing important experiences for those who are excluded from legally participating in civil society. Rooted in the traditions of sewing circles and intergenerational exchange, her participatory work provides a platform of empowerment and protest to those whose voices are often silenced.

LEANNE: Why is immigration a recurring theme in your artistic practice?

ARAM: I moved to the United States from South Korea when I was five years old. As an immigrant, I saw firsthand the difficulties that my family went through when we moved to the California's Central Valley. Seeing the treatment of immigrant laborers and their lack of access to work, education, or basic human rights made me want to work toward change—both in immigration policy and in the way people talk about immigrants.

As an undergraduate, I took art classes at UC Berkeley for fun. I studied with Ehren Tool, a ceramic artist and veteran who creates cups with war imagery on them and then gives them away for free. He's given out over 22,000 cups. War can feel so far away for most people, and being able to see these images of war on a household item like a cup creates an intimate relationship. The idea is that it will create a connection to the atrocious images of war, or it will spark a conversation. His cups are a tremendously powerful gesture. I became interested in art when I could see how political it could be, so I dedicated myself to grad school at the School of the Art Institute of Chicago in fiber and material studies.

ARAM HAN SIFUENTES, *Official Unofficial Voting Station: Voting for All Who Legally Can't*, 2016. | Photo: Brandon Bullard. Activation by Brandon Bullard at the Heidelberg Project in Detroit, Michigan.

I come back to textiles-sewing practices over and over again in my work. When my parents immigrated to the United States from Korea, they were highly educated but had such difficulty finding jobs. They don't speak English well, and their education credentials didn't translate. They came here not knowing what they would do, but someone in the tiny Korean community in the Central Valley gave them part-time jobs in their dry-cleaning business. Eventually they opened up their own dry-cleaning store, which they still have today.

My mom, who is very artistic, became the store seamstress, doing all the alterations and tailoring. She was always bringing work home, even though they spent more than twelve hours a day at work. I learned how take out zippers, make buttonholes, and mend. That's why sewing is linked to my identity and very political for me. The people working jobs in the garment industry are predominantly immigrant women—and Asian American women specifically. That connection speaks to the immigrant experience, and it speaks to my immigrant experience.

In 2016, I created the Official Unofficial Voting Station, a project that made it possible for those who cannot legally vote to do so. I'm doing it again now, in 2020.

Noncitizen immigrants of color are my network, my neighbors, and my family. I like creating artworks that not only talk about the immigrant experience, but are for immigrants. When you think about the art world, it's not necessarily one that immigrants feel we have access to. These works [I create] can live inside of museum and gallery spaces, but they also exist intentionally outside of these spaces.

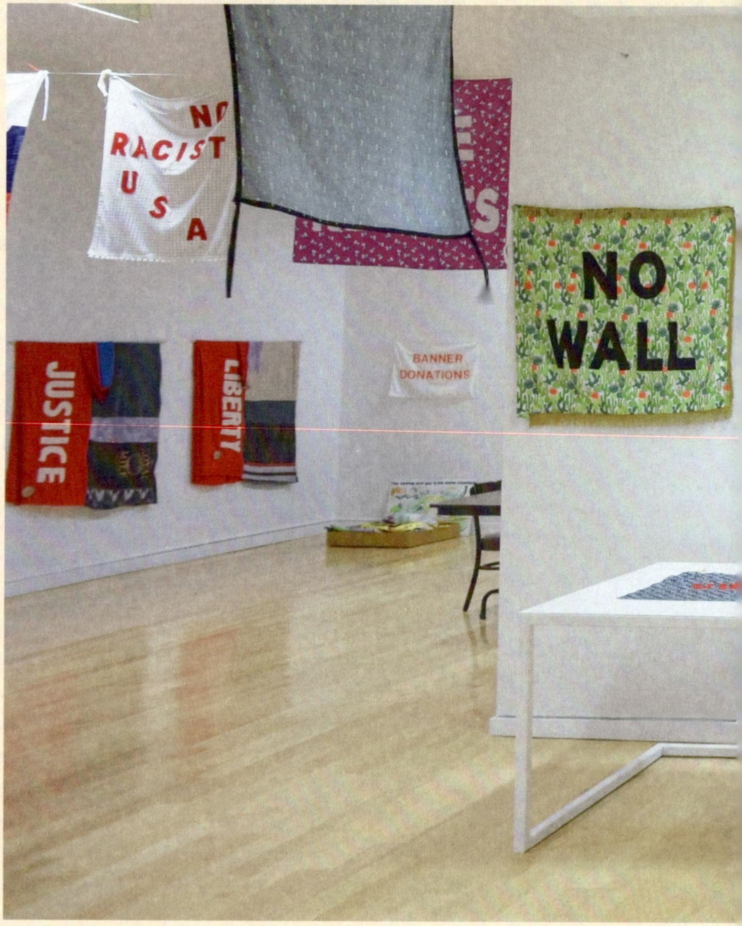

In 2016, at the Jane Addams Hull-House Museum in Chicago, I created the Official Unofficial Voting Station and some protest banners as part of this installation. With the results of the 2016 national election and the protests that erupted the next day, I continued making banners. I couldn't easily go to those protests because of my one-year-old child and my noncitizen status. It was precarious.

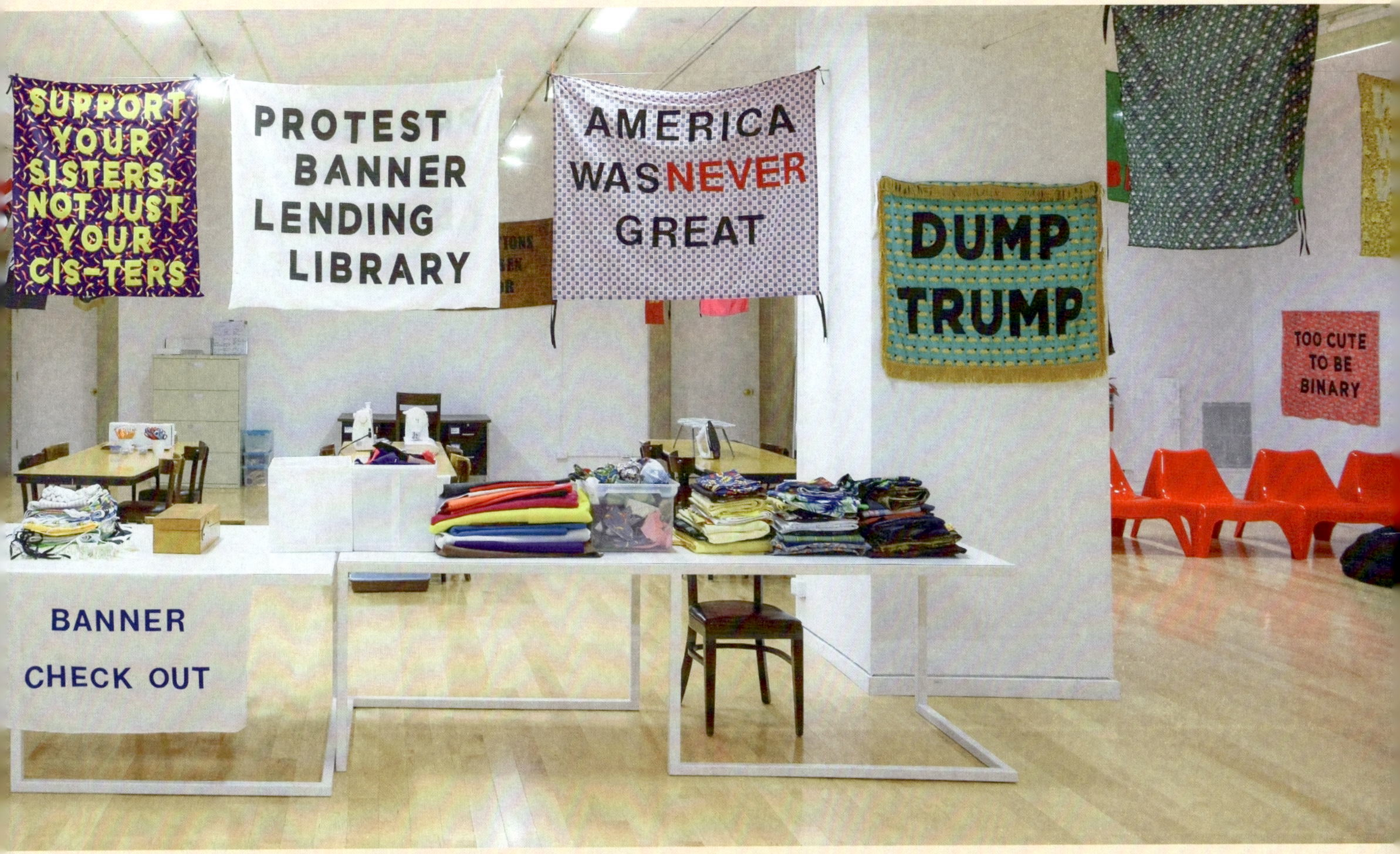

ARAM HAN SIFUENTES, Protest Banner Lending Library, 2016. | Photo: eedahahm. Installation photo from the Chicago Cultural Center, Chicago, Illinois.

I was inviting other people to make these protest banners with me. There was a moment when it was like, "Okay, we made all these banners, but who's going to take them out to that protest that's happening tomorrow?" And nobody could go, for reasons like my own: being undocumented, having small children. The way that protest often gets talked about is like, "We all have to go out in the streets and fight!" There isn't that other part of the conversation about how it's not a safe place for many people. Who gets to protest, and who can't protest? Why did we create all of these banners when no one could use them?

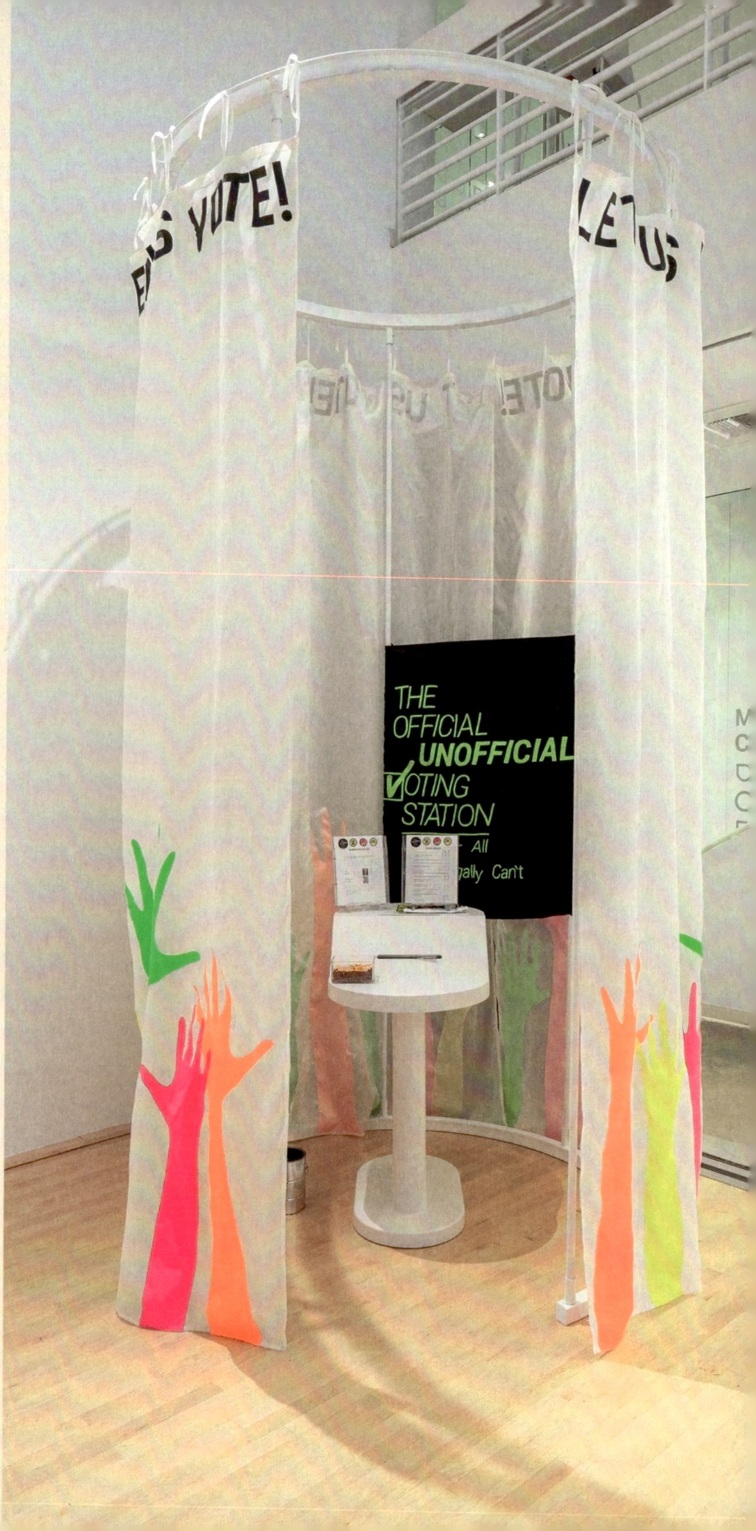

RIGHT: ARAM HAN SIFUENTES, *Official Unofficial Voting Station: Voting for All Who Legally Can't*, 2020. | Photo: Nash Baker. Moody Center for the Arts, Houston, Texas.

FAR RIGHT: ARAM HAN SIFUENTES, Protest Banner Lending Library, 2019. | Photo: OffThaRecord x Steer. Home Is Here: March for DACA & TPS.

It occurred to me that if there was a lending library of the banners, we could use them to support each other. While we did not feel safe to go out to protest, we felt a need to make these banners and slogans to express our feelings and needs. When I posted photos of the protest banners on Facebook, I heard from people who said, "How do I get one?" "I want one." "I'm going out, I need one." And so on.

Today, people using the library can check them out and carry the voices of those don't who feel safe. The project has grown and continues to be a very active lending library.

LEANNE: Tell me about the experience of bringing people together to make banners. I imagine there must be a big range of artistic skills.

ARAM: The method for making the banners is simple. I use a fusible web interface, which is like glue for fabric. If you know how to iron and cut with scissors, you can make a protest banner. The steps are very easy; it's the kind of art access where anyone can become an artist. It's accessible; you can make a protest banner, donate it to the library, and it could go in an exhibit at a museum. The workshops are a place where people can learn the steps and then teach this practice to other people, and then the project grows.

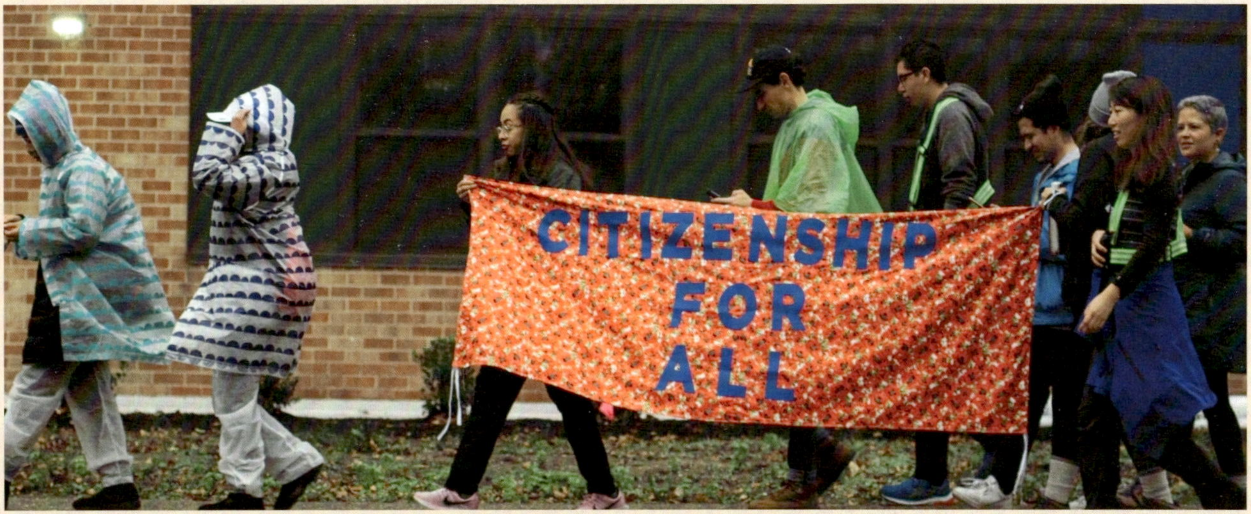

These workshops are equally—if not more—important than the final finished pieces. The environment that they create is important; we're coming together to support one another in protest. We have to recognize that coming together in this way means that everything doesn't always align politically. I have people come who make things that I don't agree with—and isn't that the point? We're supporting each other in our individual political views, and we support each other's right to protest.

LEANNE: It strikes me that you are creating a historical time capsule, whether the banners make it back to your library or not.

ARAM: The idea of use is most important to me. If someone donates their banner to the library, it is never for sale. It will live in the library and be functional. When I've done the project at different sites such as museums, it comes with the stipulation that any banners created and donated by the participants will enter that museum's collection, but they will be available to be checked out and used during the length of exhibit, or forever.

The Chicago library lives with me for the reason that it needs to be active. I catalog the banners on index cards—the person who made it, sometimes the date it was crafted, and its slogan, along with check-out and check-in dates. When borrowers return the banners, I ask them to share where it was used to compile a written history of each banner.

LEANNE: What advice would you give to someone looking to start a project that engages other people?

ARAM: I always encourage people to think about their own lived experiences. That's always a really excellent starting point. A lot of my art projects start from me just talking, drinking, and making jokes with friends. Like,

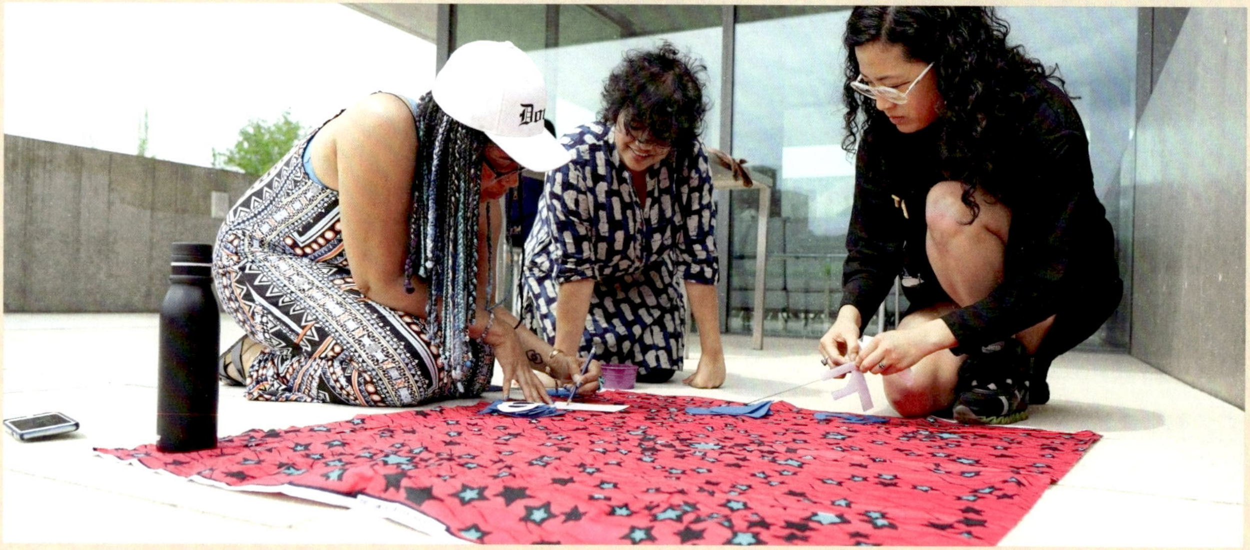

"Oh my gosh, I hate this thing. I want this thing to exist, right? Oh wait, I could just make that!" That's how the voting stations happened. I was like, "I really want to vote. How do I vote?" And then I realized, "Wait, I'm an artist and I could make voting stations for people who can't legally vote!"

If you want to see something in the world, I'm sure there's a ton of other people who also want to see it. Being silly is an excellent starting point. That's part of the joy and fun of art projects and creative practices. As an artist, I get to create the sorts of things that I want to see in the world.

ABOVE: ARAM HAN SIFUENTES, Protest Banner Lending Library. | Photo: Michael Thomas. Protest banner–making workshop at the Pulitzer Arts Foundation, St. Louis, Missouri.

ARAM HAN SIFUENTES *is a fiber and social practice artist who works to claim spaces for immigrant and disenfranchised communities. Her work often revolves around skill sharing—specifically sewing techniques—to create multi-ethnic and intergenerational sewing circles, which are a place of empowerment, subversion, and protest. Aram is a 2016 Smithsonian Artist Research Fellow, 2016 3Arts Awardee, and a 2020 MAP Fund Grantee. Her Protest Banner Lending Library was a finalist for the Beazley Design Awards at the Design Museum (London, England) in 2016. She earned her BA in Art and Latin American Studies from the University of California, Berkeley, and her MFA in Fiber and Material Studies from the School of the Art Institute of Chicago. She is currently an adjunct associate professor at the School of the Art Institute of Chicago, and the 2020–2021 Artist-in-Residence at Loyola University Chicago.* **aramhansifuentes.com**

CHAPTER 2

GET COMFORTABLE WITH YOUR CREATIVE VOICE

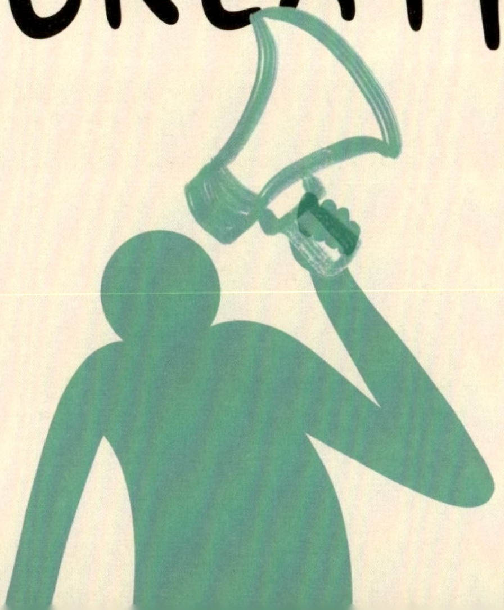

Your creative voice is your point of view as an artistic person. It reflects who you are, what you believe in, and what you have gleaned from a lifetime of discovery. Your personal politics, skinned knees, bold ambitions, quiet observations, and unusual obsessions are all wrapped up in how you express yourself. Even if you are unsure of what your creative voice is at this moment, I believe that if you consistently show up to make creative work, eventually you will find the themes that recur in the things that you make.

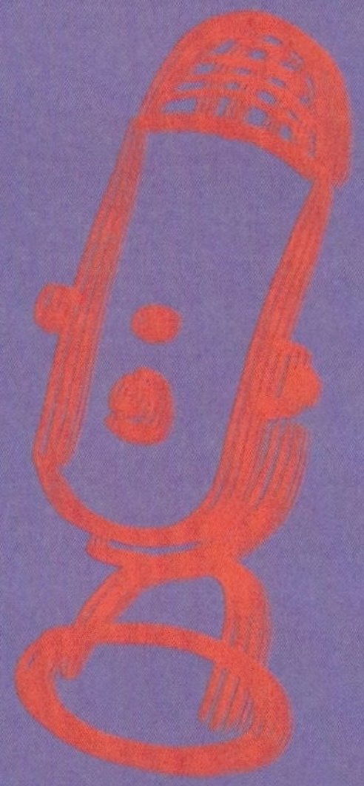

Some artists have spent a lifetime studying their craft and mastering art-making tools and processes under traditional apprenticeships or schooling. Others may have developed their drawing skills by doodling on Post-it notes at the office or making home movies with friends. However you come to the act of making creative things, be aware that everyone struggles with impostor syndrome from time to time. There is no one path to becoming a creative human. Creative style blends personal taste, acquired skill sets, given or found talent, and your unique mission.

The painter Georgia O'Keeffe once said about the act of creativity, "Whether you succeed or not is irrelevant, there is no such thing. Making your unknown known is the important thing."

BUILDING A CREATIVE PRACTICE

Whether you envision your project as an all-consuming endeavor or a side project, all creative projects require sustained focus and hard work. Maintaining a sustained focus on who you are as a creative person can be a difficult thing to achieve in your busy life, but it is essential to unpacking what it is you need to make.

A creative practice is a commitment. Simply put, it is a routine that you show up for regardless of whether you had a terrible day at work, are exhausted from changing a flat tire, or haven't gotten over a newly broken heart. A creative practice is the ultimate tool in helping you build trust and enthusiasm for your own work. You need to be your project's biggest advocate. Creative work is not only the exercise of bringing something into existence, it is also the exercise of making it exist for yourself.

Finding the time and space for focus and creativity is something that even the most experienced artists and designers contend with. Usually, they've found ways of carving out time, despite the odds. Even when we have the best intentions, we find our calendars full of necessary distractions, like dentist appointments, parent-teacher nights, grocery shopping, caretaking, homework—never mind the bigger stuff of life, such as layoffs, emergencies, births, and deaths. Commitments are part of life; amidst the ups and downs of juggling them all, you will need a strategy to build and protect your practice.

My creative practice looks like getting up early on weekday mornings and writing three pages longhand on a legal pad while I drink my first cup of coffee, before I go to my day job. I'm particular about the sheets of paper—they need to be pulled from a legal pad so they can go directly into the recycle bin. While I have a lot of fancy notebooks, there is something to be said about using materials that don't feel precious. A creative practice does not need to be fussy or complicated, but you do have to consistently show up for it.

PROMPT

What Does Your Practice Look Like?

What parts of your current routine inspire creative thinking in you? Take a few moments to jot them down. What parts help you the most? What would you like to do more of?

WHAT A SUSTAINED CREATIVE PRACTICE LOOKS LIKE

- A commitment to showing up to create regularly. For some people this is every day, for others, every week.
- The ability to experiment without the expectation of achieving something.
- A collection of inspirations—for example, a selection of Instagram accounts to follow, a scrapbook of magazine clippings, a small library of art books, or a bulletin board full of your sketches.
- A dedicated space, whether it be a desk or a closet, or an on-the-go kit that will allow you to set up your work wherever you go, such as a backpack or sewing basket that contains all the tools that you need.
- A journal or a sketchbook to hold your notes. A journal could also take the form of scraps of paper on a bulletin board, pencil marks on offcuts of wood or other found objects, or a social media account about your process.

CASE STUDY

FOCUS ON YOUR MISSION

A CONVERSATION ON

The Horrible & Wonderful Project

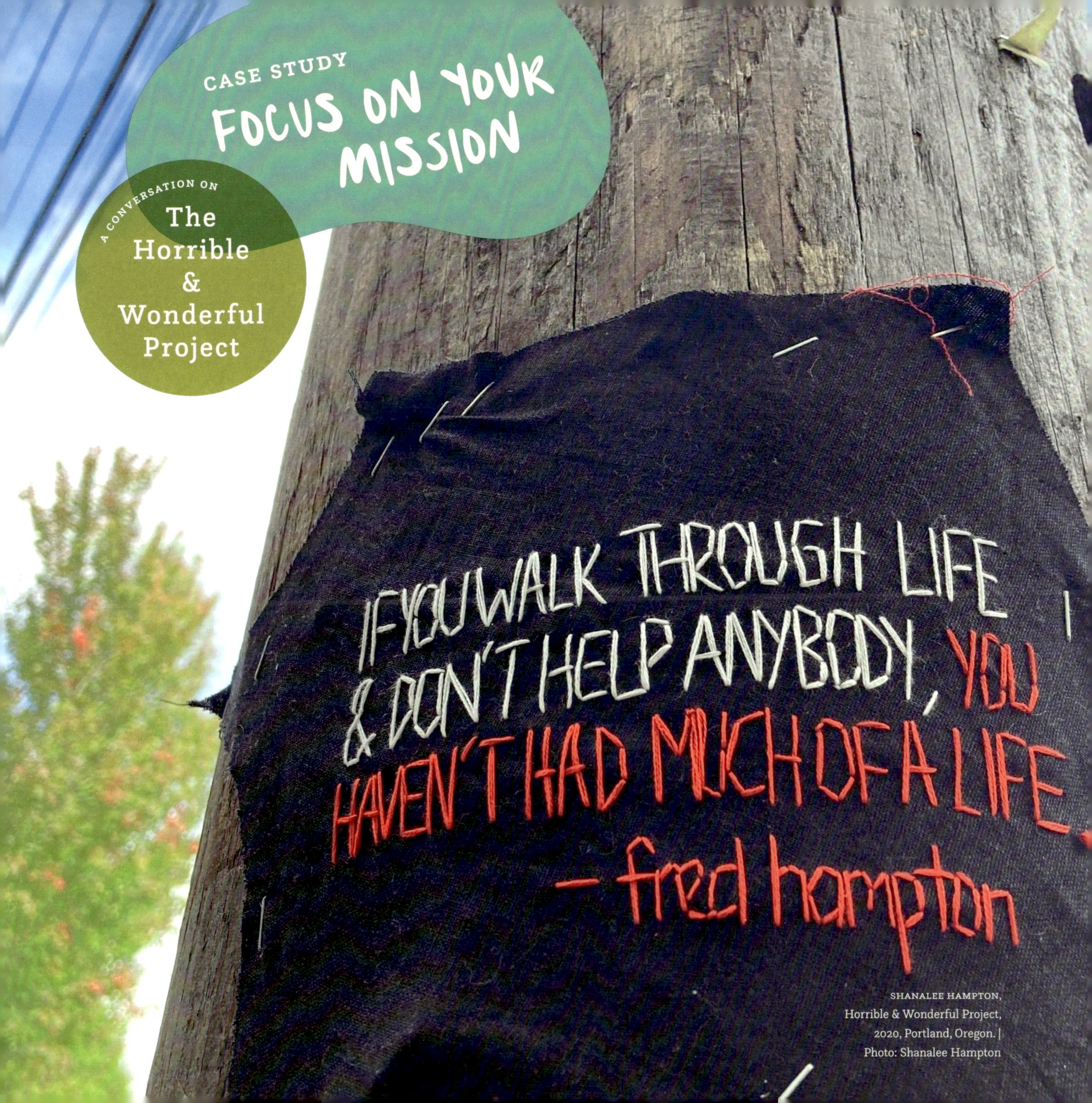

SHANALEE HAMPTON, Horrible & Wonderful Project, 2020, Portland, Oregon. | Photo: Shanalee Hampton

Embroidery artist Shanalee Hampton is someone who found her creative voice gradually, as a craft artist who has moved her practice from pop culture to rallying cries. Her Horrible & Wonderful Project is a call to action for her fellow citizens of Portland, Oregon. Tiny pieces of cloth tacked onto telephone poles address a wide range of issues, from gun violence to ruminations on kindness. Driven by love for humanity and anger over social injustice, these tiny works show how something as small as a stitch can be a loud statement.

LEANNE: When did you discover that your craft could be tied to activism?

SHANALEE: I was aware of the concept of craftivism and art as activism for a long time, but I didn't realize, "Oh, I can do that," until I actually started to call myself an artist. I began to realize the possibilities when I started to think of my craft as art.

In 2018, I attended an inspiring show called INTO ACTION! in Los Angeles that was about political art and spanned many mediums. On my way home to Portland, I saw a storefront banner in Oakland with a quote by Toni Cade Bambara: "The role of the artist is to make the revolution irresistible." That became my mission statement. My work now needs to be in one of two categories, love or rage, and needs to make the revolution irresistible.

LEANNE: Your stitchings have been visible in Portland, Oregon, a seemingly liberal city, during a year when citizens' voices have been silenced by police brutality. Embroidery is typically thought of as a quiet medium, but you've used your art to touch many who are in social, political, and health crises.

SHANALEE: Portland has a reputation as being progressive, and in many ways it is, but performatively so. The politics of the mayor and most of our city council are neoliberal. It is not an easy place for Black, brown, and other non-white people. Oregon has the most active hate groups of any state, and a large antifascist community has been working to defeat those groups for years. Portland's police have a long history of sympathizing and collaborating with white supremacists, as well as employing them. A substantial number of Black men and children have been murdered by the Portland police. When George Floyd was murdered, I don't think anyone paying attention was surprised at how hard Portland's protesters went.

I've gotten so many messages from people in Portland about how my street art installations have changed their day or changed their mind. I've also had them slashed and left in tatters. That can be discouraging, but the good messages more than make up for it. Executing this project has only deepened my love for Portland. It's a complicated place, but there's a lot of heart and potential here.

LEANNE: You've mentioned that you had to work up the nerve to post your work in public, but it's gotten easier with practice. Can you offer any guidance for emerging artists who want to do street art projects like yours?

SHANALEE: What a rush those first few posts were! But I now recognize that as a white lady, I've got a lot of privilege walking around in broad daylight, stapling things to poles. I go unnoticed a lot. I didn't realize that at first, but over the last year, we've all learned a lot about our privilege. Now I'm more determined than ever to use that privilege for good.

Learn what your city's laws are regarding street art, ignore them, pay attention to your surroundings, be nimble, be respectful of other street artists by never covering up their work, and if you're white, know that you can do what you're doing with little risk, and use your powers for good.

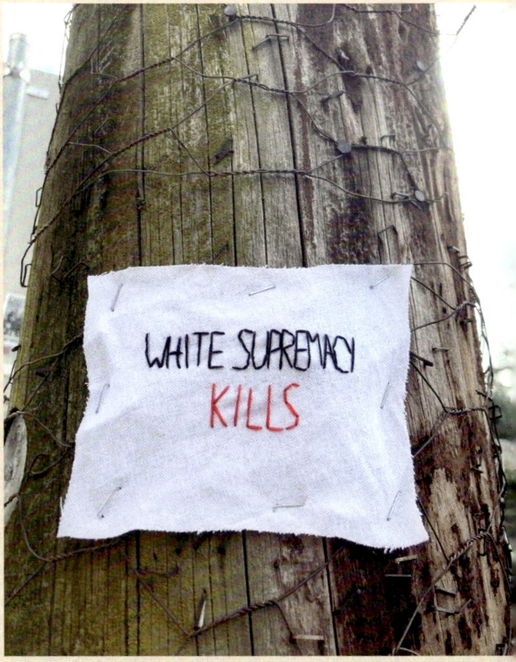

SHANALEE HAMPTON, Horrible & Wonderful Project, 2020, Portland, Oregon. | Photo: Shanalee Hampton

---

SHANALEE HAMPTON *grew up in Chicago, where she eschewed arts and crafts, much to her mother's disappointment. In 2003, she discovered that she had actually picked up a skill or two from her self-sabotaged craft attempts growing up and began making mixed-media art, to some degree of success. In late 2006, she began making jewelry and hair accessories with silk and cotton yoyos, vintage repurposed items, and a bit of grandma chic. Over the summer of 2013, she began selling embroidered hoop art in her online shop. Embroidery had been her go-to craft for gifts for years, ever since she learned how to embroider as a small child, hated it, then later discovered a real love for it. Over the last six years, Shanalee's work has become increasingly political. She tries making things that inspire people to do better, be better for the world.* **shanaleehampton.com**

NO ONE WORKS ALONE: NAYSAYERS, CHEERLEADERS, AND GUIDES

If you're scared to make things that might offend the delicate sensibilities of friends, bosses, and neighbors, I have news for you: no one is paying as much attention to you as you think they are. They really aren't.

Andy Warhol once said, "Don't think about making art, just get it done. Let everyone else decide if it's good or bad, whether they love it or hate it. While they are deciding, make even more art."

I once visited an exhibition at the Morgan Library about Warhol's days as a self-published writer and illustrator. They included a small case of all of the rejection letters he had received from book publishers, each one featuring a grave misspelling of his name. This amusing piece stood in stark contrast to the enormous amount of print collateral that Warhol designed: hand-drawn bookplates and bookmarks; invitations to self-hosted art shows at his favorite ice cream shop, Serendipity 3; watercolor illustrations of shoes and cats. Warhol the superstar was known to be prolific, but all these scraps of paper made me understand that he had been doing all of this even as a young man, when no one was watching. Take a note from Andy: be prolific even when you don't have an audience.

Whether they are friends or strangers, people who genuinely care about you and your creativity will support you, no matter how weird your ideas or how many U-turns your creativity takes. Your allies might include a best friend from childhood, a stranger who shows enthusiasm during a random chat, or someone who buys your work. Look for people who are excited about your ideas—they will be out there.

You may also sometimes find people who are negative about your creative work. These naysayers are the folks who have bruised their own artistic egos somewhere along the way. If someone is pulling you away from the work that you genuinely want to do, you need to ask yourself whether they truly have your best interests in mind. Are they speaking from a sense of their own fear?

Traditionally, teachers and guides are people who have taught you in a classroom, but they can also be found among the folks you count as friends and collaborators. They are the ones who bring you articles related to subjects you're interested in and check in with you to see how your work is going. You might have the nagging feeling that they often ask you questions you're unprepared to answer. These people push you, sometimes without even knowing it. Treasure these relationships; they are essential to you and your artistic well-being.

Each of these types of people can help propel you forward; fans will encourage you, teachers and guides will encourage you to take it to the next level, and naysayers? Naysayers will make you acutely aware of who your project is for and who it isn't.

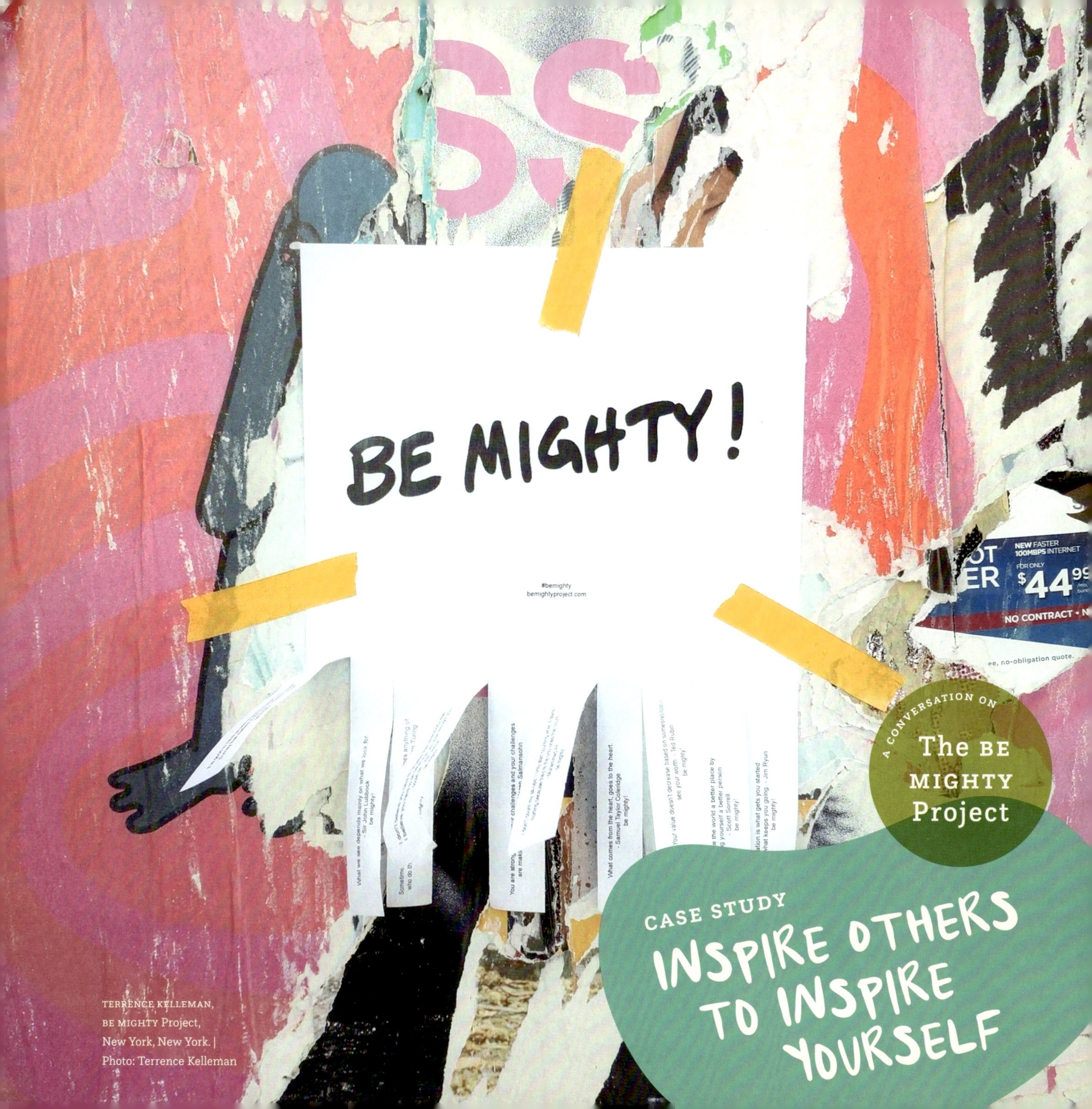

A CONVERSATION ON **The BE MIGHTY Project**

CASE STUDY

INSPIRE OTHERS TO INSPIRE YOURSELF

TERRENCE KELLEMAN, BE MIGHTY Project, New York, New York. | Photo: Terrence Kelleman

On a snowy afternoon in New York City's garment district in 2015, I came across a flyer with the bold words, "BE MIGHTY!" along with tearaway tabs bearing inspiring quotes. This small delight felt like a personal treasure guiding me forward, and I carried my little tab in my coat pocket like a talisman as I wandered around the city. Little did I know that BE MIGHTY was a street flyer project established by artist and entrepreneur Terrence Kelleman that very year. The BE MIGHTY Project aims to spread seeds of strength, positivity, and courage, one flyer tab at a time. Over 600,000 quotes have been distributed across the city, inspiring countless acts of mightiness in New Yorkers and visitors alike.

LEANNE: Why did you start the BE MIGHTY Project?

TERRENCE: It was the culmination of seeing a lot of street art and flyers on light poles in New York City. I was thinking, "My god, I want to do something like that." The first was a one-off on my birthday in 2015. I was not expecting it to get the reaction it did, but instantly a bunch of people were posting it on Instagram. So, I thought, "I'll do another flyer, and then another ..." I was going through a difficult time, and I needed the quotes to say something positive. The act of giving back can be empowering, even though we might not feel that way.

LEANNE: Do you have a favorite memory of the BE MIGHTY Project so far?

TERRENCE: One of my favorite moments was when I was putting up flyers and this lady carrying three bags of groceries said, "Hey, are you Mr. Mighty?" She put her groceries down and gave me a huge hug, saying, "Oh my god, you've saved my life three or four times with these quotes!" A lot of the time people message me and say, "Wow, I found the perfect quote right at the time that I needed it." I've come to believe that this is not an accident. These paper flyers are taped up randomly and usually fall off in a few days, but that one person finds the right quote, regardless.

LEANNE: Your project is an ephemeral one; you put flyers up, but you don't necessarily know when they'll come down. It could be in the next hour, or it could be a year later.

TERRENCE: Before I became an artist entrepreneur, I was a performance artist and did body art. You have one shot at documenting this ephemeral thing and then that's it. You're only going to remember it the way that you captured it through the document. I love the way that my work changes, degrading over time, and the fact that there might be something like one little tab left, hanging off. Or that people graffiti over it. It's all that random chaos of the city that I love, and in documenting it, you're finding it and framing it in a certain way that says something about its ephemeral nature.

I feel like the project will continue to grow for as long as I need this process in my life. Artists create things so they can understand the world. And for me, this project has been a long process of creation, but also of self-discovery. As long as I need it to grow, I'll keep doing it.

LEANNE: What advice would you give someone who wanted to start an ambitious art project?

TERRENCE: I would use the Theodore Roosevelt quote that I've been putting on flyers since the beginning: "Do what you can, with what you have, where you are." Sometimes we think we need a certain device or tool or camera to get started. It's just an excuse so that you don't do anything. You just have to start with what you've got.

TERRENCE KELLEMAN *is the inventor of the Mighty Wallet, the first Tyvek wallet, and the founder of Dynomighty. He is an inspiration junkie and creator of the* BE MIGHTY *street art project, which weekly distributes flyers with quotes of inspiration around* NYC *and online, hoping to inspire others to go for their own hopes, goals, and dreams.* **bemighty.com**

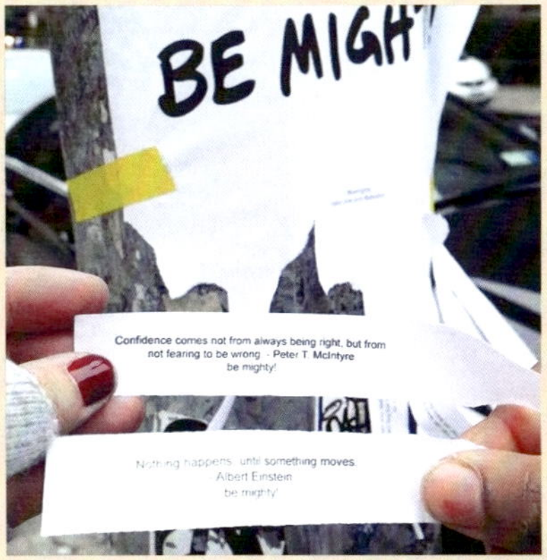

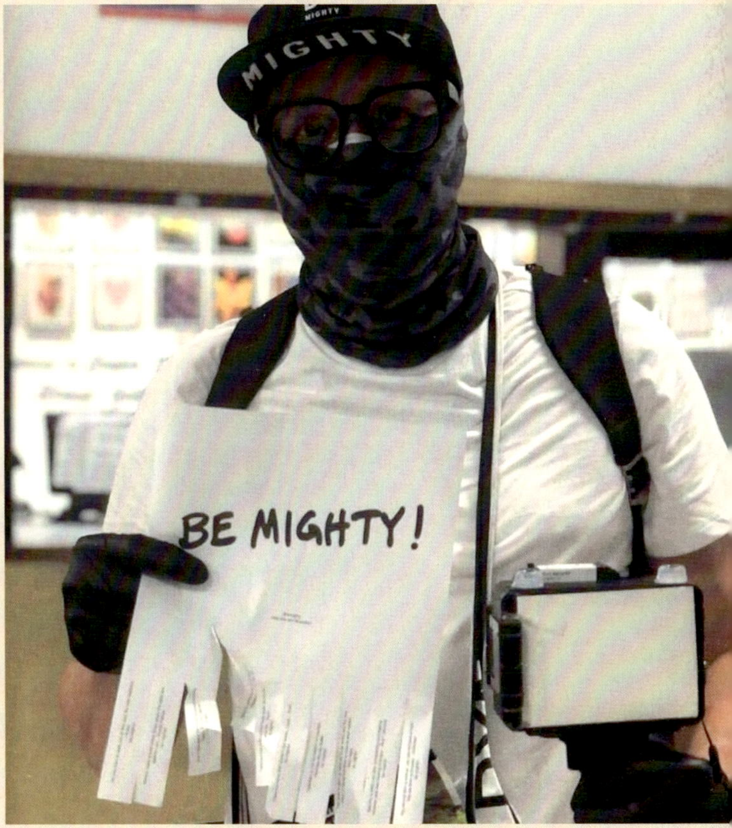

TOP AND BOTTOM:
TERRENCE KELLEMAN, BE MIGHTY Project, New York, New York. | Photo: Terrence Kelleman

Track Your Time

When you get curious about your practice, you will find more time. I keep a day planner to track the times when I do creative work. Months later, I can go back and see that I always tend to have more social plans in the third week of the month and that I'll often drop out of doing creative work for a good four to five days. For years, November has been my least productive month, but it is also when I absorb the work of others, with increased visits to craft studios and art galleries. Get to know your patterns; this will enhance your creative life.

TRY IT ALL: A MULTIDISCIPLINARY APPROACH

Creative people, particularly creative instigators, do a lot of different things. If you can't decide between embroidery and welding, silk-screening and writing—don't! In my experience, creative people like to express their creativity through many different mediums; one carries over to another. Explore the idea of being interdisciplinary (blending more than one artistic discipline) or multidisciplinary (trying lots of different artistic disciplines).

In my first year of university, I took a visual art class with a variety of different projects. I remember sketching a study of the shadow and light on a carton of eggs in cobalt-blue conté crayon; making a soft sculpture of driftwood, fabric, and glitter-flecked bouncy balls; and staying up late at night to paint thick acrylic portraits. The one thing from that class that has stayed with me is the final critique: the instructor pointed out that no matter which medium I was working in, it was possible to tell from the color and form that each piece belonged to me. That remark taught me that we all have a creative fingerprint that follow us from one medium to the next. What commonalities do you see in the things that you make?

TIME IS SOMETHING YOU MAKE

Time can be elusive to those whose lives are full of commitments. Between working full time and being part of a family and/or a network of friends, how do we make time for creative work?

My friend Katherine Soucie (see page 117) is a textile artist and is very serious about sticking to her studio days. Over the years of our friendship, I've come to understand that if she says, "I'm in the studio," she truly is focused on her studio time and is not to be disturbed. "My creative discipline is a form of self-care," she said. "It is important to have time alone to think, organize, and immerse yourself in your environment so you can focus on what it is you're trying to communicate. I value and respect the time I set aside for myself, because no one else is going to give me permission to do so. Check in with yourself to ensure one area of your practice isn't being neglected over the other. If you don't reserve the time, then the well can dry up."

Each of us finds time in different ways. I often use my vacation time for long, dedicated projects, but I also meet up every week with a small, like-minded group of friends to work on our individual projects beside one another. Perhaps there is a half hour before dinner when you can sit down and jot something down in a sketchbook. The more you start to look for pockets of time, the more you will find.

MAKING SPACE

Performers need space to move, painters need the freedom to make a mess, and crocheters can work almost anywhere. Soundproof walls, running water, good lighting—what are your nonnegotiables?

Do you need to find a space for making? Here are some suggestions:

- Contact your local community centers to find temporary space.
- Book a free room through your public library.
- Does the local college/university host artists-in-residence?
- Find your local makerspace.
- Ask your local art school or civic theater if they provide discounted rates for cultural workers.
- Know someone with office space? Ask if the boardroom can be borrowed after hours.
- Is there an empty storefront or shopping mall near you? Ask for cheap rent.
- Do you live in a tourism region full of parks, wedding venues, or ski lodges? What happens to these spaces during the off-season?
- Do you know someone who can lend you a cabin, garage, or yurt?
- Pet sit! Filling the kibble bowl for a family's pet can give you access to some extraordinary spaces.
- When in doubt, set up on your back porch, laundry room, bike room, or closet.

DON'T GET STUCK ON SUPPLIES

Art supplies can be expensive. Don't feel that you need to buy everything you possibly can just to get started. Sometimes the best photos are taken with a borrowed camera. Your painting doesn't know if your watercolor paints are secondhand. In a pinch, you can use cardboard as a canvas. If you are struggling for proper supplies, celebrate these shortages as constraints that will ultimately make you a stronger creative.

And don't give up. If you ask around, you will most likely find more art supplies than you need. Put up a poster in your local coffee shop. Join an online group to barter and trade. I've asked for castoffs on Facebook Marketplace, Craigslist, and Kijiji.

TRY THIS

Keep the Ideas Flowing

How do you sustain excitement about a project? Wind the act of creativity into your day. Spend your first waking moments jotting down a few ideas in a notebook. Spend a half hour before bed free-associating ideas. Find touchpoints throughout the day that will remind you of your work, even when you can't get to it directly.

- Schedule a regular time and place for working on your project in mini sprints, such as the ten minutes during your morning coffee or the time you spend waiting in line at the grocery store.
- Start a process notebook to capture details that support your idea.
- Summarize your idea in one to two sentences. Use this to start your manifesto.
- Find a reliable friend who will listen as you describe the project to them. Ask them to respond only with the word "why?"
- Make a sound recording of your project on your phone. This could include the ambient noise from the area where you want the project to take place, musical elements you are thinking of adding, overheard conversations, or your own narration.
- Use social media productively; find work by other artists on similar themes and make comparisons.

EXPERIMENT FREELY

Let yourself and your art-making be a little bit absurd. Try making something that you would be absolutely mortified to show to another person.

Trusting your own creativity means suspending personal criticism, even for a few minutes, while you make something. There is no rush to get to the finish line; take time to experiment. Prove to yourself that the thing you're not sure will work actually won't work. The worst that could happen is that it won't work. But maybe it will!

Editing a project too early might cause you to walk away in frustration before your idea is fully formed, so remember, you don't need to have a critical eye when you are just getting started. Allow yourself the freedom to discover, with a plan to refine the work in the future.

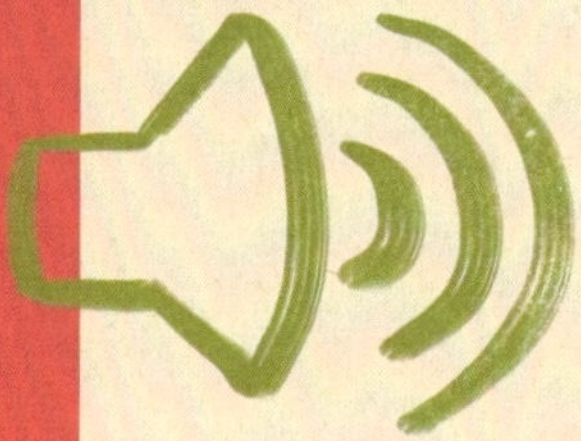

CASE STUDY

BE TRULY YOURSELF

A CONVERSATION WITH

Meg Lewis

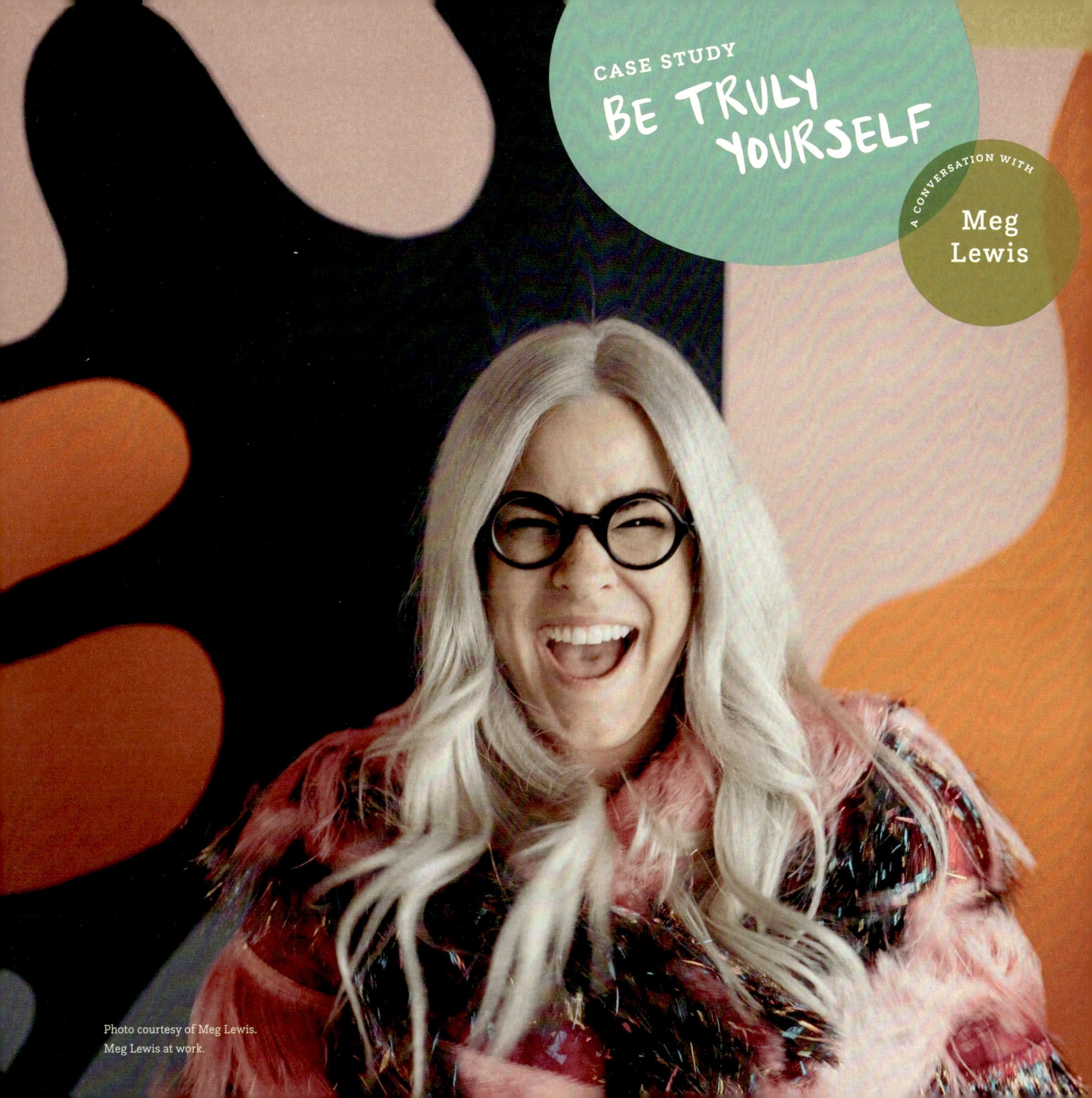

Photo courtesy of Meg Lewis.
Meg Lewis at work.

Meg Lewis's personal style first caught my eye when I came across one of her comedic dances on Instagram. My first impression was "This woman is confident!" I was struck by how fearless Meg was in leveraging her memorable visual style and wit across an enormous collection of media and platforms, such as creative spaces, sculptures, creative self-help books, podcasts, and brand projects. Once based in New York City, she now supports others as a creative coach and educator from her home in Minneapolis, which she has called "the kindest city in the world." Meg uses her design skills to help individuals to become their most authentic selves. We discussed her journey as a creative person and how she has built a career by recognizing her own strengths.

RIGHT: Photo courtesy of Meg Lewis. Meg Lewis at work.

LEANNE: Did you have an aha moment when you discovered that you could use many creative disciplines in your work?

MEG: I did. I think it's pretty rare to have such an epiphany, but I was in my mid-twenties, a few years into my career as a freelance designer, and I realized that I was not enjoying it. At a certain point, I realized, "This is not working."

I thought back to all the things that I did like working on, and I made a list of what those things were and their qualities. I discovered that what I wanted was a combination of two things: more creative freedom to work in a style that I had fun doing, and working with people who enjoy their jobs. In that moment I decided to push through the fear and work on projects that reflected this. As soon as I was able to start doing my work my way, everything just fell into place.

LEANNE: You are open to taking risks. How does this work when you are collaborating with other people who may be a bit more risk averse?

MEG: I often start things by myself, because I've learned that I am the one who is most excited about them. Due to my confidence level, it usually works out fine. I really like starting things by myself, where I know I'm not going to have to worry about other people's fear holding me back. I just sort of hurtle myself at the sun very quickly, and I don't let anything get in my way. I love collaborating with other people, so I always develop a plan for how I can bring other people in while supporting them and lifting them up.

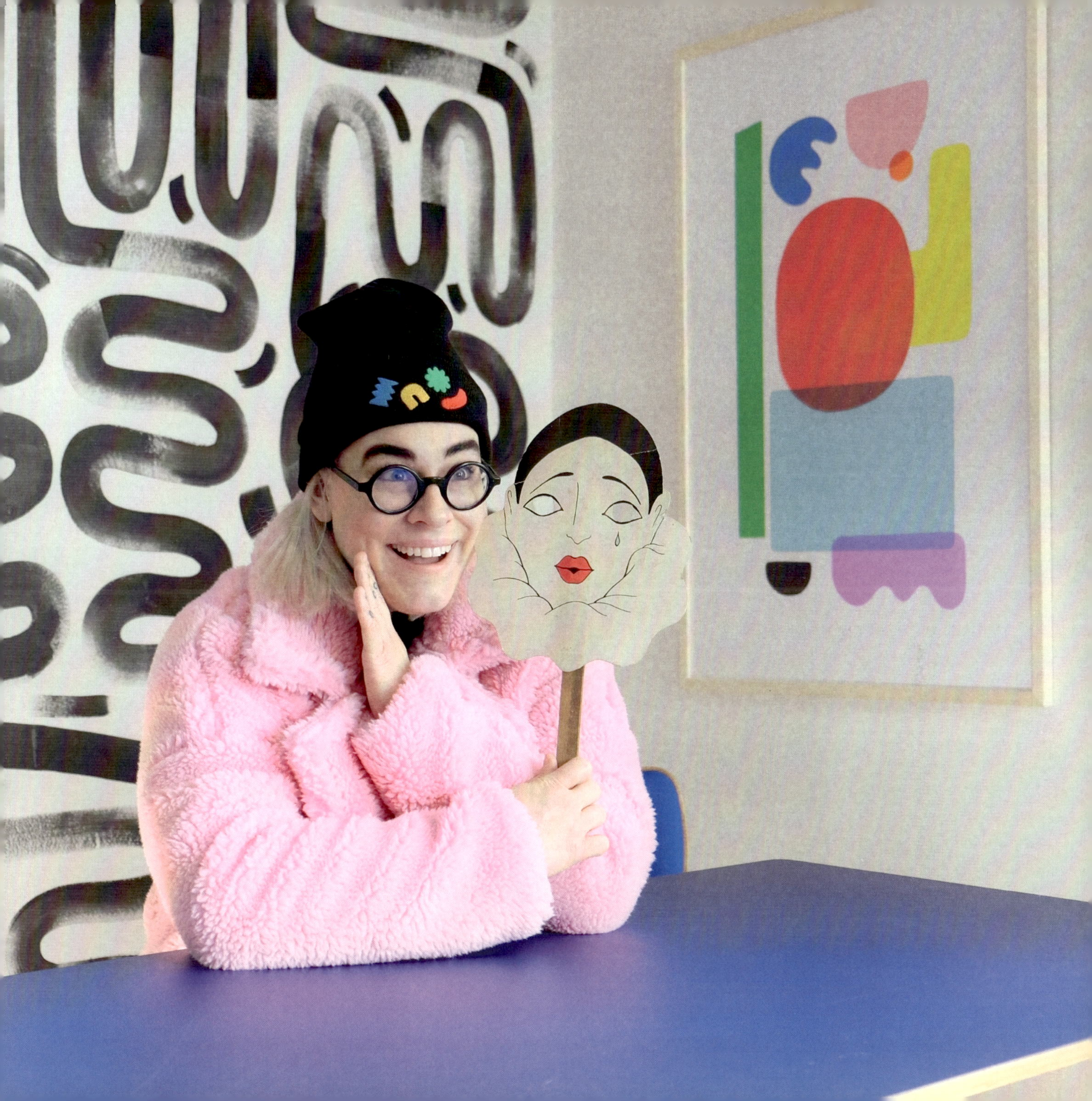

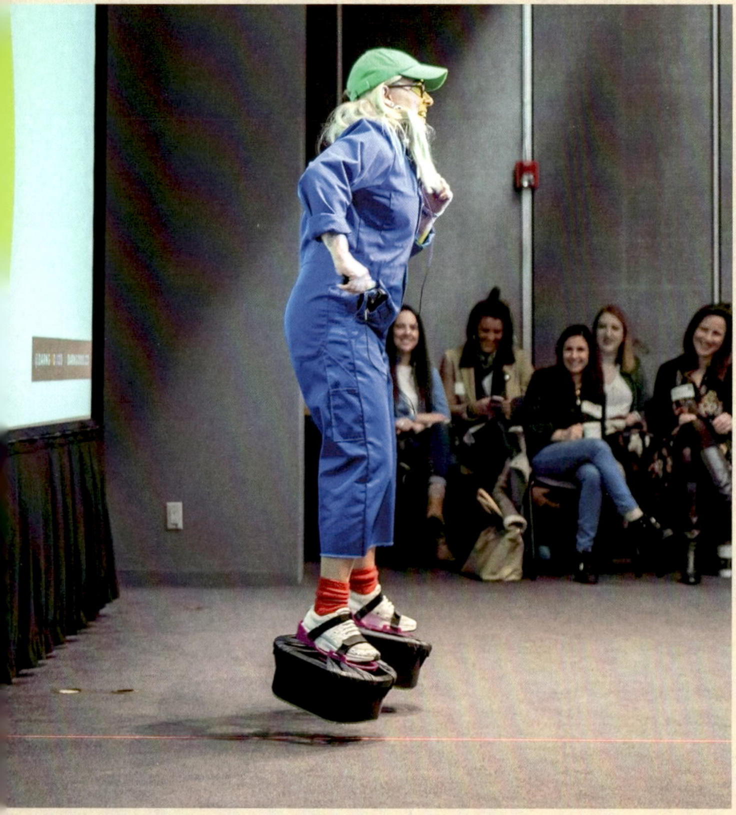

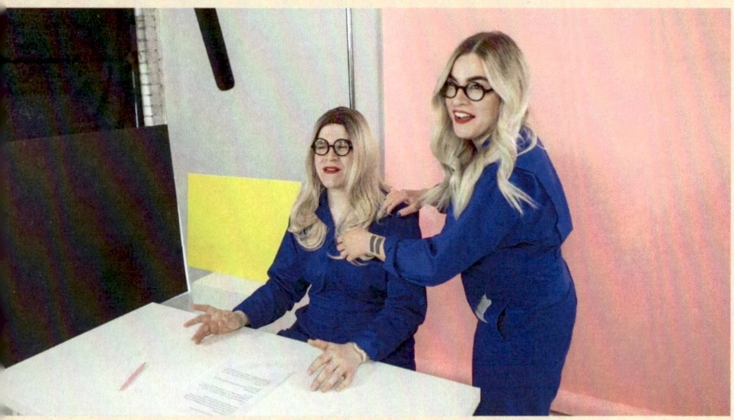

LEANNE: When do you know that it's the right moment to bring other people in?

MEG: One of the interesting things about my work is that I celebrate myself and express confidence in my style. I also spend a lot of time with individuals, getting them excited about what they can offer the world that nobody else can. We can each have our own little island where we're doing our thing, but there is room for everyone to succeed independently.

LEANNE: You've had such a prolific career, and you do so many different things, from podcasting to storytelling to speaking. How do you prioritize what you want to do next?

MEG: I'm an up-for-anything person. I wake up every day and I'm like, "What do I feel like doing today?" I listen to my intuition and just kind of follow whatever I'm feeling the most fulfilled by. I think the most important thing that I've done for many years is what I call "strategic play." I focus on what I have the most fun doing.

One of the things that bums me out about humans is that people put such an emphasis on success or failure. Even though I've had creative businesses come and go throughout my career, I've never once thought of them being a failure. Change led me to become interested in

TOP AND BOTTOM:
Photos courtesy of Meg Lewis.
Meg Lewis at work.

something else, or it led me to change myself. I've never really moments where I think, "What a waste of my time." Everything I've done has always led me to something else. It's always worth it.

LEANNE: Do you have any words of advice for creatives trying to find themselves?

MEG: One of the things that's been on my mind lately is the concept of labels, like what do you call yourself? Every human has to deal with this—are you are a fine artist, or a painter, or an illustrator, or a graphic designer, or a writer? I learned how to become a designer in school, and at the time, I felt like that should be my whole career. I would call myself titles within that field—logo designer, brand strategy designer, product designer—but now, as I've started to embrace every aspect of my personality and skill set, I've realized that I have a lot more to offer the world.

I'm calling myself a designer and a comedian. So what if I don't have any traditional comedy training outside of childhood? As a kid, I went to comedy camps and acting schools. When we think of a comedian, we think of somebody who does stand-up or is in an improv troupe. And that's not me, but I do have a comedy podcast and a comedy video series, so I should be able to call myself a comedian, too. Once we start to realize that labels are just labels, our minds can open up all sorts of possibilities.

MEG LEWIS *is a designer, comedian, performer, and educator working to make the world a happier place. Experience her work at* ***meglewis.com****.*

NO FAKERS: TRENDS DO NOT MATTER

Art and culture trends come and go. Flash mobs, black velvet paintings, parking spot installations, free hugs stations, no-pants subway rides, renaissance fairs, salons, tiny houses, art cars—every cultural movement has a moment, and some people find their place in them. Others do not, and that's okay. If you feel indifferent or ambivalent toward an artistic trend that sounds like a good idea because everyone else is doing it, it is probably not your jam.

Today's provocative could be tomorrow's boring. Be inspired by trends, but don't get swept up in them. Art is not a paint-by-numbers activity. Find the projects that make you genuinely curious about the world.

PROMPT

Find Your Influences

Whether you're new to making art or are an experienced creator, everyone can benefit from getting familiar or reacquainted with our muses. Some, like Andy Warhol, who loved to make films, books, and portraits of celebrities' likenesses, carry their artistic muses with them through their lifetime. Others, like Picasso, who went through a blue period, go through phases of work in which they focus on working in one particular medium.

Here is an exercise to help you reacquaint yourself with your influences. Answer these questions quickly, without overthinking, but be sure to write down the answers. You may surprise yourself.

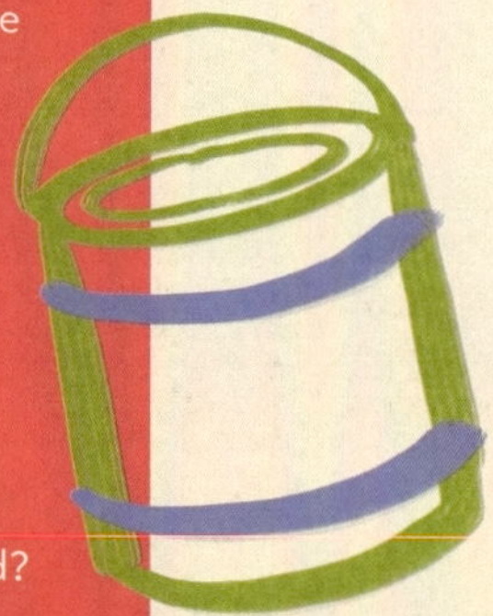

1. Who are your favorite artists or designers? Why?
2. Which creative medium would you choose above all others? Why?
3. Who inspires you? Why?
4. What symbols do you tend to doodle? Why do you think this is?
5. What enrages you?
6. What is the most astounding piece of art that you've ever experienced? What do you remember about this experience?
7. Which colors do you favor? Why?
8. If your artistic practice was a song/texture/color/slogan/shape, what would it be?
9. Do you often think about the past, or the present, or the future? If your project could speak to one of these states, which would it be?

CHAPTER 3

WHAT ACTIVATES YOU?

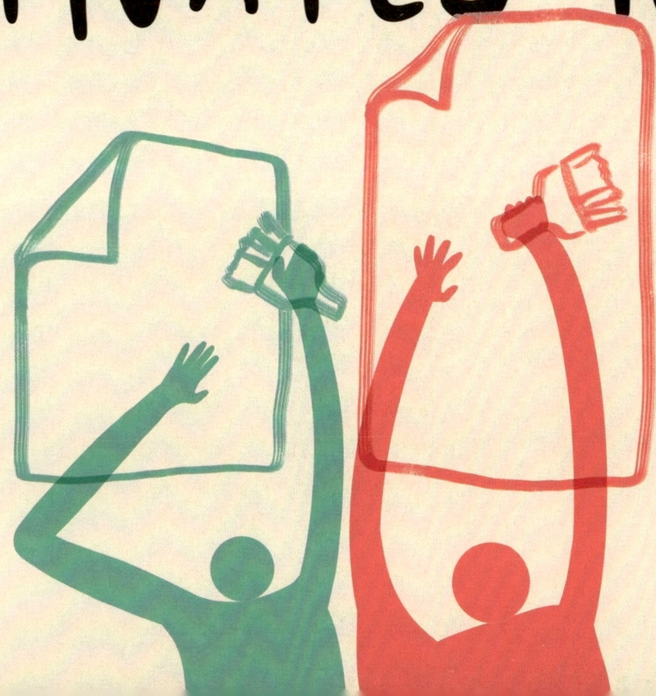

The best ideas catch us unawares when we are busy doing other things. From my interactions with different creative people, I've learned that when they first start, most don't know their passion project will become their life's work. At the outset, they are simply experimenting or following a small idea that came to them.

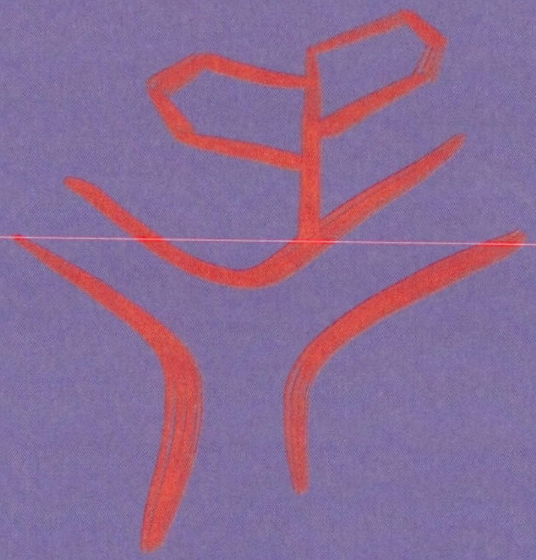

The majority of artists that I've interviewed say that only once they put their creativity into action did they discover that the work they were creating answers a deeper calling within themselves or their community. It is this driving purpose that moves them to keep creating and, in turn, returning to their projects, time and time again.

Think about what drives you in all parts of your life, and how this motivation and personal mission might carry over to the work that you make. It is one thing to make; it is another to make things that rally around a cause.

WHAT AFFECTS YOU?

We each of us have our own activist causes that we hold close. These issues often show up in our lives in the form of things that anger us, things that excite us, and things that we think about a lot. Sometimes what we are drawn to stems from our childhood experiences, our sense of what justice should look like, or our response to traumas. Your cause (or causes—most of us have many) is likely to become the focus of your work. What inspires you to speak? Which causes do you hold in your bones?

Here is a list of issues that may spark some ideas.

CONTENT WARNING: *I list some sensitive topics on the pages ahead. Readers may wish to skip to page 60.*

- [ ] ableism
- [ ] accessibility
- [ ] addiction
- [ ] ageism
- [ ] animal cruelty
- [ ] antisemitism
- [ ] artificial intelligence
- [ ] banned books
- [ ] Black Lives Matter
- [ ] body confidence
- [ ] body shaming
- [ ] bullying
- [ ] capital punishment
- [ ] capitalism
- [ ] car culture
- [ ] car-free communities
- [ ] child welfare
- [ ] children in care
- [ ] classism
- [ ] clear-cut logging
- [ ] climate justice
- [ ] consumerism
- [ ] copyright protection
- [ ] coral reefs
- [ ] COVID-19 prevention
- [ ] craftivism
- [ ] cultural appropriation
- [ ] data democracy
- [ ] Deaf culture
- [ ] decolonization
- [ ] democracy
- [ ] digital privacy
- [ ] DIY skill building
- [ ] domestic violence
- [ ] eating disorders
- [ ] education
- [ ] emotional labor
- [ ] employment standards
- [ ] endangered species
- [ ] environmental welfare
- [ ] equality
- [ ] equity
- [ ] factory farming
- [ ] food security
- [ ] fat activism
- [ ] feminism
- [ ] fossil fuel dependency
- [ ] free health care
- [ ] freedom of expression on the internet
- [ ] freedom of religion
- [ ] freedom of the press
- [ ] frontline workers' rights
- [ ] gang violence
- [ ] gender dynamics in the workplace
- [ ] generational inequity
- [ ] gentrification
- [ ] government surveillance
- [ ] gun violence
- [ ] harm reduction
- [ ] hate crimes
- [ ] hate speech
- [ ] HIV/AIDS awareness and education
- [ ] holistic medicine
- [ ] homophobia
- [ ] human trafficking
- [ ] income gap
- [ ] Indigenization
- [ ] influencer culture
- [ ] interculturalization
- [ ] intergenerational poverty
- [ ] intersectionality and human rights
- [ ] Islamophobia
- [ ] land rights

- [ ] language rights
- [ ] LGBTQ2S+ marriage rights
- [ ] literacy
- [ ] living wage
- [ ] man camps
- [ ] mansplaining
- [ ] marijuana legalization
- [ ] menstrual equity
- [ ] mental health
- [ ] migrant rights
- [ ] monetization of the internet
- [ ] neurodiversity awareness
- [ ] nuclear weapons
- [ ] open source
- [ ] opioid crisis
- [ ] organized labor
- [ ] pay equity
- [ ] peace
- [ ] pesticides
- [ ] pink tax
- [ ] pipelines
- [ ] police violence
- [ ] political criminals
- [ ] poverty alleviation
- [ ] prison systems
- [ ] proportional representation
- [ ] public space
- [ ] puppy mills
- [ ] racism
- [ ] reclaiming oral languages
- [ ] recycling
- [ ] refugee rights
- [ ] rent control
- [ ] right to choose
- [ ] right to housing
- [ ] right to self-care
- [ ] seed saving
- [ ] segregation
- [ ] self-harm
- [ ] sex workers' rights
- [ ] sexual assault
- [ ] sexualization of minors
- [ ] shopping local
- [ ] social isolation
- [ ] social media addiction
- [ ] STDs
- [ ] Stop Asian Hate
- [ ] student debt
- [ ] sustainability
- [ ] suicide awareness and prevention
- [ ] trans activism
- [ ] upcycling
- [ ] walkable cities
- [ ] war
- [ ] water rights
- [ ] wealth gaps
- [ ] wellness washing
- [ ] white violence
- [ ] whitewashing

This list is only the beginning. I'm sure there are many more topics that have come to the surface for you. What causes, issues, and movements speak to you?

TRY THIS

Write Your Own List

Once you are clear on an issue you want your work to speak to, I invite you to further explore your relationship to that topic using the exercises in the next section. Grab a pen and paper and make some time to explore your history and lived experience in relation to making creative work for others to experience.

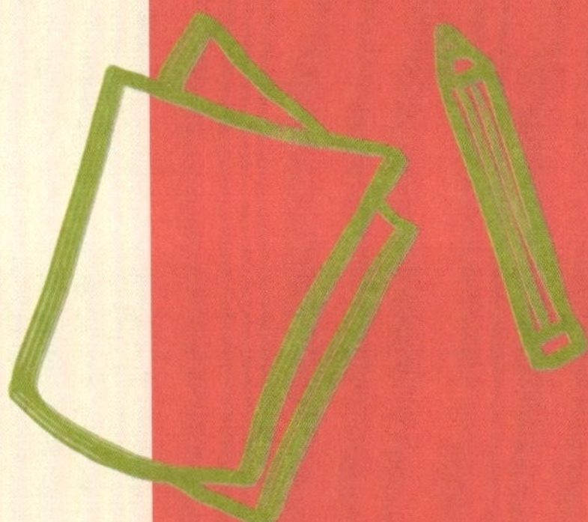

EXERCISE 1

The Personal Wayback Machine

Our creativity is wound from strands of childhood memory, trauma, friendship, milestones, worry, joy, and success. Whether you are ten years old or eighty, you have your own history. What common themes, recurring issues, and long-hoped-for dreams come to the surface? What conversational patterns arise time and time again with close friends? What sorts of stories are you drawn to read?

What is in your background that might serve your artistic expression? Probe inside the dusty corners of your memory and find what is lurking in the deep shadows there. Whatever is hanging out in the back recesses of your brain, it's probably tied closely to the causes, issues, and passions that are most important to you.

Take ten minutes to probe these questions about your childhood:

- What did you enjoy doing?
- What were you fascinated by?
- What memories of that time come back to you time and time again?
- What captivated you?
- What delighted you?
- What did you not understand?

EXERCISE 2

What Makes Your Blood Boil?

What makes you really, really angry? Not just a little upset, but full of rage? At some point in our childhood and early teens, when did you feel that things just didn't seem right? These are issues that stick with us as adults and creative people.

What rules were you given that you now know should be broken? What stories of injustice do you tend to tell family and friends over and over again? What kinds of injustice do you face in the world? For whom are you a voice? Who are you in a position to support and bolster? What keeps you up at night?

CASE STUDY:
COLLECTIVE ACTION

THE EVOLUTION OF THE RED DRESS AWARENESS CAMPAIGN & INSTALLATION

TEXT PROVIDED BY THE
KUMUGWE CULTURAL SOCIETY

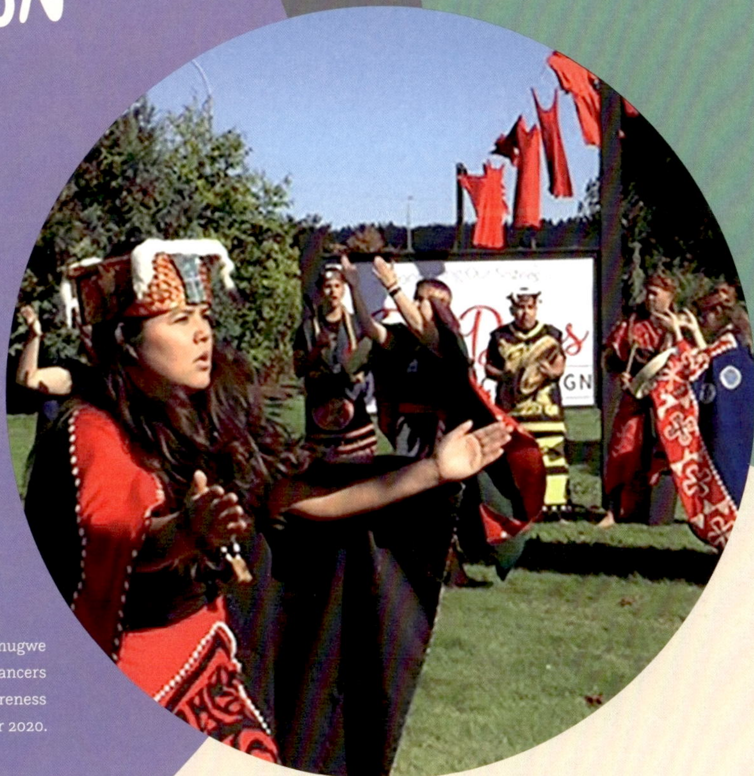

Photo courtesy of the Kumugwe Cultural Society. Kumugwe Dancers at The Red Dress Awareness Campaign, October 2020.

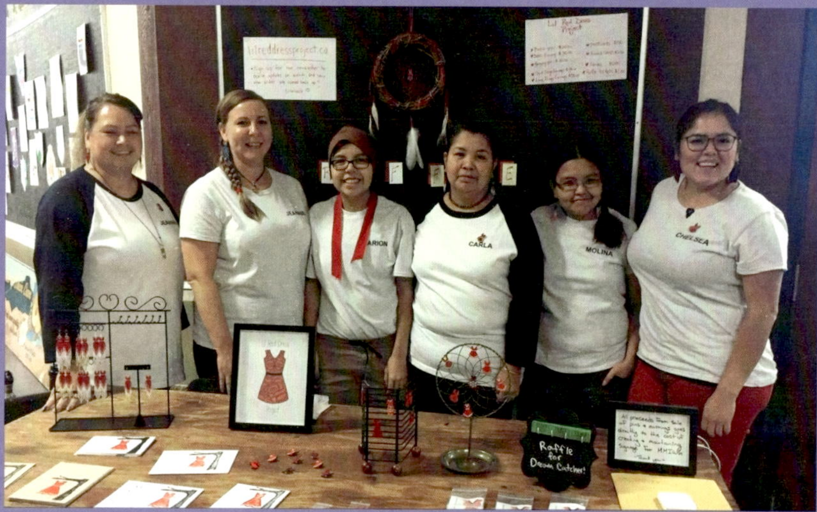

Photo courtesy of the Kumugwe Cultural Society. The Lil' Red Dress Project volunteers create stunning beaded red dress pins and earrings for purchase to help raise awareness and fund new projects.

WALKING WITH OUR SISTERS — K'OMOKS

In 2015, Walking With Our Sisters — K'omoks opened its doors to the community to experience a traveling commemorative art installation honoring the 1,800-plus missing and murdered Indigenous women and girls (MMIWG) in North America. The large collaborative art piece, created to draw attention to this injustice, was made available to the public through selected galleries and locations.

The art installation was composed of 1,763 pairs of moccasin vamps (tops), with 108 pairs of children's vamps. Hundreds of beaded vamps were created by hand and donated by hundreds of caring and concerned individuals. Their work formed an installation of the beaded vamps arranged in a winding cloth path. Viewers were asked to remove their shoes and walk on a path of cloth alongside the vamps. This powerful and impactful experience was steeped in cultural practices to honor those lost.

Each pair of vamps (or "uppers" as they are also called) represents one missing or murdered Indigenous woman. The unfinished moccasins represent the unfinished lives of the women whose lives were cut short. The children's vamps are dedicated to children who never returned home from residential schools. Altogether, the installation represents all these women, paying respect to their lives and existence on this Earth. They are not forgotten. They are sisters, mothers, aunties, daughters, cousins, grandmothers, wives, and partners. They have been cared for; they have been loved; they are missing; and they are not forgotten.

Through the combined efforts of partnerships between the I-Hos Gallery, the Transition Society, and the Kumugwe Cultural Society, and with support from municipalities, organizations, and businesses, over 5,000 guests visited the installation on the traditional unceded territory of the Puntledge, E'iksan, and K'omoks Peoples. For two years, more than 400 volunteers dedicated their time, expertise, and financial support to ensure that all activities, cultural protocols, and traditions were adhered to, making the event one of the most attended art installations in the history of the Comox Valley. When the sacred bundle of vamps left the territory, volunteers, businesses, municipalities, and organizations were honored and invited to attend a celebration in the traditional Bighouse. As conversations continued, there was a realization that this work must continue.

Learn more at ***walkingwithoursisters.ca***.

Photo: Melanie Norris. In the fall of 2020, The Red Dress Awareness Campaign & Installation was hosted by the town of Comox. A 150-foot-long clothesline of red dresses was installed in October as the fourth and final installment in the Comox Valley, British Columbia.

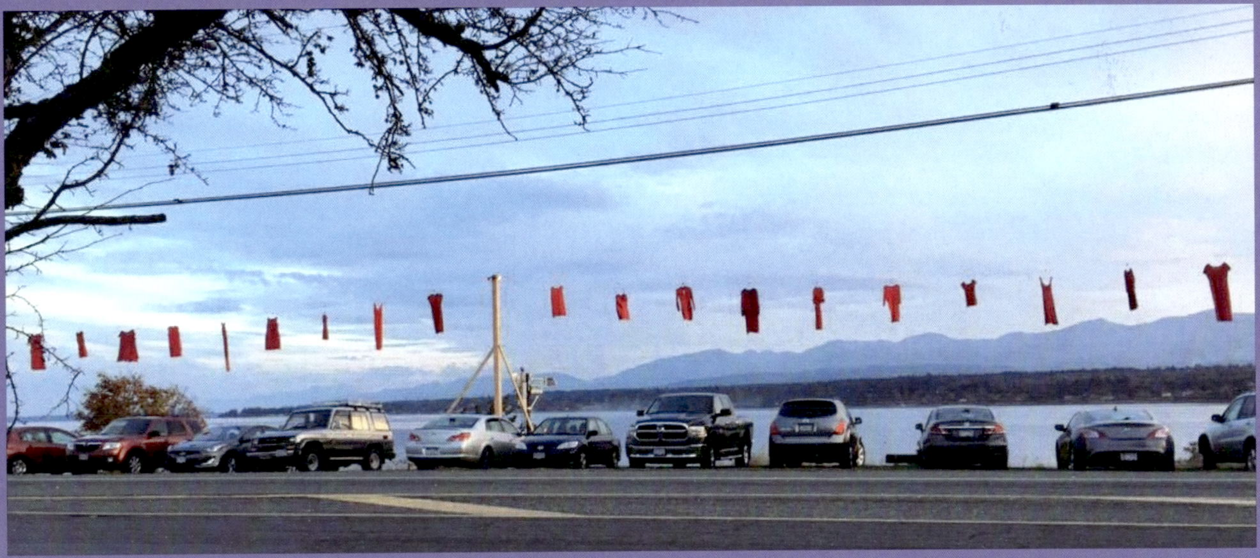

CAMPAIGN & INSTALLATION

In 2016, the organizers reunited for The Red Dress Awareness Campaign & Installation, a 150-foot installation of clothesline hung with the powerful symbol of red dresses to recognize and inform the public about the increasingly high numbers of missing and murdered Indigenous women and girls in North America. Inspired by The REDress Project, started in 2010 by Métis artist Jamie Black, which currently resides in the Canadian Museum for Human Rights in Winnipeg, Manitoba, The Red Dress Awareness Campaign & Installation occurred each fall in the first week of October for four years and was held in a different municipality in the region each year: K'omoks First Nation, Courtenay, Cumberland, and Comox. Through positive working relationships built by these groups, the project was unanimously supported and honored in each community.

A social media and print campaign invited the public to participate and hang a red dress in their own front yards and businesses. The local school districts of the Comox Valley and Campbell River became involved and developed curricula to educate the next generation, and this learning continues past the end of the project. Local politicians took notice, with the Honorable Gord Johns, Member of Parliament for the federal electoral riding of Courtenay–Alberni bringing it to the floor of the House of Commons of Canada, further raising awareness across the country.

THE KUMUGWE CULTURAL SOCIETY, nestled in between the Beaufort Range and the Strait of Georgia, in the Comox Valley on Vancouver Island off the west coast of British Columbia, Canada, began in 2007 with the purpose to promote, preserve, and advocate for cultural practices of the K'omoks and Kwakwaka'wakw Peoples. The society conducts activities to foster a vibrant cultural experience for its members, and to advocate for Indigenous Peoples to promote social change.

"How did organizers get so much support for a topic that many people know very little of, and that is not widely covered by the media? It all stems from relationships. Period. For the past twenty-five years, members of the K'omoks First Nation have shared their passion for their culture with the community in an effort to bridge the gap between the communities to foster an understanding and appreciation for the First Peoples of the Valley. Through these efforts, deep relationships and respect have formed. Undoubtedly, we could not do what we do without the endless support from our communities."

—THE KUMUGWE CULTURAL SOCIETY

THE LIL' RED DRESS PROJECT

Before the final Red Dress installation in 2019, two of the campaign board members, Carla Voyageur and Jeannine Lindsay, had a family conversation sparked by witnessing multiple billboards being erected to find a missing girl. Through their conversations came a common thought that many Indigenous families with missing loved ones would not be able to afford such signage for their own loved ones. With this in mind, they began to brainstorm ways to bring more awareness to MMIWG.

Jeannine and Carla, both avid beaders, decided to bead a red dress pin to honor MMIWG through a project they called the Lil' Red Dress Project, in light of the Red Dress Project being installed later that month. Carla created the first pin, and the rest of her family members quickly followed suit, creating many pins to spread awareness and to raise funds for billboards for MMIWG.

Support for the project grew quickly, and since launching in September 2019, the project continues to be a success. It truly is a family affair; husbands and children have all picked up beadwork and contribute by beading pins, packaging products, doing mail-outs, and helping to host workshops. A dedicated team of volunteers with a love of beading share their time and talents for the cause. Through social media and community engagement, the Lil' Red Dress Project team has been able to help support other communities and organizations to envision and create their own awareness campaigns and grassroots projects. Ultimately, grassroots projects such as these have created space for emotional, uncomfortable, and often difficult conversations, continuing a dialogue that we must have to ensure Indigenous women and girls experience a safe and prosperous future.

Visit ***lilreddressproject.ca*** for more information.

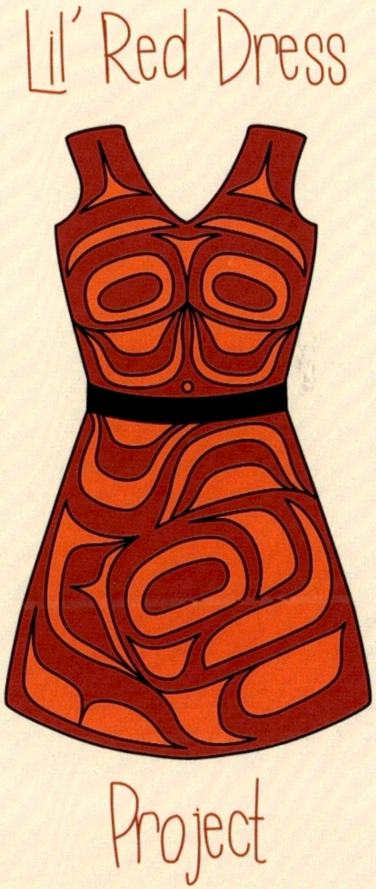

HELLO, INSECURITY

To Those Who Didn't Go to Art School

If you didn't go to art or design school, this book is more for you than for anyone else. While I appreciate the hallowed institutions and established spaces that exist to show art, I believe (and I hope you do, too) that art can be made by anyone, anywhere. We have only to look at people like filmmaker Miranda July, painter Bill Traylor, and interdisciplinary artist Yoko Ono to see that great art can be made despite access to formalized art education. Tyree Guyton, who is profiled on page 231, was originally rejected from his art school, only to later be awarded an honorary PhD for his art by the same institution.

Remember, we all start from the same place. Everyone has to start with a first brushstroke, gesture, dance, or doodle.

EXERCISE 3

Be Inspired by Your Surroundings

The places where we live and work can have a significant impact on our creativity. Whether we reside in the country or the city or somewhere in between, the environments that we inhabit impact us.

Where do you live? Who do you encounter each day? Does your lunch come from a bodega, or do you eat something homemade out of Tupperware? Do you hear birdsongs or sirens? Do you commute via rapid transit, car, or bicycle, or is it simply a short walk from your bed to your desk?

What happens where you live? If you were to capture the pulse of your community's needs, what would they be?

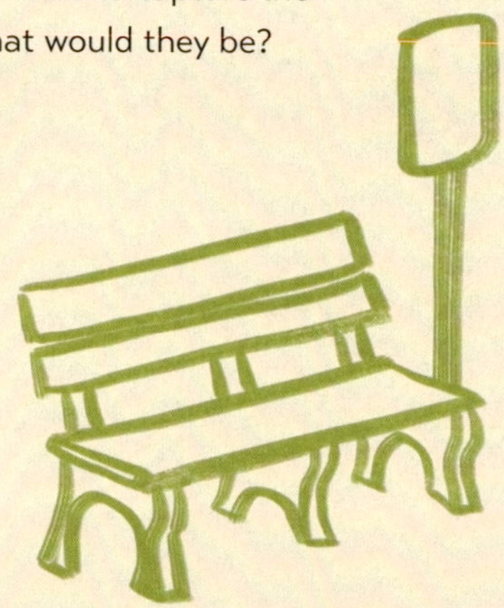

Here are some questions to probe into the place where you live:

- How can I make people slow down and notice things more? What should they be seeing?
- If I could tell people only one thing about my community, what would it be?
- What is a big truth that is being ignored?
- Who is being overlooked here?
- Is there something here that needs to change?
- Is there something about this place that should be known and/or celebrated?
- Who has not been recognized for their contributions? What would be the best way to celebrate them through art?

In Chapter 5, we will explore how to bring research to your work, and when we get there, I'll ask you to keep the following questions in mind:

- Are there unknown histories that you can highlight to help people remember?
- Who used to live here?
- Who used to have a stake in the place where you live?
- Who can you reconnect with here, and who from the past might the community learn from?
- What is the story-before-the-story that might need to be acknowledged?
- Who previously claimed these lands? What names did they give this place?
- How has this place changed? Why did this happen? What intentions were behind the change?
- How have I changed this place? What impacts, good and bad, do I have on it?

Check Yourself

When doing work that speaks to social justice themes, we must remember to check ourselves. For example, racism makes my blood boil, but as a white cis woman, I cannot speak to the lived experience of people of color. However, that doesn't mean that I can't address racism in my creative work. When I consider my own relationship to who I am in a society built upon systemic racism, it is my responsibility to figure out how to make a difference through the experience that I can own.

There is no single way to tackle a tough issue, but it is vitally important to consider who and where you are in the cycle of injustice when tackling tough topics. Make projects that focus on who you are and what you are uniquely positioned to speak to.

CASE STUDY

BEAR WITNESS

A CONVERSATION ON

The Tiny Pricks Project

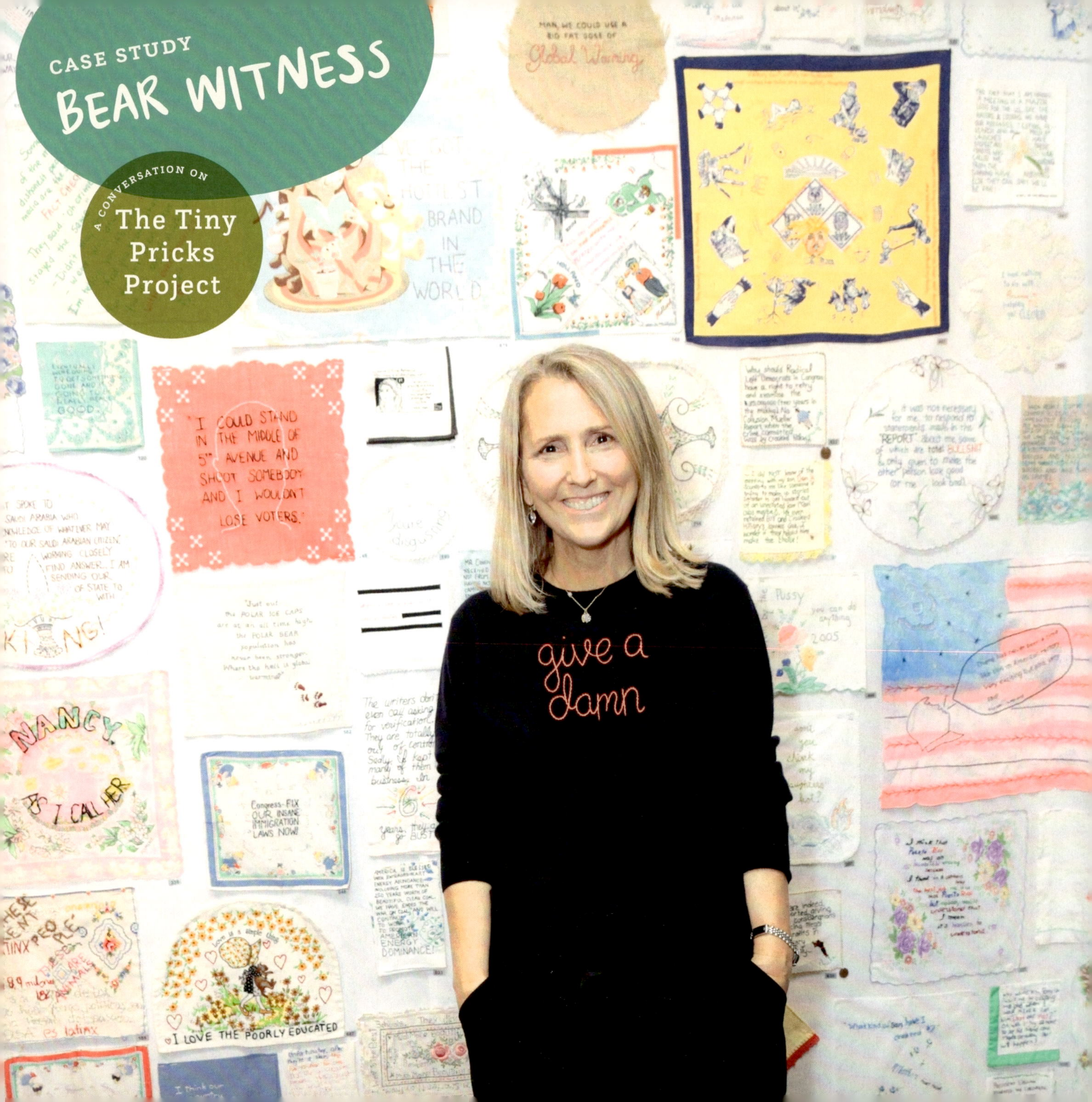

Looking back on 2020–21, the end of Donald Trump's presidency of the United States was a whirlwind of hyperbolic tweets, grandstanding, and threats to democracy. By facilitating hundreds of volunteers, the Tiny Pricks Project captured the bizarre and hurtful words of "45" in stitches, seeking to reframe Trump's words and the movement against them in fancywork. This textile-based historical record juxtaposes truth and fiction in stitchwork, a medium traditionally associated with "women's work." The collection can be viewed online and has been exhibited in San Francisco and New York City. Artist and curator Diana Weymar's work is a testament to how using art to record current events can help magnify ill intentions and injustice.

LEANNE: Do you have any advice for emerging artists who are looking to gain community participation in their own creative projects?

DIANA: Follow the work. If you work hard and are serious about it, people will help you. If your idea is a good one, you can take it out in the world with confidence. The reception to this project has been tremendous. This is a challenging time, and people are grateful for a productive way to be political.

LEFT: Photo: Yvonne Tnt/BFA. Diana Weymar, founder of The Tiny Pricks Project.

RIGHT: *The Best Thing That Ever Happened to Puerto Rico Is President Donald J. Trump*, The Tiny Pricks Project. | Photo: eedahahm. Embroidery by Dana Robson (Instagram: @aquarabbit).

LEANNE: Has the project surprised you in any way?

DIANA: With over 5,000 pieces, there are many surprises, but the greatest thing might be that I wake up every morning, seven days a week, and still look forward to working on it. I'm so inspired by the Tiny Pricks Project community. I didn't realize that the medium would be so generous. Every single piece is amazing. For a medium that has a reputation of striving for perfection, it also works well with imperfection.

LEANNE: The past year has been a period of rapidly reacting—emotionally, physically, and artistically—to the sudden changes brought about by the pandemic. Can you tell me if this has brought any change to your project?

DIANA: Tiny Pricks already had the tagline, "Desperate Times, Creative Measures" before COVID-19, but I had no idea how true this would become! I accept virtual submissions so that people can participate without going to the post office. The high stakes of the Trump presidency brought a further need for this project. There is a sense

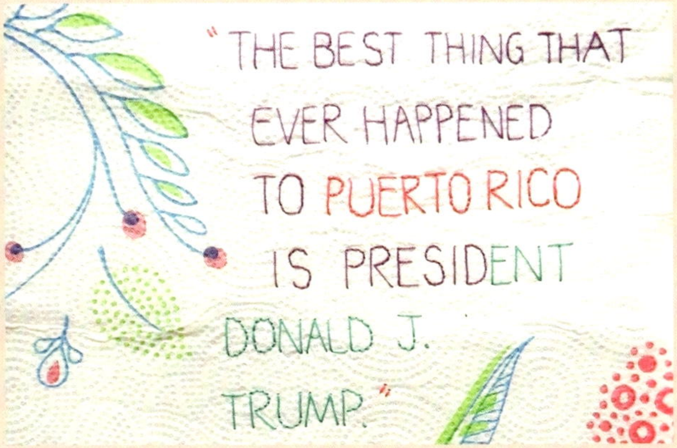

of urgency to document our habits, feelings, and how we've lived. With everyone glued to the news cycle, the project provided an essential outlet to counterbalance feelings of helplessness.

LEANNE: Do you ever receive pieces that you feel don't work with the political aims of the project? If so, how do you deal with this?

DIANA: I accept every piece. Some pieces are challenging to post, but I feel that they all belong. In 2020, the project was opened to include positive language from other sources. It felt important to give people some relief from Trump's words, and to capture a larger historical context.

LEANNE: What do you hope that the Tiny Pricks Project achieves? What do you hope people take away from it?

DIANA: I would like the pieces to remain together as a collection and be viewed as a quiet but beautiful protest against the language of Trump's presidency. I hope what people take away is the concept that something good and beautiful can come out of anything.

DIANA WEYMAR *has worked in publishing and film. She lives in Victoria, BC, and has four children. She is a graduate of Princeton University, where she studied English and creative writing. Diana created and curated Tiny Pricks and Interwoven Stories, which are both international, public textile-based projects.* **tinyprickproject.com**

LEFT: *Drain the Swamp*, The Tiny Pricks Project. | Photo: eedahahm. Embroidery by Danielle Otis (Instagram: @otis.danielle).

RIGHT: *I Want Great Climate*, The Tiny Pricks Project. | Photo: Nelson Hancock. Embroidery by Diana Weymar.

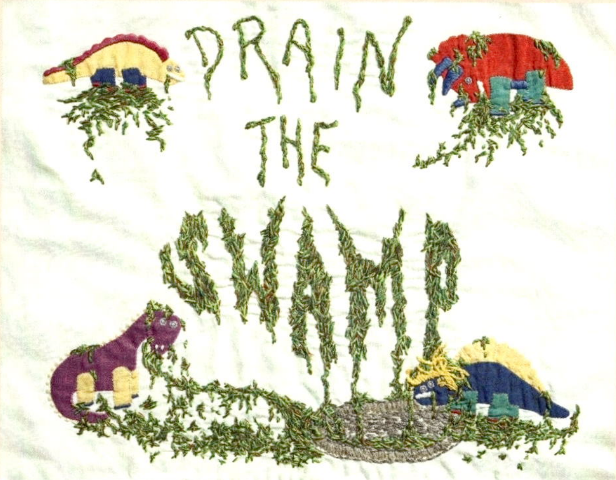

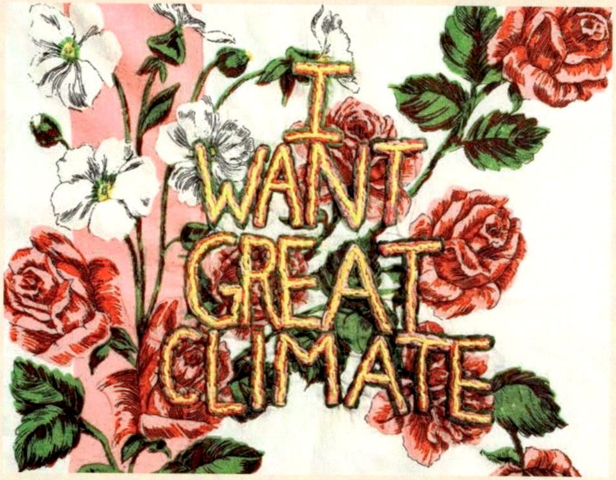

EXERCISE 4

What Time Is It?

A few years ago, I was struggling with a problem with an event that I was planning. My friend Mark was offering a listening ear. He asked me bluntly, "What time is it?" His question threw me for a loop at first, but it was the right one. My problem was not a big deal; what was an issue was my failure to focus on the event's desired outcome and its relevance to my audience. I had to ask myself, "What really needs attention in the world right now?"

Here are some questions that might help you discover what time it is:

- Who needs some love? What can I do about it?
- What change needs to happen in the world?
- Who needs my help and support most urgently?
- What is truly important?
- If I weren't here tomorrow, would it matter to other people?
- If you had only one contribution to make to the world, what would it be?

Conversely, what could get thrown out right now? Take some time to identify what seems unimportant in the face of the struggles around you:

- What emotions are in the air right now?
- Do I agree with the current politics of the day?
- What can I create to help bring about the world that I want to see?
- How are the people around me feeling? What are currently their deepest concerns?
- Can others see themselves in my art? Why or why not?
- Who needs to join in? How can I use my creative expression to invite them to the table?
- How can I take care of myself and provide methods of care to others in this project?

THE SCOPE OF IT: DEFINING PARTICIPATION

The following section is an exploration of different project forms that you may want to explore. For the purposes of this journey, I'm going to assume that you've come to this book with your artistic skills in your back pocket, so I won't detail possible mediums. I trust that you love making something and that you'll deduce how your medium adapts to this form once you spend some time experimenting in your practice.

Projects that call on a community to participate can take many forms:

- A community working together under the direction of artistic facilitation to create things like community quilts, yarn bombings, or group performances. One example of this is the Quarantine Quilt Project (see page 158).
- A project made (by an artist) out of items discarded by a community and created with community labor, such as Thomas Dambo's troll project (see page 20).
- A project that allows a community to tell stories about itself. For examples, see the Poetry Society of New York's Typewriter Project (see page 175), which invites New Yorkers to contribute their own words to a long typewritten scroll, or Candy Chang's Confessions, which asked thousands of participants to share their inner thoughts via private booths where they could write a confession.
- A project that can supply tools for a community to use, such as the Protest Banner Lending Library (see page 28).
- Acts of exchange. Can your project invite skill sharing, the trading of goods, or the swapping of labor?

PROJECTS CAN SHAPE-SHIFT

It might take a while to start to see how your project will come together, but I hope that eventually, you will have an aha moment of your own, like Meg Lewis did. Keep the faith while you work on your ideas.

You don't need to have all the answers right away. Give yourself permission to tool around. Dip your toes first into the murky water of your ideas; don't commit to wading in until you are ready.

Sometimes your project will shape-shift and take on a different form. If this happens to you, go with it. The path to something successful is often paved with haphazard misstarts and moments of doubt. Most artistic things that you try to make will let you down a little bit. To paraphrase radio host Ira Glass, as a developing artist, it can be disappointing when your artistic ambitions don't yet meet the level of your artistic tastes. Becoming skilled at what you want to do takes time. Some of the projects that you think up may never get finished, and some of them may not turn out. Despite this, I hope that each of your ideas and attempts moves you a little bit closer to realizing what it is you want to make.

CHAPTER 4

COCONSPIRATORS UNITE!

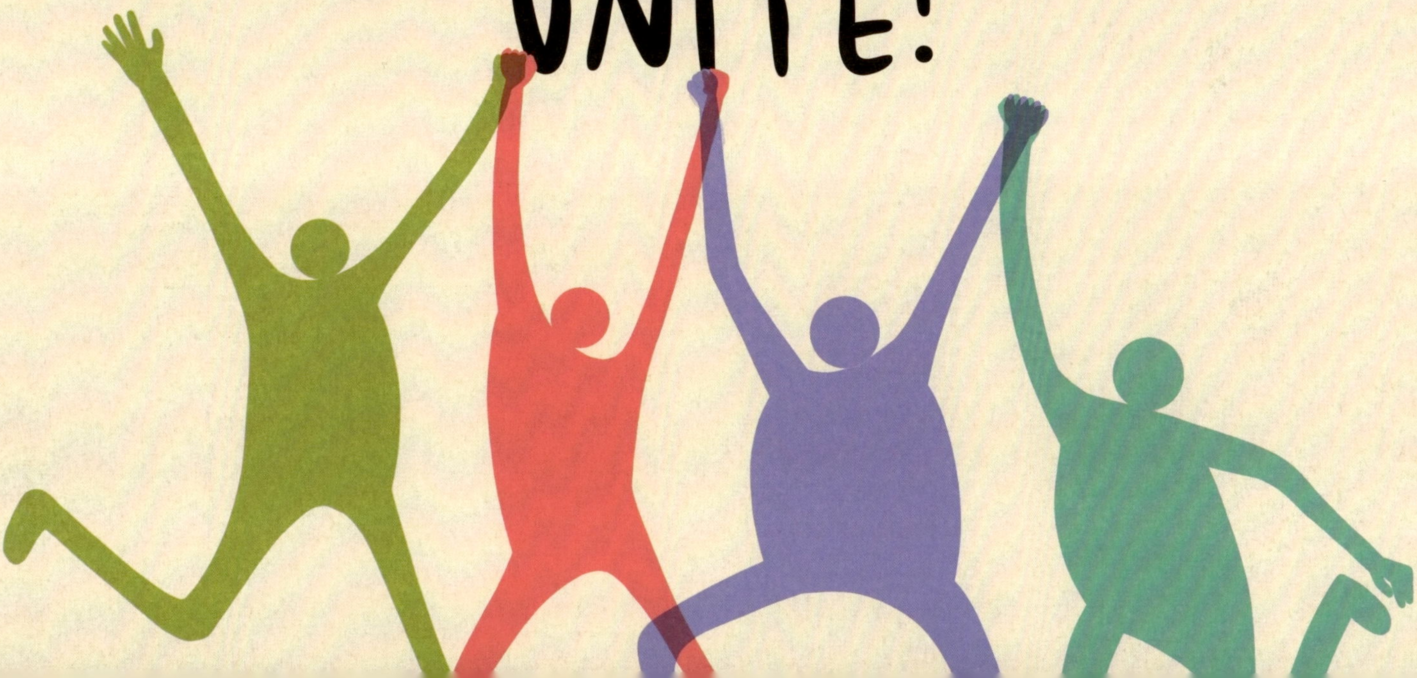

While popular culture may idolize the artist as renegade loner, history reveals that great creative teams have always had an immense impact on the world. The Wright brothers taught humans to fly; John Lennon and Yoko Ono gave us the legendary "bed-ins" for peace; Jean-Michel Basquiat and Andy Warhol made incredible art together, and Elton John and Bernie Taupin wrote songs that we still can't stop humming.

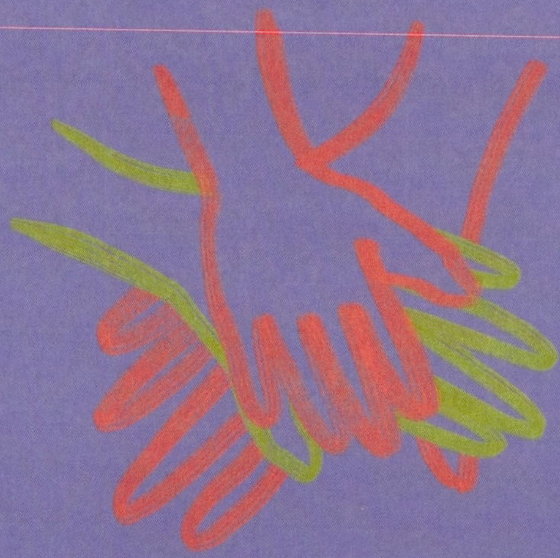

There used to be a vegetarian restaurant in my neighborhood that had terrible service, but delicious nachos. On one side of the restaurant, facing the street, was a large mural with a quote by Margaret Mead: "Never doubt that a small group of thoughtful, committed citizens can change the world. Indeed, it is the only thing that ever has." In short, you need to find your coconspirators, those folks in your life who will not only collaborate with you, but scheme, and daydream, and help you take things up a notch.

If you consider the artists and creators you admire, you'll likely see that most of them have other people to brainstorm and collaborate with. You can find their names listed in the liner notes of albums, cited in interviews, tagged in social media posts, and mentioned in award acceptance speeches. Think of the collaborations between musicians Lady Gaga and Tony Bennett; filmmaker Pedro Almódovar and composer Alberto Iglesias; and fashion designers Elsa Schiaparelli and Jean Cocteau, to name a few. Whether lifelong or short-term, collaborations between artists have resulted in unforgettable cultural contributions.

Fostering a partnership with one or several coconspirators is one of the most important things you can do for your creative life and your creative projects. Collaborators are our strongest critics and confidants. While most others will only experience the polished end result of a project, our collaborators are with us through the messy stages of our creative journeys. They're the ones who know what it really takes, the ones who stay up late with us, who drag art supplies across parking lots in the rain, who share our worries, and who continue to love our projects, despite knowing about all the quirks and hardships involved. Great coconspirators encourage us to push past our limits, and they help us to keep going when we don't know what to do next. Most importantly, everything that coconspirators do for us—we do the same for them. In essence, good collaboration is a relationship of mutual respect and admiration, and sometimes a friendly challenge to push you out of your comfort zone.

NO CREATIVE PERSON IS AN ISLAND

If you want people to support your work as a creative, remember that you have to support their work, too. No matter how shy or intimidated you may be, being part of a creative community is vital. This means that you should go to that book launch, buy that piece of art, comment on that social media post, visit that gallery exhibition, and be a megaphone for the creatives around you. Genuinely show up for other people and their work before expecting them to show up for you. You don't need to personally enjoy everyone's work, but you do need to recognize that you and every person around you plays a vital role in creating an audience and an appetite for creative work.

Take some time to get to know who is in your creative community. Listen to what excites them. When you are passionate about someone else's work, you'll find those who feel the same way. There is no competition in creativity; when we see what is possible within others, it gives us insight into what might be possible in ourselves.

Is It a Collaboration or a Commission?

A word of caution: There is an important difference between someone doing you a favor to make your project real and true collaboration. Collaborators are not merely there to fill a need that you can't afford to pay for; they are colleagues who offer you a true meeting of minds.

Once you've thought about what you might be looking for in a collaborator, consider how you will find them. Our ideal collaborators might be right in front of us, but often, it takes a bit of hunting to find them.

EXERCISE 5

Be Clear about What You Bring to the Table

While our first instinct is usually to seek out people who do the exact same thing that we do well, some of the best working relationships are between people with complementary skills.

Take an inventory of your skills. Are they hard skills, like drawing, writing, or public speaking, or soft skills, like patience or negotiating? Be honest with yourself about what your weaknesses are, as well. These gaps may give you some insight into what qualities you may want to seek in a collaborator.

- What do people tell you that you're good at?
- Which skills could you improve?
- What qualities in a collaborator would help fill in your weaknesses?
- Why would someone want to work with you? What can you offer them?
- What is your working style? For example, do you like to meet face-to-face or online? Do you want to work on certain parts of a project in isolation, or be involved in the entire project from beginning to end?
- Whose projects do you admire?
- Who has expressed enthusiasm for your work in the past?

CLOSE TO HOME

Think about who you know. Write a list. Who in your circle might be interested in working with you? Who do you really want to work with? Is it your best friend? A friend of a friend? That person you volunteered with years ago? The coworker who runs off at lunch to make interesting things?

You may come up with a list of names that surprises you. Sometimes there are creative collaborators in our circles who have been overlooked and are just waiting for us to uncover their talents. I've often been pleasantly surprised to find someone come out of the woodwork exactly when I wished for someone to help fulfill a specific project goal.

HOW YOU KNOW IF YOU'VE FOUND THE RIGHT COLLABORATOR

- Their art interests you.
- They don't see things exactly the same way you do.
- You trust them to share their opinions with you and agree with what they have to say.
- You share an understanding of who will lead. It might be natural for one person to take on the first steps of organizing, giving pep talks, and leading the charge. In other situations, this labor might be shared among different people.
- You can be completely honest with them.
- You both know that it is okay if you don't agree with each other.
- You both agree not to invite other collaborators into the group without consensus.
- You have mutual respect for each other's skills.
- You each have access to complementary networks of people.
- You agree on the desired impact you want this project to have.
- You have a shared vision for the beginning, middle, and end of the project.
- You share the same activist goals.
- You have an understanding of how you both like to work.

If you both desire the same impact, you'll both be happy with where the project goes—even when it ends up in an unexpected place.

CASE STUDY

A SHARED VISION WITH DIFFERENT PERSPECTIVES

A CONVERSATION WITH **Mustaali Raj** and Minahil Bukhari

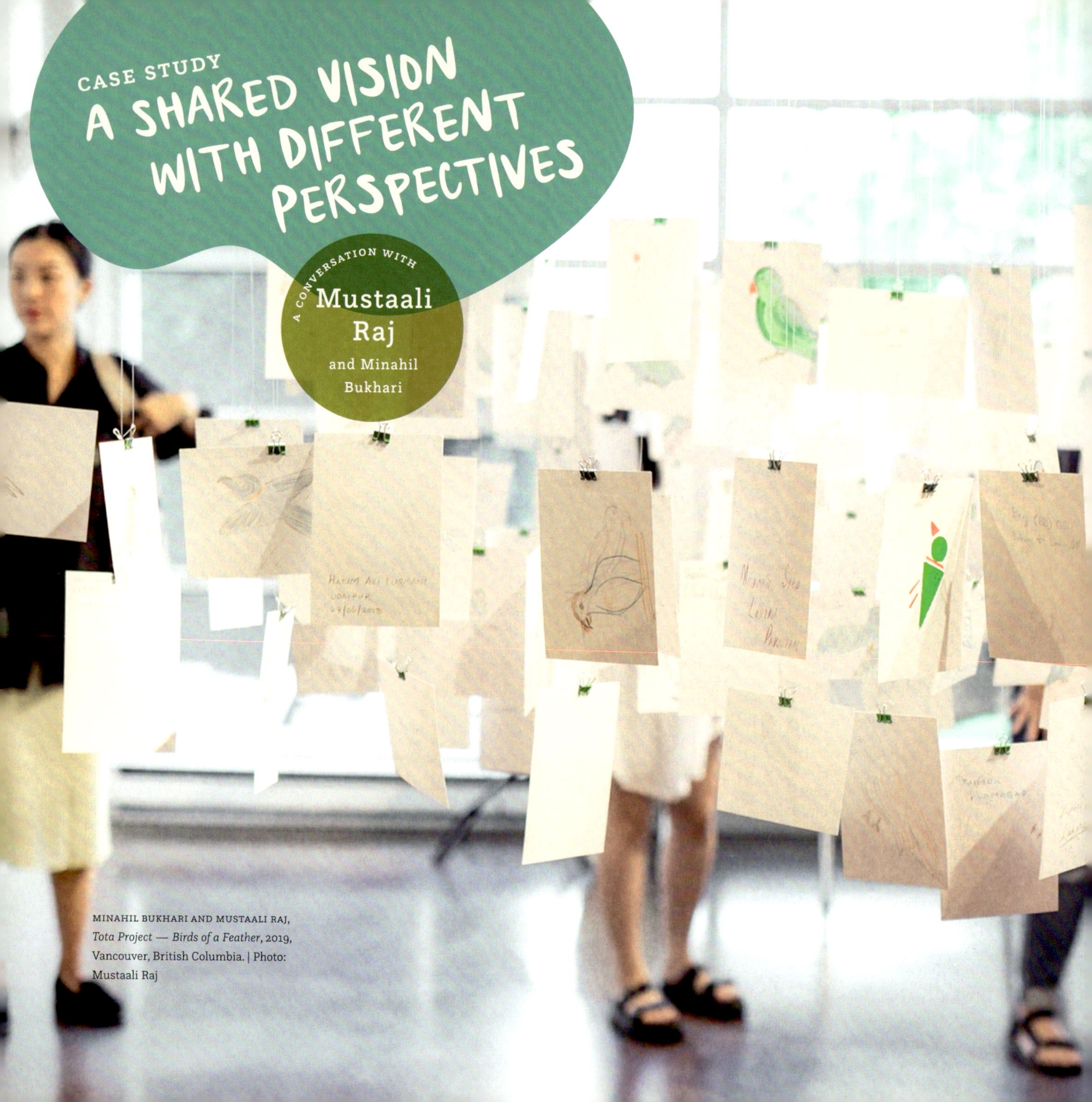

MINAHIL BUKHARI AND MUSTAALI RAJ, *Tota Project — Birds of a Feather*, 2019, Vancouver, British Columbia. | Photo: Mustaali Raj

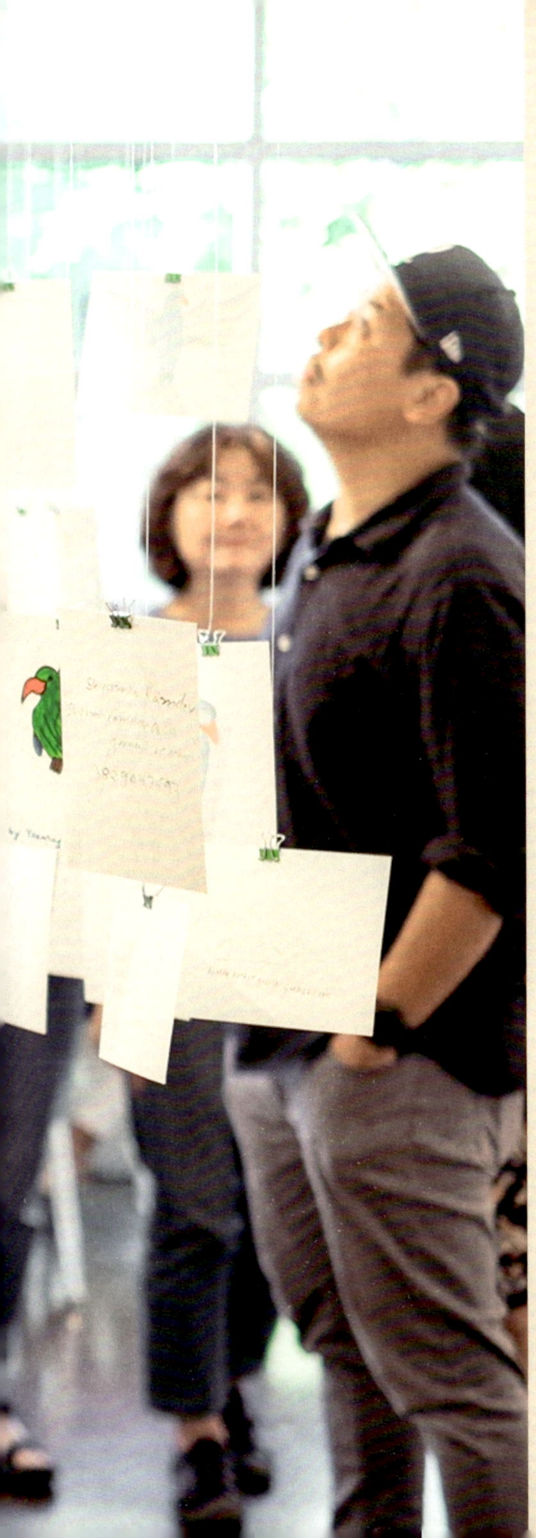

I was struck by how Mustaali Raj and Minahil Bukhari are both husband and wife and a highly creative pair of collaborators. Drawing from their respective cultural and artistic backgrounds, they have worked together on a variety of projects, including Tota Project — Birds of a Feather, a participatory drawing project that collected drawings of parakeets by people from both sides of the India–Pakistan border. Each of the 130 parrots represents "each participant's individuality while retaining a collective sense of belonging—a postcard flock." This work is one of a series created by the couple while traveling that challenges the borders and boundaries of their respective homelands, seeking a collective sense of belonging. Likewise, Mustaali and Minahil work together with a shared vision while also maintaining their own cultural and artistic identities. While they are global travelers, they live in Vancouver, Canada.

LEANNE: When did it occur to both of you to collaborate artistically?

MUSTAALI: As a creative couple, we often collaborate by bringing diverse perspectives from our respective fields into projects. Minahil's fine art background and my graphic design practice pair nicely together. We each look at things from our own lens to reach a common goal. Sometimes she takes the lead, sometimes I take the lead, depending on whose expertise is needed at the moment.

LEANNE: With Tota Project — Birds of a Feather, you engaged people in both India and Pakistan to draw the rose-ringed parakeet, a bird whose habitat extends beyond human borders. What did you learn from interacting with folks in both countries?

MUSTAALI: The concept behind the Tota Project was to nurture a sense of shared identity within the larger South Asian communities, bringing people together through creative connections. One of the highlights for us as artists was the joy people felt while drawing the parrot. For many, it had been ages since they had put pencil to paper, and it was refreshing to see this childlike curiosity come alive in their expressions. As a group activity, multiple people

PARTICIPATE

↓

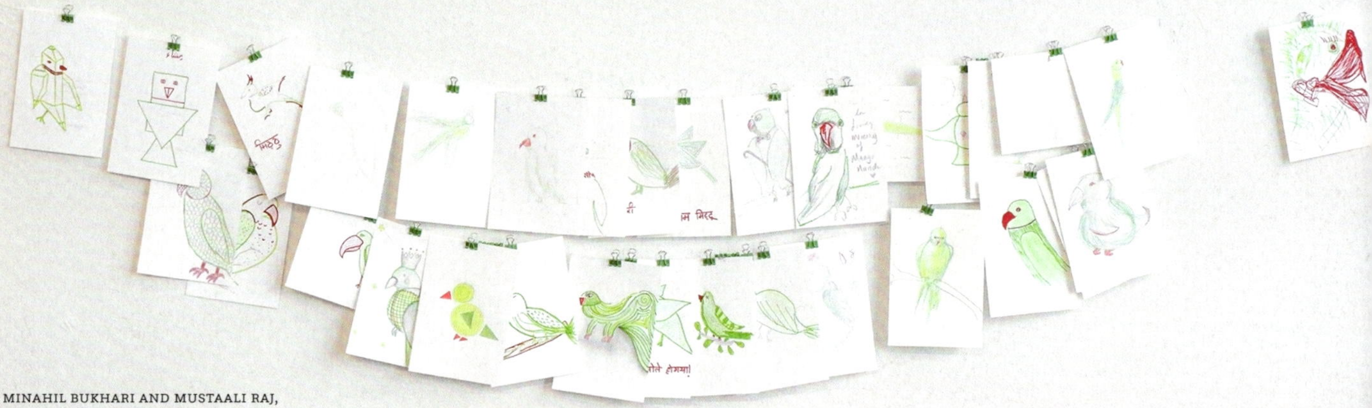

MINAHIL BUKHARI AND MUSTAALI RAJ, *Tota Project — Birds of a Feather*, 2019, Vancouver, British Columbia. | Photo: Mustaali Raj

were drawing parrots together. There was a sense of collective participation—"we are in this together"—that even brought strangers to gather at a table. There was a genuine curiosity to know more about the other drawings, especially those from across the border, leading to in-depth discussions about the reality at hand. Initially, the process was just supposed to be a personal archive of drawings, but the results were far greater than our initial expectations. Hence, we decided to showcase the whole collection as an exhibit.

LEANNE: Can you offer any tips for how emerging creatives should approach potential partners and pitch them an idea?

MUSTAALI: The first step is to come up with an idea or concept that you are genuinely passionate about. If you approach potential partners with a plan in place, they are more likely to get engaged. Outline key tangible benefits of the project, not just for yourself, but also for the potential collaborators and partners. It's equally important to define the impact it will have on the intended audience. When you can show partners that your project will also benefit them in some way, they are more likely to get excited about it, too. That benefit could be monetary, promotion/advertising, or maybe it's just a feel-good campaign. Remember, you have to be the driving force to bring the project to life, even if you get others involved. Lastly, don't be afraid to reach out; sometimes you have to talk to several people or organizations before things click into place.

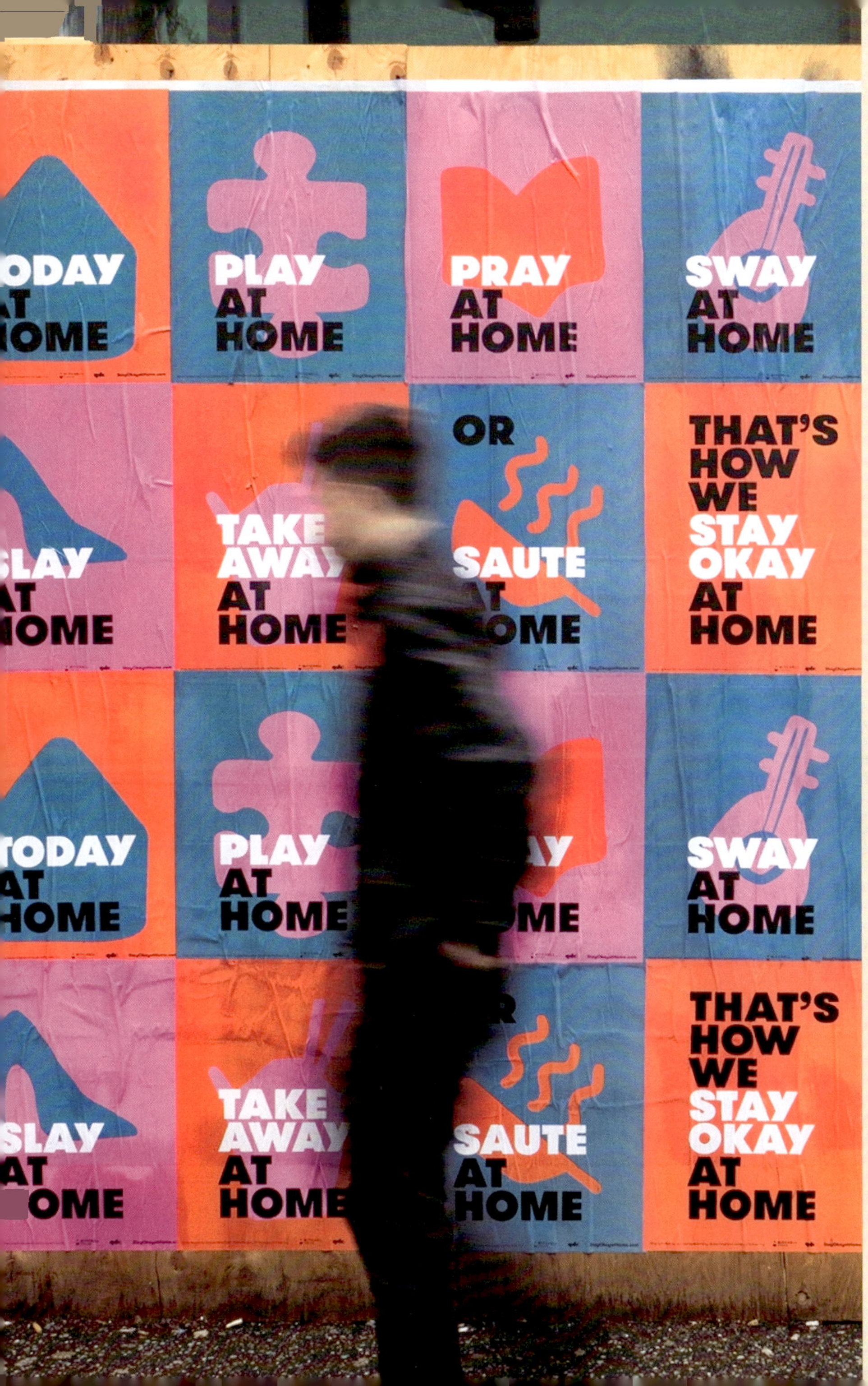

Stay Okay at Home

This project fostered positive and lively inspiration for activities to do at home. The outdoors had an eerie, empty feeling, but these large vibrant posters brought a bit of joy back into the streets of Vancouver while encouraging people to stay okay at home.

LEFT: DESIGNED BY MUSTAALI RAJ, executed in partnership with Mitchell Press, GDC BC, and the Poster Guy, *Stay Okay at Home*, 2020, Vancouver, British Columbia. | Photo: Mustaali Raj. Due to the COVID-19 shutdowns and lockdowns, there was an emphasis on encouraging people to stay at home. This poster campaign helped support public safety campaigns.

Line of Control

In the summer of 2018, Mustaali and Minahil traveled to both India and Pakistan, their respective birthplaces. These two countries share a common history, heritage, and political tension. The poetics of this conjoined relationship between the countries became apparent when they visited the Lahori Gate in Delhi and the Delhi Gate in Lahore. Moments in their travel emanated this sentiment so perfectly that they decided to capture them through the lens of their camera. This led to the beginning of the Line of Control series, which captures history, moments, architecture, and subjects that mirror one another across the India–Pakistan border. *lineofcontrol.org*

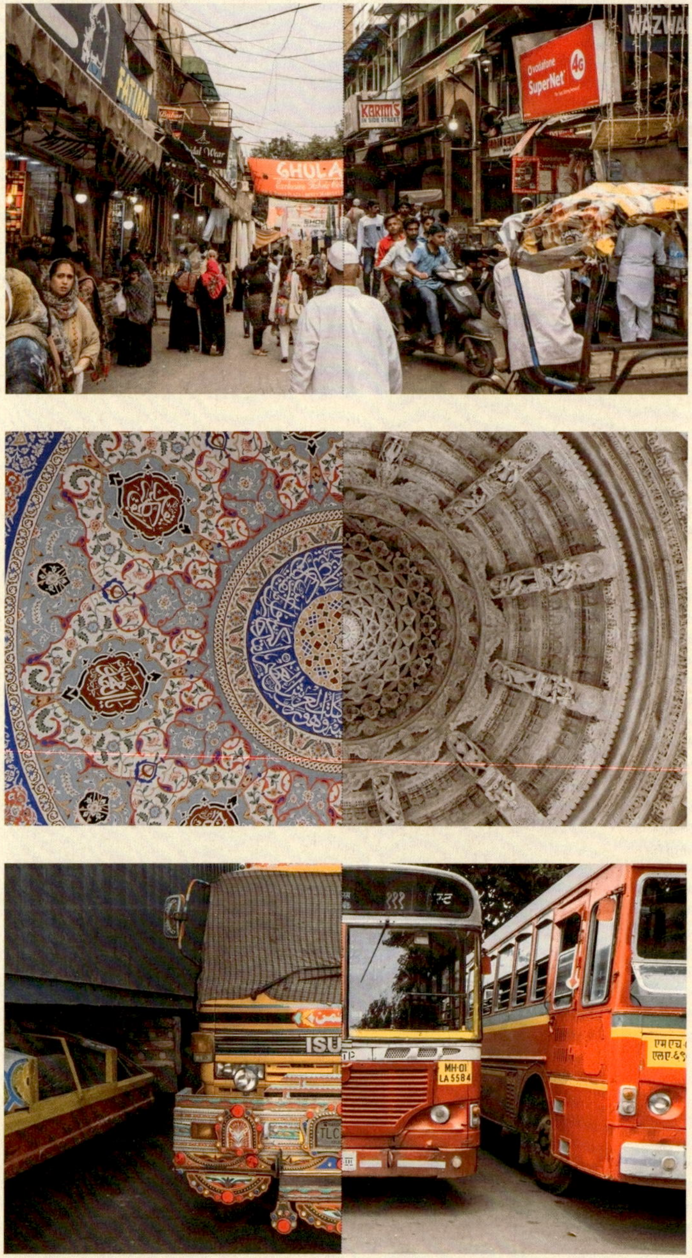

RIGHT: MINAHIL BUKHARI AND MUSTAALI RAJ, *Line of Control*, 2018, India and Pakistan. | Photos: Mustaali Raj

MUSTAALI RAJ is a visual artist, art director, and graphic designer with a multidisciplinary practice. As an engineer-turned-designer, his creative process is a cohesive blend of left- and right-brain thinking. Being both a third-culture kid and an avid traveler, his sense of belonging extends well beyond geographic boundaries. This multifaceted sense of belonging and set of experiences play an important role in exploring the intersection of identities through his work. Mustaali's projects have been internationally recognized by numerous publications, media outlets, and award shows. **mustaaliraj.com**

MINAHIL BUKHARI is a Pakistani Canadian artist with an interdisciplinary practice that approaches projects with a lens of intentionality, conceptual thinking, and global contextualization. Alongside her fine art practice, her media include photography, interior curation, styling, and art direction. Minahil enjoys working the sweet spot between fine art and accessibility. She has created multiple large-scale installations immersing and engaging the viewer's bodily presence. She has received multiple awards, and her works have been widely exhibited in Canada. **minahilbukhari.com**

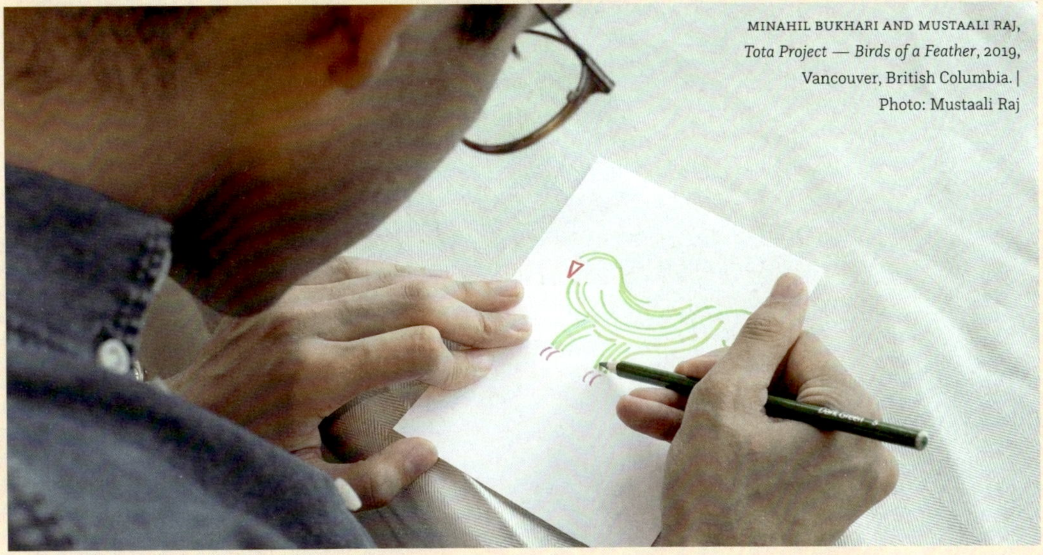

MINAHIL BUKHARI AND MUSTAALI RAJ, *Tota Project — Birds of a Feather*, 2019, Vancouver, British Columbia. | Photo: Mustaali Raj

SOMETIMES YOU HAVE TO LOOK FAR AND WIDE

What if it seems that everyone else has found their artistic soul mate, yet you are still looking? Finding collaborators can take work. One of the best things you can do is to get serious about spreading the word—tell everyone. The more you share exactly who you are looking for, the more likely you'll get an introduction to the right person to collaborate with.

WAYS TO FIND COLLABORATORS

- Make a post in your social media accounts.
- Ask friends.
- Tell your barber or hairdresser or pet groomer.
- Post an open call on a community website.
- Post on professional websites for arts councils, craft guilds, art school alumni, art studios.
- Put up a poster at your local library or art school.
- Find a meet-up group or a community center group that works in the medium(s) you are interested in.
- Be brave and reach out to someone whose work you admire.

If this last suggestion seems intimidating, note that there would be no Poetry Society of New York (page 172) if Stephanie Berger and Nicholas Adamski had not taken a chance on each other. This is how Stephanie described her first impressions upon meeting her eventual longtime collaborator: "Nick and I met in grad school at the New School. We both sat next to the teacher and across from each other, but we were not friends. We're very different people. I was like, 'Oh, he's your classic charming kiss-up who talks a lot.' I was more of your typical nerd; I wanted to learn as much as possible. I'd wanted to start the Poetry Brothel for some time. I've always been operations oriented, but I had little experience in event logistics. A mutual friend recommended Nick. He was writing his thesis on erotic poetry and planning events and parties. I invited him for a drink to talk about the concept. It was funny because we had dismissed each other, but we had instant creative chemistry once we were engaged in conversation. Our skills balance each other's out so well."

MEETING UP

The goal of meeting a potential collaborator for the first time is to decide whether you are a good match. Be safe: if you didn't connect through your own social networks, choose a well-populated public place to meet. (A note to underage readers: Never meet up with a stranger alone. Inform your parent or guardian of the meeting and make sure to take an adult with you.)

The location you choose should be a comfortable place to talk. Look for somewhere that has good lighting and a low noise level and that doesn't mind hosting you for a few hours. Coffee shops with long hours and big tip jars are great places to meet. Remember to always compensate the staff working there. With luck, the space may become your ongoing meeting place. If the cost of meeting in a restaurant is prohibitive, community spaces, public parks, and public libraries are great options.

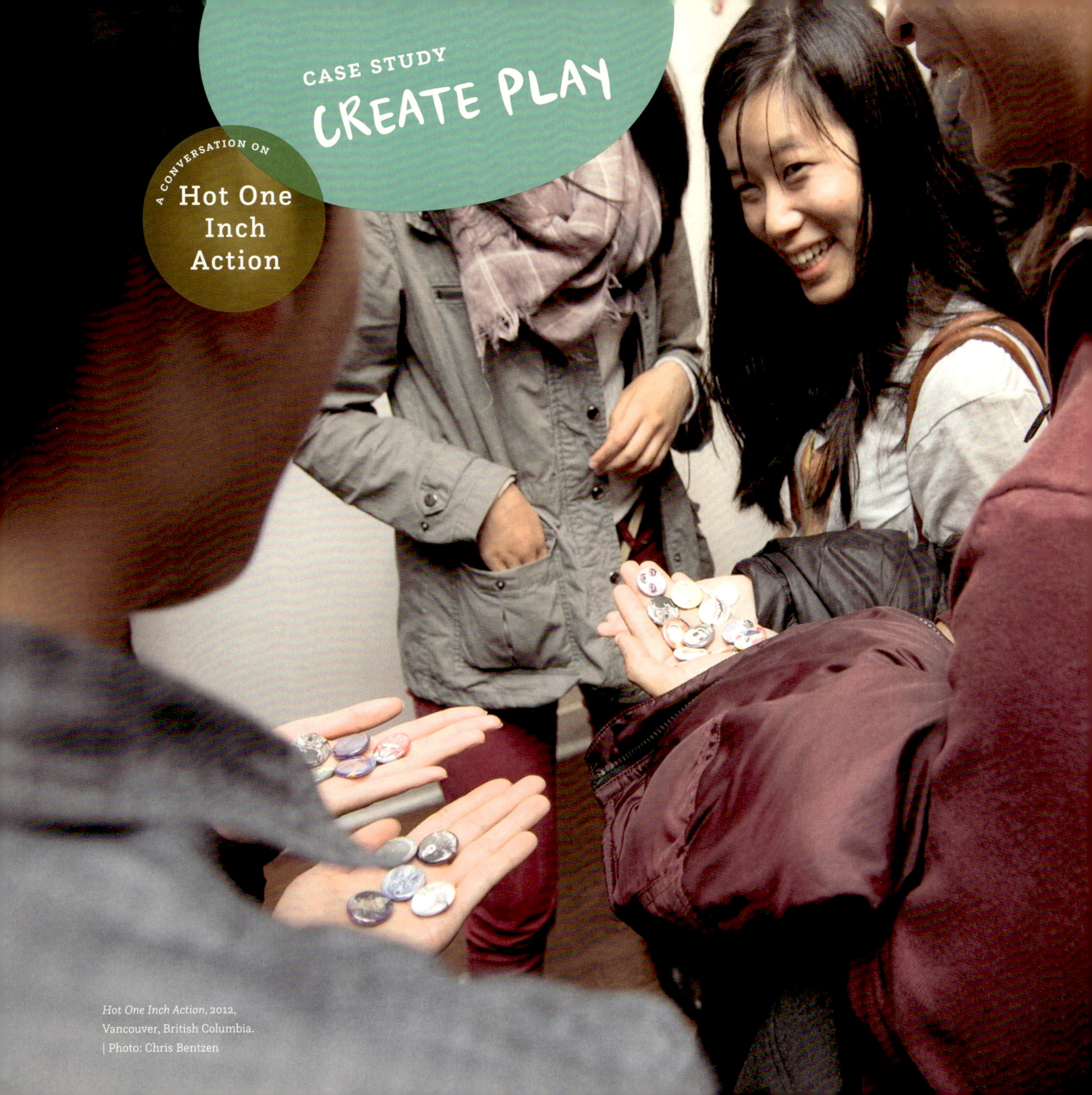

Hot One Inch Action, 2012, Vancouver, British Columbia. | Photo: Chris Bentzen

For more than fifteen years, Chris Bentzen and Jim Hoehnle curated an enormously fun art show called Hot One Inch Action in Vancouver, British Columbia. Hot One Inch Action subverted the traditional experience of art openings and art collecting: the art was extremely affordable and was selected for purchase at random, and art patrons bartered with each other within minutes of buying the art, raising its supposed value and desirability on the spot. At each art show, the artwork of fifty artists was reproduced in miniature on limited-edition one-inch buttons. For a mere five dollars, attendees were invited to reach into a large box covered in pink fun fur and draw a chance selection of pins. After purchasing their buttons, patrons traded them with other attendees to collect their favorite works. Hot One Inch Action stands as a prime example of creatively bending the rules of traditional passive interaction with art while creating an opportunity to break down social barriers.

RIGHT: *Hot One Inch Action*, 2012, Vancouver, British Columbia. | Photo: Chris Bentzen

LEANNE: How did the idea for Hot One Inch Action and the collaborative partnership between the two of you come about?

CHRIS: I had an art show in 2003 that included one-inch buttons. Jim approached me at that show to work together to produce a group art show featuring art on one-inch buttons. Everything came together pretty easily after that. The name of the show was kind of a joke at first, but we couldn't think of anything better, so we went with it. Fifty artists just seemed like a good number. The first show in 2004 was an experiment, and when it worked, we knew we'd found the right combination. And then we just kept doing it every year for fifteen years!

JIM: I had been coproducing festival events that focused on cycling advocacy with a group called PedalPlay and was looking to see if I could do something different. I had read about an art event where people were buying one-inch buttons that featured local art from a gumball machine at a gallery event. One of the unexpected results of the randomness that generated was people trading the buttons. It sounded fun. Around that time, I bumped into Chris at his art show and pitched him the idea. We had a few meetings, tossed around some ideas, and our show was born. There were a lot of changes in the first five years, but we eventually settled on a formula that worked. For example, we had live bands and DJs at first, but then we just played music because no one cared about anything but the buttons!

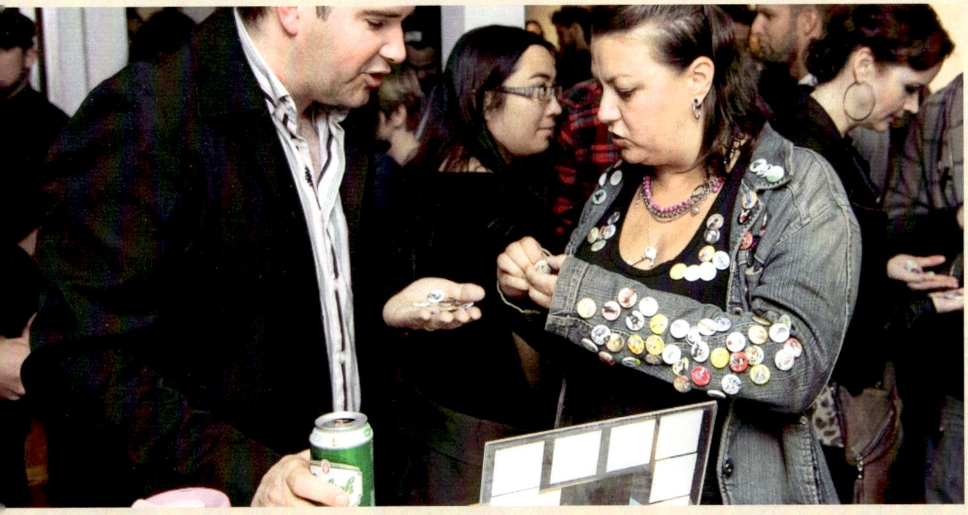

From 2004 to 2018, Hot One Inch Action was the original, one-night-only show of button art and social interaction from Vancouver, BC. The tiny work of fifty different artists is reproduced on one-inch buttons. Buy a mixed bag of five random buttons for five dollars. Want a specific button? Trade with other people at the show. How bad do you want that button?! That's when the hot action starts. Created and hosted by Jim Hoehnle and Chris Bentzen.

LEANNE: What advice would you give to emerging producers who are planning projects that involve active participation from audience members and possibly engaging people with a set of rules?

CHRIS: Don't force participation. And if the rules are complicated, forget it. It should be easy to explain quickly. It also got easier for us every year—returning collectors became our ambassadors. People who had experienced Hot One Inch Action before would teach newcomers the rules of engagement.

JIM: Keep it simple and stick with it. Our show grew steadily successful because our core concept didn't change. People knew what to expect and what to pitch to their friends if they wanted company for a fun night.

CHRIS BENTZEN *is an artist, gallery space and event curator, and professional creative.* ***bentzen.ca***

JIM HOEHNLE *is an artisan, noise musician, and event producer.*

TIPS FOR MEETING VIRTUALLY

If you are meeting a potential collaborator online, be sure to give the meeting just as much care as you would in real life.

- Before the meeting, send them an email to confirm the details and provide a few notes so they know what to expect from the conversation. Check your time zone and theirs. Be sure to clarify which platform you will use for the meeting.
- Mute your phone's ringer and any other distractions. Your attention should be on the person you're meeting with.
- Place a notepad or sketchbook and a pen next to you. Be sure to jot down notes as you chat. Details that you'll want to remember are sure to come up.
- Don't make them wait; log on early.
- Be honest about your situation if you don't have access to a quiet solo workspace; if you expect to be interrupted by kids, pets, or roommates during the call, let them know up front.
- Don't feel that you have to launch into the nitty-gritty of the project in the first few minutes of your conversation. Take some time to get to know them.
- Don't forget to end the call with an agreement to follow through on next steps and a thank-you for their time.
- Don't be too disappointed if you don't make a connection, or if they are unable to envision the project as you see it. This just means that there is a better match for you somewhere else out there.

SWEET CHEMISTRY: COMPATIBLE COLLABORATIONS

How can you tell if you have great creative chemistry with your coconspirators?

- They are keenly excited about your ideas, and you are keenly excited about theirs.
- You keep the same hours and have the same kind of availability.
- You are willing to do the hard work of creating together, whether you live in the same city or half a world apart.
- You know that working with them will continue to bring surprise and delight.
- You look forward to your next exchange with them and keep scraps of things that you think may inspire them.
- You are amazed at how easy things seem to be when you work together.

THE MORE, THE MERRIER: WORKING WITH A GROUP

If you have ever suffered through a group project in school, you've probably realized that working in a group is very different than working in pairs. The great thing about artistic collaboration is that you get to choose who you want to work with. When a number of people come together, there is as much power in collective creativity as there is opportunity to discover conflicting viewpoints.

How do you know whether a group of people will work well together? Talk it out. Here are some things to discuss:

- Will you agree on actions by majority vote, or by consensus?
- Will there be defined roles and responsibilities?
- Who will be the spokesperson?
- Do you need a manifesto?
- Who will pay for supplies, space, insurance (if needed), etc.?
- What will the main method of communication be?
- Who "owns" the end product?
- How will you collectively document your process?

Before you start, develop a plan together so that you each have a map to refer to when decisions and possible conflicts come up. Clear understanding of your collective goals will ensure that you make the right choices when you need to.

GOT PRIVILEGE?

Remember in Chapter 3, when I asked you to look at your lived experiences and your motivations to create? One of the best things that you can do as a potential collaborator is to take on the continual work of learning to be a better ally. We all have inherent biases that we need to check. If you are not familiar with the concept of privilege, take the time to learn what it is, how to recognize it, and how it may impact your potential collaborators. Empower yourself—we must all be committed to learning and unlearning systems and protocols that cause oppression and to finding the resources to do so without putting the burden on those who experience that oppression.

Be open to being challenged. Those of us who enjoy privilege need to be aware that our lived experience may be quite different from that of our collaborators. Make it your mission to listen carefully when your ideas are critiqued by those who have different experiences than you.

LIMITED-TIME COLLABORATION

Sometimes you just need people to show up and help. Posting an open call for collaborators is a great way to find them. Blog posts, handbills, posters, and social media channels are easy ways to spread the word. Some collaborators will follow you through a lifetime of creative work. Others may be there for only a day or two. In every case, I hope that you'll learn new things from one another that you can take with you into future endeavors.

WHAT DOES MUTUAL SUCCESS LOOK LIKE?

Everyone has their own idea of what success is. Your outlook can be a result of your upbringing, your aspirations, and your financial circumstances. Unpacking what mutual success looks like will go a long way toward setting up a stellar collaboration.

Host a frank conversation with your collaborators on what success means to each one of you. Is it simply executing something and having an enjoyable day? Encouraging true community participation? Inciting activist-led change? Is it fame and future opportunities? Whatever your goals are, they should be shared by all collaborators.

NO WAY: NONNEGOTIABLES

What would make you (or any of your coconspirators) walk away from a project? We all have different things that are important to us. Some may value complete creative freedom over funding. Others may require rehearsals to be scheduled around their childcare needs. Sometimes, a person only wants to collaborate on one project, not subsequent projects. While it is impossible to foresee all nonnegotiables at the start of a relationship, I recommend having a discussion about your no-gos before you fully engage in creating with each other.

Nonnegotiables change over time, and checking in with your partners every so often will ensure that your collaboration has longevity.

DISTANCE MAKES THINGS STRANGER: CHECK IN REGULARLY

Recognize when your collaborator needs a day or week off, but don't let the time between your connections dwindle. One of the greatest challenges of working with other people is when the time between meetings stretches a little too long, and one or both of you forgets where things left off, exactly. Like losing your spot in a book or a TV series, it may take some time to come back and immerse yourself in the plot again.

If you can't meet face-to-face, figure out some way to keep the conversation going, such as text messages, exchanging photos on social media, phone calls, keeping shared calendars and/or collaborative documents, and mutually set deadlines.

STRUGGLING? ASK THE HONEST QUESTION

There will come times in the life cycle of a project when you and your collaborator are not working well together. This may happen because one of you shows more passion for the project than the other, or because you don't share the same vision or desired outcome for the project. Or, perhaps they are struggling with a difficult situation such as depression, addiction, a breakup, extra work hours, or a personal loss. If you find yourself engaged in a project but not getting traction from your partner, treat your collaboration like a relationship and talk to them. If you can identify the problem together and be willing to work with each other in a respectful manner, the two of you can work out a solution that works for both of you.

BE READY TO BE SUCCESSFUL

Sometimes projects can suddenly expand beyond our wildest dreams—you may receive a dream commission, get a ton of press, or become an acclaimed success overnight.

What happens if your collaborator is excited to do a ton of press, but the others are camera shy? What happens if you are suddenly granted a windfall? Would you divide it up according to division of labor, or reinvest it back into the project? What if you are asked to tour with the project, but only half your team is available? It's good to think through variety of scenarios that could come to pass and workshop possible reactions.

PROMPT

Ask for Feedback

The best way to provide feedback is to be clear, direct, and kind.

- How can I better support you in this project?
- Do you think this is working?
- I notice [blank], can you tell me why that is?
- If you could change one thing about this collaboration, what would it be?
- Is the project looking the way you envisioned it? Why or why not?
- How long would you like to work together? Is there an end point for you?

No project is perfect, but inciting dialogue with those you work with is a sure way to keep the project alive and to ensure a positive experience for those involved.

PROMPT

Be Prepared before It Happens!

- **PRESS:** who will be the voice of your project?
- **RECOGNITION:** a classic trope of stories about the music industry is that conventionally attractive bandmates are featured in press photos most often. How would you handle this if/when it happens?
- **OWNERSHIP:** if someone needs to walk away, will that mean the end of the project, or is there a longevity plan?
- **DISAGREEMENTS:** how will you handle them? Will you have a mediator on standby?
- **MONEY:** how will it be spent, received, saved, and divided?
- **COPYRIGHT:** will you permit work from the project to be used outside of the partnership?
- **TRAVEL:** are you all willing and able to travel, given the opportunity? Would you be okay with only part of your team traveling?
- **DIVISION OF PROPERTY:** when your collaboration ends, who ends up with the supplies?
- **DEATH:** if one person perishes, what is the plan for their work and for the other collaborators?

DON'T FORGET TO BRING HOME FLOWERS—FOSTER THAT RELATIONSHIP

Creative coconspirators need to think of each other as partners, and partnerships flourish when each person pays attention to the other. Take the time to learn what your coconspirator needs to be creative. Is it a certain work-space? A time of day? What makes them perform at their best, and how can you help them with that?

Great coconspirators show up with surprise snacks, new opportunities, thoughts they've scribbled in their note-book outside of a meeting, an inspirational book they know you'll love, or a great new song that will kick off your meeting. They know your inside jokes, how you like your coffee, and whether you are gluten-free. Don't forget to woo your creative partners from time to time.

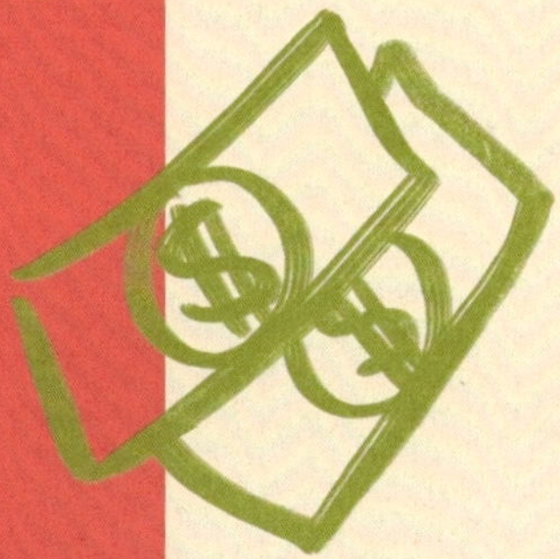

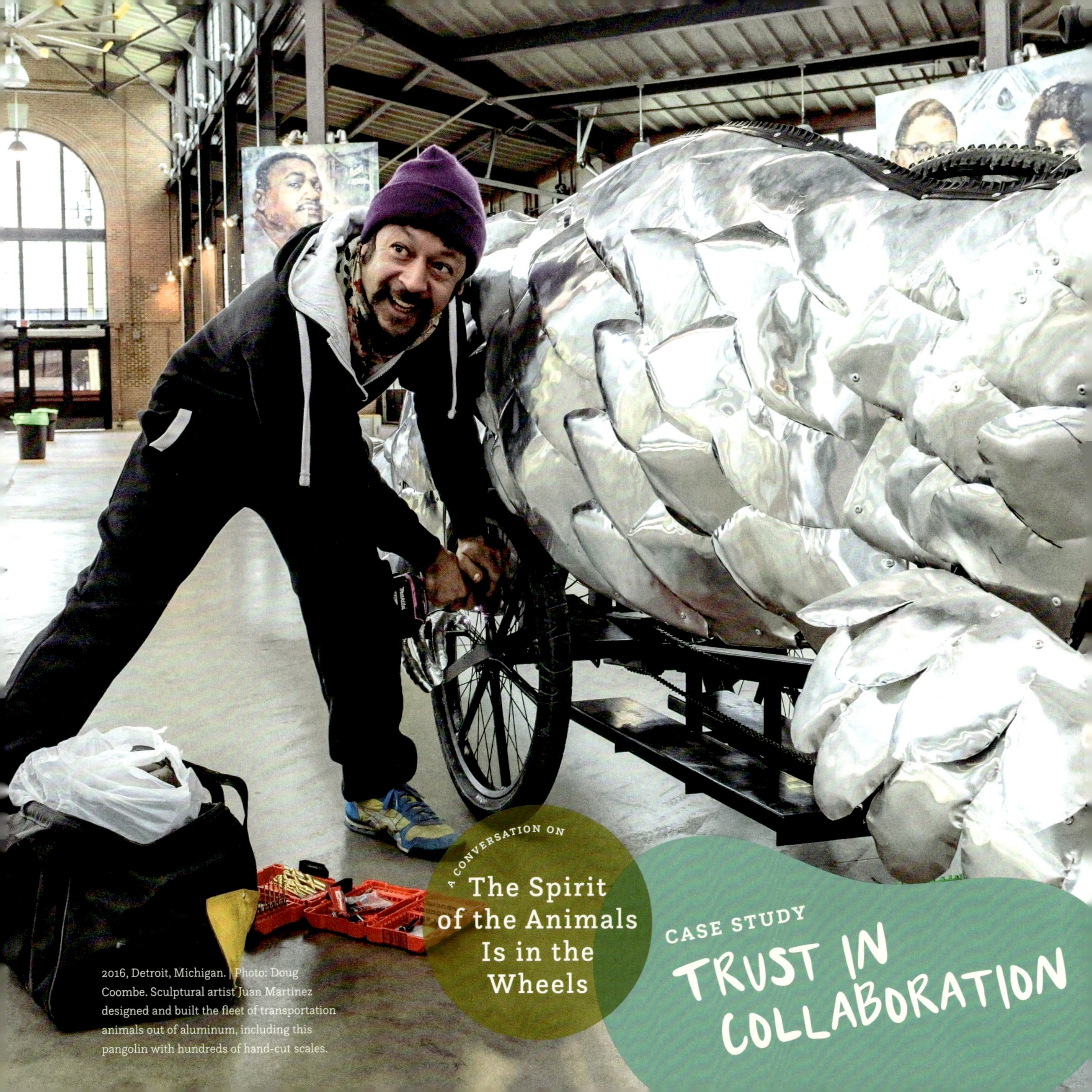

A CONVERSATION ON

The Spirit of the Animals Is in the Wheels

CASE STUDY

TRUST IN COLLABORATION

2016, Detroit, Michigan. | Photo: Doug Coombe. Sculptural artist Juan Martinez designed and built the fleet of transportation animals out of aluminum, including this pangolin with hundreds of hand-cut scales.

I can't help but smile every time I think of The Spirit of the Animals Is in the Wheels. This fleet of shiny, pedal-powered, fantastical animals was created by Juan Martinez and Dave Eggers. From Dave's conception of a fleet of animal bikes steered by adults to Juan's execution of highly elaborate metal sculptures, this incredible partnership resulted in a scaled pangolin, a bison, and a rhinoceros clanking through the streets of Detroit, transporting kids through the Eastern Market neighborhood. These animal bikes make it possible for middle school kids to travel from their local schools to the 826michigan after-school literacy and tutoring center, one of nine 826 centers that Dave has established across the US. These magical beasts are enjoyed by the residents of "Motor City" as a public art project and transport system for 826 literacy and writing students to travel throughout their neighborhood. Universally conjuring joy in all who see them, they also tour across the US, visiting art spaces, schools, and community venues.

RIGHT: 2016, Detroit, Michigan. | Photo: Doug Coombe. 826michigan executive director Amanda Uhle takes children for a ride on the pangolin.

LEANNE: How did The Spirit of the Animals Is in the Wheels come about?

DAVE: About fifteen years ago, I was watching the pedicabs on the Embarcadero. At the time, I was drawing a lot of bears and bison, and the shape of a fully loaded pedicab seemed very close to that of bison and bears—that big, lumbering shape in motion. So I asked Gate Five Group in the Bay Area to build a bear out of an old pedicab. They created one using foam and fur, and it was light and rideable. But I thought maybe a metallic bear would be interesting, so I commissioned a different group, Gizmo Art Production in San Francisco, to create a steel bear-bike that could fit about four people—which was successful. Around that time, Amanda Uhle, my partner in Michigan, connected me with Juan Martinez. He took the idea into new territory, creating more delicate and sculptural versions of the animal bikes. Juan is a true artist.

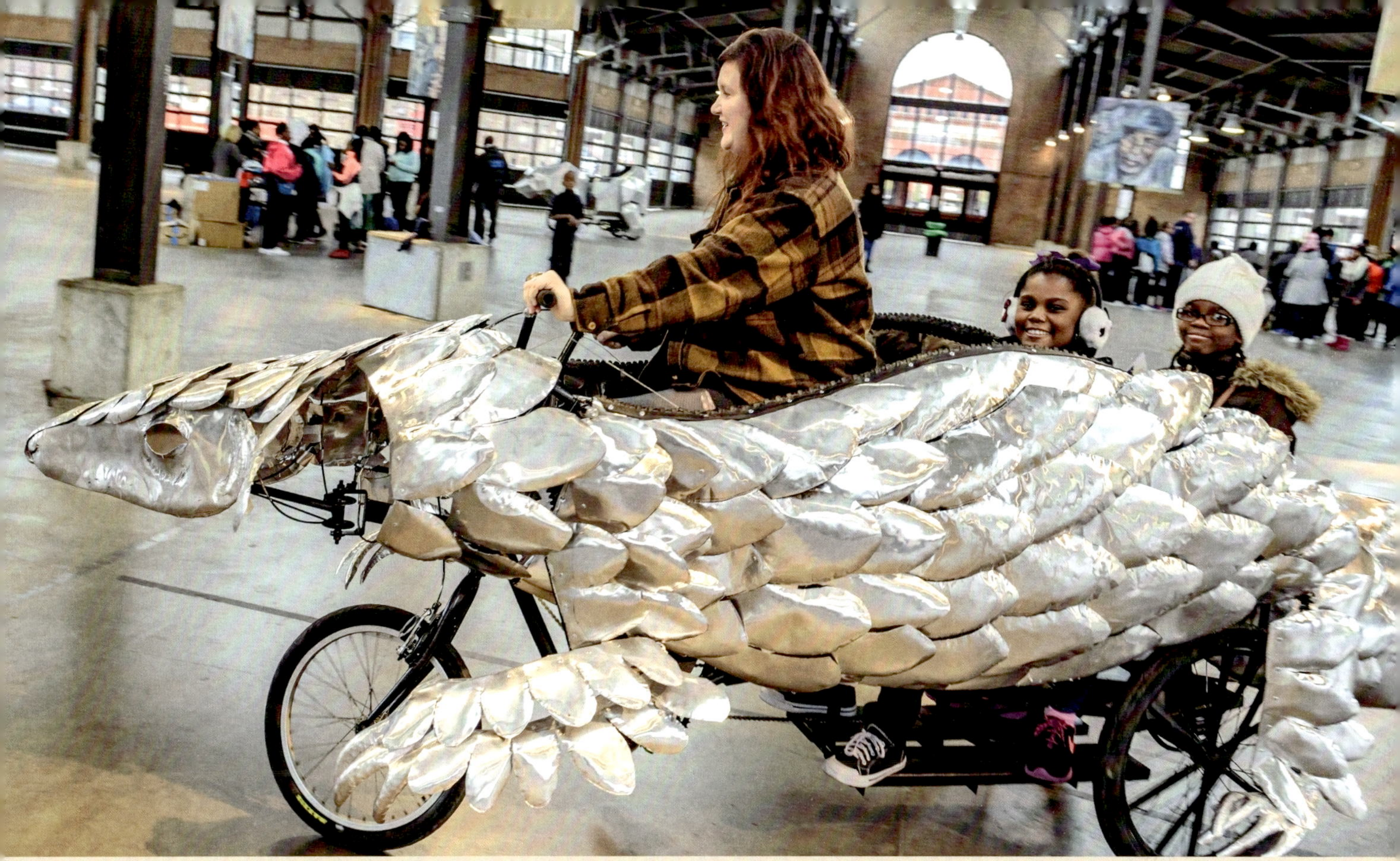

LEANNE: Why is it important to you to make art that people can use?

JUAN: Given the nature of the art world, it is too easy for spaces like galleries to be elitist. These sculptures counteract elitism in the best way: these creatures are larger than life and can't be cooped up in a gallery. They're meant to roam free, out in the streets! When I take them to outdoor events, I love that kids get to use their bodies to interact with my sculptures physically. It's almost impossible to find that kind of experience in a gallery.

LEANNE: Not only do the sculptures look great, they each accommodate adult drivers and small passengers. How did you go about working out this creative problem?

JUAN: Dave gave me a napkin sketch and pretty much left me to figure it out. I pride myself on finding simple solutions to complex problems. I only had a month to build the bison and the pangolin, so there was no time to do prototypes. I made sketches and scale models of cardboard and baling wire for the key moving parts. Mostly I didn't overthink it, just kept a steady pace and trusted my instincts.

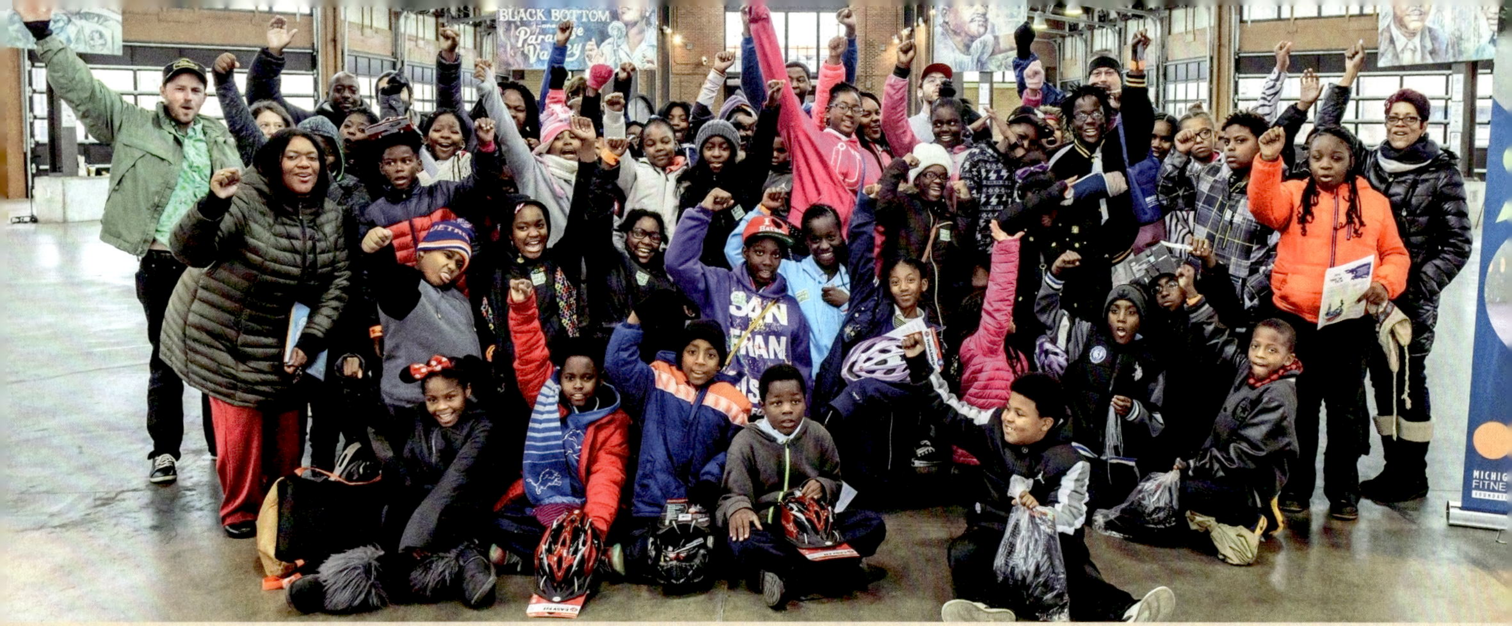
BLACK BOTTOM
Paradise Valley

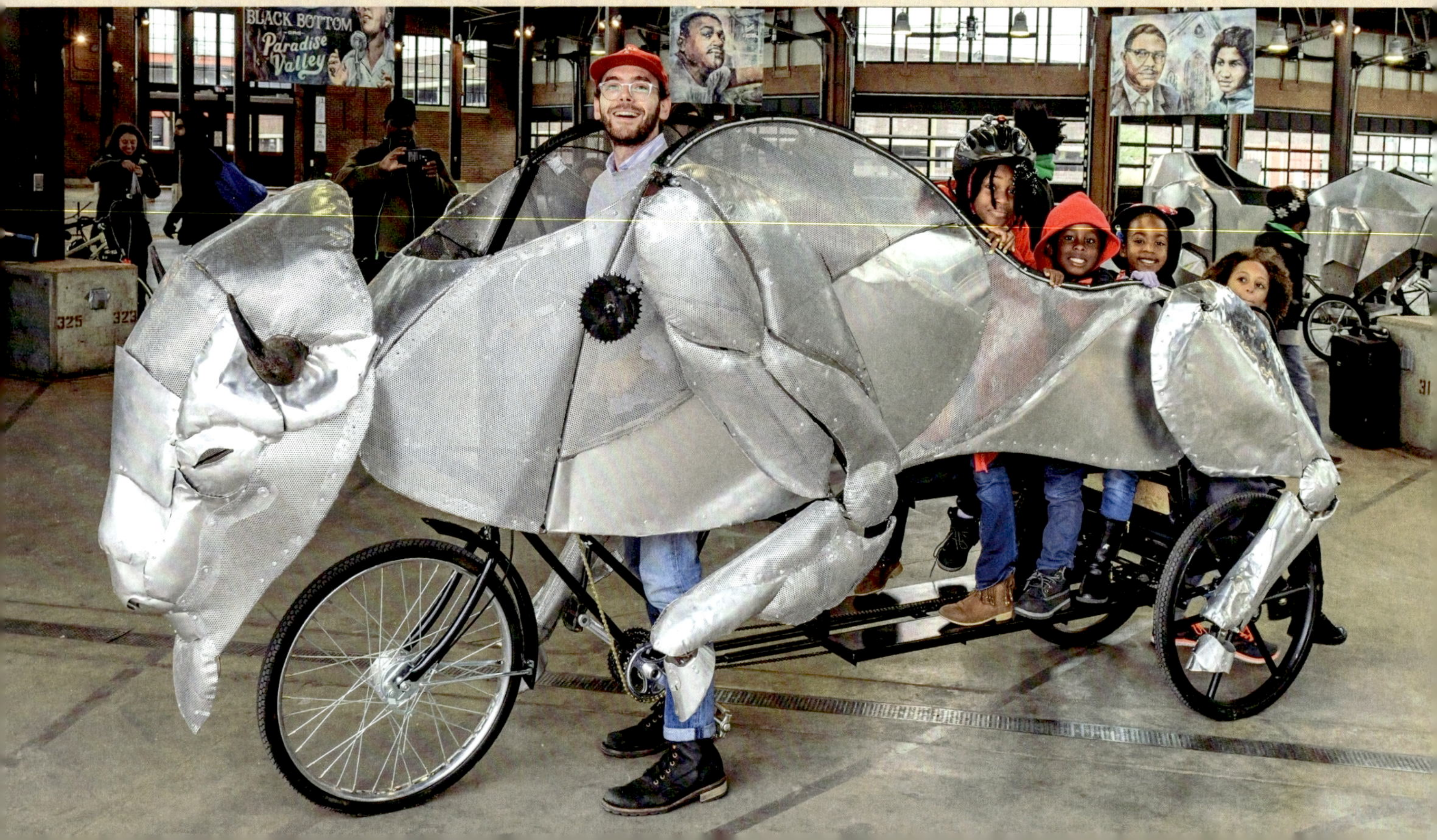
BLACK BOTTOM
Paradise Valley

TOP LEFT: 2016, Detroit, Michigan. | Photo: Doug Coombe. The children of 826michigan who enjoy The Spirit of the Animals Is in the Wheels.

BOTTOM LEFT: 2016, Detroit, Michigan. | Photo: Doug Coombe. The aluminum bison, designed and built by Juan Martinez, was created to transport children to 826michigan, a literacy and tutoring center.

DAVE: The sketches I gave to Juan were so basic. The idea was simple: make a bike that looks like a bison. It's up to Juan to interpret the idea, to make it his own. I love standing back and seeing what he creates.

LEANNE: Juan, I understand that you now have a team of Detroit-based artists working on the fleet of sculptures. What is it about the city of Detroit and the creatives who live there that make this project possible?

JUAN: Detroit is not a very expensive city to live in—though unfortunately, that is changing. The affordability factor gives people more time to work on things they'd like to do instead of things they have to do to survive. I moved here because there was a lot of space and time to do the things I want. There are a lot of homegrown events here; people have to make their own fun.

Detroit has adopted the bike animals as its own, and Detroiters are proud that they were made here. We've found that people seem to love sharing the road with giant moving sculptures. I've never received so many cheers and thumbs-ups. I have a policy that if there's no rush, I'll always stop and answer questions about the bikes.

LEANNE: Do you have a favorite story about the project that you'd like to share?

JUAN: One of my favorite memories is of taking the animals on their first test-drive around my studio in East Detroit. I got to meet everyone within a five-block radius! People came out into their front yards as soon as they saw me coming. That's when I realized what an effective project this was.

DAVE: The first time I saw Juan driving the bison with kids inside, on the streets of Detroit, I was knocked down flat. The joy in those kids! Months later, I was in Detroit for an 826michigan fundraiser and got to drive kids and donors around Eastern Market in the bison bike, and the way people stop on the street, cars screeching to a halt to take pictures ... it is something. Juan's

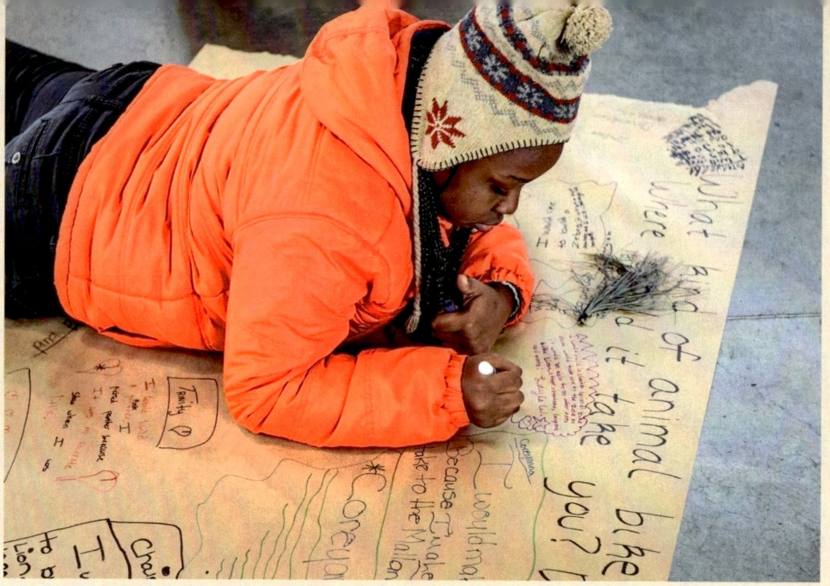

2016, Detroit, Michigan. | Photo: Doug Coombe. An 826michigan student brainstorms different types of transportation animals.

creations are so otherworldly in their beauty and how they move that people are hypnotized.

LEANNE: What do you hope that the project achieves?

JUAN: I love that Detroiters are proud that these bikes were built here. I hope that children and adults are inspired by them to build ludicrous and beautiful things.

JUAN MARTINEZ *creates sculptures that live and work among us, drawing from his experience as a science illustrator and a fabricator working with metal, wood, and other materials. His work has been exhibited at Art Basel Miami,* MOCAD, *and in public and community spaces in Detroit, Los Angeles, and beyond. Juan's artistic practice is informed by his commitment to community, with an emphasis on empowering and equipping Detroit youth for extraordinary futures. He is a cofounder of the Beehive Design Collective and the Austin Bike Zoo.*

DAVE EGGERS *is the author of many books, including* The Circle, The Monk of Mokha, What Is the What, A Hologram for the King, *and* The Lifters. *He is the founder of* McSweeney's, *an independent publishing company based in San Francisco that produces books, a humor website, and a journal of new writing,* McSweeney's Quarterly Concern. McSweeney's *also publishes Voice of Witness, a nonprofit book series that uses oral history to illuminate human rights crises around the world. Dave is the cofounder of 826 National, a network of youth writing and tutoring centers around the United States. Numerous other organizations worldwide operate with inspiration from the 826 National model. Trained as a painter, Dave's artworks have been exhibited at the Museum of Contemporary Art Detroit, the Nevada Museum of Art, the Biennial of the Americas, and numerous other galleries and art spaces. He is winner of the Muhammad Ali Humanitarian Award for Education, the Dayton Literary Peace Prize, the* TED *Prize, and has been a finalist for the National Book Award, the Pulitzer Prize, and the National Book Critics Circle Award.*
daveeggers.net/spirit | 826national.org

CHAPTER 5

LEARN MORE: DO YOUR RESEARCH

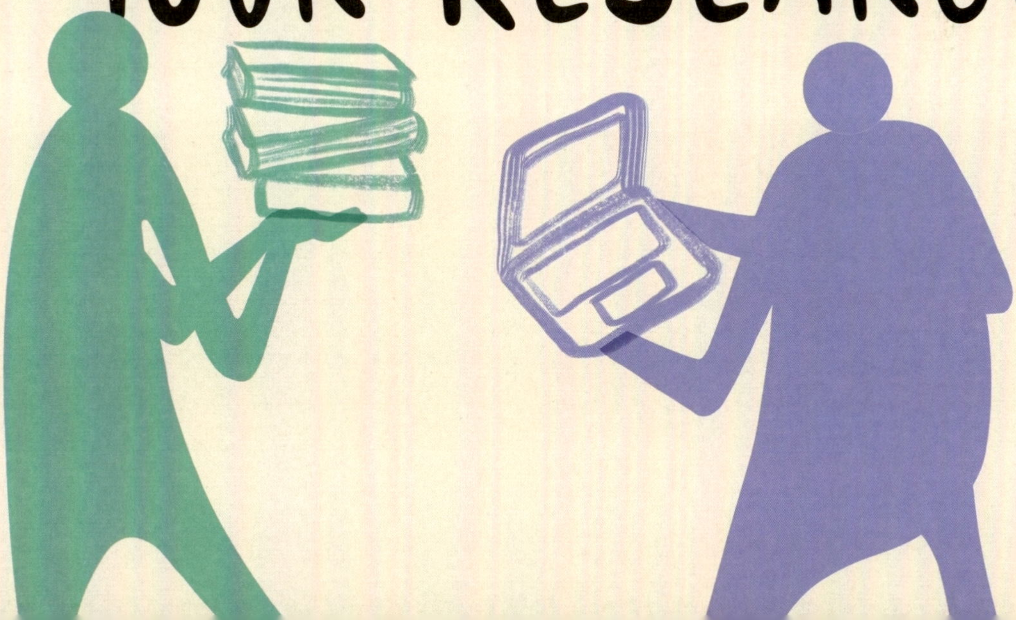

Doing research might sound boring, but really, it's just learning more about the thing you are curious about.

Academics consider research to be creating new knowledge or using existing knowledge in new and creative ways. Your research will allow you to unravel your assumptions and dig into your subject matter on a deeper level, seeing it from a number of perspectives. Be open to what you might discover as you conduct your research—you never know what surprise might change the direction of your project.

PAY ATTENTION: MAKING INFORMED WORK IS IMPORTANT

A community project can touch or ignite a number of different sensitivities. From politics to social identity, you will need to think critically about the hows and the whys of launching your creative project. Knowing more about the community, materials, and subject matter that you wish to work with will enable you to engage meaningfully with your audience and your participants.

Research can be a confidence booster. Expect to be challenged, excited, daunted, and amazed!

Whether the project is big or small, it can sometimes seem like there is never enough time. Research is just like any other part of the creative process; you have to take the time or make the time. Book it into your calendar; take yourself to the library; write that email that you've been procrastinating about.

It is helpful to have creative collaborators who can help with the research process. One of my collaborators, Laura, is excellent at helping me create boundaries around my research. She lets me know when enough is enough. Mandy, who I've collaborated with on books, enjoys interviews, but doesn't like to make the first contact with interviewees. We've split duties so that I've taken the initial steps to reach out, while she's written the interview questions. Our partnership works well when we each take on our preferred tasks.

CASE STUDY

RESEARCHING RADICAL HOSPITALITY

A CONVERSATION WITH

Sara Clugage

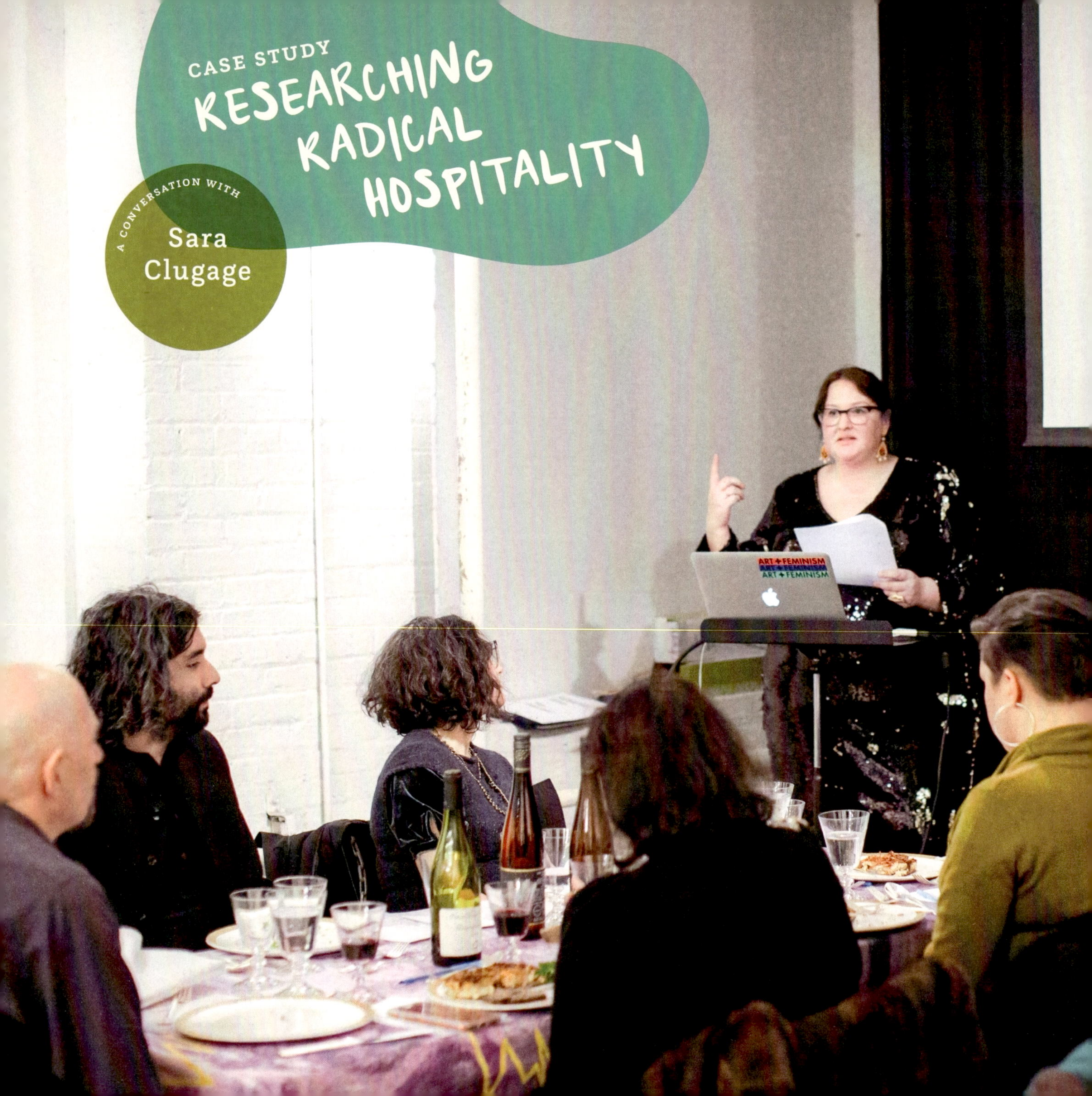

Sara Clugage, a multidisciplinary artist, writer, editor, and publisher, inspires me. Based in Brooklyn, New York, she hosts a series of salon dinners that investigate the role of food in art history and the sociability and organizing capacities of artistic communities. Since they began in 2015, these events of "radical hospitality" examine the cultural and economic models of art salons at various points of art history, such as the centenary of the Russian Revolution, Napoleon's reign, and 1730s London. Historical accuracy and research reigns supreme in Sara's artistic process. She shows us how research, even dull research, can lead to the most intriguing ideas.

LEANNE: How did you come to host these historical salon-style dinner parties?

SARA: I got on the dinner train after researching amateur work in the arts. The global art market works the same as other late-stage capitalist industries. It operates by promoting very few people to high-earning capacities, while exploiting a vast army of volunteer and amateur labor. Most who work in the arts are unpaid or underpaid. That's also true of my work. Upon leaving grad school, I had to describe myself professionally, which occupied me with the question: "Is making art a form of work, even when it's uncompensated?" It's important to say that I don't earn a living from anything I do. I have family money, so I have the incredible luxury of engaging in self-directed or collaborative projects while having my bills paid. The way I experience work is significantly different from that of my peers. That makes the question of work even more pressing to me. The refusal of art institutions, publications, and markets to value the creative labor of my peers keeps many of them in poverty.

One of the first research subjects I developed along this line was the evolution of the word "dilettante." That word came to English from the Italian in the mid-18th century, largely thanks to a group of English men who founded a club in London around 1732, the Society of Dilettanti—which still exists today. Early Society of Dilettanti members were art historians avant la lettre; they were enthusiastic students of Greek and Roman classical history in a period when archaeology, starting from the excavations of Herculaneum and Pompeii,

SARA CLUGAGE, *Gilded Age New York: A Wealth Inequality Dinner*, January 20, 2019, food, lectures, trivia. | Photo: Liz Ligon, courtesy of Sara Clugage

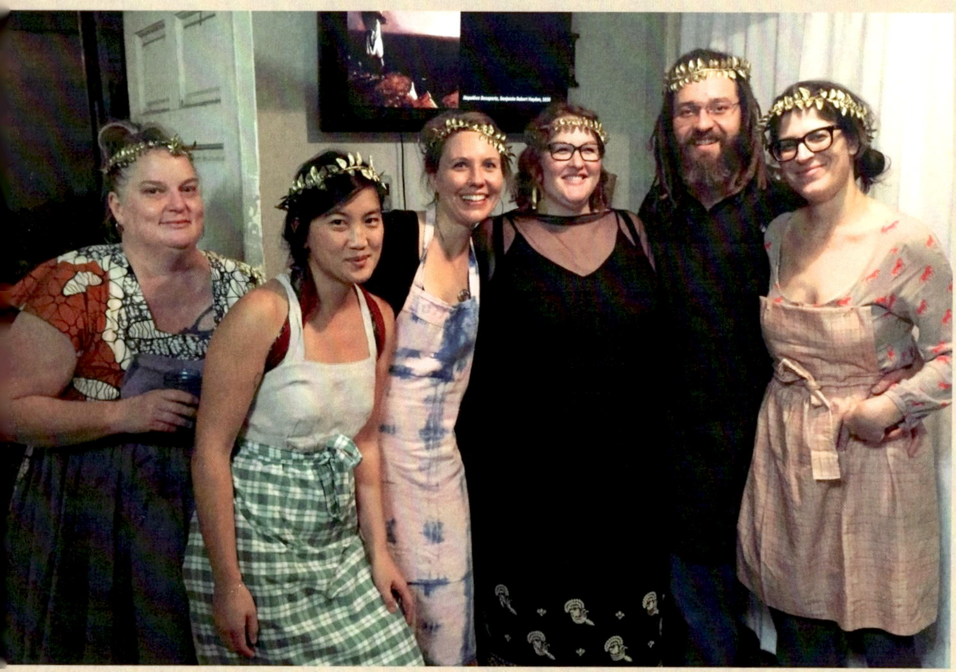

SARA CLUGAGE, *Napoleon Salon: Dinner in the First Empire*, February 2, 2017, Los Angeles. | Photo courtesy of Sara Clugage. Kitchen crew at Thank You for Coming. From left to right: Carole Frances Lung, Cynthia Su, Lauren A. Ross, Sara Clugage, Jonathan Robert, Laura Noguera.

was just beginning. I find them fascinating because they were, by definition, amateurs; art history did not yet exist as a professional field. The Dilettanti was also interesting because their history throughout the 18th century is a series of grand ambitions and spectacular failures. They helped to define the emerging professional disciplines of archaeology and art history, but because of their perennial incompetence, those disciplines then left them behind.

I was reading old Dilettanti meeting minutes from around the turn of the 20th century, and it was so boring. To keep engaged, I started making some of the food that they might have eaten during these meetings, going off accounts of other British clubs and tavern menus. That quickly became the most exciting part of the research—you can tell so much about what a gathering is like by examining what people eat. And what the Dilettanti ate influenced their decisions. Those meeting minutes are full of complaints about the expense and quality of the food, next to reports on who was behind with their dues.

The food also says something about the routes that art took to get to London in a period when individuals were collecting what would become the founding collections of the British Museum. Art travels the same trade routes that food does. I hadn't thought before how you could learn about money and power and influence through what foods appear where and at what time.

I held that first salon dinner in my apartment and invited friends. I sent out selections of readings ahead of time and expected people to discuss them—and they did! But as I moved on to the next dinners, I decided that these should be public events to ensure a broader base of participants and I needed to supply the necessary historical information myself instead of leaving it up to the guests to prepare.

The first public salon took place at Thank You for Coming, an LA restaurant partly run by two artists, Cynthia Su and Laura Noguera. It was called "Napoleon Salon: Dinner in the First Empire," covering the years 1800–15 in Paris. At the Napoleon Salon, I hit upon a method that's stayed mostly the same since. The dinner is served in several courses, and for each course, I give a short lecture on that food and why it's important to the history or art of the period. After we've cleared that course, we play a round of trivia, which is a fun way to bring us back together as a group. At the end of the night, the winner gets a prize.

I was glad to have a chance to revisit Napoleon as a subject, because the second dinner took place in February 2017, soon after Trump's inauguration. The points I had been pressing about how art-making works under autocracy were newly relevant; Napoleon's skillful manipulation of the press, his recognition that his power depended on the glory of an ever-expanding military empire, and his pugnacious character all have striking parallels to Trump. It took me a while to notice that all the themes I was choosing were related to new types of nationalism. Artist community–organizing around political themes is often tied to a political sea change, like the rise of a new nation, or a regime change.

LEANNE: How do you prepare for each of these salons?

SARA: I start by picking a theme and researching the history of the period. It usually takes me a year: I read books, look at relevant archives, and consult with experts. When I have a rough grasp of the story I want to tell, I start teaching myself to make the food. For every salon but the Napoleon Salon, my coeditor at *Dilettante Army*, Christine Elliott, has come on board. We test recipes and figure out what will be possible to make given our constraints. Christine most often runs the kitchen crew on the night of the dinner. She is a magnificent partner.

For the last two salon dinners, I've also reached out to guest speakers, who provide a range of expertise.

SARAH CLUGAGE, *Gilded Age New York: A Wealthy Inequality Dinner*, January 20, 2019, food, lectures, trivia. | Photo: Liz Ligon, courtesy of Sara Clugage

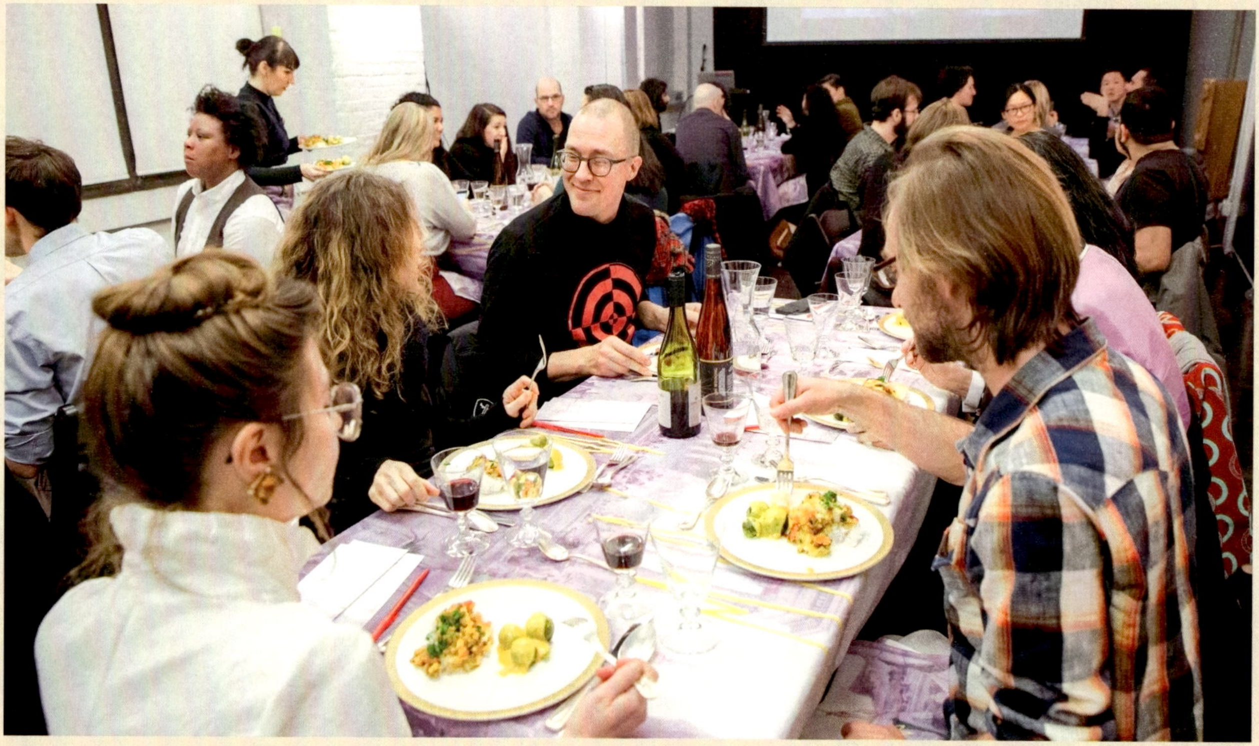

I design the table linens, and then I rope in friends to help cut and sew. We find a venue, rent the dishes, and recruit some folks to work in the kitchen or make specialty foods. We print the menus and the trivia sheets. We spend three to five days cooking. I sometimes wonder why I thought it was a good idea for me, a naturally anxious person, to get into large-scale event planning. But nothing catastrophic has happened yet!

LEANNE: One of your salon discussion questions is, "Does creative dissent matter?" In your experience, does it?

SARA: I do think creative dissent matters. Artists can inspire new ways of looking at the world. Creative and novel things catch people's attention, and the people who make them can direct that attention toward injustices. That's often the first step toward change. Importantly, though, attention is not the same as action, and so while creative dissent matters, it is not enough, on its own, to effect change.

I try to hold two competing truths in my mind at the same time: art matters, and art does not matter at all. In a time of great political urgency driven by the climate crisis, increasing nationalism, a global pandemic, and a long-overdue reckoning of racial injustice, I am determined not to stop thinking about what change might be possible and to go past that to actively work for change. To that end, it's vital to me that the work I do be useful to people.

SARA CLUGAGE *lives and works in Brooklyn, where she is the editor-in-chief of* Dilettante Army, *an online journal for visual culture and critical theory. She writes about craft, food, politics, and theory, and she often teaches workshops on craft and Wikipedia as part of the Wikipedia campaign Art+Feminism. Clugage acts as a director for the Craft Advanced Research Projects Agency (CARPA). Since 2015, her practice has centered on a series of salon dinners themed on the economic models and culinary styles of different periods in art history. Find out more at* **saraclugage.net** *and* **dilettantearmy.com**.

BE AWARE OF RESEARCH ETHICS

The ugly side of research is that it can be used not only for good, but also for bad. Unfortunately, research has sometimes presented so-called "evidence" for undoing a community's values, as in early colonial exploration and art. Unhealthy power structures can exist between the artist-researcher and any communities that are under study. Learning about a community and how they may want to participate will ensure that your efforts are mutually agreed upon and, hopefully, lead the way to mutually beneficial results.

The methods of the field of community-based research (CBR), which service designers in public health often use, can also be applied to artistic research. Here are some of the basic guidelines:

- Ensure that you have a shared method of consent, agreed upon by you and the community. Consider using a consent form or working with a community guide to ensure that consensus.
- Respect anyone's right to withdraw at any point in time, as well as their right to take their contributions with them.
- Understand that the community may wish for you to learn specific protocols and customs before conducting any research.
- Recognize that communities have their own identities and visions of success.
- Recognize that communities are a collaborative partner in the work of research. Their input should be considered in all phases of a project.
- Ensure that the project creates a mutual benefit for everyone involved. What are you giving in compensation? What further invitations can you provide for participation? What knowledge should return to the community?
- Have you provided your contact information so that participants can get in touch with you if they have doubts, retractions, or guidance?
- Have you shared what you think will be the result of this research?

The field of research ethics and community-based research is vast and changing all of the time. If you desire to work with CBR methods, I recommend reaching out to those in your community who have experience with it. Offer to assist them with their work so you can learn from their expertise.

RESEARCH METHOD ONE: CONDUCT INTERVIEWS

The best way to become an expert interviewer is to practice being one. Interviews are challenging generally, and to conduct a great interview is a master skill. Frankly, the only way to start learning how to interview someone is to practice.

To begin, try writing a list of questions that begin with the five Ws: who, why, when, what, and where.

Open-ended questions allow the respondent to give you thorough answers rather than just yes or no responses. The best interview questions allow for the respondent to share their experiences and opinions.

You can't go into an interview expecting someone to provide you with the answer you want. However, if you go in with the intention of deep listening, you may discover things that enchant you, enrage you, or push you into doing even better work for your project.

PREPARING FOR THE BEST INTERVIEW POSSIBLE

- Before the interview occurs, introduce yourself. Let the interviewee know what you are trying to accomplish with this informational interview.
- Establish consent. Is the interviewee comfortable with your method of recording (for example, if you're making audio or video files)? Do they know how the information will be used or distributed?
- Make sure the timing is convenient for the interviewee. You want their full attention.
- Be gentle with those whom you interview. Understand that you are being gifted information—you are not extracting knowledge. Keep watch of their comfort levels as they speak to you; there may be times when you need to stop asking questions.
- Respect interviewees' time and willingness to participate. Make sure you tell them ahead of time how long you will need and don't go longer than that. (Most people begin to show fatigue after twenty to thirty minutes.) When you are close to exceeding the allotted time for the interview, ask the subject if they are okay to continue for longer (if required).
- Monitor the subject's emotional energy, as well as your own. If your interviewee's demeanor changes, they may feel that they've exhausted the subject or told you everything they think you should know. There is no harm in ending a conversation early.
- Recognize that you are not going to be able to ask every question that you want to.
- Thank these people who are giving you their time. If someone has gone out of their way to help you with your project, you owe it to them to offer your thanks and anything else you can do to help them with their work.

TRY THIS

Keep Track with Mind Maps

I find that I remember things better when I take notes, but I make my recordings visual in some way. Not only do small doodles help me to learn things, I've found that creating mind maps is a great way to keep track of ideas and to connect seemingly disparate concepts. Look for similarities and differences, and let juxtapositions, in turn, guide your research.

A mind map can take any shape you want. You can use a rough pencil sketch or a digital drawing. The contents of a mind map should never be precious; just get your ideas down on paper first. A mind map is a tool for connecting ideas. Refinement comes later. Keep these documents for your eyes only.

CASE STUDY

REIMAGINING PUBLIC SPACE

A CONVERSATION ON

Alley-Oop

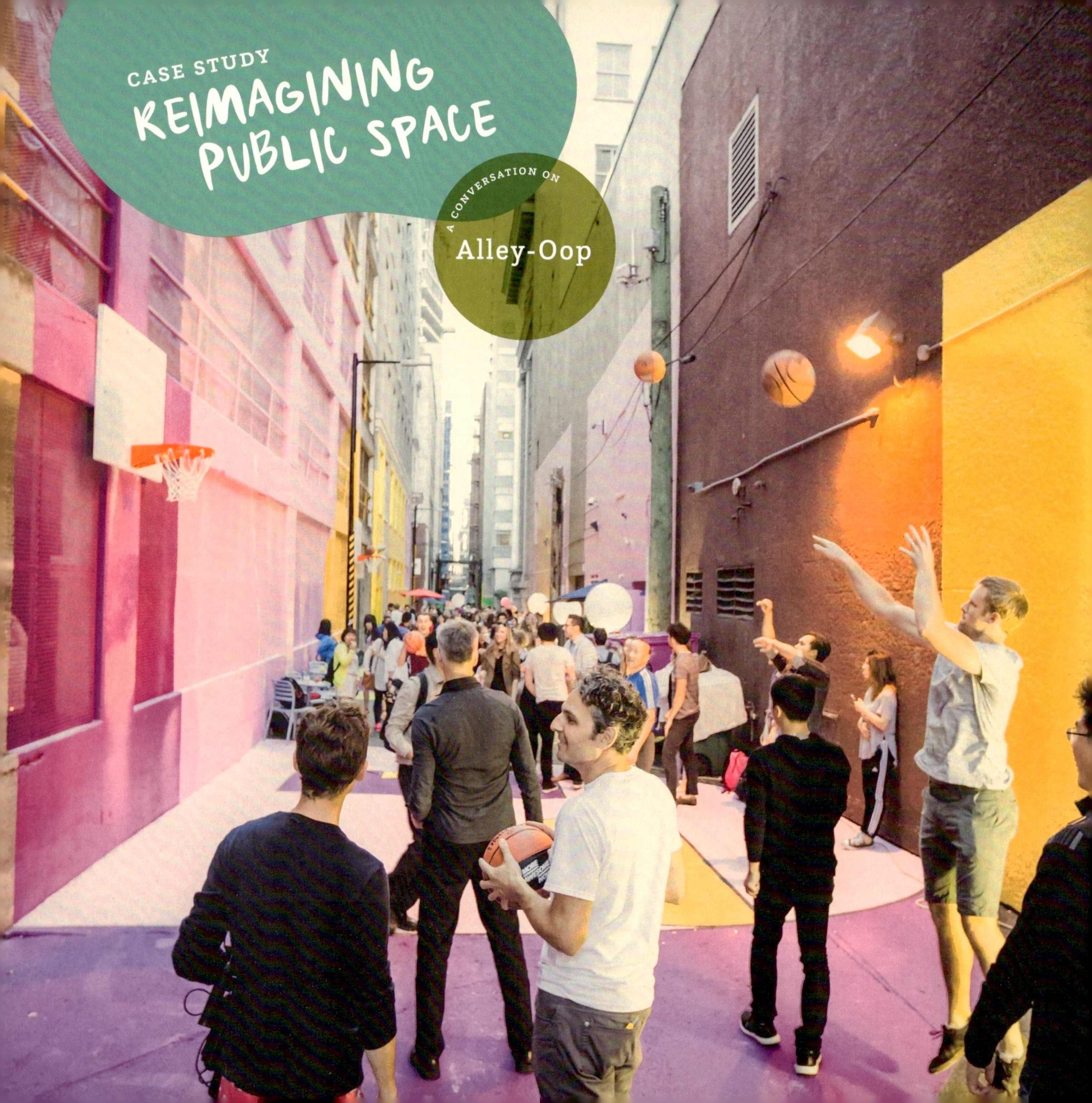

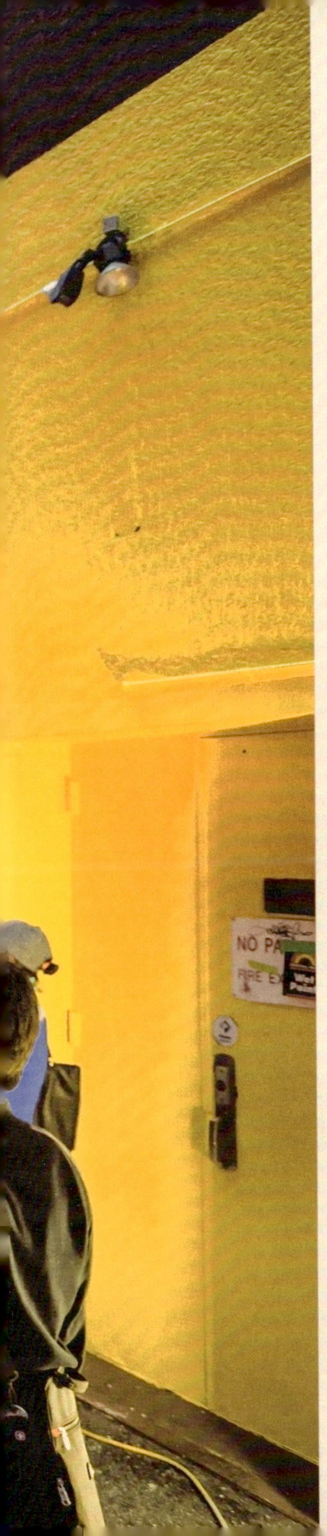

You cannot ignore Alley-Oop. Launched in 2016, this urban alley space painted in lemon yellow and searing bubble-gum pink has become a spot for people to gather, connect, and play. Situated in the middle of downtown Vancouver, British Columbia, this transformative project has become a model of public placemaking, an example of how you can create radical change even in the most ordinary and overlooked spaces. Curious to find out what it takes to execute such a radical project, I spoke with Melissa Higgs, principal of HCMA Architecture + Design, whose firm created the alley as a passion project alongside project partners from the City of Vancouver and the Downtown Vancouver Business Improvement Association (DVBIA).

LEANNE: Activating a back alley into a public space is a radical idea, particularly in a city like Vancouver that has major wealth disparity and one of the world's most expensive property markets. How did you get these stakeholders to see your vision of the "More Awesome Now" alley?

MELISSA: In Vancouver, we don't have enough places for people to gather in our city. It's not reasonable to think we can purchase more park space, because land costs are so high. Laneways are just such an obvious way to go about finding public space. Partnering with the City of Vancouver and the DVBIA, we looked at what could activate laneways as public space. What can we give a lane that can't exist on a sidewalk or other spaces?

The first alley, Alley-Oop, is in Vancouver's business district. There's lots of lawyers and accountant-types walking around. We wanted the idea to juxtapose the yin and yang of the serious and the playful. The finance people can be rushing around on the sidewalk, but then there would be this secret space for chilling out, playing, and connecting in behind.

2016, Vancouver, British Columbia. | Photo courtesy of HCMA. Alley-Oop is part of the More Awesome Now Laneway Activations by HCMA Architecture + Design, in partnership with the City of Vancouver and the Downtown Vancouver Business Improvement Association.

BELOW: 2019, Vancouver, British Columbia. | Photo courtesy of HCMA. Ackery's Alley behind the historical Orpheum Theatre is part of the More Awesome Now Laneway Activations by HCMA Architecture + Design, in partnership with the City of Vancouver and the Downtown Vancouver Business Improvement Association.

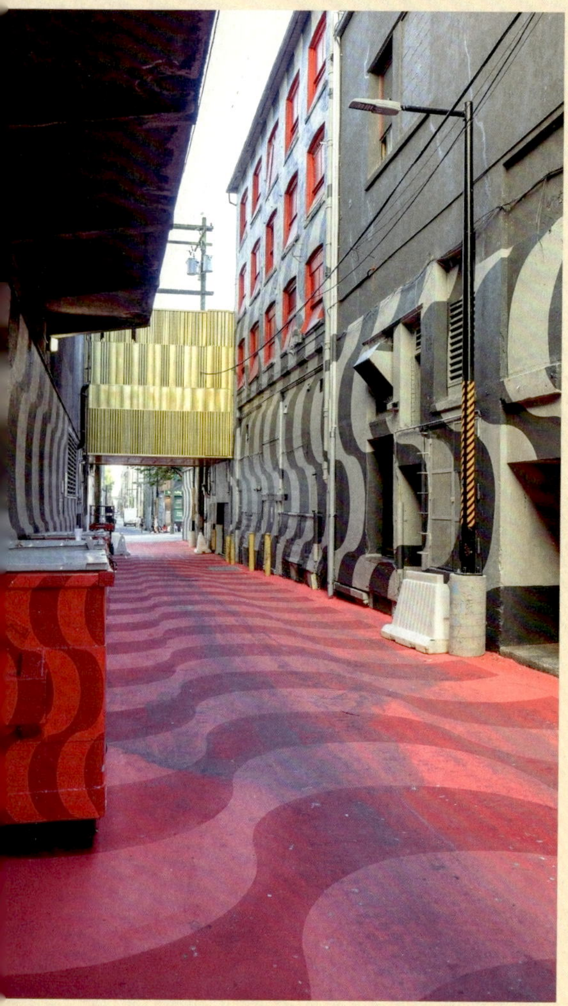

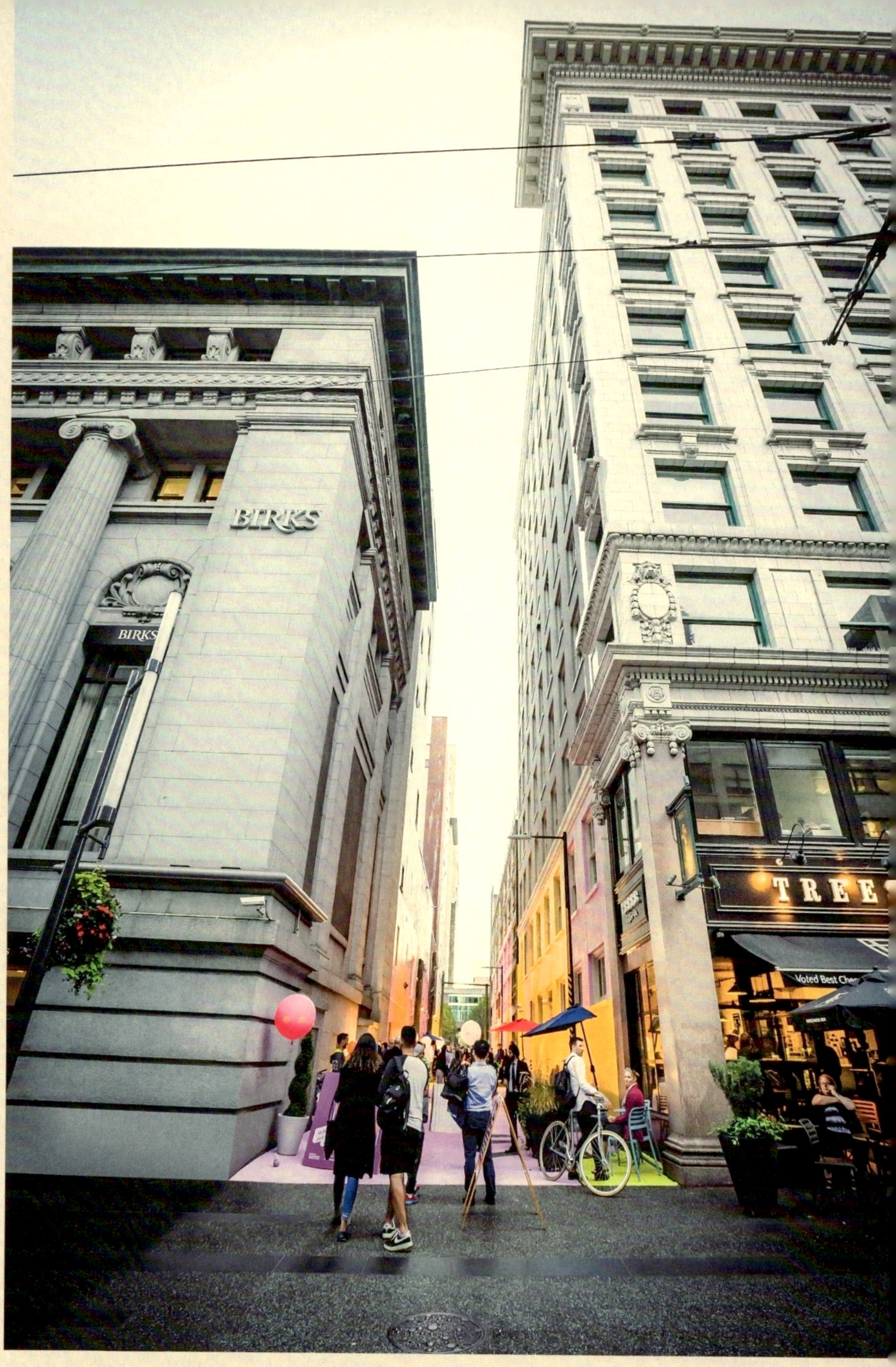

The inner laneway needed to reflect something very different than what was going on on the sidewalks, and we came up with the idea of play. We made a hyper version of it: hopscotch, basketball hoops, and some smaller playing areas. And the bright pink and yellow colors! There was quite a bit of nerding out on what the right colors would be. How do you make it inviting, eye-catching, and warm, but still authentic?

LEANNE: I imagine that you did have to adjust your vision a bit in response to having many stakeholders.

MELISSA: Yes, in terms of working with the community to make it happen, we conducted a lot of engagement workshops for tenants to understand what it would look like. We wanted to paint the mural walls higher, but there are some thresholds around people's comfort level regarding how much we would paint. The City of Vancouver was a great partner in the project. They were on board, but there were still many questions that we had to answer around permits, liability, and electricity, for example. Projects like this take perseverance and conversations, the stuff that artists in the public realm have to deal with all the time.

LEANNE: Was there a moment with this project when you knew you had succeeded?

LEFT: 2019, Vancouver, British Columbia. Photo courtesy of HCMA. The theme of the Alley-Oop laneway is "play." Part of the More Awesome Now Laneway Activations by HCMA Architecture + Design, in partnership with the City of Vancouver and the Downtown Vancouver Business Improvement Association.

MELISSA: First, it is highly visible. I take the SkyTrain (Vancouver's rapid transit), and there is a station right across from Alley-Oop. It's so striking to see the alley and the bright color pop up between buildings when you pass by—and it always seems to be active. The BIA collected metrics on foot traffic in the alley for six months, before and after the opening. Pedestrians tripled, and the number of women using the alley doubled, which is a signifier of its feeling safe.

LEANNE: Since Alley-Oop, you've completed a second project in Ackery's Alley, in Vancouver's entertainment district behind the historic Orpheum Theatre. What learnings did the firm take from one project to the next?

MELISSA: We were excited to make an alley that was an extension of a performance space and an extension of the activities inside the theater. It has been activated by the Public Disco, an inclusive dance party project, and many others that host events there. We are looking forward to seeing how artists use the space after the pandemic.

We are now thinking about what will make future alley designs successful. How can we make a network of alleys between buildings that people can move between? Alleys take up so much real estate in the city, and the services that they hold, such as garbage and recycling, still have to happen, but can't we make those places work for people as well?

Learn more at: ***hcma.ca*** and ***vancouver.ca/streets-transportation/laneways.aspx.***

RESEARCH METHOD TWO: WHAT IS THIS PLACE?

For projects based in a chosen place, I recommend visiting the spot where you intend to execute it. Take photos of every interesting thing that you see. What types of architecture, window decor, or colors stand out to you? Take some time to explore what the place is like at different times of day and in different weather. How does the light change? What do you hear at different times of the day? Does the foot traffic change? What is beautiful in this space? What is neglected?

Here are some methods that I like to employ when thinking of place:

- Look at street signs and maps. Find out why the space was given the name that it has.
- Was there a different name before the current one? City planning archives, libraries, and history websites can give you some context for how names may have changed over time.
- What kind of work has changed this place? What leisure activities have been enjoyed here? Who had free access to this place? Who did not?
- What major and minor events occurred here? How can we reconcile the history of the past with what we know today?
- Who lived here? Which communities did they belong to? What were the first businesses in the area?
- What do people not know about this place? What should they know?
- What sorts of plants grew here? Are they still here now?
- What famous people came from here? Which side of history were they on?
- Who do you not see in this place? Why? What could your project do to include them in this space?
- Is the place public, privately owned, or government property?
- What are common nicknames for this place/area? Why is it called that?

Beyond these questions, there are other ways to explore places that do not show up in traditional research: look at census records, newspaper advertisements from neighborhood publications, amateur photo archives (online or elsewhere), business directories, city planning records, typological maps, bylaw documents, and how other artists have conveyed a sense of place in their own projects.

RESEARCH METHOD THREE: INHABIT THE EXPERIENCE

What senses might a person need to experience your project? How will your project be experienced by people of radically different backgrounds?

- Would your project's desired experience be different if participants were thirty years older than you, or ten years younger?
- Does one's eyesight, vocabulary, or physicality impact how they will experience this project?
- How many of the senses (taste, touch, sight, smell, sound) does your project appeal to? What are the alternatives to relying on these senses?

- Does this project (or any part of it) speak only to someone of your own age, gender identity, race, or cultural background?
- What can you change to make this project accessible to more people?

RESEARCH METHOD FOUR: LISTEN

Record ten minutes of silence in the place where you will do your group project. Listen to it later with your eyes closed. Even in a supposedly quiet area, you'll likely discover that it's far from completely silent. What do you hear? What sounds could you add or create to enhance or change the atmosphere?

What kinds of sounds do you hear—natural ones, or human-made? Do they seem to be consistent with this space over time, or are they occasional occurrences? Are there voices? What are they saying or singing? What emotions do you hear?

Consider recording audio in the place over time, whether hourly, over the course of several weeks, or yearly. Listen to the recordings together and compare and contrast. What can you learn about this space just from its sound?

RESEARCH METHOD FIVE: THE MEDIUM CAN BE THE MESSAGE

Sometimes learning more about the history of the tools that you work with can create new ideas for your work. A painter might research the history of pigments to find out how the properties of the color blue have changed throughout the ages. A puppeteer may explore European pantomime traditions to understand the history of drama with non-emotive faces. A crocheter may look into the historical connections between manufactured lace, royalty, and prostitution to understand the relationship between handicraft and the how society valued women's work, worth, and time.

Dig into your research and ask bold questions, for example: Where did textile recycling start? Do yarn bombs damage trees? How was Vantablack (one of the darkest pigments in existence) developed? Which art tools were invented by women?

RESEARCH METHOD SIX: MAKE UNUSUAL JUXTAPOSITIONS

Sometimes fascinating concepts come about by researching two seemingly unrelated things to find out how they come together. Embroiderer Penny Nickels compares her stitchwork to the printed marks made by early lithographers and has investigated how shorthand for making marks in both disciplines have informed each other. Sara Clugage's public salons and dinners conjure the delight of artist salons while also sharing detailed knowledge about classicism.

Often, creative ideas are the result of merging several seemingly unrelated things. What crossroads and juxtapositions do you need to research? Do you think you can find any commonalities between the subjects? Why or why not?

RESEARCH METHOD SEVEN: CONSIDER SCALE

There is something to be said for examining your project's smallest component part (a stitch, a brushstroke, a pixel) and considering how one small building block can become part of a larger chain.

Take inspiration from the idea of making things bigger; what could your project look like in its most significant form? Could it cover a bridge, take over a building, challenge Godzilla? What dimensions of space would you need to engineer this? How much material would it take? What would it cost? How would you get people there? What would be the impact of the project artistically, environmentally, socially?

Conversely, how would your project work if you scaled it down? Could it still be effective? Could you adjust the amount of effort you are planning to put into it? Could you change one thing to make it work better?

I invite you to explore the logistics and impacts of planned projects both large and small.

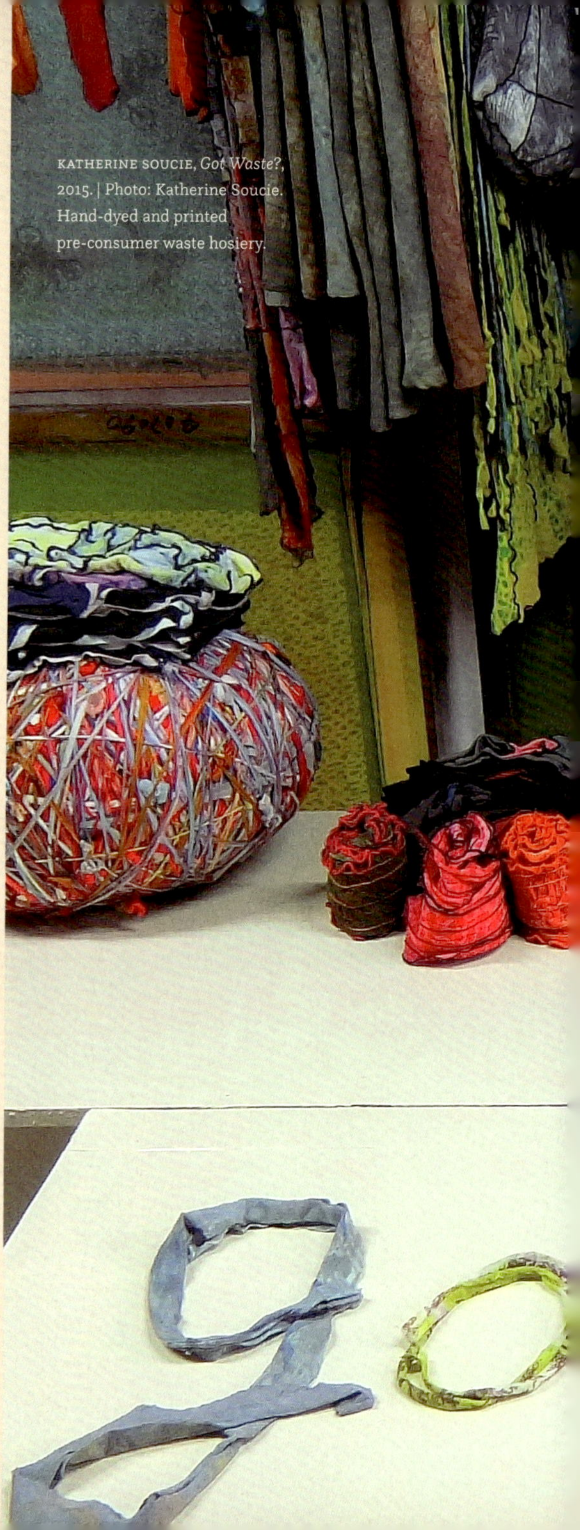

KATHERINE SOUCIE, *Got Waste?*, 2015. | Photo: Katherine Soucie. Hand-dyed and printed pre-consumer waste hosiery.

CASE STUDY

EXPANDING MATERIAL PRACTICE

A CONVERSATION WITH

Katherine Soucie

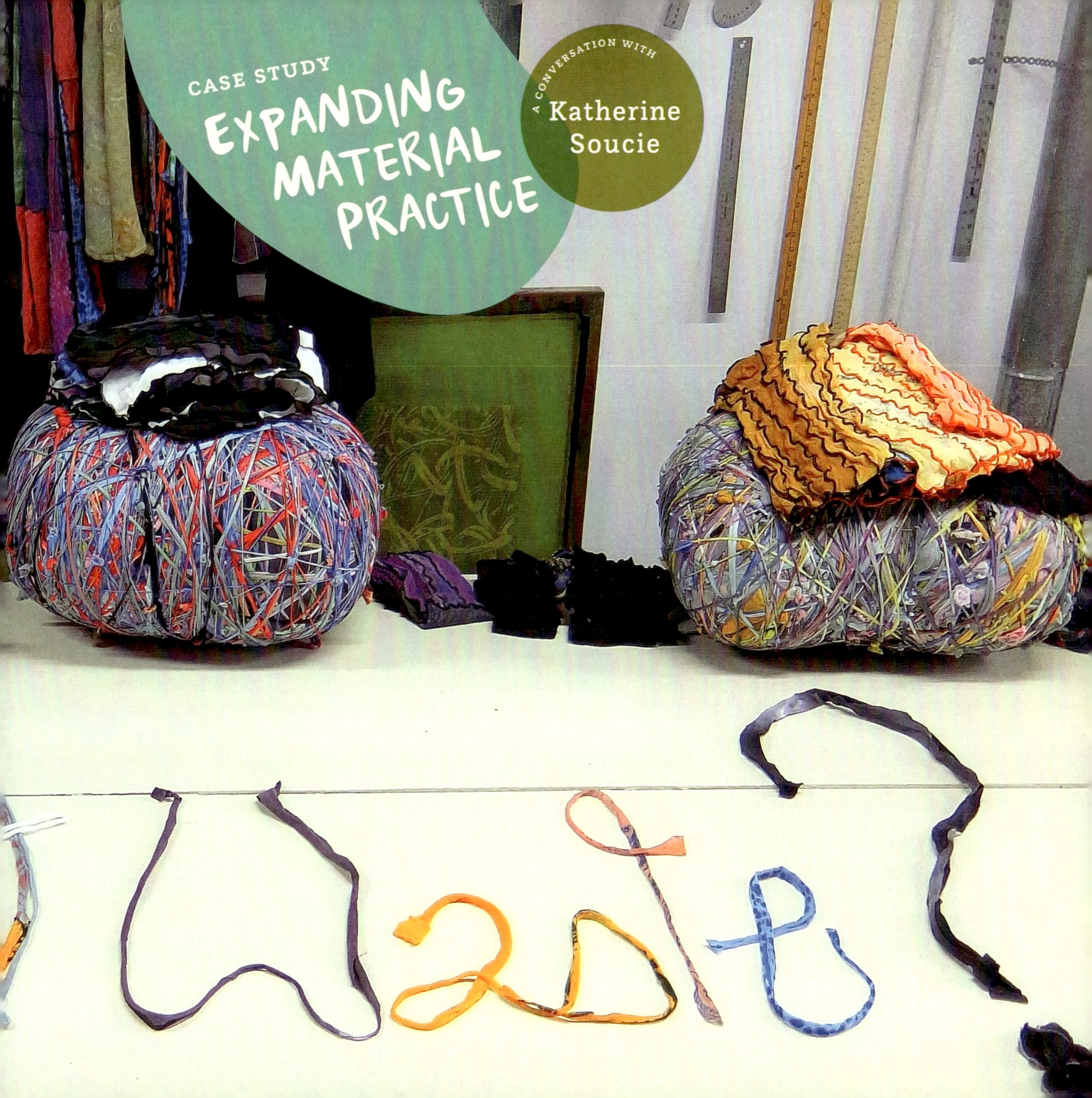

Based in London, England, Canadian artist Katherine Soucie gives waste textiles a second life by transforming them into incredible sculptures and wearable fashion. As a zero-waste artist, she not only works to eliminate material waste, but also gives the waste fiber from her own practice a third life by supplying it to other artists to use. Her material practice has included a rug maker, a potter, and a craft program at a seniors' home—each felt that they could incorporate Katherine's leftover fiber in their work, further lengthening the chain of sustainable production, while also providing her with further opportunities for creative research.

LEANNE: As a textile artist who uses pre-consumer waste materials, you've further increased your practice's sustainability by providing other artists and makers with your scraps. Your hand-dyed fibers have been integrated into handmade rugs, pottery, and even crafts made by senior citizens.

KATHERINE: Textiles is about building community. In my early years of material research and development with waste textiles, I didn't consider sharing my textiles and offcuts because I was so focused on experimenting with what I could and could not do with them. It wasn't until I was approached by others curious about using the materials that I embraced the concept. This made me realize that what I was doing was much bigger than my practice alone. If I wanted to help motivate creative usage and the reuse of textile waste, specifically with waste hosiery, this was a perfect opportunity to see how others could reimagine it. It's important for others to bring their experience to a material, regardless of medium or application. I realize I'd had a one-way conversation with my medium before others began to work with it. Their participation has enabled me to have a much bigger conversation about the valuable role of waste textiles as a tool for research and creative material resources.

LEANNE: You have collaborated with Salome Nieto, a butoh dance artist, many times. How do you know when a collaborative partnership is right for you?

KATHERINE: My collaborations are rooted in a shared language and value system. We speak and see things the same way, then we both work together intentionally to produce a shared vision. You must be aligned in your intention to support each other's contribution. The support you give one another in the process provides you with the creative freedom to feel less vulnerable, which in turn helps continue to drive the collaboration. When the collaboration is right, ideas, creativity, and material forms naturally come together.

LEANNE: You are excellent at documenting your artistic process and materials. How do you work this into your practice regularly?

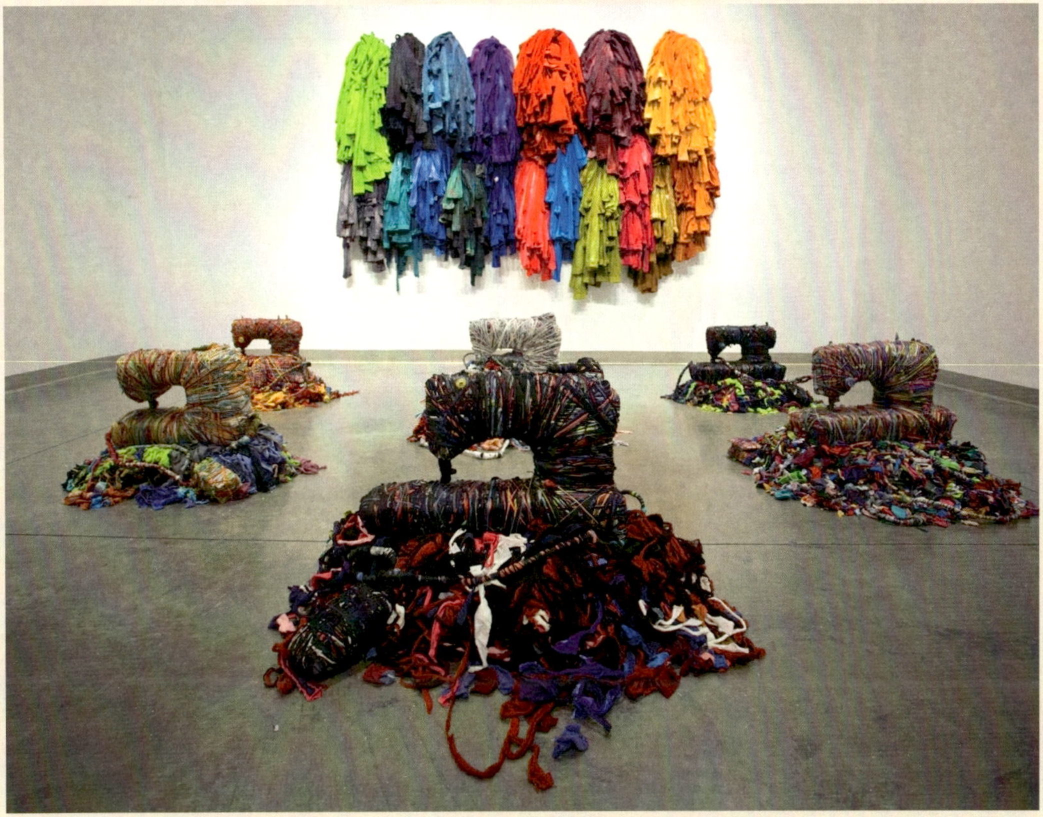

KATHERINE SOUCIE, *Raisons D'etres*, 2015. | Photo: Rob Matharu. Seymour Art Gallery exhibit, North Vancouver, British Columbia.

KATHERINE: I am someone driven by process. My training in fashion design taught me how you need to document each step, or else you may forget an essential step or ingredient in your design process. When I went in to study textiles, my love for the process expanded, though it is a very different approach; some applications are organic and improvisational, while others require rigorous attention to detail due to their chemistry. When I began to learn more about textiles, it broke me right open as an artist. It is a field of study that allows you to transition between linear and nonlinear ways of creating, researching, and documenting. Fashion training is very linear, so it's like textiles were the missing key ingredient in how I approach research and documentation.

It's important to find what resonates with you and let that guide how you research and document. There is no wrong way, except copying that of another. This is not to say someone else's journey can't inspire you, but it is good to find out what drives you and adapt that into a formula for organizing your thoughts and your process.

TOP: Photo: Katherine Soucie. Katherine Soucie's studio is a place where she experiments.

BOTTOM: Photo: Rob Matharu. Katherine Soucie in her studio.

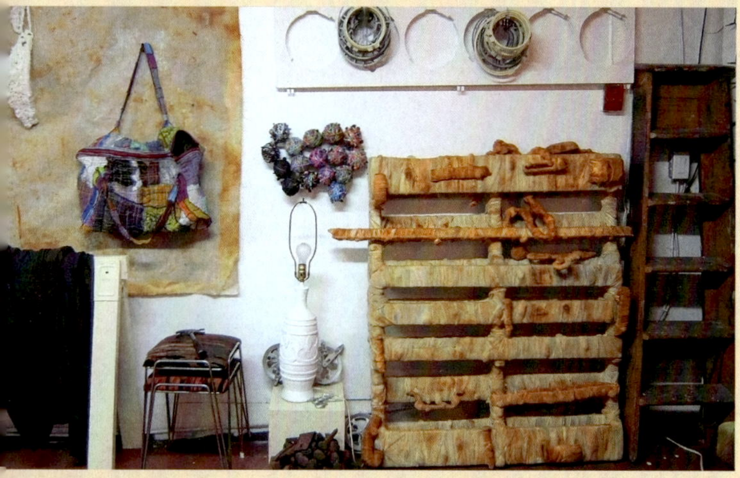

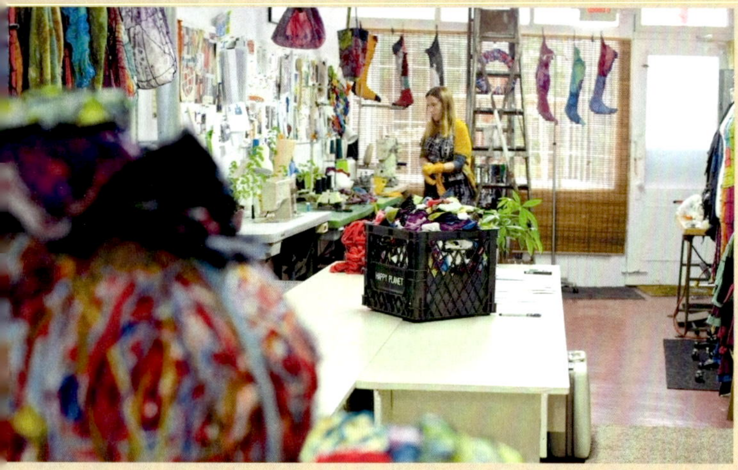

KATHERINE SOUCIE *(BAA, BFA, MAA) is an award-winning Canadian/UK artist, designer, and educator who specializes in transforming textile industry waste into new textiles for her studio, Sans Soucie. She studied fashion design in London, England, and Toronto, Canada, before furthering her studies in textiles and applied art in Vancouver. Since 2003, her experimentation with textile industry waste and zero-waste textile research has resulted in an extensive body of work, for which she has received numerous scholarships, grants, and awards. Her work has been showcased and exhibited in Canada, the US, Hong Kong, China, Australia, and the UK. As an educator, she has taught textiles in fashion, art, and design departments in Canada and the US. She was the visiting lecturer in textiles at the Ernest G. Welch School of Art & Design at Georgia State University and the former program director of fashion at LaSalle College Vancouver. She recently launched* The Material Revolution (thematerialrevolution.com)*, a podcast dedicated to creating awareness about textiles to inspire knowledge, encourage creativity, and build material community.* ***katherinesoucie.com | sanssoucie.ca***

RESEARCH METHOD EIGHT: TAP UNLIKELY SOURCES

You never know where you might learn more about your subject. Here are some places you might not think to look for information:

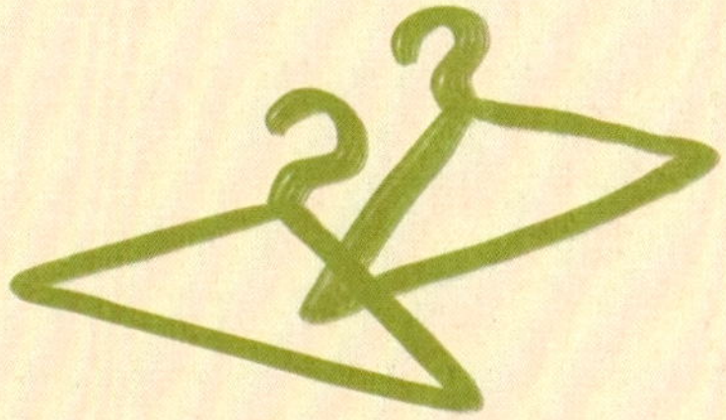

- Visual research can be done using social media hashtags. Use both geolocation tags and relevant keywords to search for your subject matter.
- Artist-run centers, gallery archives, and community libraries often provide access to books, zines, and other ephemera that you may not find elsewhere.
- Antiques shops and fairs often display rare objects that you may not find elsewhere.
- Subject-specific museums, their websites, and their archives can be a treasure trove of information. There are museums devoted to transit history, tenement life, writers' houses, coal mining, sex, textiles, design, pop culture, games, taxidermy, laborism, and witchcraft, among many other subjects. Many museums have digitized their holdings, allowing you to view their collections online.
- *The Farmer's Almanac*, a classic periodical that provides farmers with long-range weather predictions, can give you a sense of the temperature and climate of a given time and place.
- Many libraries keep cartography, ephemera, and photography archives.
- Story circles may give you access to oral histories that you won't find in books.
- Theater costume shops may be a source of historically accurate clothing.
- Radio recordings can take you back to the feeling of a time and place.
- Many colleges, universities, and art schools allow the public to access their lending library for a small fee.

THINKING CRITICALLY ABOUT WHAT YOU'VE COLLECTED

Ultimately, research is not only the collecting of materials and ideas, but the ability to take what you've gathered and form a theory about it. Not everything that you collect will serve your project, but ultimately, the act of collecting knowledge will help you determine what is relevant to you and your work.

The world is constantly evolving, and it is up to the creative researcher to be aware of these shifts. When looking at information, be careful to understand the viewpoint of the sources. Media has its own bias, as does publishing. Our current collective understanding of power dynamics, equality, and social health differs from what it was even a few years ago. Ultimately, you will need to consider the source of the information you've collected and its biases when you decide how to apply it to your creative work.

BE PREPARED TO CHANGE YOUR MIND

"Murder your darlings" is an often-quoted piece of advice that you should not fall so deeply in love with aspects of your creative work that you refuse to edit them. Remember, you create for an audience, and the best way to reach them is to make your work speak directly to that audience. Research will often indicate that one or more aspects of your project should change; don't let the headiness of creativity get in the way of creating compelling work.

How do you know if you need to change something? Here are some warning signs:

- Research proves it untrue.
- You have to work extra hard to explain your project.
- You know in your gut that something's wrong, but have spent so long on a specific aspect that you don't want to change it.
- Changing the problematic aspect might make the whole piece fall apart.

Changing your mind is humbling. It can feel embarrassing. But remember, changing your mind actually means that you are responsive to the needs of your audience. Don't be afraid to murder your darlings when your research indicates that you should. Follow the research, and you'll be better off for it.

ENOUGH IS ENOUGH: SET CONSTRAINTS

Research can be something that you dread, or it can be a love affair. Some of us love to meander in research—much like the impulse of doomscrolling,[1] there will always be one more book to read, one more Google search, one more interview. You might grow an appetite for research that is never satisfied—but that won't take you all the way to execution. Recognize that although you might never feel you've reached the point of having done enough research, you will eventually be able to recognize synchronicities and patterns in your research.

Like all things artistic, I recommend putting some constraints on your research: decide how much you think your project needs, when you will begin, and when you will need to stop and move on to the next stage of your project. As with all creative endeavors, you will eventually have to make a judgment call about what to keep and what to discard from your research process results. Your collaborators will have opinions as well. Research undertaken for your project should invite exciting debate.

As you move forward, consider what you are looking to explore or accomplish. Do you wish to ask a question based on your research, or do you wish to make a statement that is a culmination of that research? Are your sources balanced and varied? Do you trust them? Are you able to defend the findings of your research?

1 In May 2020, during the global COVID-19 pandemic, *Urban Dictionary* defined "doomscrolling" as "obsessively reading social media posts about how utterly f*cked we are."

Librarians Make You Smarter

Librarians who work in public libraries want to help you unearth the information that you're looking for. They can access archives from other libraries' collections, discover historical photos, and locate music, maps, and ephemera. Go in with specific questions, and I'm willing to bet you will find a librarian who would be thrilled to help you.

One way to work through your research findings is to gather everything together—audio files, transcripts, ephemera, screenshots, visuals. This collection may inform or be part of your final artwork, or it may serve as inspiration for a new set of questions. What stories and patterns emerge when you see all of your research in one place? How do you make sense of it altogether?

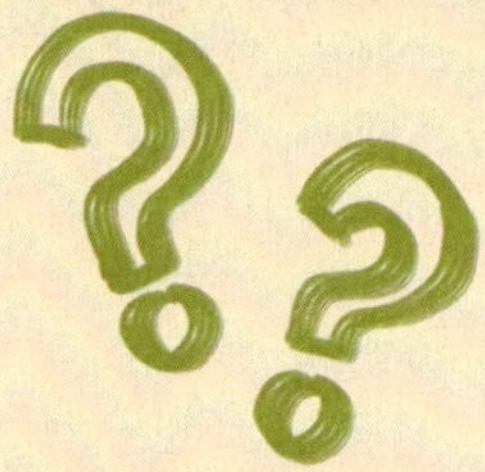

Lastly, when you see the entirety of your research, what form comes to mind for the project? Will you produce a piece of visual art, sound, or dance? Will it be an essay, a series of social media posts, or a rock opera? Will it inspire a sculpture or a community workshop?

However it manifests, it may or may not be what you pictured before you began. Your research is truly what you make of it.

CHAPTER 6

PRACTICE MAKES PERFECT: ITERATE AND PROTOTYPE

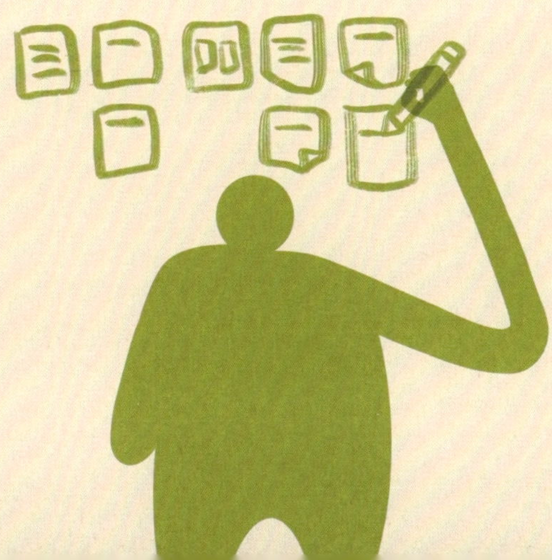

You may have put a lot of work into your project, but still feel like you haven't made the progress that you expected to. Having doubts about your next steps is normal. Welcome to the messy middle. When you are uncertain of what to do next, take the time to test out whether your project is feasible. Think of this stage as a dress rehearsal to put your project through its paces and see how it works artistically and logistically.

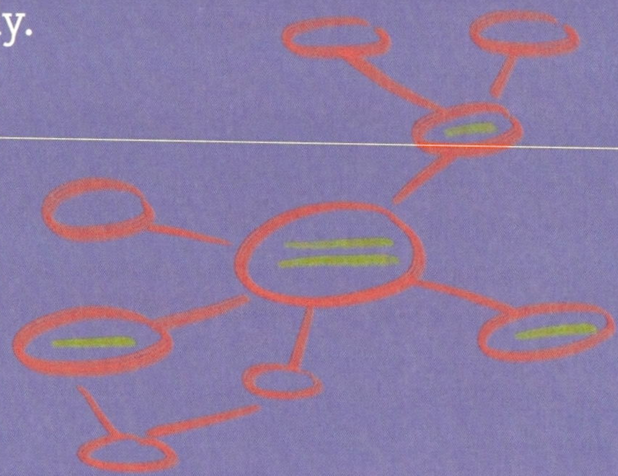

So many of us hesitate to make the things that we want to. In the face of creating something extraordinary, all sorts of excuses seem to come up—we need an art studio, or a bigger workplace, or a new set of tools. You may well need these things as you bring your project to life, but chances are you need less than you think you do.

You cannot design a project solely in your head; you must use your hands to execute it. In the practice stages, you should feel free to fail miserably. Remember, mistakes will teach you something. Even when things seem challenging, what *doesn't* work will help you find new ways to approach a problem.

Chats over coffee with your project partners might build friendship, but you won't understand each other's working styles until you actually make something together.

BRAINSTORMING: A JUDGMENT-FREE ZONE

Drawing from your research, host a brainstorming session with your collaborators. Be prepared to generate a ton of ideas without casting any editorial judgment. The worst thing that you can do is to censor yourself or others. The best ideas often develop from the most absurd and outrageous thoughts. Focus on quantity over quality—spitball those ideas! When the brainstorm is complete, you can pick the strongest contenders from the mix.

Write every idea that comes up and put it up where everyone can see it, whether on a big piece of paper, a whiteboard, or a bunch of Post-it notes. If there are more than a few of you, consider designating someone to be the moderator, with the role of reminding others when they start critiquing rather than presenting ideas. Banish phrases like "no," "I don't agree," "that's dumb," "that won't work," and "but ..." These inhibit brainstorming and hinder others from fully contributing their ideas.

There is no one right way to brainstorm, but here are a few techniques that can help you develop your ideas:

- Set an objective or a goal for each brainstorming session. You don't have to ideate the whole project; instead, you may want to choose one aspect to focus on, such as a central thesis or visual style.
- Set a timer to encourage rapid ideation with a deadline.
- Brainstorm on the move—walk, bike, or hike.
- Hold your session somewhere inspiring, such as a place with a great view.
- Have a round-robin, encouraging each participant to build off the last idea in succession.
- Go visual! Instead of words, use only drawings.
- Put on some background music to inspire you.
- Employ phrases like "Yes, and ..." to connect new ideas to the ones suggested by others.
- Remember to take breaks when you need them.

Once you've finished your brainstorming session, don't forget to document the results. A photograph of your notes will make it easier to remember the session.

Set the Tone

Have you given any thought to what mood you want your project to convey? Participants or viewers will develop their impression of the work based on the clues you give them. What emotions come to mind when you think of your project? What emotions do you want it to inspire?

Colorific

Color communicates volumes, whether it's through a pleasingly complementary palette or through our associations with colors (such as orange for safety, gold for royalty, red for festivity, and green for Ireland). How might the use of color make your project stand out even more? How might your project change if you changed the color palette?

Hear Me Out

Does your project have a soundtrack? A heavy metal soundtrack will not give someone the same impression as a series of birdcalls might. If someone were to make a movie about your project, what would be on the soundtrack?

UNDERSTANDING YOUR IDEAS

What if you and your coconspirators have landed on several ideas, but you can't agree which one works?

I believe that the best thing you can do in such a situation is to step away for a day or two so that each of you can reflect on the process so far. As we discussed in Chapter 3, the best ideas are the ones that keep coming back to you.

Brainstorming can be addictive, but ultimately it's only helpful if you actually use some of the ideas you generate. Here are some tips for moving your brainstorm into action:

- Seek similarities within your collection of ideas. Work with your coconspirators to lump similar thoughts together. Encourage further discussion about why certain things go together or do not.
- Rank your ideas by number. Eliminate the ideas that nobody likes.
- Determine a litmus test of whether an idea relates to your project. Is it possible? Does it support your activist cause? Does it reflect your research?

Decide what's next. What can you move forward on? What makes sense to implement? Do you have a consensus among your team of merry creative bandits? If you don't, it may be time to host another brainstorming session.

CASE STUDY

PLAY IN PUBLIC

A CONVERSATION WITH

Luke Jerram

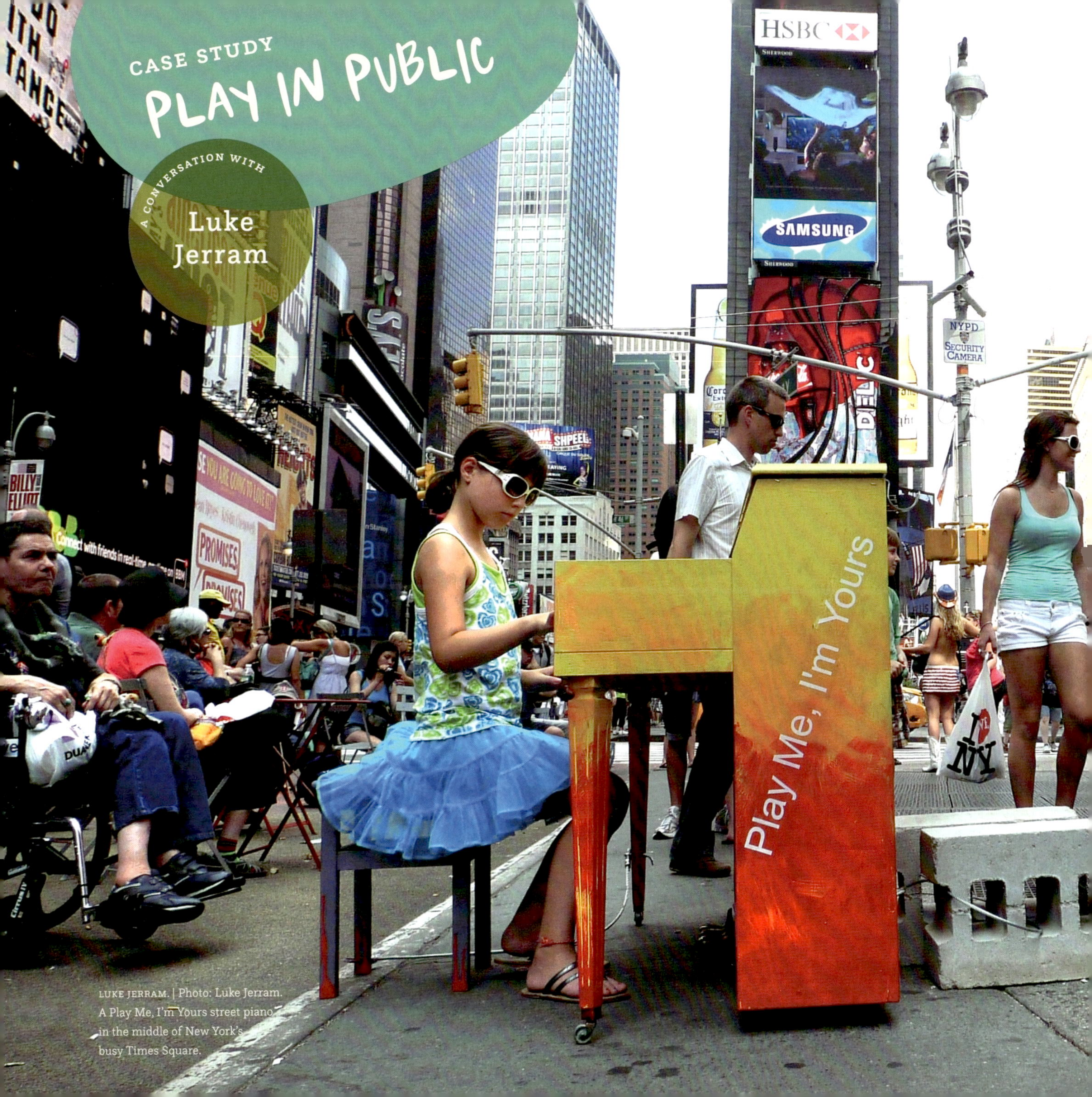

LUKE JERRAM. | Photo: Luke Jerram. A Play Me, I'm Yours street piano in the middle of New York's busy Times Square.

UK artist Luke Jerram's sophisticated projects seem to be born of an unlimited imagination. To look at his body of work is to be astounded. How the heck did he come up with that? His projects looks simple, but require a master hand and countless hours of scientific, medical, or engineering research. From glass microbiology artworks which are collected in museums throughout the world to a mile-long Slip 'N Slide, many of Luke's projects invite the public, curators, or other artists to actively engage with the work while having a great deal of fun. His work inspires me to think bigger about what is possible.

LUKE JERRAM. | Photo: Sally Reay. A Play Me, I'm Yours street piano under a pagoda in Shenzhen, China.

LEANNE: How did you begin your career as an artist?

LUKE: My first successful installation twenty years ago was called Retinal Memory Volume. This artwork creates an illusory sculpture using the biological mechanisms of the viewer's eyesight. The artwork had success touring festivals globally and launched my career.

From that initial success, various festival directors requested artworks that were similar, but different. I discovered that it was possible to be an artist who stumbles across one good idea, then continually exploits it for the rest of their career. Some artists seem to get stuck doing the same thing, basically, for twenty to thirty years. I didn't want that.

I learn from my artworks as I develop my ideas. I often reinvent my practice by throwing away the things I've learned so far, making my body of work very diverse. My works look different from one another, but there are connecting narratives that have emerged gradually over twenty years. I often consider myself five artists in one. I am the artist who does glass sculptures of viruses, but I am also the artist who animates the street with sound and public participation.

LEANNE: You have created a large body of participatory artwork. What attracts you to this sort of work?

LUKE: I studied sculpture and performance art in university. During time-based performances, I often found that the performer who was on the stage was having more fun than the audience, who were merely observers. I wanted to flip the idea of the passive consumption of art on its head and prioritize the public by giving them a compelling and active experience.

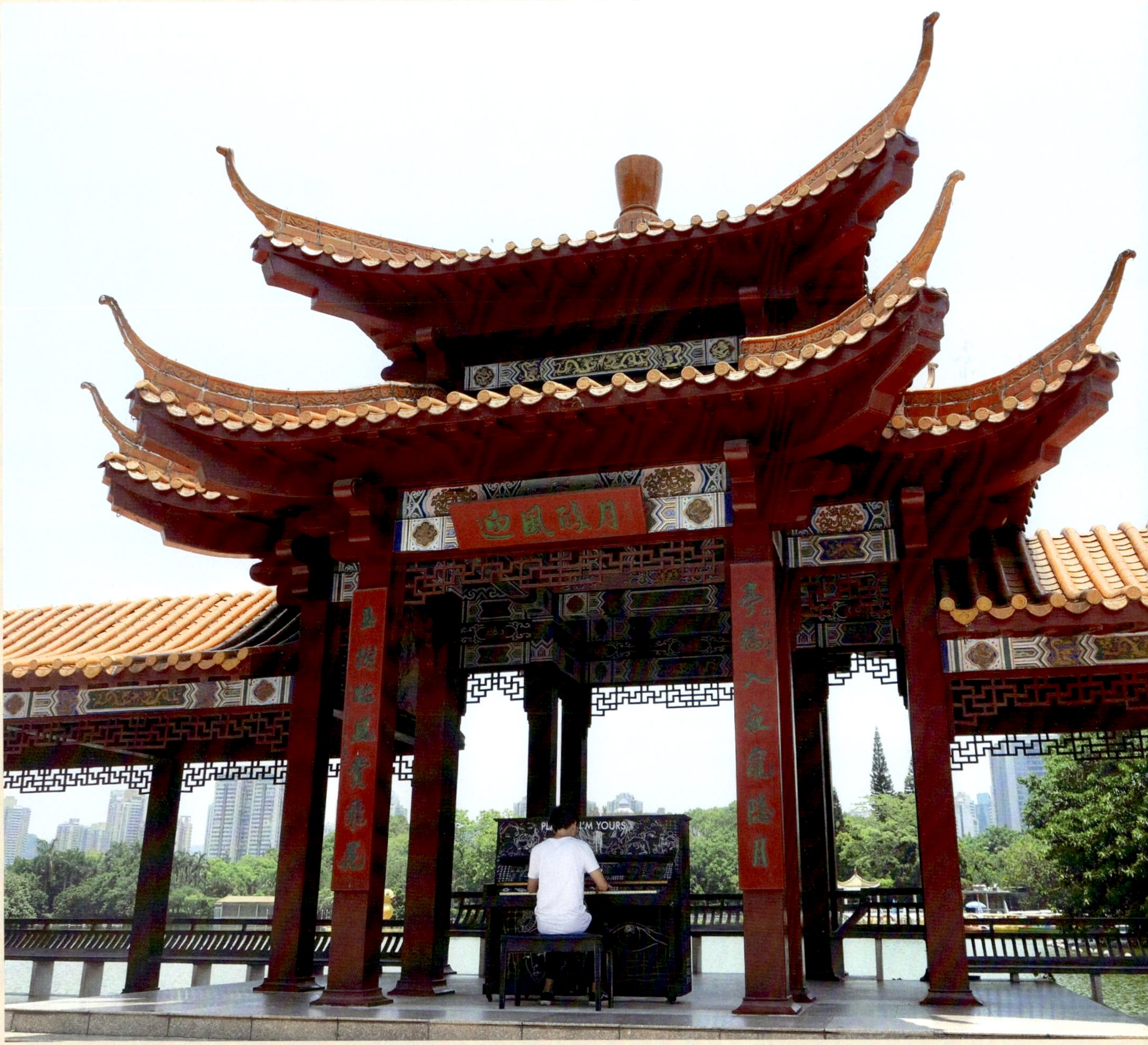
I'M YOURS

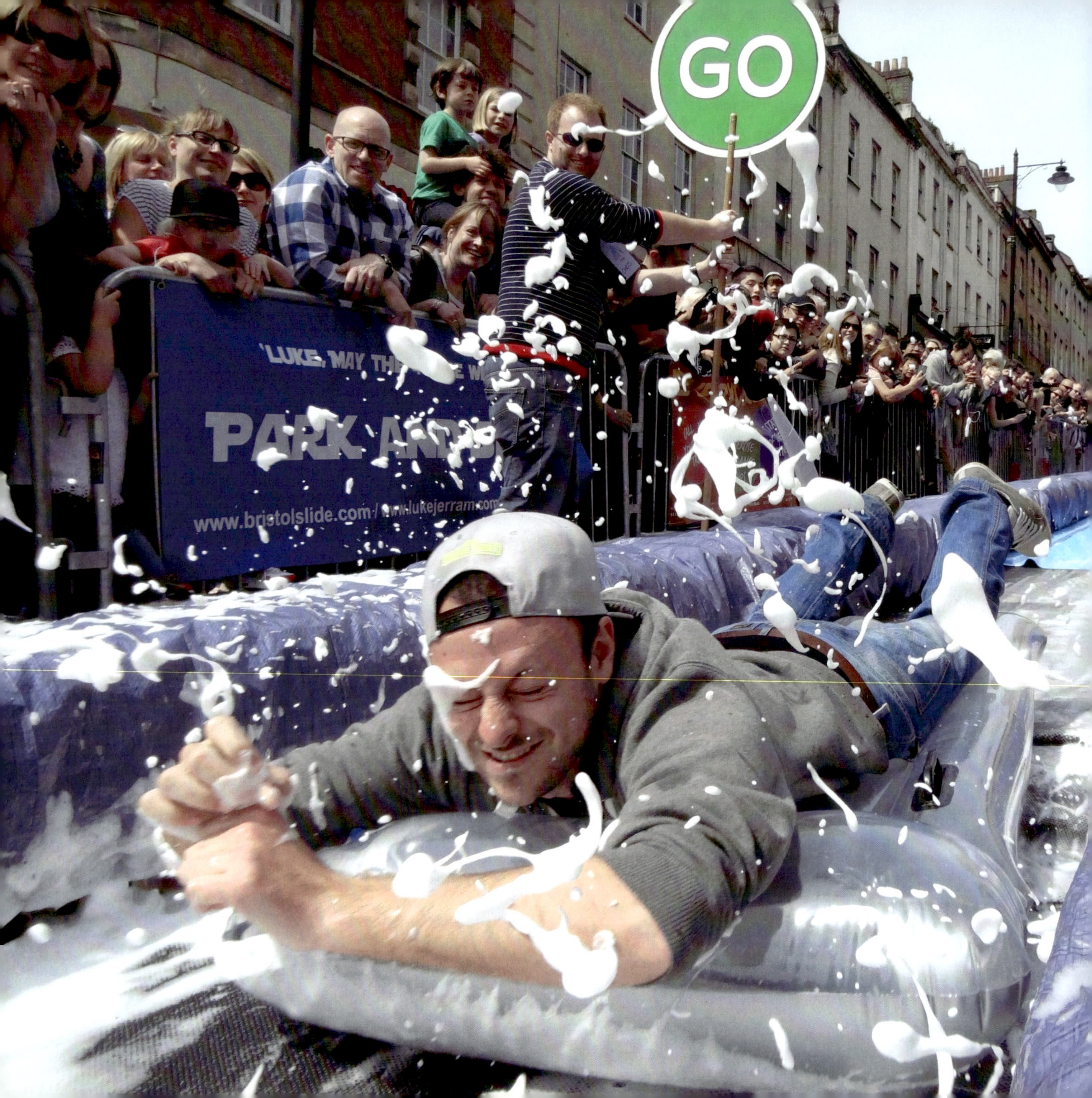
GO
www.bristolslide.com/

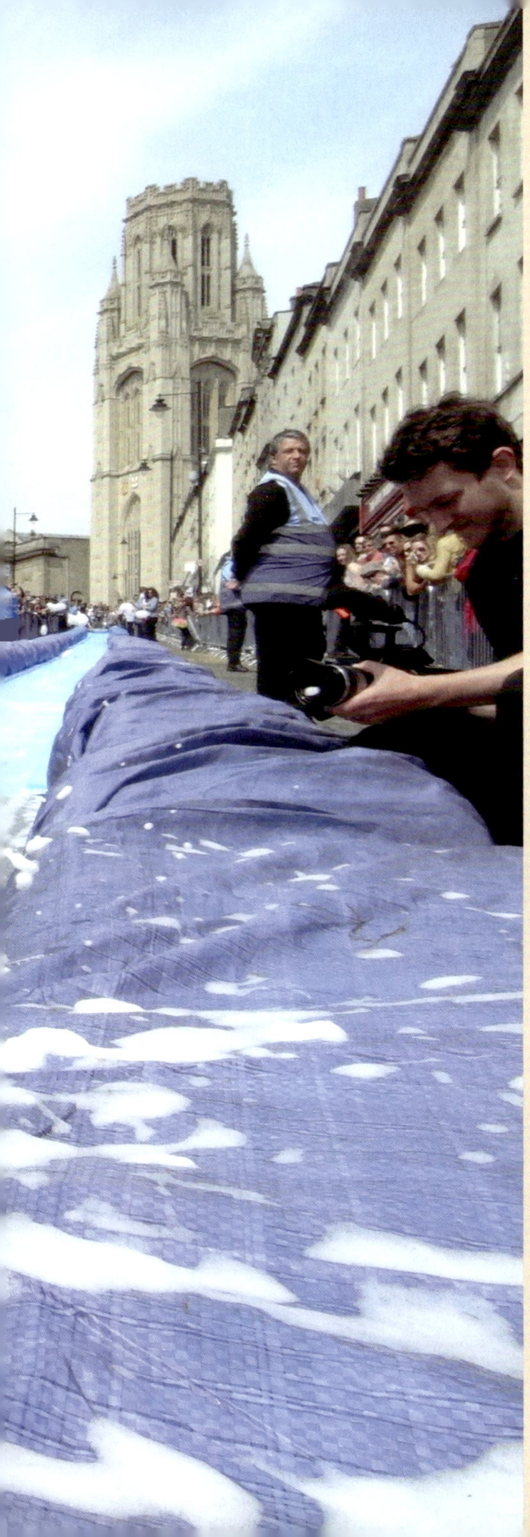

Projects like Play Me, I'm Yours, my street piano project, turn ordinary people into street performers. They become the center of attention. I like to leave space for other people to be creative within my artwork. Their participation brings enormous power and energy to the work.

I am never entirely sure what artwork will truly be like until it becomes public. The presence of people can change the perception of the work. For example, Park and Slide, a giant 95-meter [300-foot] waterslide that I designed to run down the middle of the high street in Bristol, was just a strip of plastic with some water. Then 30,000 people turned up, and it became artistic with the interaction of the public. I love that people become the vital ingredient to complete the artwork.

LEANNE: There must be obstacles to overcome when working around city bylaws and international borders. What challenges have you faced?

LUKE: There can be issues, but there are also beautiful surprises. People have given marriage proposals at our street pianos. We even led a change in the United Kingdom's music licensing laws when we installed the Play Me, I'm Yours street pianos in UK cities. The license to put a piano on the street or even in a pub was complicated. It required a huge volume of paperwork that was over an inch thick. We inspired this issue to be raised in the House of Lords in the UK Parliament, and they have since changed the music licensing laws. With art, you can have a political impact. Homeless people have gained employment through the pianos. Some have been discovered caretaking the pianos, and others have been scouted while performing. People have gotten

LUKE JERRAM, *Park and Slide.* | Photo: Luke Jerram. On May 4, 2014, this giant 300-foot waterslide was installed on Park Street in Bristol as part of Make Sunday Special and the Bristol Art Weekender. Running for one day only, it was an event that people of the city remembered for many years. 96,573 people signed up for their chance to slide; through a random draw, 360 lucky people were issued tickets.

recording contracts. The pianos have created endless possibilities. Ten years ago, we took Play Me, I'm Yours to China. At that time, the cities that we worked with didn't have much temporary public art. They didn't know what it was. The street piano project opened the door for artists to do more public work there.

The relationship with art is different in every city. For example, we were working with an American city on Play Me, I'm Yours and we discovered that our partner had only placed our street pianos in wealthy, predominantly white areas of the city. Once I learned how segregated the city was, we found out

LUKE JERRAM, 2008, Brazil. | Photo: Luke Jerram. A Play Me, I'm Yours street piano in a busy São Paulo train station.

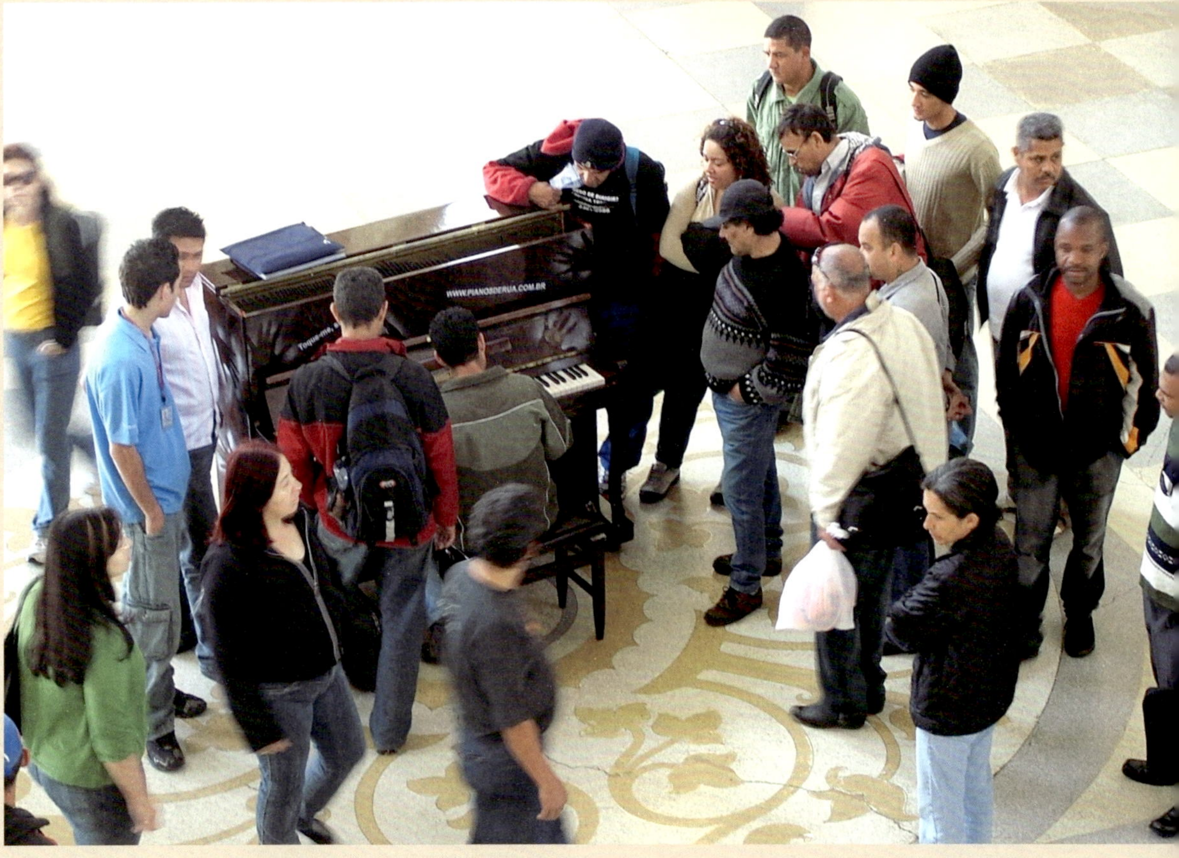

that entire communities had been excluded. As an artist working with partners, you often don't discover this kind of information until it's too late. In 2019, we had 117 exhibitions in twenty-five countries, and I learned that with this sort of reach, my attention can be spread too thin, and I have to work against that.

LEANNE: Your projects are incredibly complex. Do you use many prototypes in developing your work?

LUKE: I use a lot of prototypes. Every object around you has had over 50,000 hours of testing. For something like a cell phone, there might have been a hundred prototypes made to get it to the point where you could have it in your life. Artists don't often have that opportunity to make forty prototypes and do 20,000 hours of testing. I like to learn from failure. I think that being willing to fail is critical to growth as an artist.

LEANNE: Your work often needs to be scientifically accurate, not only to the public but also to scientists like biologists, geologists, and astronomers. Do you conduct your own research or have assistance?

LUKE: Both. Generally, I'll do the work myself in order to be able to understand the conversations I need to have with scientists. Many of my artworks are made in collaboration with scientists or engineers. I enjoy learning the language and methods from these different practitioners—it keeps my life interesting to explore different disciplines. I can have conversations with an astronomer one week, and I can speak with a microbiologist the next.

As a kid, I would take radios apart to work out what was inside, and they would never quite go back together correctly. I often give workshops to kids in which we bring in loads of objects and get them to take them apart. We encourage them to ask questions, such as, "Why is it made of plastic and wood? Where is it being made?" Children and scientists are equally curious.

I try to make artwork that can be appreciated by all sorts of different people. They react differently to it depending on who they are. If you are a four-year-old child, you'll enjoy simply making sound on a street piano. Whereas if you're a concert pianist, you're going to interact with a piano differently. It's the same way with the Museum of the Moon; the artwork can be appreciated by many different people. I had a little girl who came up to me and said, "Will you put the moon back afterward?" She thought that I had stolen the real moon. It was adorable. This was in contrast to meeting astrophysicists, who had been studying the moon for years, in tears because they could see the moon in real life for the first time. They needed a hug.

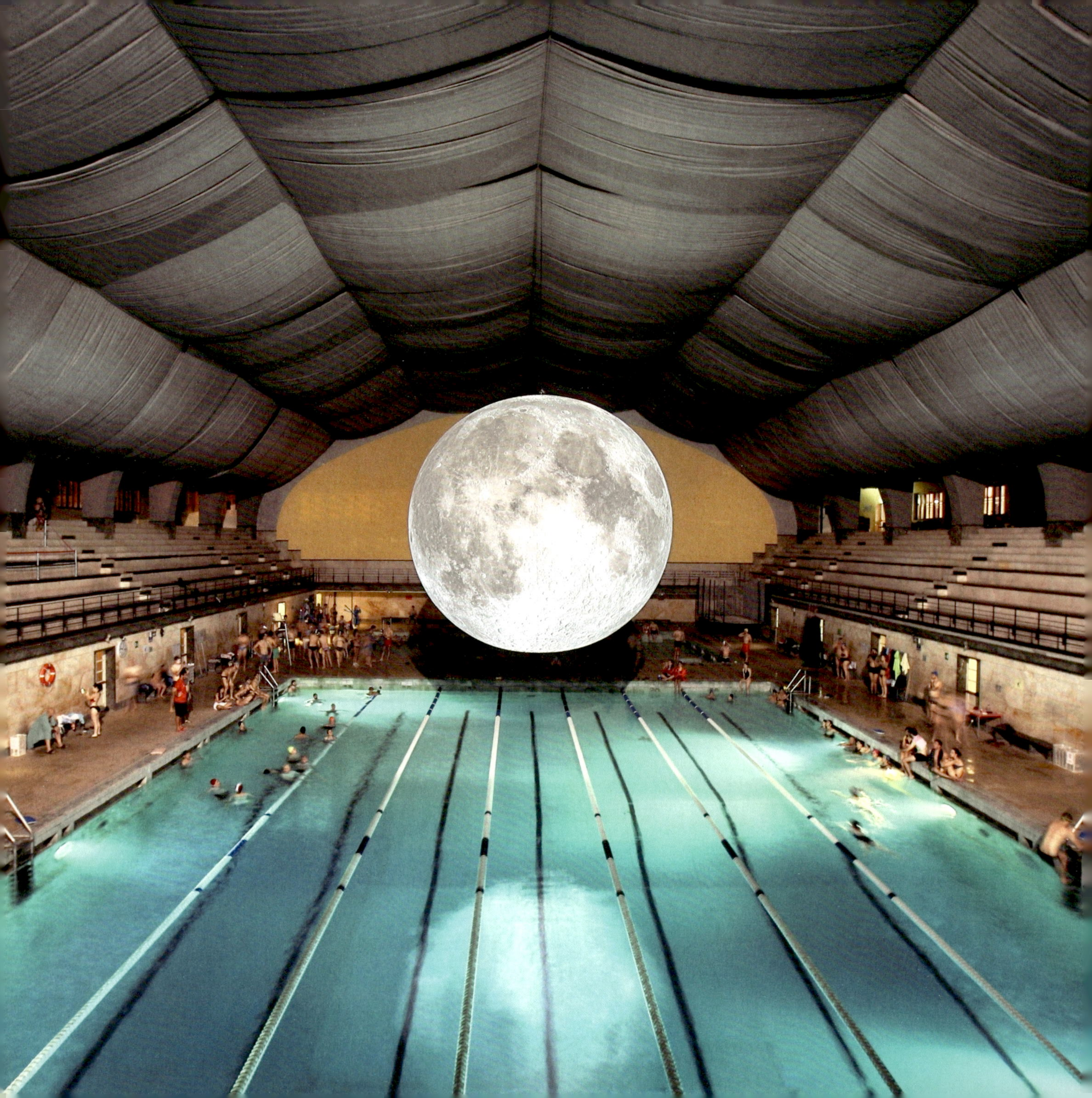

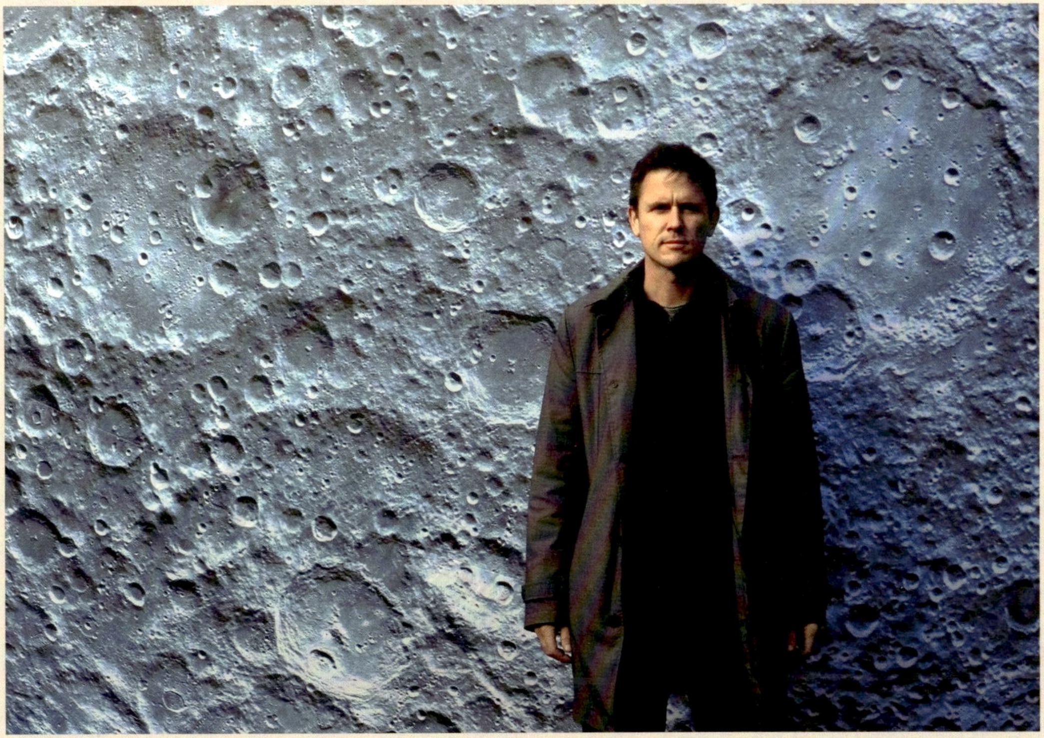

LEFT: LUKE JERRAM, *Museum of the Moon*, 2019, Milan. | Photo: Andrea Cherchi. Museum of the Moon is an adaptable piece of art that has been installed inside public spaces such as pools, parks, and cathedrals, allowing people to come in contact with the moon in an intimate and unusual setting. The work was exhibited in many countries, including France, Belgium, the United Kingdom, India, and Canada. In Milan's Piscina Cozzi, Museum of the Moon allowed the public to swim under a celestial experience by night and day.

ABOVE: LUKE JERRAM, *Museum of the Moon*, 2019. | Photo: Luke Jerram. Luke Jerram in front of Museum of the Moon.

LUKE JERRAM'S *multidisciplinary practice involves the creation of sculptures, installations, and live arts projects. Living in the UK but working internationally since 1997, Luke has created a number of extraordinary art projects that have excited and inspired people around the world. He is known globally for his innovative arts practice and large-scale public artworks. With many of his artworks in permanent collections, including the Metropolitan Museum of Art in New York and the Wellcome Collection in London, he also tours his installations in art festivals and museums. Working with some of the most established cultural organizations to create his artworks, in 2019 alone, he had 117 exhibitions in twenty-five different countries around the world. In 2020, he was awarded an honorary doctorate from the University of Bristol and was made an Academician of the RWA and Fellow of the Royal Astronomical Society.* **lukejerram.com**

THUMBNAILS: THE POWER OF RAPID SKETCHING

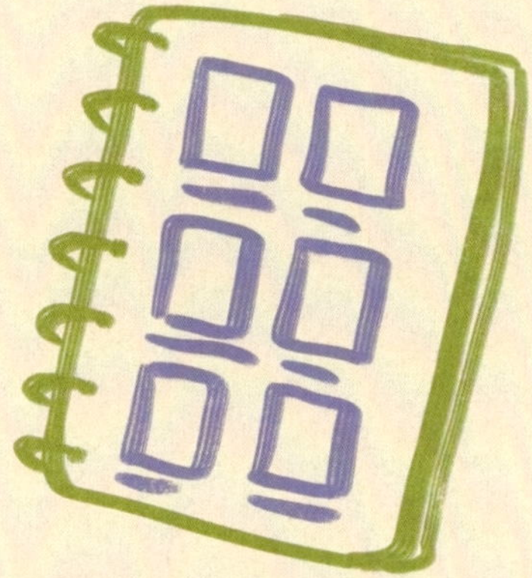

Drawing is another way you can work out your ideas. Much like brainstorming, creating small, thumbnail-sized sketches can be an effective way to refine your idea. This technique, often used in the design industry, is helpful for rapid idea generation.

Artist Tyree Guyton (see page 231) uses drawing to plan his bigger projects. He said, "I keep a notebook of three-by-five-inch drawings with me. I'm always talking and thinking about these little case studies. These little drawings first start with a thought. I have to listen to this creative muscle. It is like being in a holy place. I put it on paper, and I have the ability to make it tangible."

Thumbnail sketches are a visual shorthand—don't worry about your drawing skills. The goal is to render your idea in as little detail as possible, making many sketches in quick succession, changing a small detail or two in each. The goal of thumbnail sketches is to generate ideas quickly—do not correct your drawing. If you don't like something, move on. Most designers create fifty to a hundred tiny sketches per project to work out their ideas.

Once you're happy with your thumbnails, look over your ideas. You may want to pick one or two to create larger renderings of that you can finesse and share with your coconspirators.

PROTOTYPES ARE DREAMS IN ACTION

How do you know that your fantastical project will work in real life? One way to find out is to build a model or a prototype. A prototype is a rough draft. Consider it an early sample or model that allows you to test a concept or process. Prototypes allow someone who does not live inside your mind's eye to see what you see.

A few years ago, I visited the Victoria and Albert Museum in London and came across an incredible collection of scale models of theatrical productions made from paper. At first glance, all you see is the beautiful rendition of a stage set, but as you walk around the exhibit, you realize that each model is made out of a dirty old cigar box. I loved how these simple models can express exactly what the set designers wanted them to. These miniatures truly made each set design come to life.

A prototype allows you to test your project without investing significant time, money, or expense. A prototype will also allow you to change course and try new things as new ideas come to you.

MAKE IT REAL USING YOUR MEDIUM OF CHOICE

Pick your medium. There isn't a single way to prototype or to execute your project. Why not try the following:

- Render a visual project through thumbnail drawings, test photos taken with a phone camera, napkin sketches, photo collages, or a mood board.
- Test an experiential project by making chalk or tape markings on the ground, shoebox dioramas, miniature builds out of modeling clay or paper, or cardboard replicas.
- Trial movement projects by shooting short videos of the performance or by staging a dress rehearsal in a different space of the same size.
- Craft miniature versions of interactive public projects by employing audio recordings, site maps, internet conversations on social media sites, or quick exchanges with strangers.

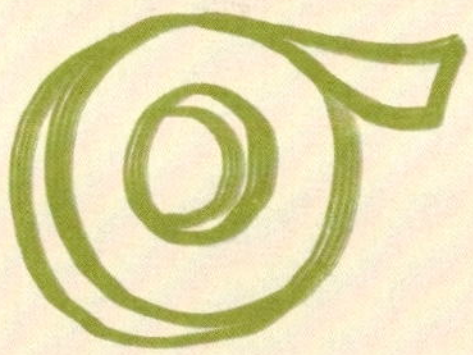

A Word of Caution on Illicit Activities

Some activist projects have a greater effect when they take place in unsanctioned spaces. If your project is one of these, be sure to have a conversation with everyone participating so that they understand the potential consequences and liabilities.

TESTING IT OUT

As creators, we often think that we can control the outcome of our projects. Most of the time, we do not have this level of control, but if you have trust in your project, one of the most exciting things that can happen is that you'll achieve results you did not expect. Don't forget to keep a spirit of play and experimentation as you test out your ideas. Often the best results come from being open to letting things take their course.

As artist Terrence Kelleman (see page 43) said, "Trust your gut—when you go through the process of creating, there will be part of you that knows what feels right and what should be discarded. The stuff that you get rid of isn't bad; it's just not as connected to the project as the other stuff."

SCOUT IT: UNDERSTAND YOUR LOCATION

If your project takes place in a location that you've found—by prior arrangement or by stealth—you will want to ensure that the site works properly for your needs.

It's not enough to see a location once. I recommend visiting a place several times a day over several weeks and under different conditions of light, weather, and human interaction. Observation can help you discover unanticipated obstacles, such as heavy foot traffic when the workday and/or school day ends, loud delivery trucks, high theft patterns, or a dog walker with an armful of unruly pups.

If you are using a space that belongs to others, make sure you have a conversation with them about logistics to agree on what will occur in the area. If people are kind enough to host you, do your best to ensure that they don't receive any surprises or legal challenges.

If the project is an immersive one, you'll need to stand in the space for a long time to determine how it may work for you and to anticipate any challenges that might come up. Is the sun in your eyes? Is the ambient sound low enough not to be distracting? Is the ground muddy? What surfaces can you apply materials to? Where can participants work? Is there access to electricity, water, washrooms? Put yourself in the place of potential participants. What will the experience be like for them when they get there?

CHECK YOUR ACCESSIBILITY

When testing your project, it is essential to consider how accessible your project is. Consider it with and without mobility, sight, and hearing. How will it work for people of different heights? Consider it with different languages and reading levels. Do the entrances and exits of the space make it easy for people to come and go? How can you make everyone welcome?

I once created a community embroidery project at a Maker Faire in which I invited anyone to come and stitch on a communal canvas. I thought I was so clever, fashioning a DIY standing embroidery table out of a five-by-four-foot canvas stretcher and using two IKEA shoe racks as easels so participants could stand together and stitch. For the first few hours, I was pleased with how well it was working. People were stitching and talking, and the artwork began to take shape.

Later that afternoon, a woman in a wheelchair told me that she would have liked to participate, but the project was not accessible for her. If I'd considered accessibility beforehand, I could have developed a setup that would have allowed her to participate. I wonder how many other people I excluded that day with my design choices.

SAFETY FIRST

While your art might be edgy and provocative, please ensure that participants and viewers can engage with you without experiencing bodily harm. Fire exits exist for a reason; ensure that you do not block them. Likewise, if you have an installation in a public place, it is up to you to do due diligence to ensure that it is safe for participants. Look around: loading zones often have large vehicles backing into them; back alleys could have needles lying on the ground; ponds with waterfowl can look pretty, but birds can quickly get territorial. Remember that you want participants to remember what you created together, not a trip to the emergency room.

A CONVERSATION ON

The Global Angel Wings Project

CASE STUDY

CREATE A PLATFORM FOR OTHERS

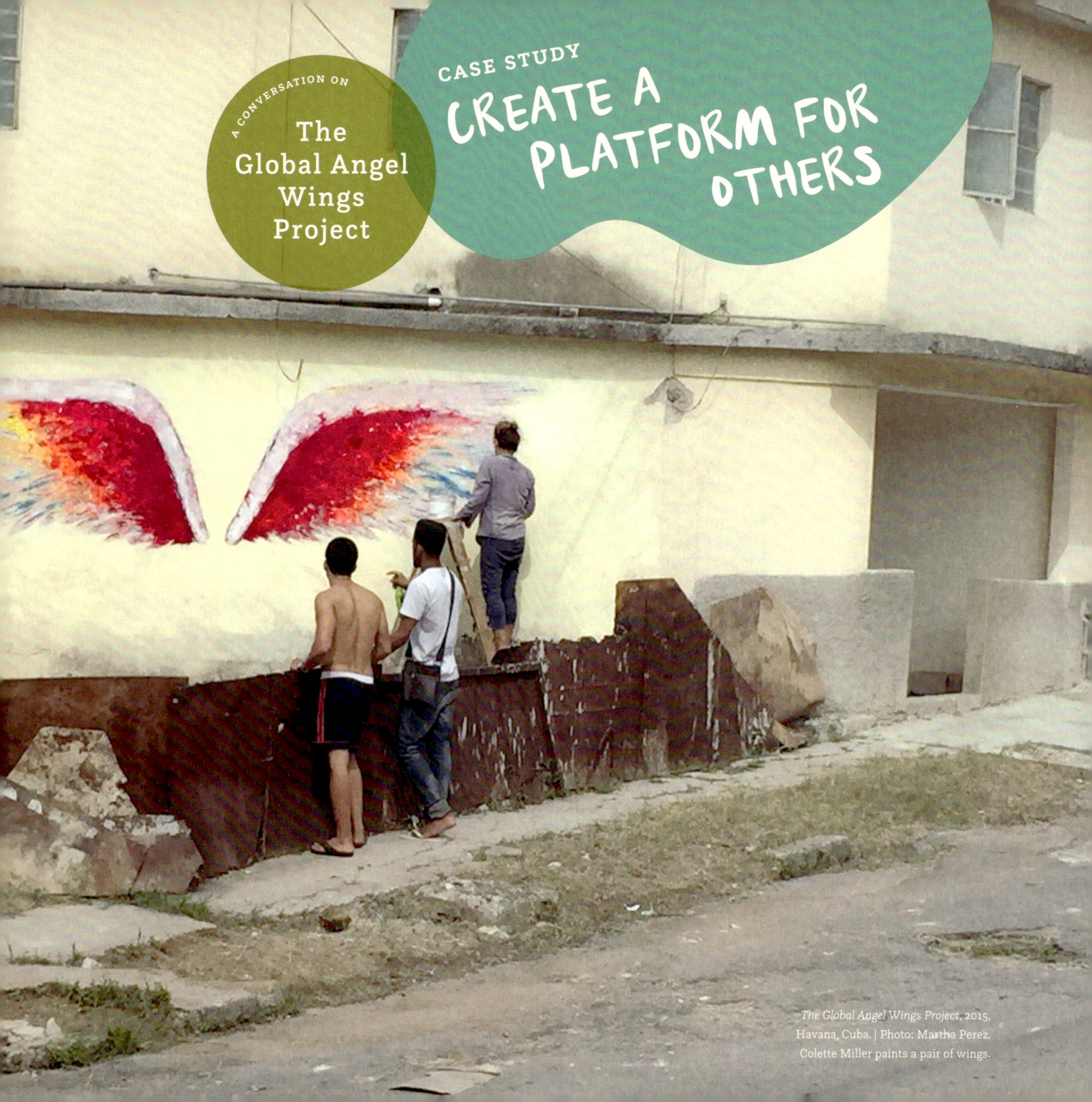

The Global Angel Wings Project, 2015, Havana, Cuba. | Photo: Martha Perez. Colette Miller paints a pair of wings.

Colette Miller created the Global Angel Wings Project in 2012, in the streets of Los Angeles, the City of Angels, to remind humanity that we are the angels of this Earth. The wings are human-sized interactive public art that people can take photos with, thus become becoming part of the artwork. The public response—from people of all sorts and backgrounds—was natural, immediate, and spontaneous. You cannot help but notice the delight of those who pose in front of the wings, from giddy schoolchildren to politicians. Colette's colorful interactive murals invite people to connect with something fanciful, even just for a minute. Since 2012, she has been painting angel wings across her city of Los Angeles and around the world, creating space for the public to interact, reflect, and experience joy. Her work shows that something simple can have great impact.

LEANNE: Tell me about the experience of creating the first public artwork.

COLETTE: My early installations were self-authorized. The first time, my friend Stevie "Casual" Bryant stood looking out for police. We wanted to make sure that we were not arrested or fined. I chose buildings that seemed available to use without creating damage. I thought that my wings would enhance the scenery. With my first project, I had help from Stuart Noble, who had worked with Shepard Fairey and other street artists. He was a semipro at putting up posters and paper wheatpaste and showed me the quickest way to get a piece up and then saunter away casually. I didn't sign my name to the first pairs of wings, as I was nervous about the repercussions. I had placed them without permission. I also wanted to remain anonymous because I felt that I was creating these divinity wings as a gift for humanity.

The first weekend that the wings were up, there happened to be a street festival right near the mural. I was hanging with Stevie, who had kept guard the night before. When we walked around the corner, we saw a line of people—old people, young people, and everyone in between—all of them waiting to take a photo with the wings behind them. Someone had even left a step stool out front for the children to use.

Stevie and I found a vantage point high up in a parking garage across the street to watch all the activity. We were absolutely joyous. I had an aha moment: I had hit on something bigger than myself.

LEANNE: Why wings?

COLETTE: I had been meditating a lot on humanity, the human experience, and the divine in us, or our "true selves," as yogis call it. Images of large wings popped into my mind. I'd imagine them on walls as I drove around LA, the City of Angels. So I acted on that impulse and made them large enough for people to wear them. I didn't have financial or legal help at the beginning. I just believed in my idea and myself, and I acted on it.

I traveled to areas that had been traumatized, and for healing, I put up wings under my own auspices. I visited Baltimore after the riots, war refugee camps in France, and abandoned areas and alleys in Kenya, Africa, where street kids slept. In Kenya, a few of the kids' friends had been murdered by the villagers, burned to death and

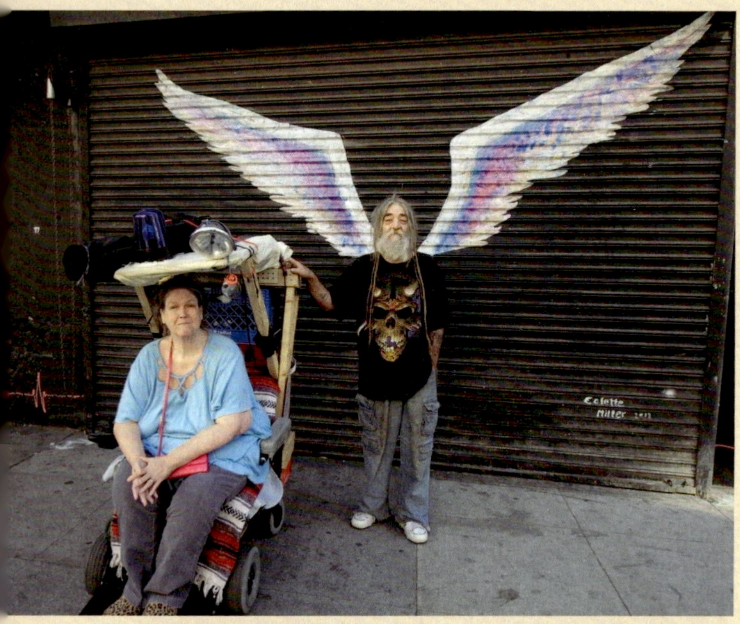
Colette Miller

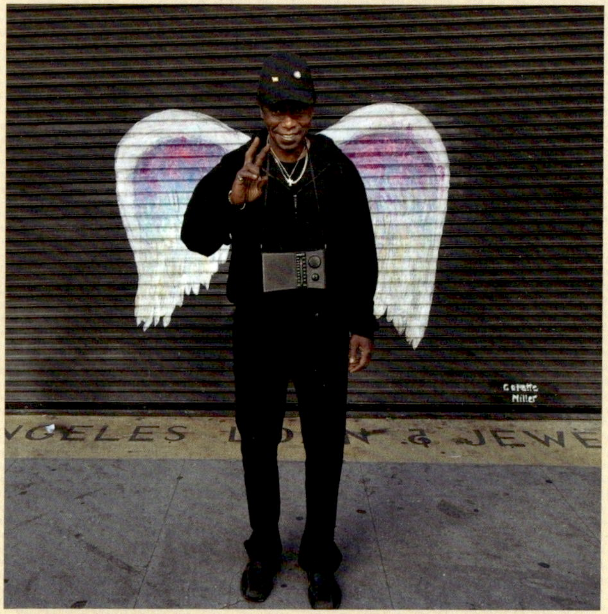
Colette Miller

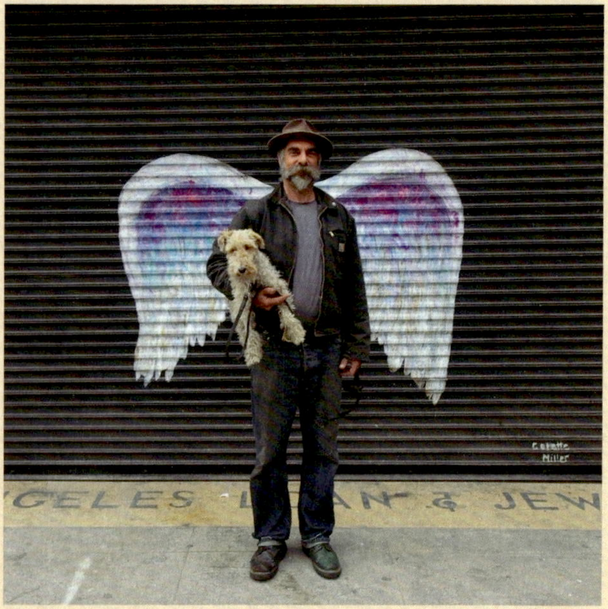
Colette Miller

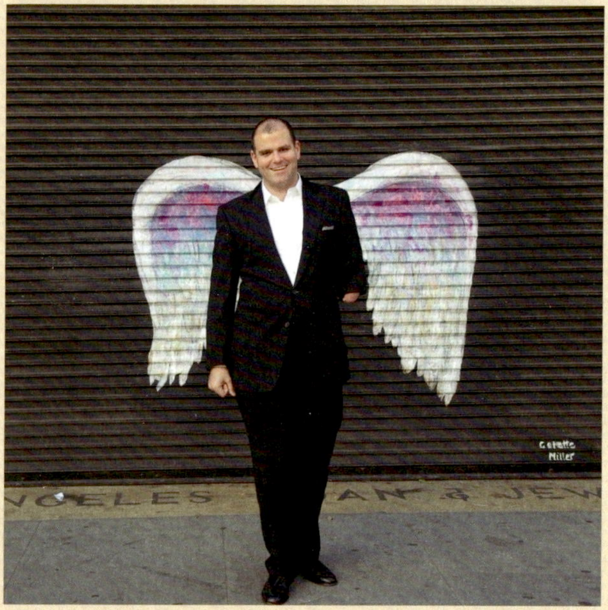
Colette Miller

The Global Angel Wings Project, Los Angeles, California. | Photos: Gary Leonard. Every person who poses before one of Colette Miller's paintings becomes a unique angel.

accused of stealing. To heal, they started a community boxing club outside Nairobi and named it the Kayole Wings Miller Boxing Club.

The experiences I've had painting wings in different locations are all special to me: the orphanage in Jiaxing, China, when the kids gathered around and hugged me; the kids in Kenya naming their boxing club with "Wings"; the Burj Khalifa in Dubai, the highest building on Earth; the amazing culture of Japan; special places in Europe; and my home base of the City of Angels that embraced the idea and my art.

LEANNE: You've stated that although the wings may not change people's minds, you hope they will give people pause.

COLETTE: My intent was for others to reflect on their higher nature—our kinder, better selves. The angel inside all of us. The wings are a relatable universal symbol. They cross cultures, religions, and classes. The culture of each place is different, but the similar reactions of the people are unifying.

COLETTE MILLER *created the Global Angel Wings Project in 2012, in the streets of Los Angeles, the City of Angels. They were painted to remind humanity that we are the angels of this Earth. They are human-sized interactive public art, wings that people can take photos with and thus become part of the artwork. Colette has painted angel wings globally, in Kenya, Australia, England, Japan, France, Cuba, Mexico, China, and the US. Some are commissioned and others gifted, but the wings themselves are free to the world, never owned by anyone, not even Colette, though they are of her provenance and her work. Find out more at* ***colettemiller.com*** *and* ***globalangelwingsproject.com****.*

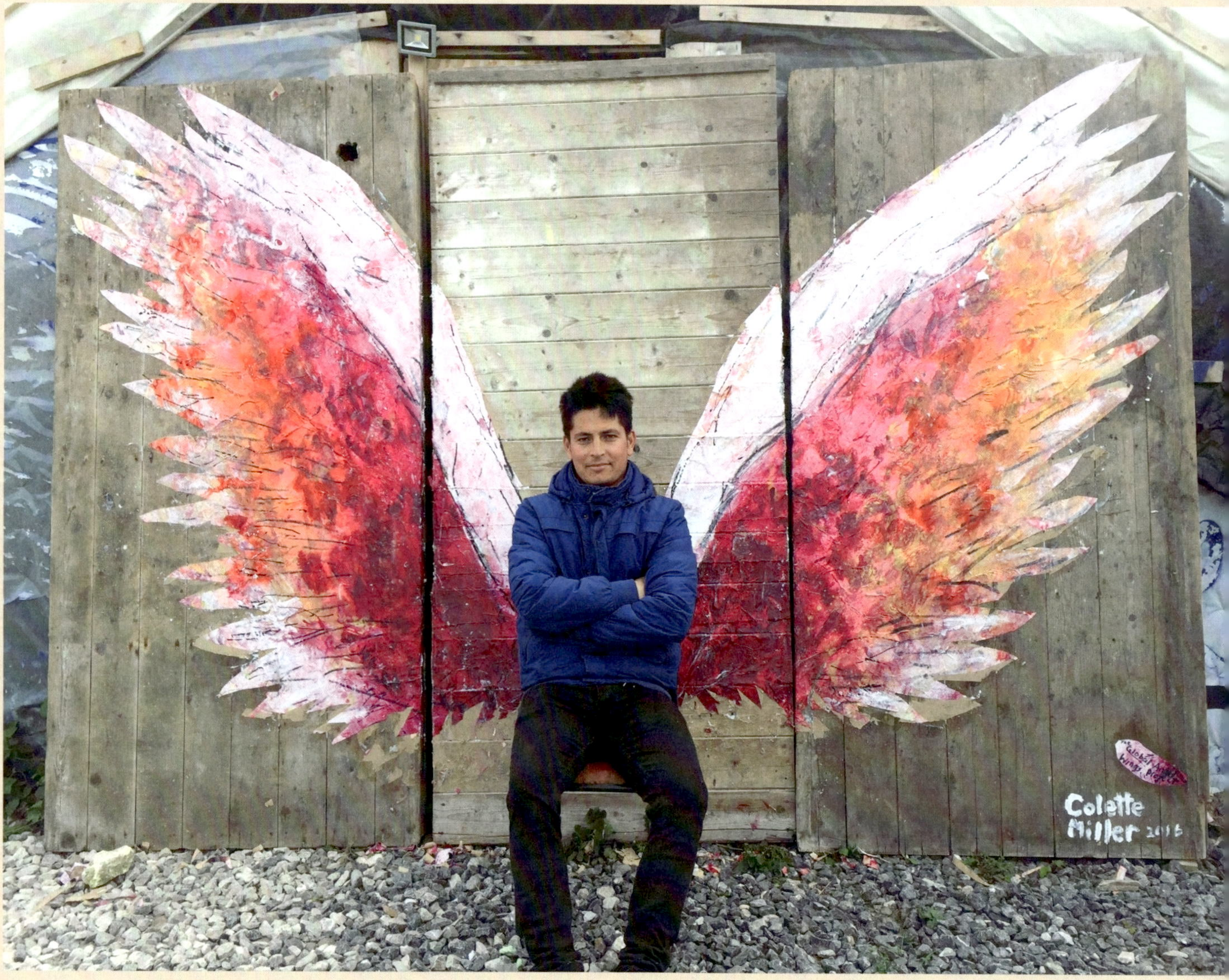

COLETTE MILLER, *The Global Angel Wings Project*, Calais, France. | Photo courtesy of Colette Miller. Calais Jungle refugee camp / Camp de la Lande.

BUILDING YOUR ARSENAL: GATHER SUPPLIES

What materials do you need to execute your project? I recommend making a list as you go. Some of these items will be essential, others just nice to have. As you start to build an inventory, it will become clear which items you have ready access to and which your group may need to purchase or find. I generally try to spend as little money as possible on project materials, as the budgets of creative projects are never quite as large as we desire.

It's also good to understand your nature when it comes to execution. Are you a minimalist or a maximalist? Sometimes it helps to be partnered with a coconspirator who has different tendencies.

I'm a maximalist when it comes to executing projects. I like to be a bit over the top, and I always have extra supplies on hand. A few years ago, my creative collective, The Imprint, decided to stage a literary dinner party where participants could write stories on paper place settings. To make it feel like a real dinner party, we decided to outfit long tables with tablecloths and candlesticks. In the days leading up to our event, I found myself shopping in thrift stores for dozens of brass goblets. I worried that I didn't have enough decor until my coconspirator Laura gently but firmly reminded me that we had enough material for participants to get the idea they were at a dinner party. Left to my own devices, I would have tried to kit out our table with forty perfect place settings, a porcelain cornucopia, fake bouquets, and a lusterware statue of a sheepdog, even though our time to source materials and our limited budget did not afford this. In the end, Laura was right: the simplicity of a few candlesticks and goblets made our table work, and our participants did feel like they were at a dinner party. I was grateful for Laura's guidance as we packed up at the end of our event day. A suitcase that doesn't contain forty brass goblets is much lighter than one that does.

I've learned that things don't need to be perfect for them to work. Your project is likely not going to be 100 percent your original vision, but sometimes a bit of duct tape and twine can make it 100 percent in the eyes of those who experience it. As you start to envision the final execution, be aware of what you can let go of and what is essential. Have frank and honest discussions with each of your coconspirators about what elements will make or break the project.

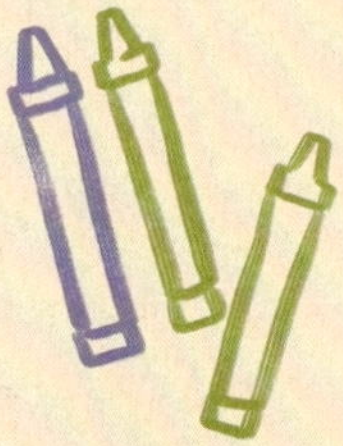

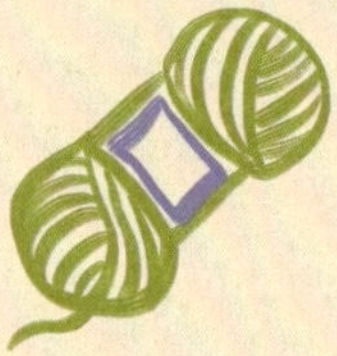

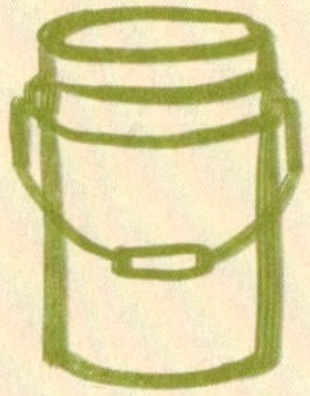

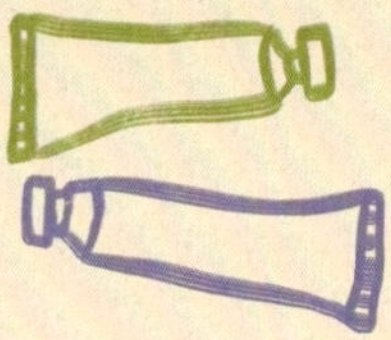

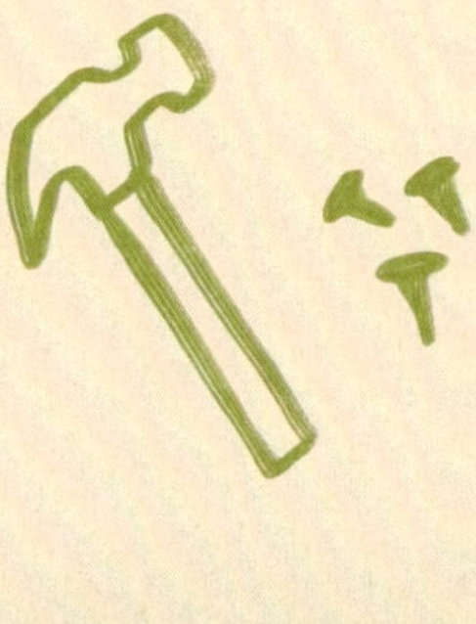

Here are some good places for sourcing supplies:

- People sell supplies on online message boards like Kijiji, Craigslist, and Facebook groups.
- Hardware stores and industrial building supply stores often have samples, discounted paints, carpet remnants, and vinyl offcuts that are out of fashion.
- Kids' art workshops and community centers may be willing to sell gently used supplies for cheap.
- Look for businesses that specialize in reselling waste as artist materials or that offer tool libraries.
- Thrift stores and hospital auxiliary shops can be a fantastic source of fabrics, props, old electronics, hand tools, and costumes.
- Fiber enthusiasts usually have more wool than they will ever use. Post in fiber-specific message groups online or put up a poster at your local yarn store. Explain what you need the materials for.
- Newspaper printers may be able to supply you with offcuts of newsprint.
- Bakeries often have large white ten-gallon buckets to dispose of.
- Your local scrapyard likely has cheap metal items for sale.
- Fancy wine stores may have beautiful wooden wine boxes to donate.
- Dollar stores are an excellent source of cheap paintbrushes, presentation cardstock, glue sticks, and cheap tablecloths (often needed to protect surfaces in community centers).
- Your local library or college resource centers may have video, photography, or sound equipment that you can borrow. Some even offer editing equipment, musical instruments, and recording studios.
- Word of mouth: tell everyone what you need until you find someone who can help you.

DON'T GET DISTRACTED BY WHAT'S NEW

When we're in the final throes of testing out work, things can start to feel challenging. Don't despair. Recognize that any feeling of overwhelm that you are having is likely part of growing creatively. Remember, if you don't stay the course, no one else will. Make this thing real!

When things get tough, it is natural to want to deviate. Perhaps you or one of your creative coconspirators will come up with a shiny new idea. But beware of distractions! Does this new idea build on and improve the project that you've been developing? Yes? Great, then you should pursue it. No? Then it's not the time. You already have a project in front of you, and you've committed to it. Put that shiny new idea in your mental lockbox for later. You can take it out once you are done with this project and see if you still are enamored of it. True love waits.

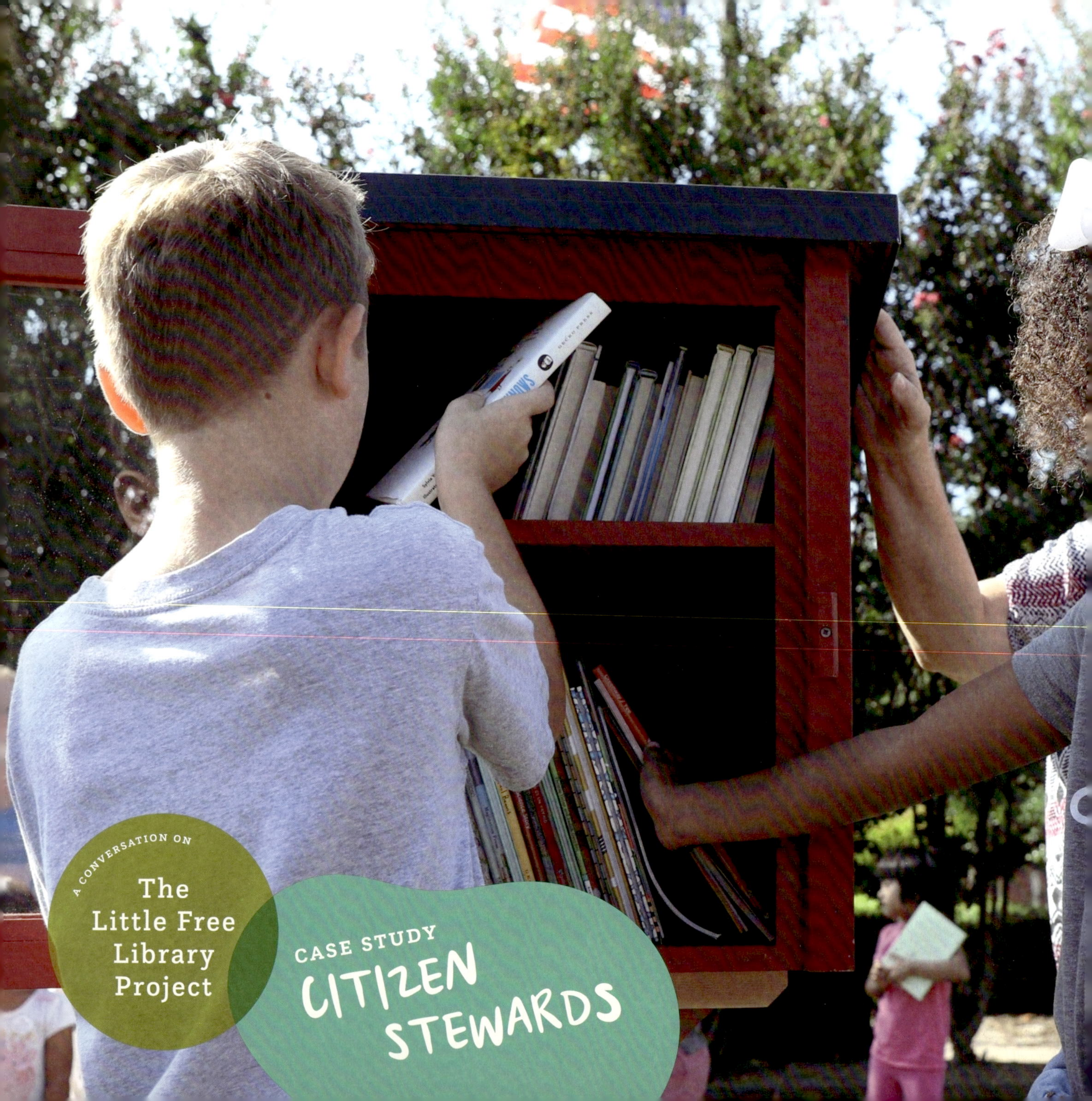
A CONVERSATION ON
The Little Free Library Project
CASE STUDY
CITIZEN STEWARDS

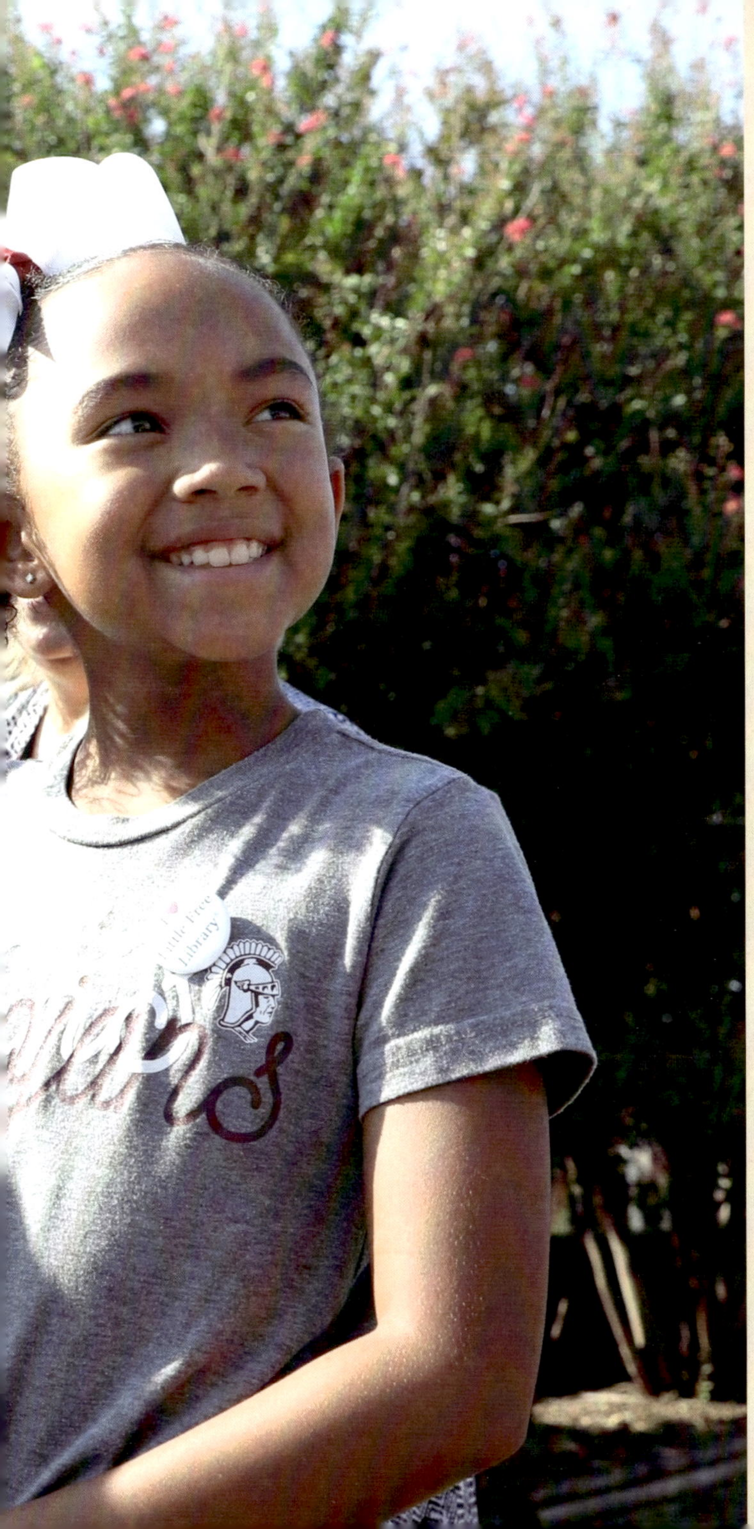

I know that you've seen them—the little free libraries that have been popping up just about everywhere. The Little Free Library Project grew from one little library to a nonprofit organization that leads over 100,000 citizen-run libraries worldwide and promotes literacy, creativity, and community around the world. If you want to scale up a project, look no further for example than the Little Free Library Project, which supports a volunteer steward network with resources for launching libraries, engaging your communities, procuring books, and other essential steward activities. Each Little Free Library steward has the autonomy and freedom to operate their library in a way that meets the needs of their community, creating a local movement and a global movement at the same time. I spoke with Margret Aldrich, director of communications for the Little Free Library Project.

LEANNE: How did the Little Free Library Project come about?

MARGRET: The first library was built in 2009 by Todd Bol in Hudson, Wisconsin, as a tribute to his mother. It immediately struck a chord as a beacon of literacy and community. Little Free Library was established as a non-profit organization in 2012. Today there are more than 100,000 Little Free Library book-sharing boxes in over 100 countries—including Italy, Australia, Brazil, Sudan, and Japan. The common thread between Little Free Library volunteer stewards, wherever they may be, is that they share a love of reading and a dedication to the common good. A Little Free Library has a unique way of bringing people together through books.

Photo courtesy of Little Free Library.

The creativity of Little Free Library stewards is boundless. We've seen Little Free Libraries that look like rocket ships, robots, movie theaters, and more. A favorite library of mine stands in Coeur d'Alene, Idaho, and was carved from a 110-year-old cottonwood tree. That not-so-little library has interior and exterior lights, and you can walk inside it to peruse the books. Another favorite was built by Dr. Russell Schnell for the Atmospheric Research Observatory at the South Pole. It was the first Little Free Library in Antarctica—which means there are now little libraries on every continent! It's also wonderful to see creative locations for Little Free Libraries that help provide equitable book access. Barbershops, laundromats, hospital waiting rooms, and bus stops are all inventive spots for little libraries.

LEANNE: The Little Free Library Project fosters relationships with stewards, those who tend and protect their little libraries. What do stewards need to support their work?

MARGRET: It's important that Little Free Library book-sharing boxes in different parts of the world reflect their local communities and the needs of those communities. Each library is championed by a local volunteer steward who ensures that it is running smoothly, but a Little Free Library works best when the community understands that it belongs to everyone, and everyone can work together to make it a thriving, shared resource.

Learn more at ***littlefreelibrary.org***.

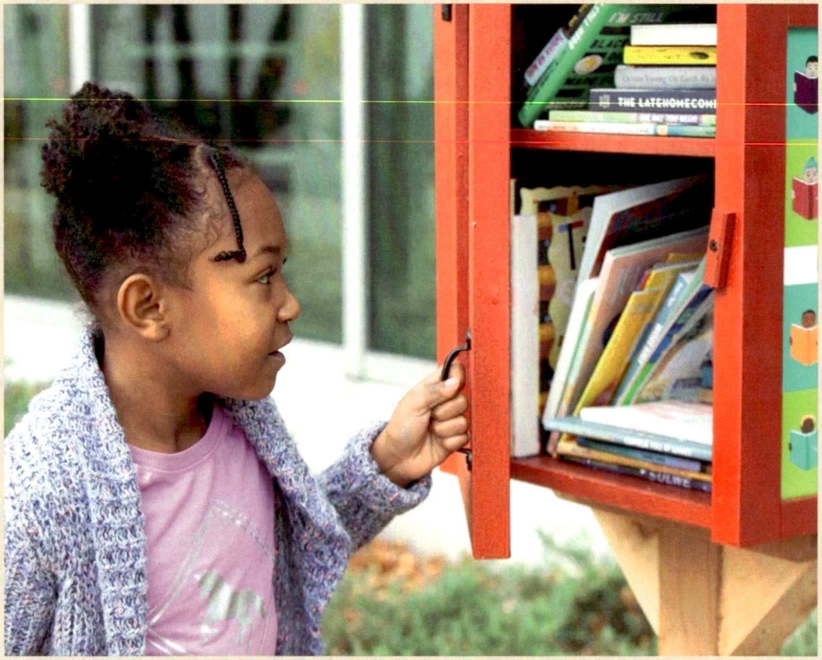

LEFT AND RIGHT: Photos courtesy of Little Free Library.

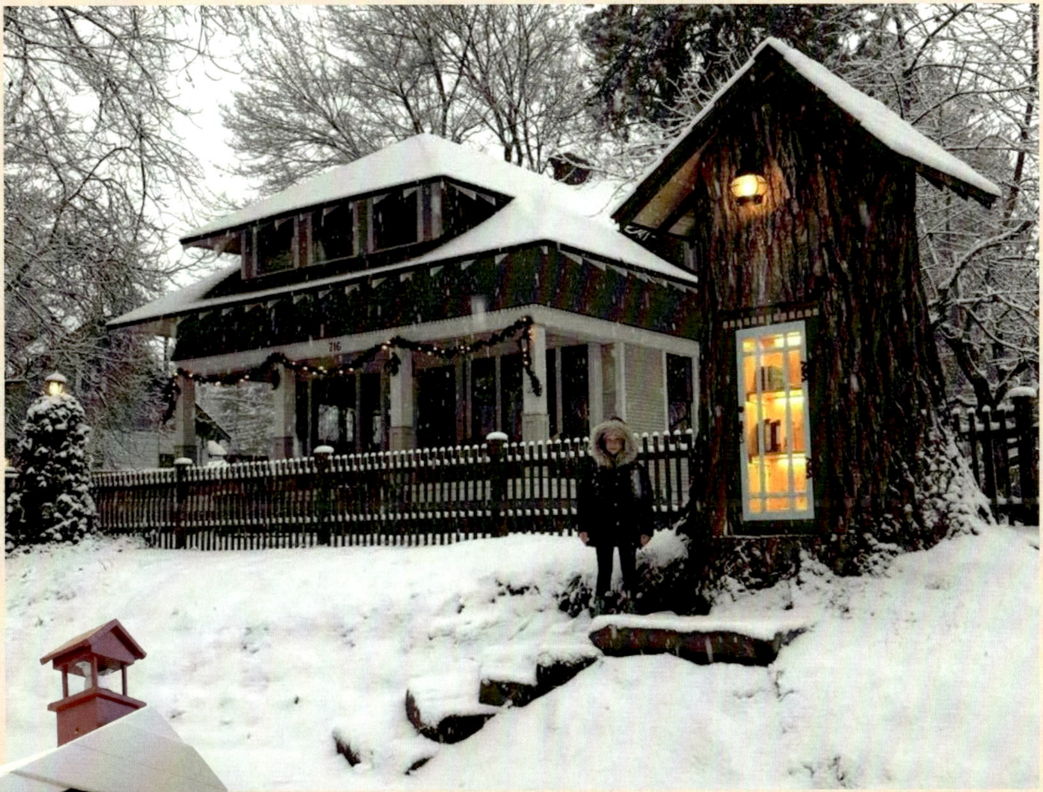

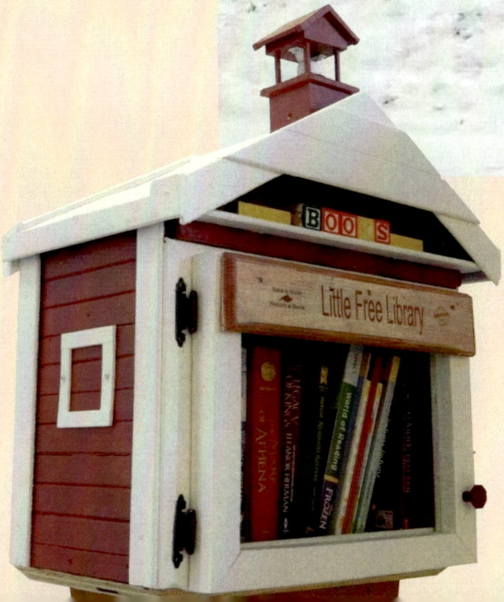
Little Free Library

SAY MY NAME, SAY MY NAME

What will you call your project? The testing stage is a great time to try out names and see if they stick. Here are some different qualities of memorable project names:

- Straightforward: it says something about your project or its aim, e.g., Little Free Library Project.
- Evocative: it conjures an image that you want participants or viewers to hold, e.g., Poetry Brothel (see page 172).
- Thematic: it suggests further projects around a greater theme, e.g., Official Unofficial Voting Station (see page 28).
- Emotional: it cuts to the heart, e.g., Before I Die (see page 187).
- Witty: it's funny, ironic, or cute, e.g., Play Me, I'm Yours (see page 129).

FIND YOUR NAME

- Make a list of every word you think might apply to your project. Use a thesaurus to find more.
- Combine one or more words.
- Does a possible acronym stand out from one or two words?
- Play off the title with a common pun, cliché, or pithy saying.
- Try a twist on the title of a popular book, movie, or song.
- Search for relevant hashtags on social media.
- Explore your artistic medium—are there interesting-sounding tools or techniques that are used in your project?

Once you have your name, you might want to check to see if it's in use by anyone else. Here are a few things to consider:

- Is it available as a domain name?
- Are any social media accounts or hashtags already using it?
- Has another artist used the name? It's worth several Google searches to find this out. Search for the title "+artist" or "+project" or "+creative" to see if anything comes up. I recommend searching major book retailers' websites as well.
- If the project is being cocreated by a community, has it been co-named by the community?
- Does it pose any copyright or trademark infringement? Copyright and trademark laws are different in every country. It is important to be aware of your country's laws and the laws of any other country where you wish to stage your project.
- Could it have another meaning in other communities or countries? If you wish to scale your project internationally, can it be understood internationally?
- Does it have another meaning in slang? *Urban Dictionary* (*urbandictionary.com*) holds slang definitions for over 7 million words and phrases—often used in homophobic, misogynistic, sexually explicit, and racist ways. Double-check that your name of choice is in keeping with your good intentions.

Test names on people not related to the project to see how they respond. Their reaction should give you a sense of whether the name is working. Ultimately, only you and your coconspirators know the right name for your project. Eventually, it will all come together!

CHAPTER 7

BE YOUR OWN MEGAPHONE: PROMOTE THAT THING

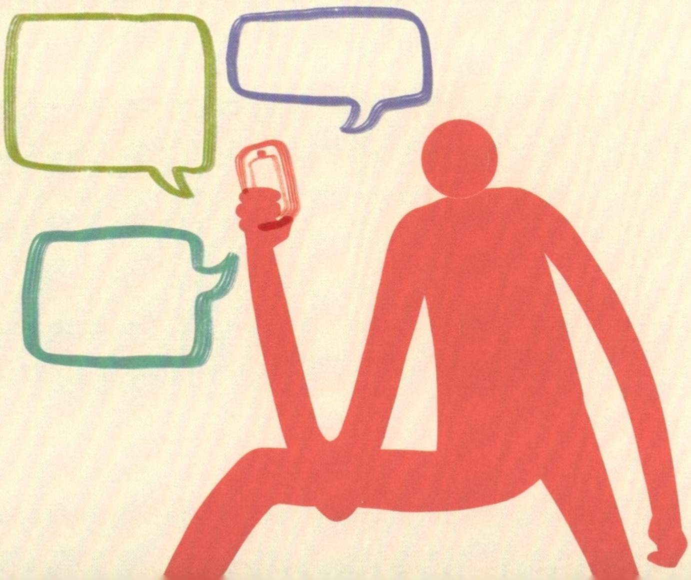

The word "marketing" is often frowned upon in artistic circles. It conjures the idea of pushy salespeople, cheesy ads, and half-truths. Marketing is often associated with negative connotations, but let me reassure you, marketing does not have to be sleazy or deceitful. It can and frankly should be a positive experience that helps you connect with your chosen audience.

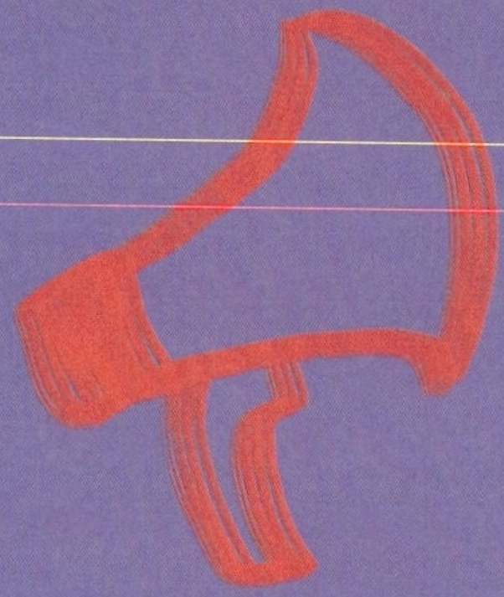

Promoting your work can become an art unto itself, and with the right tools in hand, you might even find it enjoyable. Connecting your project to your chosen audience is an act of service to that audience. Marketing makes your work visible to those you want to reach.

The good news about marketing is that you do not need a million-dollar budget, a highly connected network, or a social media manager to implement it. All you truly need is an understanding of your audience and a strategy for how to reach them. Marketing is not a dark art. It really is as simple as answering a few questions clearly and directly for those who might be interested in what you are doing.

WHAT IS YOUR PURPOSE, AGAIN?

As you begin to raise awareness about your project, you may be tempted to copy the tactics of other successful creatives. While it can help to observe how others bring attention to their work, note that their techniques may not be the right ones for you and your project. The tactics you adopt will depend on your intentions, values, budget, and availability (or that of your collaborative team). The best marketing starts with a clear understanding of how and why you want to achieve a specific goal.

PROMPT

Tell Me More

Can you answer the following questions about your project clearly and succinctly?

- What is it?
- Why did you make it?
- Who is it for?
- Why should they care?
- How will knowing about it benefit them? How will participating in your project benefit them?
- How can they get involved?

If you can answer these six questions, you are ready to begin to introduce others to your work.

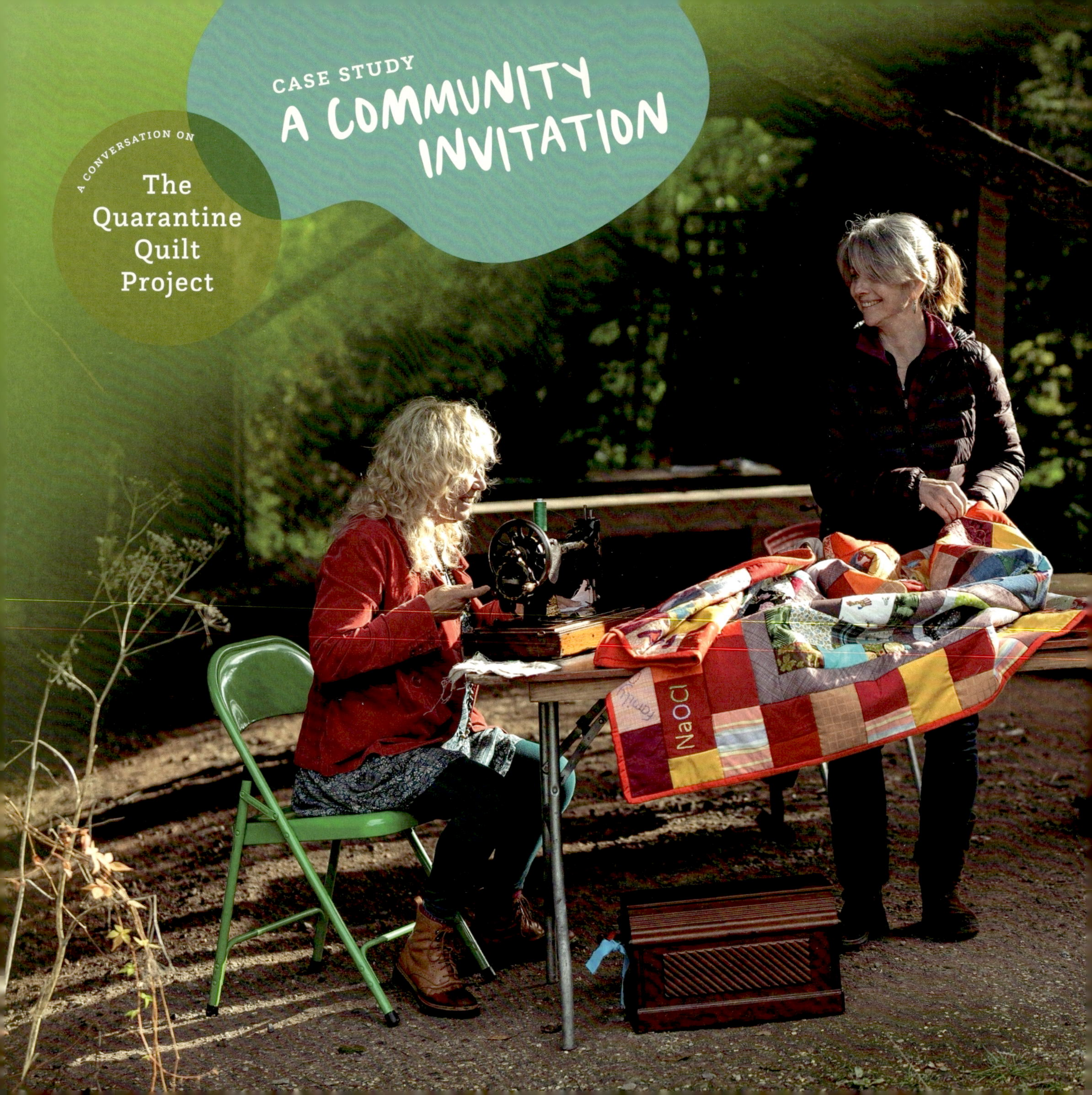

CASE STUDY

A COMMUNITY INVITATION

A CONVERSATION ON

The Quarantine Quilt Project

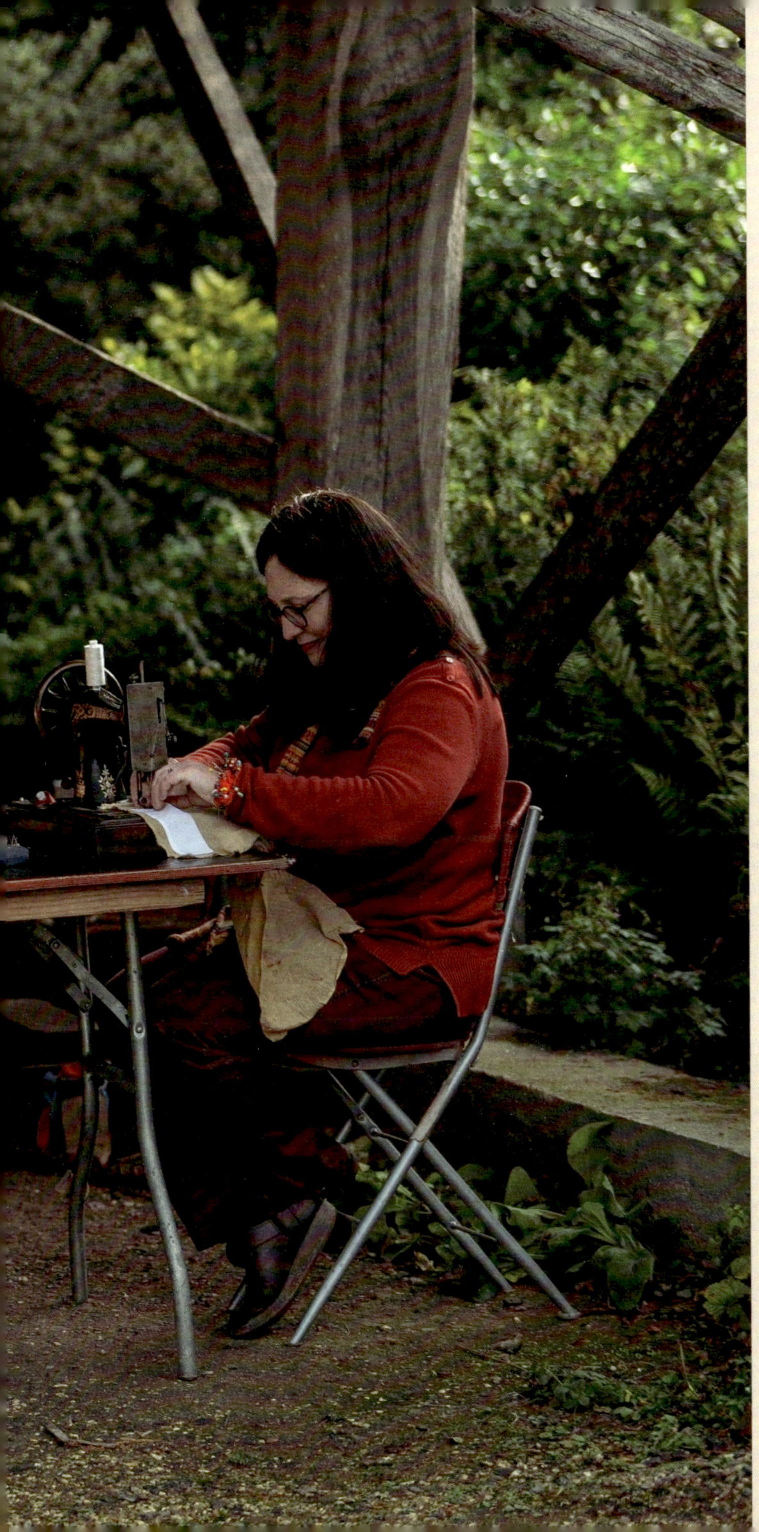

I was struck by the story of the Quarantine Quilt Project facilitated by Significant Seams, an artist collective of mental health practitioners based in the UK. How can artists who are used to working closely with the public suddenly change course in the face of an emergency? Significant Seams believes that mental health and art are relevant to everyone, and they proved themselves worthy of this mission when extending care to their community as collective members in response to the shock of the COVID-19 pandemic.

When the UK went into a COVID-19 lockdown, Significant Seams realized that anyone in their community could become a client and quickly launched the Quarantine Quilt Project. This community project, delivered by video and postal service, touched community participants and inspired further connections through artist practitioners throughout the UK. I spoke to founder Catherine West about the experience.

LEANNE: Tell me about the Quarantine Quilt Project.

CATHERINE: Mental health and art became exceedingly relevant to everyone during the pandemic. We are community artists who support people, but we couldn't go out into the community. We had to adapt quickly, so we made some training videos with our phones. We designed and created six new online courses, along with an instructional PDF of embroidery stitches, all in association with

2021. | Photo: Jim Wileman. Piecing the Quarantine Quilt pieces together.

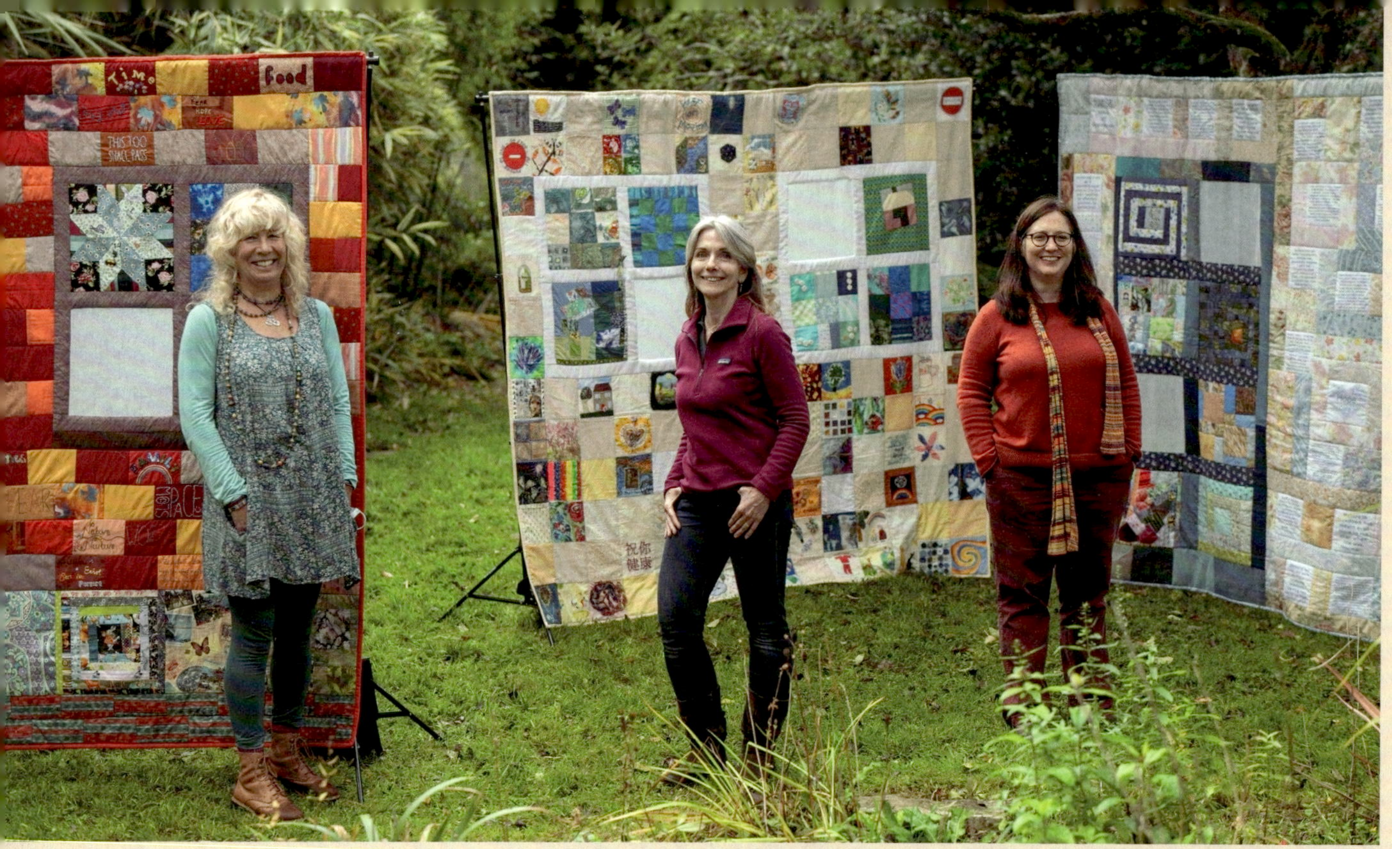

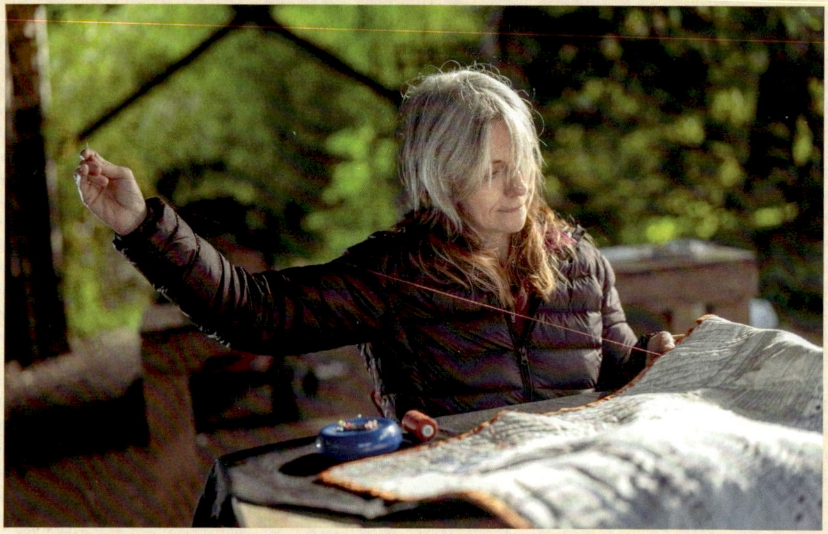

ABOVE: 2021. | Photo: Jim Wileman. The Significant Seams team with the three Quarantine Quilts.

RIGHT: 2021. | Photo: Jim Wileman. Piecing the Quarantine Quilt pieces together.

FAR RIGHT TOP: 2021. *This Too Shall Pass*, The Quarantine Quilt Project. | Photo: Jim Wileman. A patch created by a community member as part of a participatory project created by Significant Seams during the 2020 COVID-19 lockdown in the UK.

FAR RIGHT BOTTOM: Photo: Jim Wileman. Black Lives Matter patch, a detail of the Quarantine Quilt Project.

the Quarantine Quilt Project. We used social media and our existing partnerships to spread an invitation to those who were struggling with the lockdown and could benefit from participating. We sent out over a hundred kits, with an embroidery hoop, fabric pens, a needle, a rainbow of embroidery threads, and a five-page printout about our project, including instructions and a form for returning work to us.

LEANNE: Tell me about the quilts that you pieced together from all of these community contributions.

CATHERINE: We made three quilts out of squares that, when displayed together, form an installation. Over 150 patches were stitched together to represent two external walls of a home and one internal one, with quotes from the patch makers.

LEANNE: As an organizer, how do make seemingly unrelated contributions work together?

CATHERINE: When teaching patchwork for the first time, we couldn't create overly ambitious rules for people. We wanted to celebrate what they were learning. We introduced several variables that connected things, some associated with the learning outcomes that we had established. Early on, we decided to have three different sizes of quilting blocks, and we pre-curated a color palette. We knew that we might do some curation by mood. Ultimately, we came back to the idea of a shared experience. There were lots of common themes that emerged, nature being a huge one.

We received three patches from a considerable proportion of people. Multiple patches provided a means for people to explore their emotional experiences. Generally, when people did three patches, there would be one that was very literal, one that was quite figurative, and then one that was kind of symbolic.

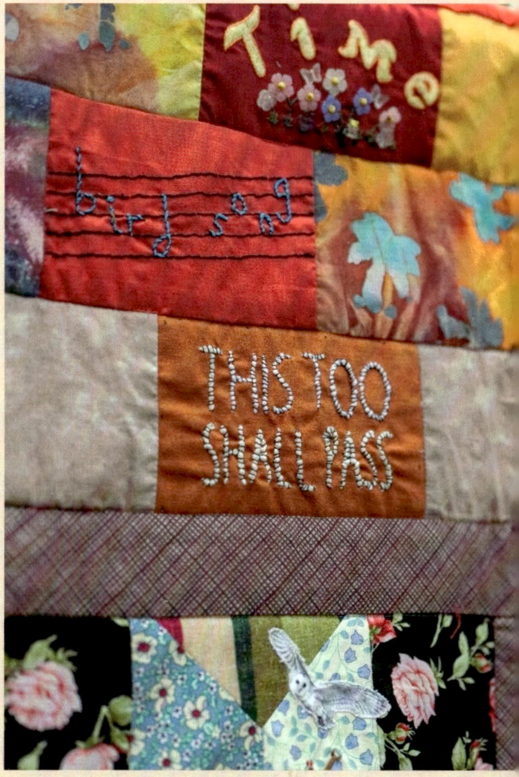

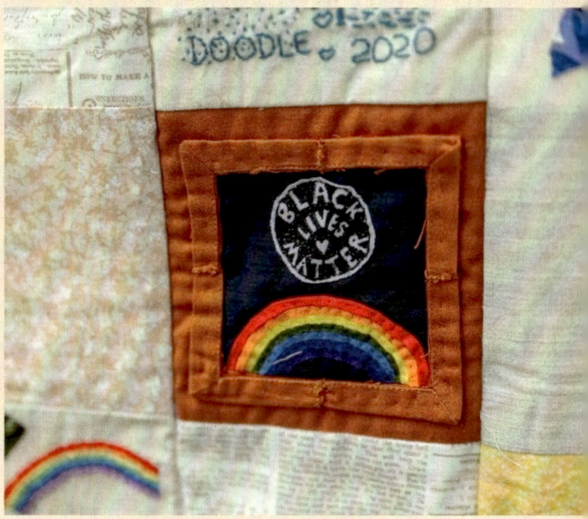

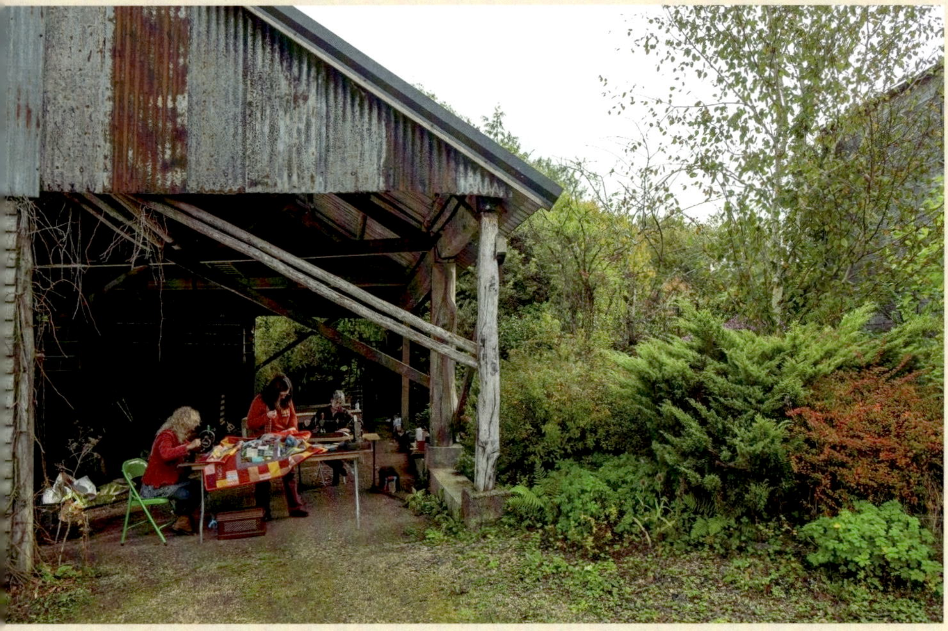

LEFT: Photo: Jim Wileman. Piecing the Quarantine Quilt pieces together.

TOP RIGHT: CATHERINE O'BRIEN WEST. *Unfurling 2020*, *Staying Connected*, 2020, soft sculpture, quilting, eco-printing.

MIDDLE RIGHT: NAOMI WRIGHT, *Exploration of Moths*, 2020, soft sculpture, relief print. | Photo: Jim Wileman

BOTTOM RIGHT: JUST SEWN STORIES, *Daily Briefings*, 2020, assemblage, cotton, thread, paper. | Photo: Jim Wileman

FAR RIGHT: Melinda Schwakhofer, 2020, quilt. | Photo: Jim Wileman

Another unexpected but beautiful thing that started to happen was that when people received a kit, they would, in turn, nominate someone else to receive one. It became a kind of pay it forward. It opened up people's abilities, not just in craft, but also in their ability to talk about other people's issues. Participants felt more connected to other people because they knew they were making something bigger than themselves, even when they couldn't interact with those other participants. Some of those who nominated others are probably friends for life now, and that's been lovely to see.

CATHERINE WEST *founded Significant Seams with an idea and her daughter's buggy. Her determination to make Significant Seams a success and the depth of her belief in the value of each person in her community routinely inspire. She brings twenty years of professional experience in marketing and fundraising with a focus on the creative industries and education. She also has extensive insight and expertise in the areas of health and well-being.* **significantseams.org.uk**

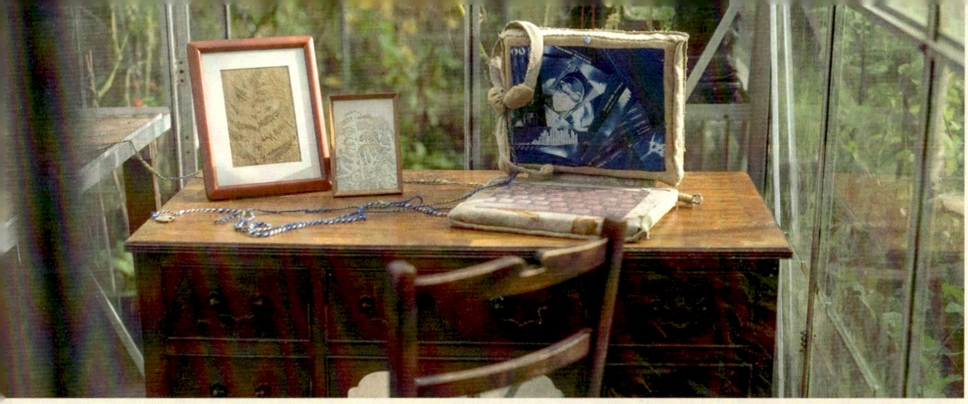

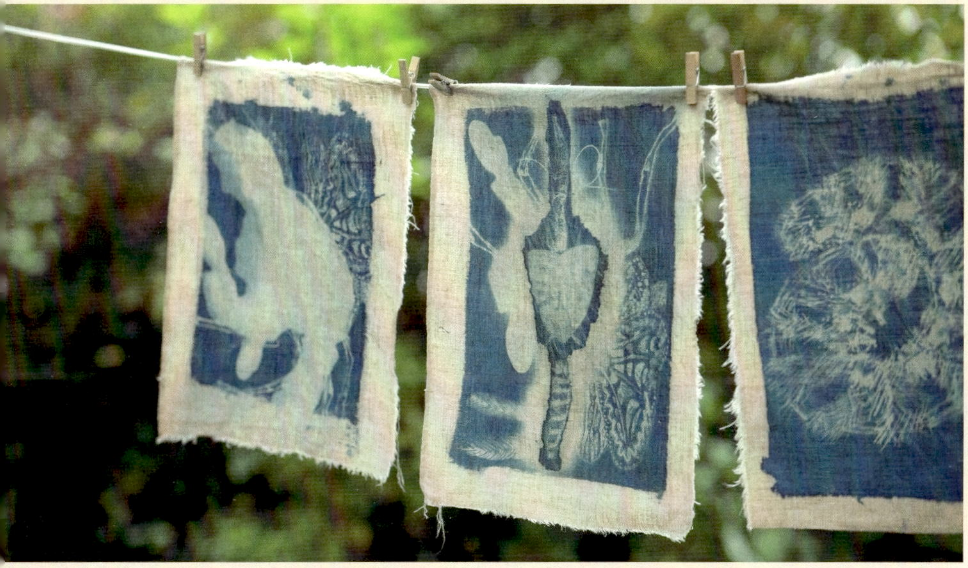

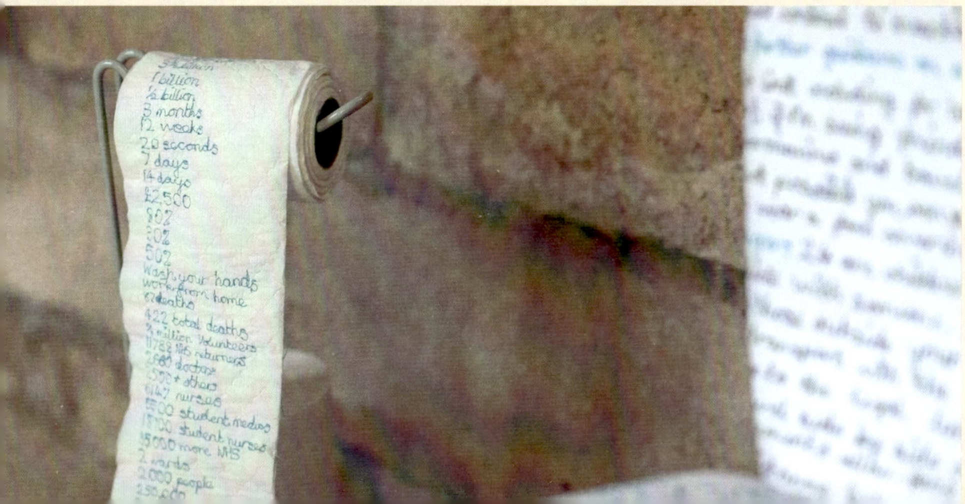

"The Quarantine Quilt Project also included new commissions from four project artists who were adapting to the COVID-19 crisis in real time: a quilt by Melinda Schwakhofer; Naomi Wright's exploration of moths and the idea of cocooning; Just Sewn Stories' funny and deeply critical piece, which stitched the statistics of the UK government's daily briefings on toilet roll; and my artwork, *Unfurling*, about experiencing emotional load, mood changes, and the fragility and focus that the time brought. My series of experimental artworks was installed in a greenhouse alongside a soft sculpture laptop representing my lifeline to family—including a sister working in a COVID ICU."

—**CATHERINE WEST**

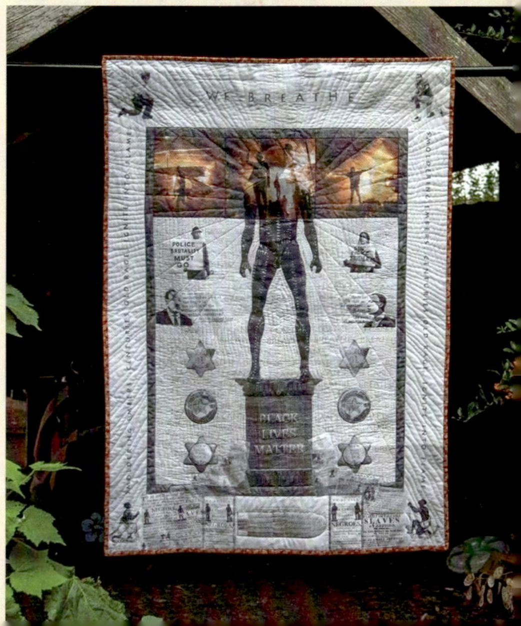

TRY THIS

Hone Your Pitch

- Try first pitching someone else's project to see what you can learn from the experience. Is it easier to talk about a different project than your own? Why or why not?
- Practice telling the story of your project to a trusted friend. Or, try telling your reflection in the mirror.
- Practice connecting with the listener. What is the benefit to the listener in learning about your project? What aspect of the project would they be most interested in?
- Forgive yourself if you mess up. Don't forget that you will have many chances to try and try again.

FIND YOUR PEEPS: CONNECTING WITH YOUR AUDIENCE

When you visualize your project, who needs to be aware of it? If your answer is everyone everywhere, it's likely that your ideas need more development. Even in participatory work, an intended audience is rarely so broad that it encompasses *everyone*.

So how do you define who your audience is? Start with what you think you know. Here is a series of questions to help define your audience.

- Is your audience of a particular age group (i.e., teenagers, kids, seniors, parents of young children, etc.)? What is their age range? Where do they live?
- What sort of media does this age range consume (e.g., social media platforms, community message boards, school bulletins, etc.)?
- Where is your project staged? Does the venue that you are using have a regular audience? Is there a community that lives close to the venue?
- What fundamental interests or politics does your project raise? If you had to put these interests into a series of Google searches, what phrases and words might you use to find it?
- Are there groups with a particular interest in the creative materials or the genre that you are using (e.g., woodworkers' unions, graphic design societies, craft guilds, activist groups, fan clubs)?
- Are there arts programmers in your community who would connect with this project? I recommend reaching out to local libraries, schools, galleries, professional societies, and arts councils.
- Is your project regional, national, or international?
- Who would be a natural fan of this sort of project? Where are you likely to find these people?
- Have you considered both online and offline possibilities?

SAY IT, DON'T SPRAY IT: CLEARLY STATE THE RULES OF ENGAGEMENT

Let attendees know what to expect. Attending a formal holiday dinner at someone's home is a very different experience than ordering pizza and playing video games. If you were to invite someone to a formal gathering at your house, you wouldn't just say, "Come over." You would share the address, time, date, and likely a few other details to set their expectations about the type of gathering they will be attending so they can prepare accordingly.

When you invite someone to participate or spread the word about your project, make it easy for them to understand your project, how it is happening, why they should care, and how to participate. Provide a concise but detailed description. Here are some examples:

> *I'm mounting a ballet about shopping at Gladstone Beach that critiques consumer behaviors of the 1940s and the rise of single-use plastic, and you should come and see it.*

> *Our collective is staging a community paint-in for a Black Lives Matter mural in Middlebury Public Square this Saturday; bring your brush.*

> *Join my feminist performance group in stand-up paddleboarding on the Tsolum River on Tuesday night. Bring a flashlight, a witch costume, and a broom. We will supply the paddleboard and give a short lesson. Beginners are welcome!*

Summarize the activity in a sentence so participants immediately understand their part in the process and are able to share the info with others. Follow-up questions are an opportunity to have a further conversation about the project. For example, they may ask, "What are we painting? Will we get arrested?" This would be an opportunity to talk about civil disobedience and the risk involved in standing up against authority. If they say, "I don't like ballet—why should I come?" or "Why should I care about the history of plastic?" this is an opportunity to educate them about sustainability and to give them some details about just how kick-ass contemporary ballet can be.

When you discuss your project with someone, observe their reaction to what you say. Are they receptive to your idea? Do they need more clarification? What adjustments might you need to make to your project pitch in order to make them interested? If you do find them expressing enthusiasm, slip them a postcard, an email address, or a social media handle that will allow them to learn more about the project on their own time. Or, if they are willing to participate immediately, sign them up on the spot!

CASE STUDY

Converting Chaos into Opportunity

A CONVERSATION WITH

Kevin Spenst

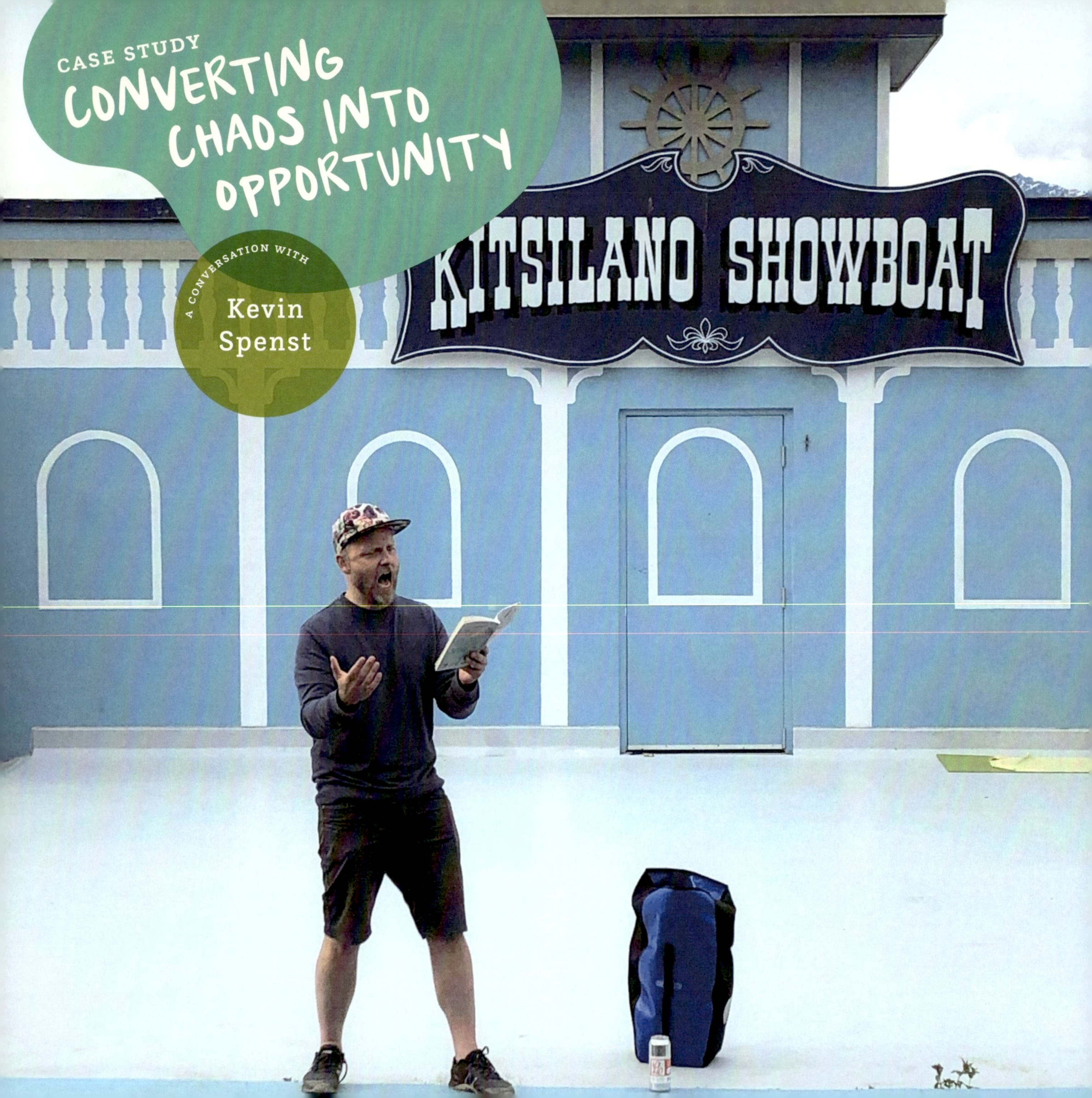

In the first few weeks of the COVID-19 lockdown in my city, my social media feed was suddenly full of Kevin Spenst, a local poet who had taken to giving poetry readings in parks, at the beach, on sidewalks, and in the entrances to apartment buildings. At a time when we were unable to gather inside, Kevin found a unique way celebrate his poetry while engaging the public in an interactive way. Instead of expecting his audience to come to him, he went to them. Kevin shared with me how this mobile reading series came about.

LEANNE: During the beginning of the COVID-19 pandemic in 2020, you hosted more than thirty physically distanced poetry readings for your book *Hearts Amok*. Can you tell me how that idea came about?

KEVIN: Earlier in 2020, I was really excited about my book coming out. I was considering the venue for my launch ... and then came March, and so did COVID-19. Reading series and book launches were shut down. I wanted to launch my book in a way that was true to how I love doing things.

When it became apparent that we could do things outside safely, it made sense to perform pop-up readings. In 2007, I did a tour where I went to fifty venues in one day. So, I thought, let's revisit the idea of pop-up readings outside. We could have small gatherings for each one, then I could go out and read to various people who wanted to hear some poetry.

I put out a call through social media to ask who wanted poetry in their front yard or backyard, or really any kind of yard. This was during our extreme lockdown time, but we must have put on ten pop-up poetry readings that day. I started serenading a third-floor balcony at a friend's place. People gathered in the back alley as I performed. Then I went to another site, and another, and then we ended up at this weird moss garden in the middle of Stanley Park.[2] I'd loved the spot when I found it in the park while I was jogging—it was so green and lush. I ended up making a stage there for my launch. I read with the poet Raoul Fernandes at the end of the day at this little secret location where we created little spots for people to listen. It was a very cool conclusion to the day that was quite different for me.

2 Stanley Park is a 1,000-acre urban park located in downtown Vancouver.

2020. | Photo: Laura Farina. Kevin performed his poetry at the Kitsilano Showboat at Kitsilano Beach to a spontaneous audience.

I ended up doing a bunch more readings over the next few weeks. I would reach out to one or two people to make sure that I had a secure reading somewhere, and then I would ask other people to participate.

LEANNE: That's the other thing I find curious about public art in the public realm. I imagine that your reading on the street may have been some people's first encounter with a poet in the flesh.

KEVIN: Yeah, there was a street artist I met in the West End, and she ended up buying a book. We chatted for a bit, and it was a really interesting random encounter. I did a reading outside of the Stanley Park Manor, which is an older building from the 1930s. It was lovely; there were lots of people that just randomly kind of came across me. The manor has a huge old courtyard, and all these apartments look down on the front walk. We had a captive audience. It was a cool spot. A lot of writers have lived there over the years.

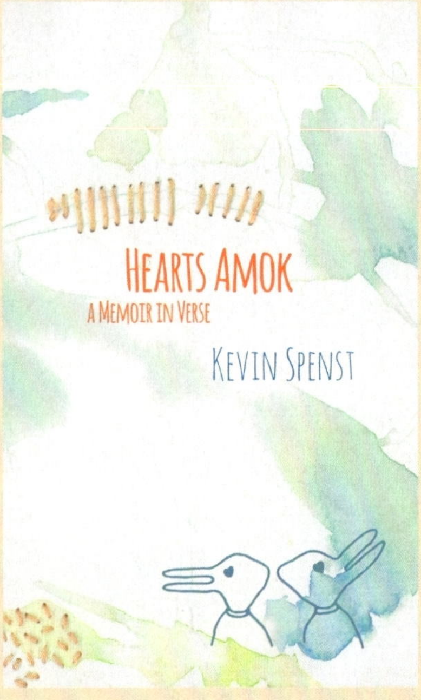

LEANNE: New artists can struggle with making their work public. There can be a fear of feeling foolish, especially when trying things that seem a bit out of the norm. How do you make yourself comfortable when trying new things in public?

KEVIN: Anyone's heart rate is going to go up a bit at the prospect of stepping out in front of a group of people. But, with that racing heart, you have the extra energy to go to another place. You might want to flee, but you can use that extra bit of natural anxiety to help you present or transform your work into something different. I think it's good for people to be reminded that everybody gets that feeling of nervousness, and it's a matter of what you want to do with it. There is something really exhilarating and fun about producing something different.

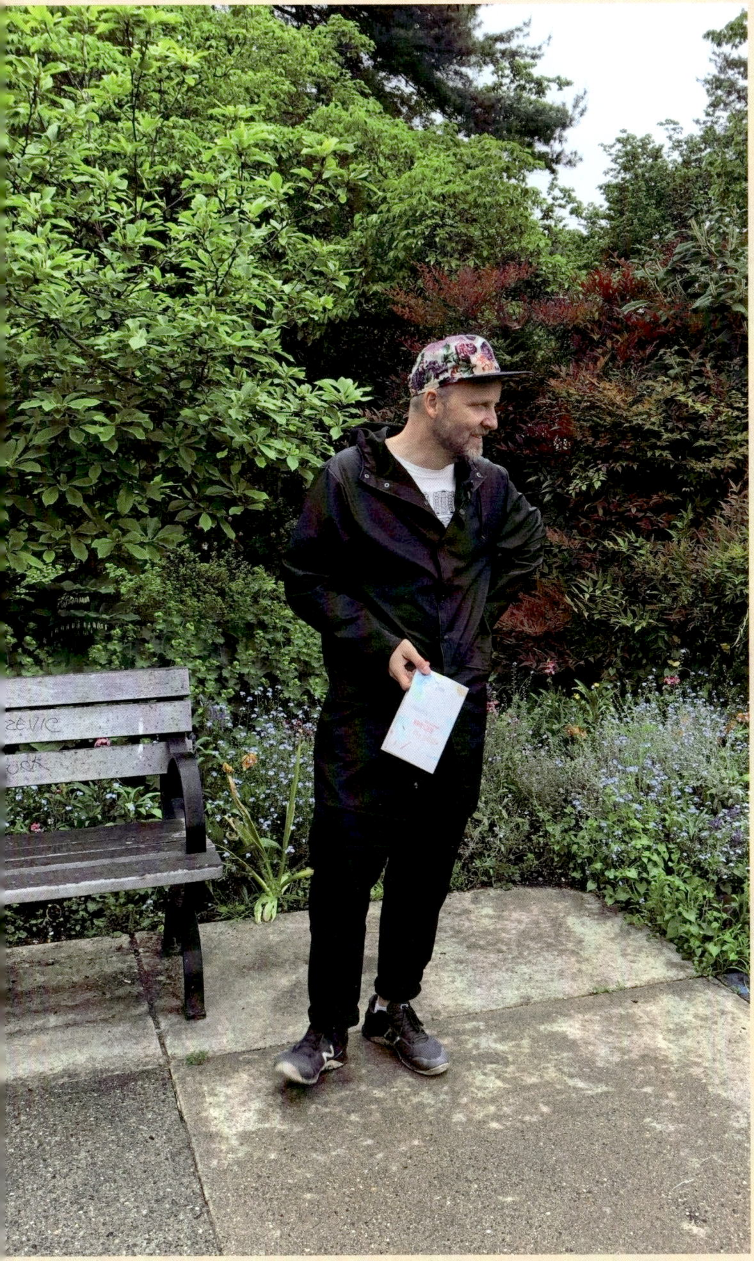

KEVIN SPENST, *a Pushcart Prize nominee, is the author of* Ignite *and* Jabbering with Bing Bong *(both with Anvil Press) and over a dozen chapbooks, including* Pray Goodbye *(The Alfred Gustav Press),* Ward Notes *(the serif of nottingham),* Flip Flop Faces *and* Unexpurgated Lives *(JackPine Press), and most recently,* Upend *(Frog Hollow Press). His work has won the Lush Triumphant Literary Award for Poetry, been nominated for both the Alfred G. Bailey Prize and the Robert Kroetsch Award for Innovative Poetry, and has appeared in dozens of publications, including* EVENT, The Malahat Review, subTerrain, Prairie Fire, CV2, The Rusty Toque, BafterC, Lemon Hound, Poetry Is Dead, *and the anthology* Best Canadian Poetry 2019. *He co-organizes the Dead Poets Reading Series and teaches creative writing at Vancouver Community College and Simon Fraser University's Writer's Studio. He lives in Vancouver on unceded Coast Salish territory.* **kevinspenst.com**

2020. | Photo: Mark Pilon. Kevin's roving poetry tour met audiences on sidewalks, beaches, alleyways, forests, and courtyards.

DRAW A FAMILIAR AUDIENCE: TELL YOUR (CHOSEN) FAMILY

When you're trying to draw an audience, does it suddenly feel like you don't know anyone? Think about the people you interact with regularly. Your list might include:

- close friends
- extended family members
- coworkers (past and present)
- classmates (past and present)
- apartment, strata, co-op, or neighborhood associations
- connections on your social media platforms
- clubs, associations, or teams that you belong to
- your local community center, community arts council, artist-run centers, or shared artist space
- your local supply stores, including art stores, knitting stores, makerspaces, woodworking shops, art-friendly coffee shops, and other entities that you and your coconspirators frequent

No matter who in your creative group is handling invitations, everyone involved in your project should commit to getting the word out to their own networks. Once your project has launched, each of you will want to see some familiar faces in the crowd.

Another thing I like to do is to ask a friend to bring a friend to an event. Having a companion will make it more fun for them to be there and it will acquaint you with more people.

CLIQUES ARE BORING: WIDEN YOUR CIRCLE

While those close to us can be strong supporters of our work, community projects require you to invite the community. When you expand your reach outside your regular circle of interaction, you'll discover new things about your project—and isn't that why you're doing all of this in the first place?

For local projects, don't forget to inform

- Your local library
- Your local bookstore(s)
- Your local community centers
- Your local newspaper (where you live now and anywhere else you may have lived)
- Your local community arts council
- Local podcasts, radio shows, or community reporters
- Your local coffee shops—especially those with bulletin boards

Make it easy for them to help you. Phrase your request to post a flyer or leave postcards behind in a way that is polite, specific, and easy to fulfill.

You might be creating an extraordinary thing, but remember that no one owes you anything. Your project might be brilliant and aim to change the world, but other people have their own needs, priorities, and focuses. Remember that every request you make is a bid for their time, influence, and knowledge. Keep your requests short and sweet, and always say please and thank you.

SHOW YOUR TRUE COLORS: EVERY ELEMENT CREATES EXPECTATIONS

Have you ever arrived at an event only to discover that your expectations for the experience were incorrect? Perhaps your false impression was shaped by a particular graphic or photo on the invitation, or by a line of copy on the website. Did you feel disappointed? Overdressed? Uncomfortable?

From social posts to invitational flyers, any promotional materials you make will create expectations in your audience. Be mindful that any collateral you produce will be the audience's first experience of the project, so consistency matters.

Take a look at what you have created—what colors do you use in your materials? What kind of typeface? Do the visual elements that you've chosen reflect the intended tone of the project? What feelings do you want your audience to have when they encounter your work? Marketing and event design all influence your presentation of your project.

PROMPT

Test Out Different Marketing Collateral for Your Project

Write the copy with a few different moods in mind. For example, is your project one that evokes strong feelings and an empowered sense of social justice? If so, then be sure that the copy you write to describe your project is the same: sharp, clear, positive, and aware. Do you want participants to have a sense of self-care? Use reassuring and soothing language. Compare how two different tones can give a different impression of the same project. From the verbal pitch that you give potential participants to the text of your website, every element a participant experiences is a clue as to how they should feel about your project.

CASE STUDY

DREAM BIGGER

A CONVERSATION WITH

The Poetry Society of New York

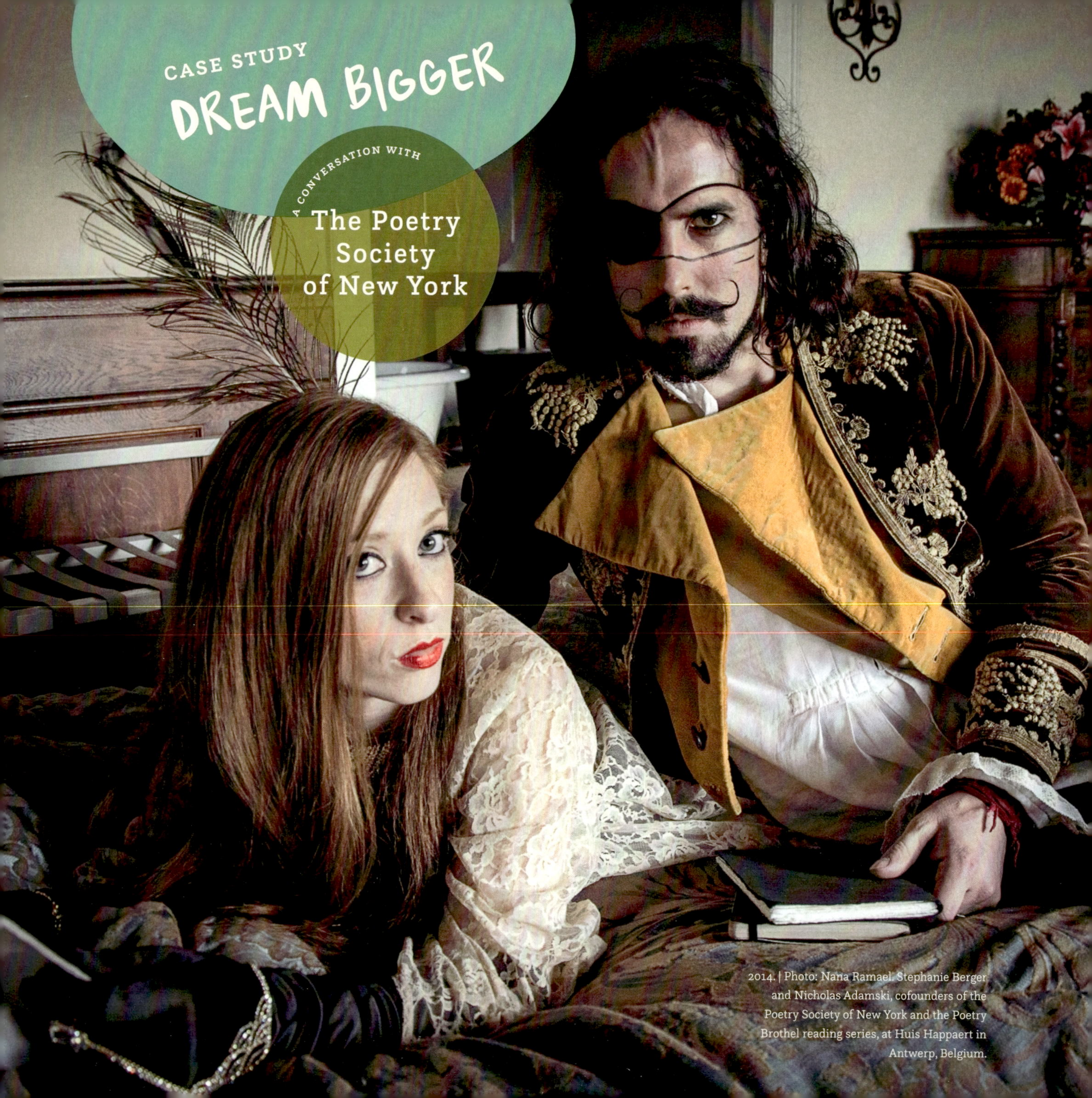

2014. | Photo: Nana Ramael. Stephanie Berger and Nicholas Adamski, cofounders of the Poetry Society of New York and the Poetry Brothel reading series, at Huis Happaert in Antwerp, Belgium.

I was at a writing conference in the Oregon Convention Center when I spotted the Poetry Society of New York's fortune-telling booth, adorned with century-old china doll heads and dried flowers. I felt like I had been transported back in time. The more I learned about the society, the more charmed I was by the Society's vision to bring the experience of poetry to the public in a myriad of interesting ways: a participatory project that brought typewriters into public parks, an international network of online poetry readings, and the infamous NYC Poetry Brothel, which has sparked companion events in cities around the world. I spoke to cofounder Stephanie Berger about her inspired collaboration with cofounder Nicholas Adamski and how their collective brainstorming has resulted in poetic and transformative experiences for the public.

LEANNE: The scale of everything you have achieved is quite astounding. Can you tell me about the Poetry Brothel, the literary cabaret series that you host? I love that it fuses poetry, activism, burlesque, live music, and vaudeville.

STEPHANIE: Oh my god, the first Poetry Brothel was crazy! I had been volunteering for a reading series at the Living Theatre while I was in grad school and was looking to dip my toe into various waters. As I already had a relationship with them, I asked about hosting the first Poetry Brothel there. They loved the concept.

We chose January 18, 2008, as the date for our first Poetry Brothel. The five-dollar admission came with a free private poetry reading and a free shot of whiskey upon entry. It was a good deal. I sent out a press release, and *The Village Voice* published a full two-page spread about the event. It had a giant photo of performer Maggie Wells reading a book in bed. The Living Theatre saw the article, and although they served alcohol at all of their events at the time, they didn't have a liquor license. They canceled our event three days beforehand because we couldn't say that we were serving liquor.

Suddenly I was running around the East Village looking for a space that would host us with only three days' notice. Finally, I found this place called the Mug Lounge. We organized a protest out in front of the Living Theatre so that people who had read *The Village Voice* could be led to the new venue. We had protest signs with sayings like, "Poetry is banned in New York City," "New York is dead." Some of the people who worked at the Living Theatre joined the protest, as they thought the situation was unfair, and we all marched up to the Mug Lounge.

I didn't know that the Mug Lounge was having a house music night that evening, which was a very different vibe from what I had intended. I'd thought it would be live jazz, so when we arrived, I was like, "Oh my god, you said that I could have an event here!" There was a DJ playing, but he was super into our event. He asked, "Can I still DJ

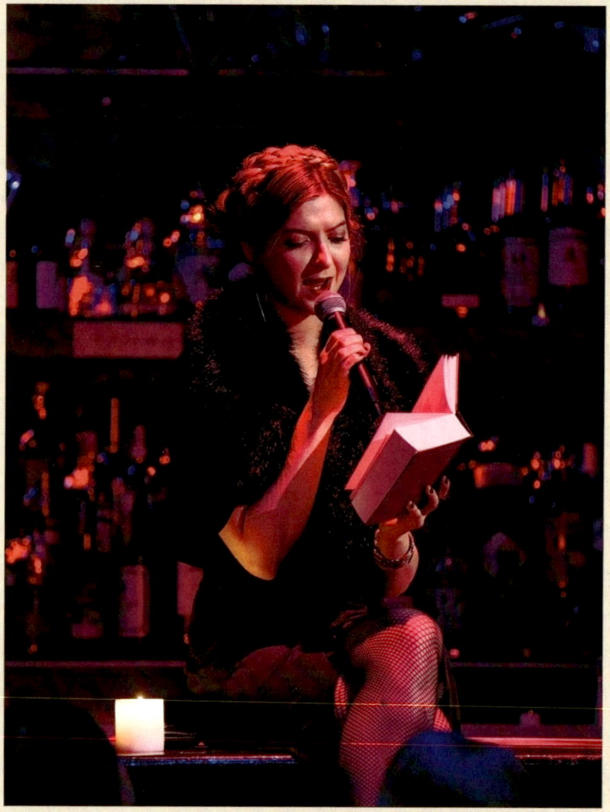 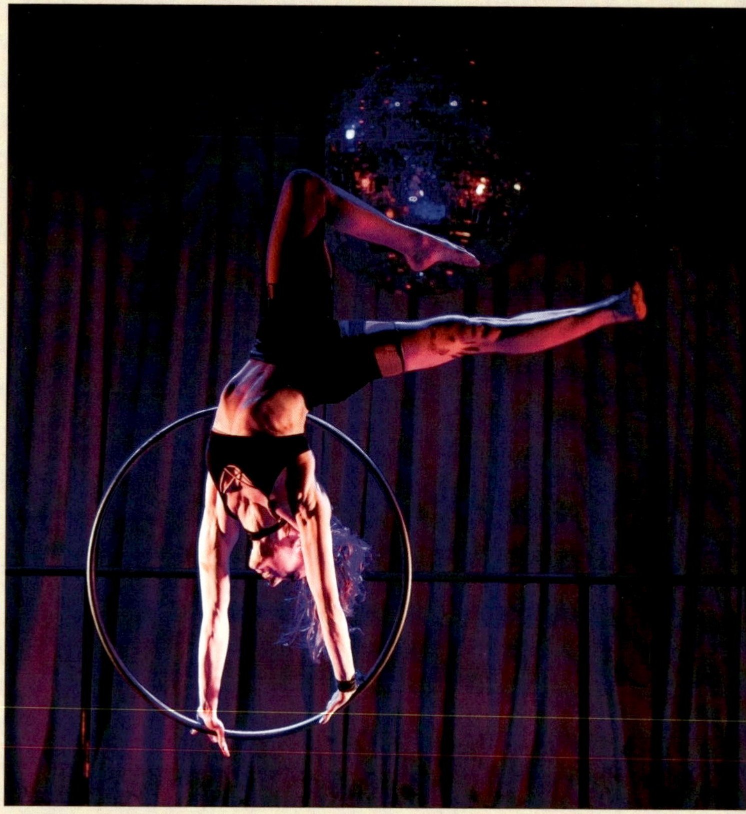

in the show?" So, we ended up having a house DJ between poetry readings and aerial acts and private readings happening in the corners.

The first event was extraordinary because we had spent a long time rehearsing for the Living Theatre. We probably did more preparation and rehearsal for that event than any other event that we've done, but in the end, I felt like what happened was very appropriate for our first event. It was also snowing that night! Everything went wrong, but the night itself ended up just being so magical. After that first night, we ended up hosting events monthly through that year. More people started coming to it through word of mouth. After six months, my roster of participants was more than I could cast in a single show.

ABOVE LEFT: THE POETRY BROTHEL, 2017. | Photo: Hannah Cohen. Jackie Braje reads her work at the Poetry Brothel at House of Yes in Brooklyn, New York.

ABOVE RIGHT: THE POETRY BROTHEL, 2017. | Photo: Hannah Cohen. Sara Solaris Zepezauer (Zepe) performs at House of Yes in Brooklyn, New York.

LEANNE: You host writing workshops for sex workers. Did that programming naturally evolve with the brothel theme, or was that part of your event's origins from the beginning?

STEPHANIE: It was part of the initial vision of avant-garde art created in Parisian brothels and how the tango was popularized in Argentinean brothels. I saw brothels as places where people could go and be their whole weird selves. That environment was a fertile ground for experimental creativity.

I was curious about the industry, not a part of it. But with the theme, sex workers started to attend and wanted to participate. Some felt like we were appropriating sex work and the community. From those learnings and checking myself, it became clear that I didn't want to glamorize things. There was a community of people I cared about who were being marginalized. I wanted to do as much as possible to represent sex workers, educate the public, and destigmatize the industry. We made a concerted effort in the first few years to incorporate those elements.

LEANNE: Can you tell me about the Typewriter Project?

STEPHANIE: We install working typewriters in parks and other outdoor gathering spaces. We like to have as many active installations as we can at any one time. The Typewriter Project was inspired by the Play Me, I'm Yours street piano project [see page 129]. In the summer that we came up with the idea, Nick and I had many meetings where we were like, "Let's walk while we meet and get our bodies and brains active." We would walk around and see these pianos all over the place, and at the same time, we kept randomly encountering vintage typewriters on the street.

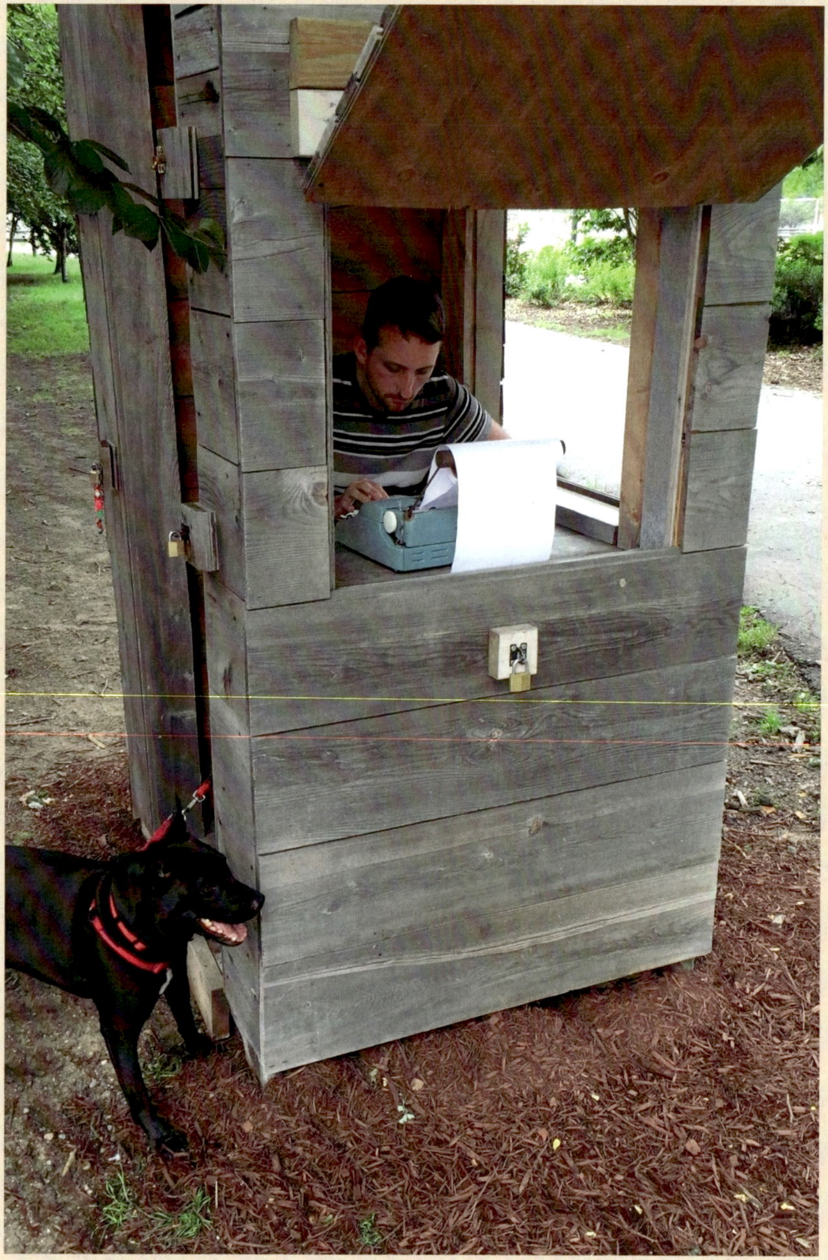

THE TYPEWRITER PROJECT, 2016.
Brooklyn, New York. | Photo courtesy of Stephanie Berger. McCarren Park.

We started talking about how neither of us plays the piano well, but we wish we could, and what if it was a typewriter instead of a piano? We talked out the idea: what if we put typewriters in the parks? But if they got rained on, that would be bad. So we figured out that we would have to build a cabin around them. We quickly realized that the project would constantly need to evolve depending on where it was installed. Different factors had to be considered, such as the availability of Wi-Fi or weatherproofing. Some of the early typewriters were beautiful, but they couldn't really handle having so many hands on them—particularly when some of those hands had never touched a typewriter before. We realized we needed a booth attendant to help them.

The technology elements have also evolved. The first installation included uploading of text to the internet, but it was kind of endless. Then we discovered that USB typewriters exist, and we contacted Jack Zylkin, who invented them, and started working with him regularly.

LEANNE: Is there a favorite moment from the project that comes to mind?

STEPHANIE: My favorite installation was the one in Tompkins Square Park in the East Village. At the time, I didn't know that the park has an active literary history. There's a tree dedicated to Allen Ginsberg where he supposedly hung out with his students, and there's a vast history of activism there. There's a large homeless population living in the park. When we initially started talking to the parks department about the project, they were like, "FYI, you guys need to be prepared. Your booth is probably going to get defaced and knocked over." We were ready for that, but the homeless people who lived in the park loved the Typewriter Project. They would type on it, chat with us, and they protected it. It became so important to the community living there.

And another thing that happened that summer was that gay marriage finally became legal across the US. It was just so incredible to see all the typed entries from that day. Everyone was so happy and writing, "Love wins." We preserved that critical moment as a historical record on the typewriter scrolls. It felt important.

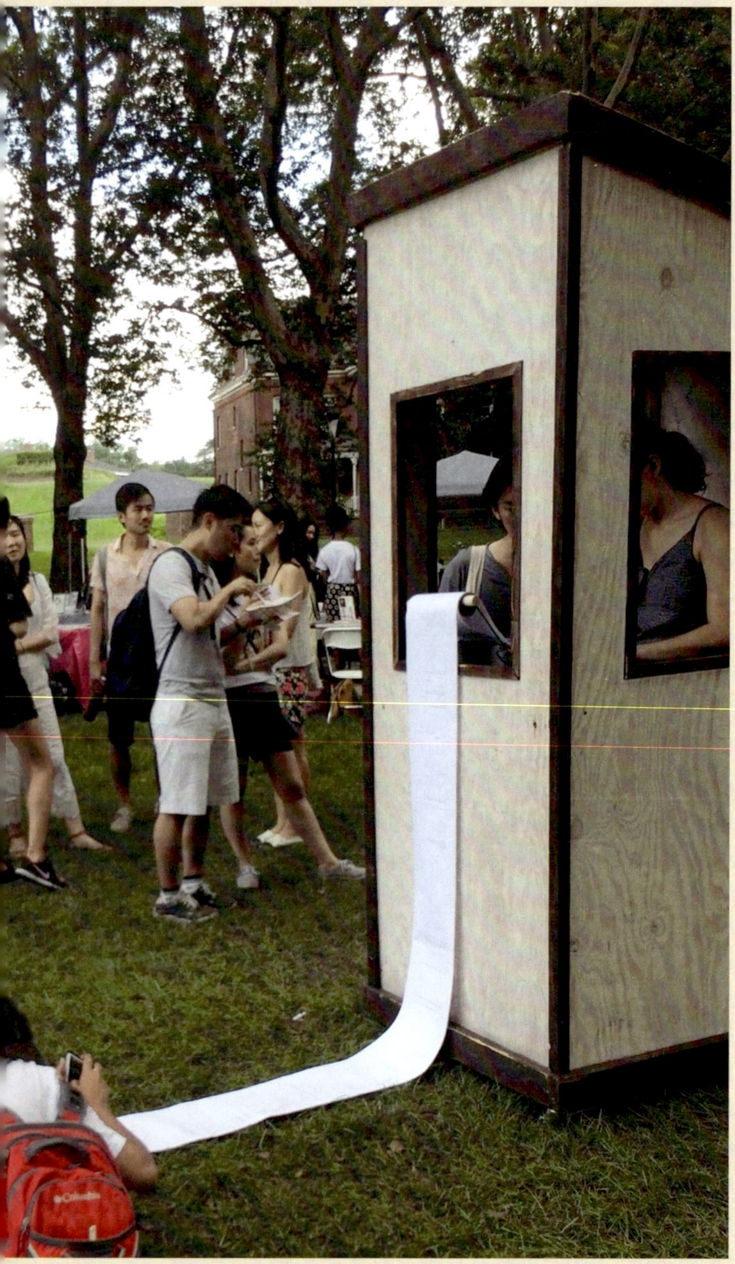

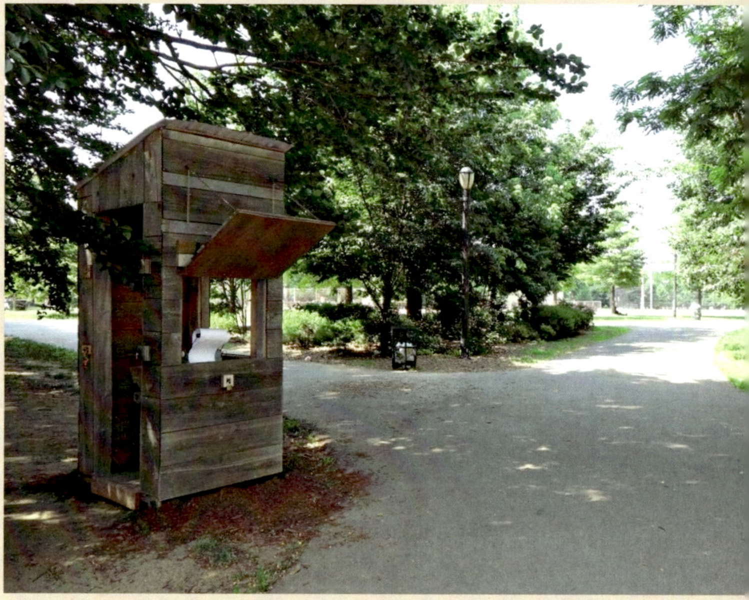

LEFT: THE TYPEWRITER PROJECT, 2019, Governors Island, New York. | Photo courtesy of Stephanie Berger. The Typewriter Project invites everyone to contribute their writing to a community record.

ABOVE: THE TYPEWRITER PROJECT, 2019, Governors Island, New York. | Photo courtesy of Stephanie Berger. Exterior of the typewriter booth.

LEANNE: Tell me about the new programming you've come up with due to the pandemic.

STEPHANIE: COVID has been difficult for the Society and for me, personally. Live events are my passion, but I have also realized that much of this work's reward is that connection with other people. Our mission is to build community around poetry and to bring it to people in unexpected ways. So many people have misconceptions about what poetry is. We approached the pivot [caused by COVID-19] by asking ourselves, "How can we carry out this mission?" We tried to approach this new environment from a place of experimentation; we have no idea what's going to hit, but we're going to try a bunch of different things and see what people respond to.

The first thing that we launched was the Poetry Stream website, which is like the Poetry Brothel; people can see who they would like to book for a private poetry reading, one-on-one, or group reading. One good thing that has come out of this experience is connecting much more with all of the people in our community internationally—Poetry Brothel people in the Paris and Bogotá chapters. Poetry Stream is international; you can buy a private poetry reading with someone in South America, you know, which is just cool.

LEANNE: It's interesting to know that other people can take your ideas and run with them, and that you trust them in that process.

STEPHANIE: Empowering people has become a considerable part of the way we approach things. Nick and I have always dreamed big. We get really excited around each other. And then we're going to launch the New York City Poetry Festival. We've already decided that it's going happen annually forever—like, what is the fiftieth anniversary going to be like? We like to get excited, dream big, and push ourselves. I think this comes from a real love of poetry. It's just the best thing; it connects people. It's an intimacy maker in a world that is increasingly disconnected and unfocused. Poetry requires focus. I want to bring that to more people and to make people understand it. Somehow poetry got institutionalized by academia, and a lot of people don't understand that like any other art form; it can be whatever you want it to be. All of it is valid, and everyone should participate in it, because it's good for your heart and soul.

STEPHANIE BERGER *is chief executive officer, executive director, and cofounder of the Poetry Society of New York. She is also a poet and performance artist. She is cocreator with Nicholas Adamski of the Poetry Brothel, the New York City Poetry Festival, and the Typewriter Project. She is the author of* In the Madame's Hatbox *(Dancing Girl Press, 2011) and coauthor with Carina Finn of* The Grey Bird: Thirteen Emoji Poems in Translation *(Coconut Books, 2014). With Jackie Braje, she founded Milk Press, a publisher and nurturer of poetic collaborations. Her work is largely collaborative, interactive, and community-oriented, and it straddles the worlds of literature, immersive theater, and public art. Stephanie earned a* BA *in philosophy from the University of Southern California, received an* MFA *in poetry from the New School, and taught in the English department at Pace University.* **poetrysocietyny.org**

BELOW LEFT: December 2016, New York City, New York. | Photo: Mark Shelby Perry, courtesy of Stephanie Berger. Members of the Poetry Society of New York at the DESIRON Showroom, New York Design Center. Left to right, top to bottom: Nicholas Adamski, Stephanie Berger, Charley Layton, Bobby Martinez, Kailey Tedesco, Jackie Braje, N.O. Moore.

BELOW RIGHT: 2019. | Photo: Max McQueen, courtesy of Stephanie Berger. Stephanie Berger and Nicholas Adamski, cofounders of the Poetry Society of New York, at the Sand Salon in Brooklyn, New York.

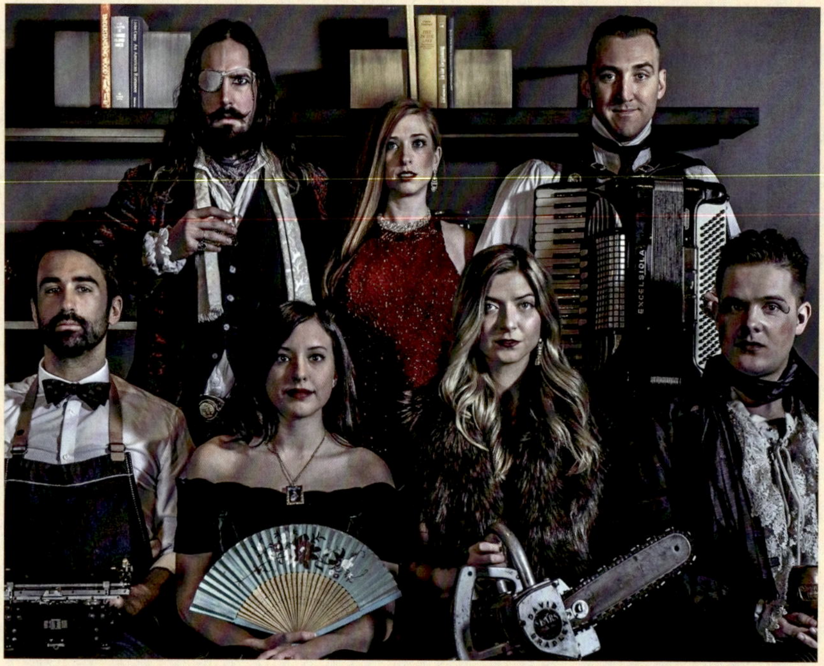

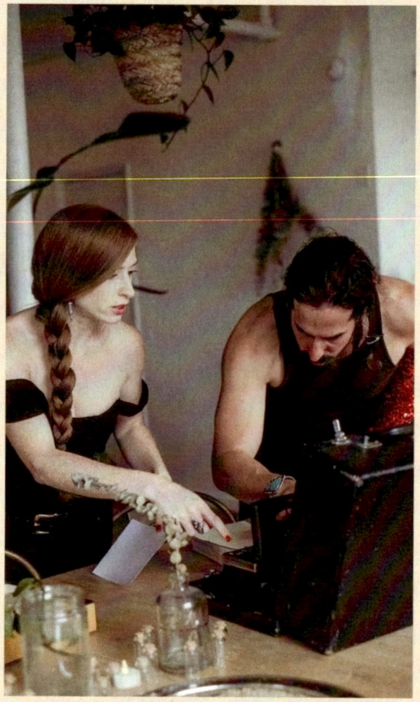

PENNILESS PROMOTION

You don't need a billboard in Times Square or a million Insta followers to get your work noticed. Consider your collaborative team and use their strengths. Who has excellent writing chops? They are probably the person who should write the press release. Who makes great visuals? Elect them to make your social media channels sing. Who is witty and fearless? Why not have them call up the local radio station and make a pitch?

Let your team grow your message by implementing some of the following tools.

PRESS RELEASES are the conventional tool for getting your project mentioned in a newspaper, television show, or magazine. A press release should usually be no longer than one page. Start with one interesting detail about why people should care about the project and include the pertinent who, why, when, what, and where details, as well as your contact information. Be sure to send your press to media four to six weeks in advance of your launch date. Select outlets that typically cover artwork or topics related to your project. The internet has a ton of examples of successful press releases, and most media outlets publish their contact information in their website footers.

COMMUNITY CALENDARS. Are there local free events calendars that could include your project? Most cities and towns have some sort of events listing associated with their local arts groups, newspapers, or magazines.

SOCIAL MEDIA has become an excellent tool for artistic promotion, and the number of platforms that one can participate on is astounding. Rather than getting overwhelmed by all the new social media platforms emerging, focus on the few platforms that you know your core audience uses. Ask influential friends to share your posts. Look for relevant hashtags or memes that you can participate in. Your desired audience already lives there.

POSTING VIDEOS OR PHOTOS of your work in progress can also increase interest in your project as it grows. If you are comfortable sharing your work as you go along, you can build a fan base for your project as the piece comes together.

EMAIL is your friend. You and/or your creative collective can put out a newsletter; otherwise, there may be existing newsletters in your community that you can submit to. Are there creative LISTSERVs such as Canada's Instant Coffee network that you can send listings to? Does your community have a newsletter put out by your local library or community arts council? Is there a professional society or guild that regularly emails their membership?

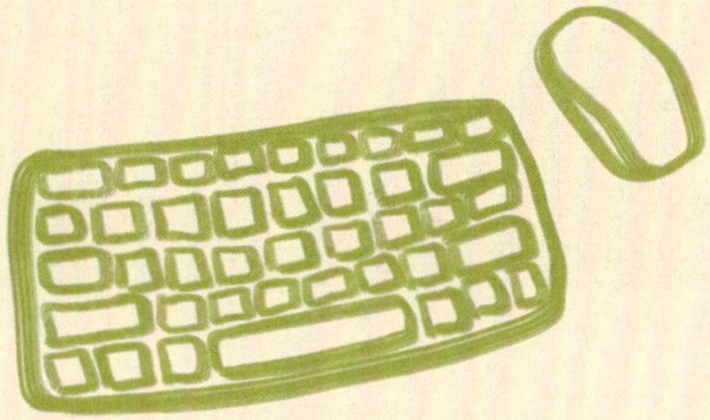

WEBSITES. Every artistic person should have a web presence, even if it is a single page on the internet. If you are promoting your event, you need to be able to send people somewhere to learn a little bit more about you and your project. If you don't have the funds to hire a designer, there are DIY templates and tools offered through WordPress, Wix, and Squarespace, among other providers. YouTube is full of online tutorials, and many public libraries offer training sessions on how to make a website. Your web presence does not need to be fancy, but you need to show up to the online party.

STRATEGIC PARTNERS. Some municipalities have a mandate to support the work of artists in their communities. Check your local government's website for free programs that offer artists digital billboards, poster distribution, or open community space. Some cities even have email lists that they post arts-related invitations to. You can also look for like-minded arts groups who may be open to negotiating promotional trades. You might be surprised at what is available to you.

PRINTED MATTER. The digital world has captivated us so much that some people can't even look up from their cell phones while crossing the street, and yet, print still matters. Posters, flyers, bookmarks, and stickers are all valuable tools for getting the word out. Professional printing can be expensive; photocopying on colored paper or getting busy with a silk screen or hand stamp can also do the trick.

GUERRILLA MARKETING TACTICS. The sky really is the limit when it comes to ideas for getting attention. What can you do that might be out of the ordinary? Could you create a temporary billboard? A wheatpaste poster campaign? What about replicating your invitation in sidewalk chalk? Or staging a parade of mascots or mimes holding signs? Outlandish acts can go a long way in capturing and delighting others to join—just be cautious and aware of whether you are breaking any local bylaws.

SAY IT AGAIN: REPETITION IS A TOOL FOR SUCCESS

One of the basic rules of marketing is that someone needs to see something three to six times to be aware of it. If you are looking to grow your audience, you will need to be persistent. Despite the fact that creative people instinctually exist on the margins of polite society as rule-breakers, surprisingly few of them consistently ask for help when they need it. If a person or group says no or does not respond after two or three messages, you should move on; they are not the person to help you. There are other fish in the promotional sea. Keep on swimming. You may not agree with every reaction or review you receive, but remember that showing your art to others is the hard work of celebrating and testing what you've made.

Promotion is never easy, but I encourage you to do it in a way that feels right to you and allows you to feel energized about your project. At the end of the day, you need to be satisfied that you've served your creative vision in a way that fits with your values and with your big and beautiful ideas.

CHAPTER 8

MAKE IT WONDROUS: EXECUTE YOUR PROJECT

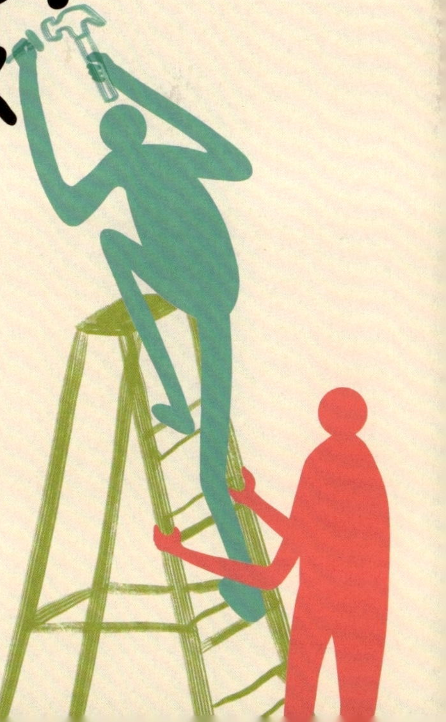

Eventually you will arrive at what you've been working toward for so long: the execution stage of your project. The act of making your project exist is thrilling, exciting, and wonderful, if a bit daunting. As your project begins to live in other people's minds, it will take on new momentum. You and your coconspirators must now gently shepherd your project to a successful conclusion.

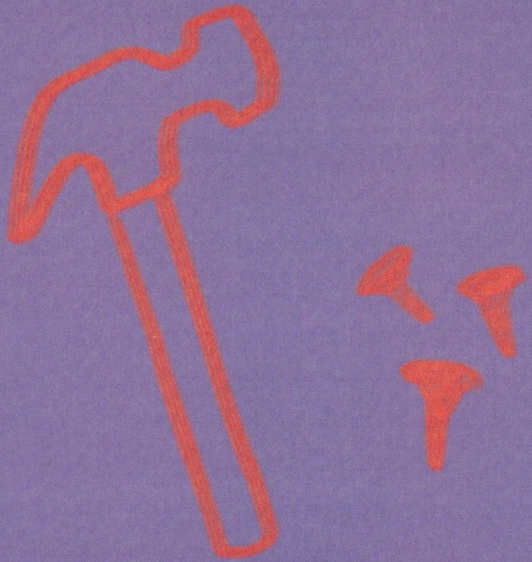

Despite all of your hard work and planning, it is normal to have some anxiety before executing your project. Why wouldn't you? You've put hours of effort and your unique perspective into creating something that is an expression of you and your values. When you make a work public, strangers are going to interact with it—and not only interact, but form opinions about it. That's not intimidating at all now, is it? Taking any project into this stage is an exercise in vulnerability. But don't let squirmy feelings hold you back.

Putting yourself out there is one of the most terrifying and gratifying things that you can do. Many people talk about doing creative projects, but there's a big difference between talk and execution. Executing work is what makes you a creative person. You've done enough planning and dreaming and scheming to be on your way and to have a strong vision about what you want the outcome to be.

TIMING IS EVERYTHING

It is crucial to give some thought to what your audience's headspace might be on specific dates and times. Public holidays, traditional workday schedules, weather patterns, and other distractions, like roadwork or public emergencies, can make or break how your audience interacts with your work.

TRY THIS

Do the Smallest Possible Task

Are you feeling stuck? Sometimes it helps to come up with the smallest possible task that you can do. Rather than dwelling on the fact that you need to get in touch with twenty volunteers and getting your mind stuck in a loop, why not write a to-do list of all their names? Don't know how to paint a whole mural? Perhaps you can begin by just choosing your first paint color. Big things can seem like they will take forever, but success starts with one small task.

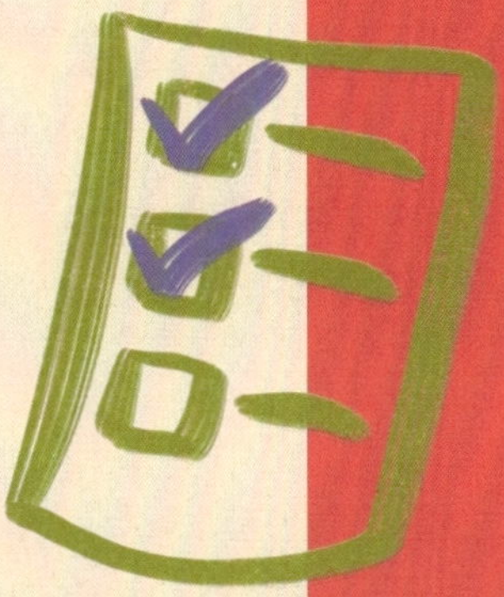

PROMPT

Who's on First? Make a Plan

Take an inventory and make a list of everyone who will be involved in the project, including their skills and their role. Take some time to review what you've written down. Is each person aware of your expectations? Have they fully agreed to be part of the project? Are you confident that they can fulfill the tasks that you've identified for them? Are there any supports that they will need?

Consider who will be participating during on-site activities at different stages. Who will be there for the setup? Who will be there all day? More importantly, who has committed to be there for the takedown? Ask in advance, and don't assume that your coconspirators or volunteers will be there at the end of the day. People tend to lose enthusiasm and often have other commitments as the day winds to a close.

Double-check before you begin: does everyone have the correct date, time, and complete address? Don't assume that they have thoroughly read your communications if you haven't received confirmation. Following up in advance will mean that things run more smoothly later. Everyone involved in the project needs to know precisely when to log on, chime in, or show up.

Consider your audience's needs:

- **LIFE CYCLE:** teenagers will be in school on weekdays, but senior citizens are likely to be available.
- **SCHEDULE:** nine-to-five office workers will likely not be available during the day or the dinner hours, and they are also unlikely to show up for something that happens at midnight on a weeknight.
- **HOLIDAYS:** are you launching your project on Christmas Day, the first night of Hanukkah, Orange Shirt Day, or the end of Ramadan? Check for holidays beyond the statutory holiday schedule—you might inadvertently be excluding whole communities with your timing.
- **SEASONS:** depending on where you live, certain kinds of weather can be prohibitive. If you live in Yukon, you're likely to brave most cold temperatures to be outside; however, the seasonal twenty-four hours of sunlight doesn't mean that participants will be up all hours of the day. Keep in mind what kinds of weather and seasonal behavior suit those in your area.
- **THE TWENTY-FOUR-HOUR CLOCK:** the beauty of online events is that they can happen anywhere and be experienced globally, but you want to know how time differences impact different participants. If it is imperative to have folks in another time zone join, consult with people who live in that time zone. Some countries practice midday siestas or have much later mealtimes than North America's average six p.m. dinner.

CASE STUDY

PUBLIC RITUALS

A CONVERSATION WITH

Candy Chang

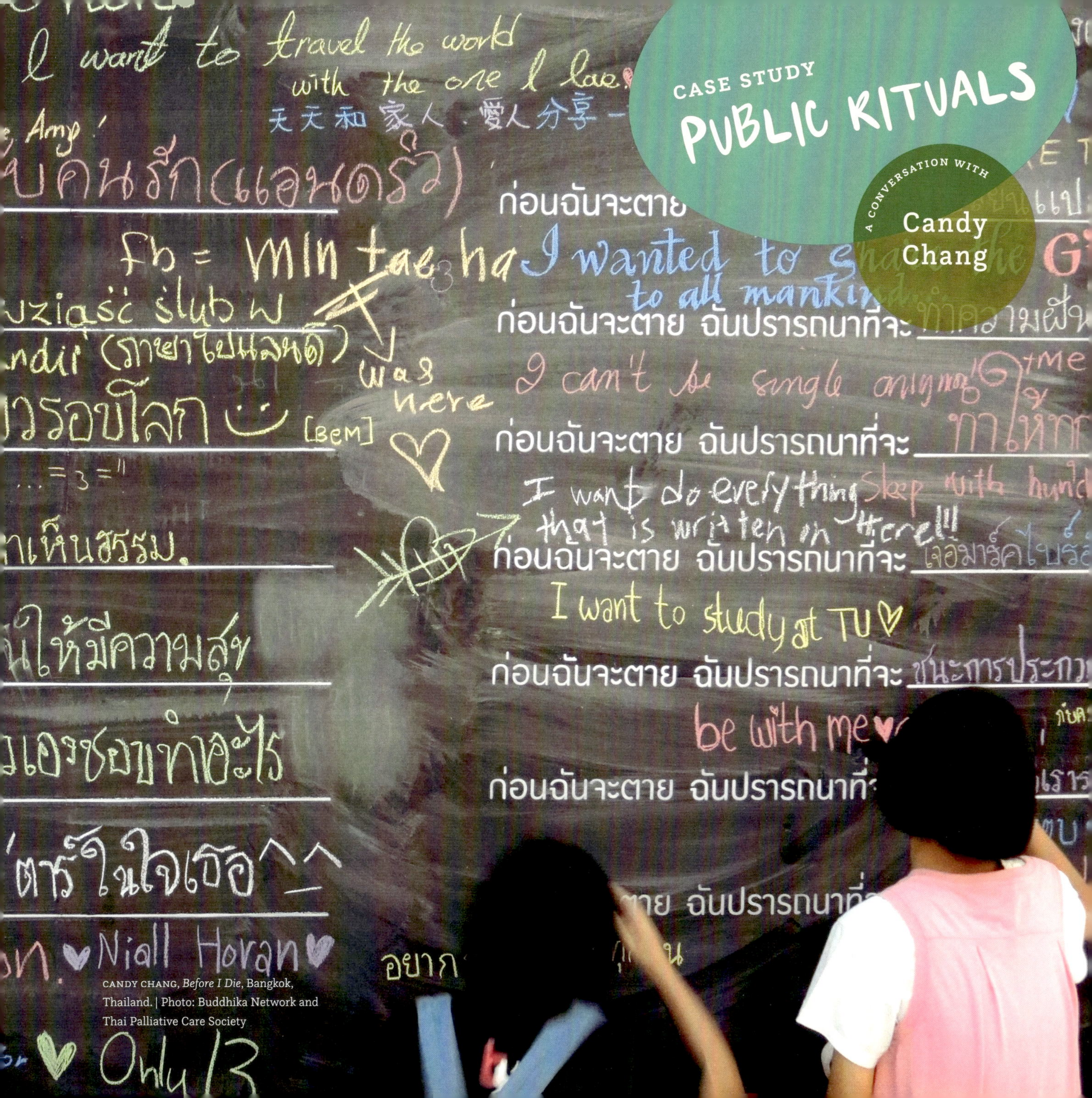

CANDY CHANG, *Before I Die*, Bangkok, Thailand. | Photo: Buddhika Network and Thai Palliative Care Society

Participatory artist Candy Chang activates public spaces throughout the world that explore public rituals and the aesthetics of the handwritten word. By creating rituals that unpack the complexities of our inner lives, her installations often include anonymous reflections from participants, captured in their own writing and reproduced through video and mixed media. Above all, Candy is an artist who knows how to engage with people. In 2011, she created the public artwork Before I Die: A Memento Mori for the Modern Age, which invited participants to consider their mortality and reflect in a community setting on what matters most. Since that first wall in her home city of New Orleans, more than 5,000 Before I Die walls have been executed in seventy-five countries. Participants' handwritten reflections are poignant, funny, aspirational, and everything in between. Candy's body of work strives to highlight anxieties, hopes, pains, and moments of grace in the 21st century.

BELOW: CANDY CHANG, *Before I Die*, New Orleans. | Photo: Candy Chang

TOP RIGHT: CANDY CHANG, *Before I Die*, New Orleans. | Photo: Candy Chang

BOTTOM RIGHT: CANDY CHANG, *Before I Die*, New Orleans. | Photo: Kristina Kassemv

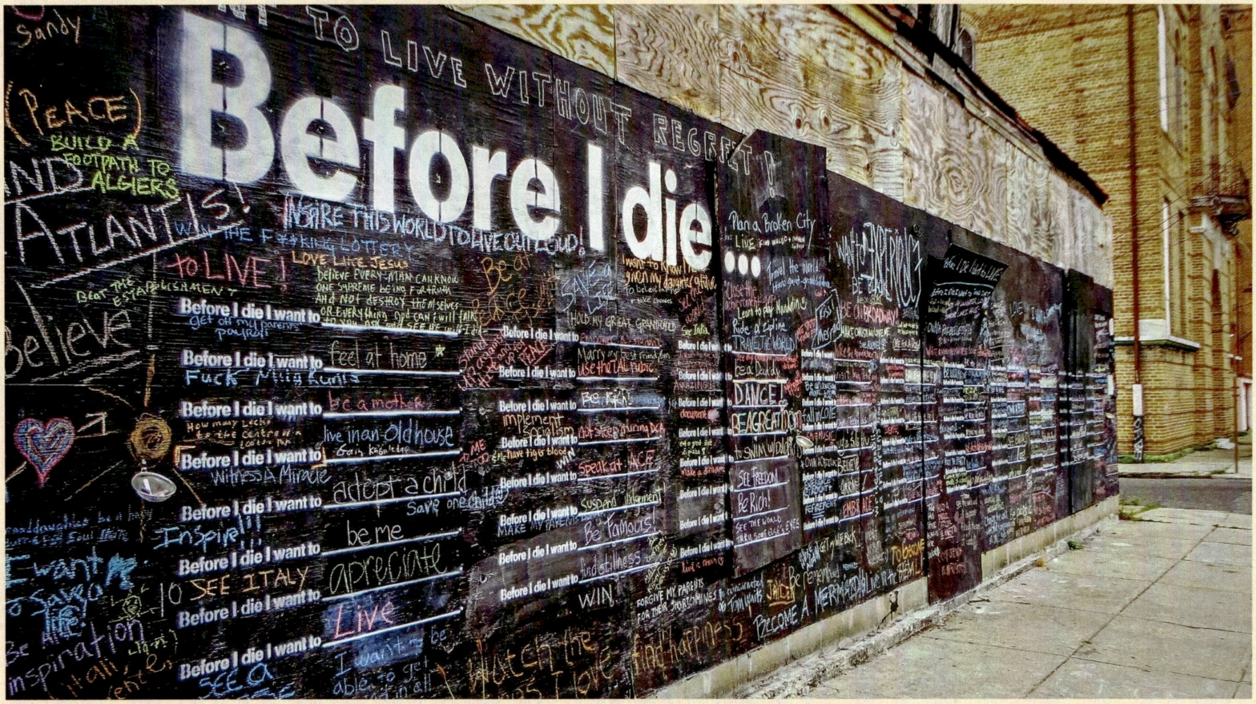

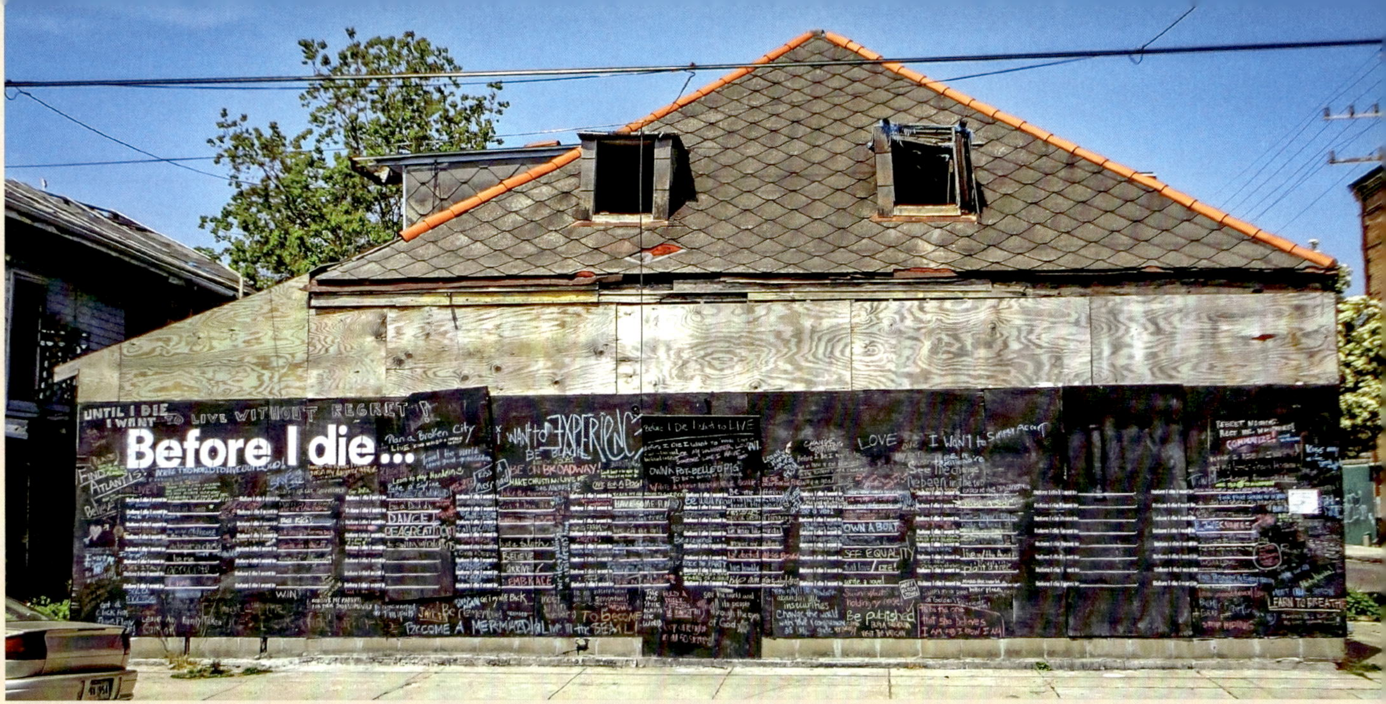
Before I die...
BECOME A MERMAID
LEARN TO BREATHE

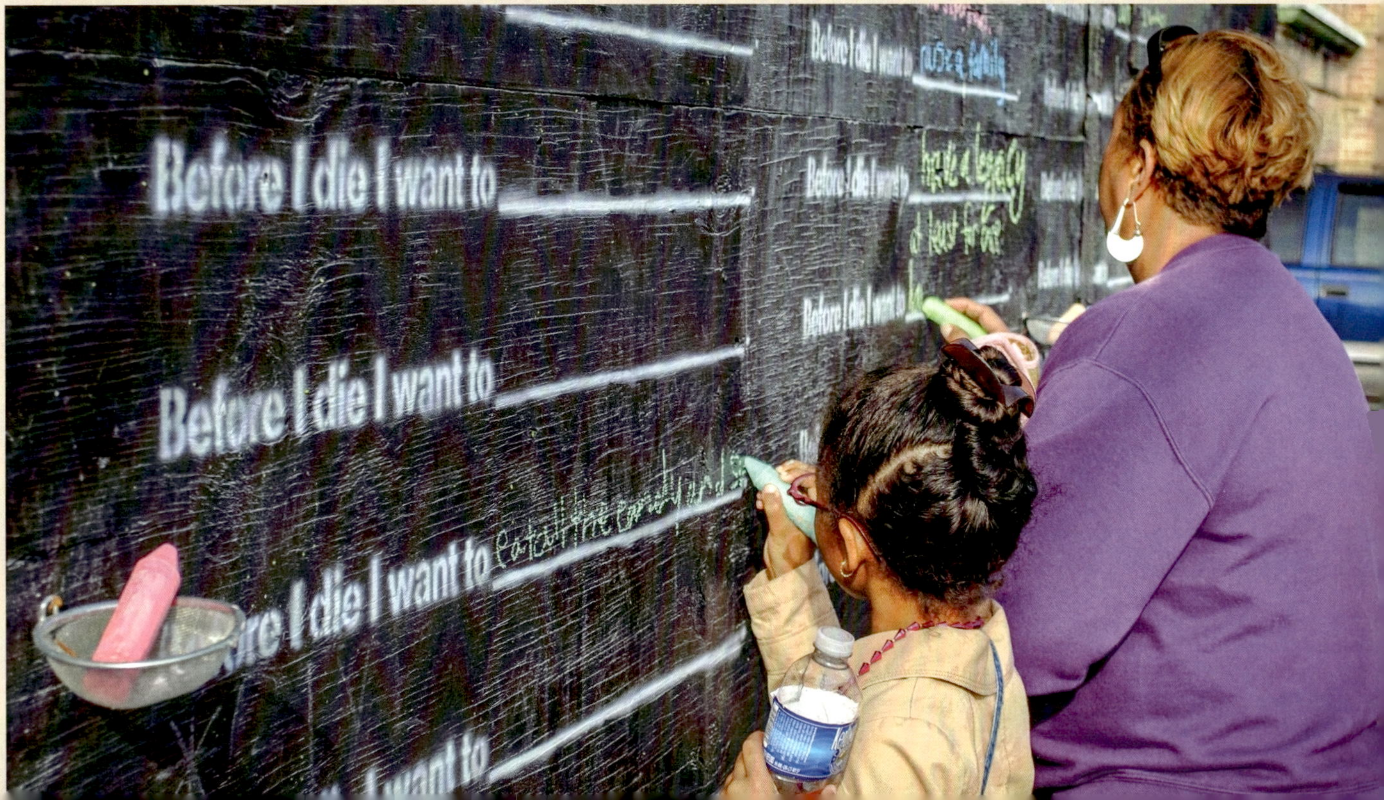
Before I die I want to
Before I die I want to
Before I die I want to

LEANNE: Tell me about your first experience creating an art project in a public space.

CANDY: The first time I made art in public, I was arrested! I was a teenager spray-painting a corny sunset by the train tracks. I never did that again, but I continued to use simple tools like stickers, stencils, and chalk to share more with my neighbors. These cheap tools made it easy to experiment on the fly, and some projects would have fizzled out if I hadn't used them.

For instance, I made "I wish this was _______" stickers for people to share their hopes for neglected spaces. I put boxes of stickers in businesses and invited people to tag their responses online. Few people did—it was too much to ask—so I posted grids of stickers on vacant buildings. I tweaked the experiment so it was easier for people to share and so that I had control documenting responses. I photographed hundreds of meaningful responses this way, and the project ended up in the Venice Architecture Biennale.

That lesson still serves me whenever I'm stuck: keep experimenting, stay nimble, and roll with the punches. When my thinking gets tortured, I try to consider what I can do to gain a little insight. I remind myself that I don't have to figure everything out. That's too much pressure. Just try something small, see how it feels, and make new decisions from there.

LEANNE: Why is it important to make art that exists in public places?

CANDY: I studied urban planning and started creating participatory work because I'm an introvert. These projects were a way for me to ask my neighbors things I was too shy to ask in person. They were a way for the quieter people to share just as much as the loud ones. It was only later that I realized the anonymous prompt also allowed people to share in vulnerable ways without fear of judgment. Anonymity led to honest reflections on anxiety, grief, and other topics that can often feel so isolating: "I want to get my wife back"; "Impressing other people is killing the true me"; "I tend to seek numbness out of fear that I will be overwhelmed"; "My dad died, and I'm afraid I'll be sad forever."

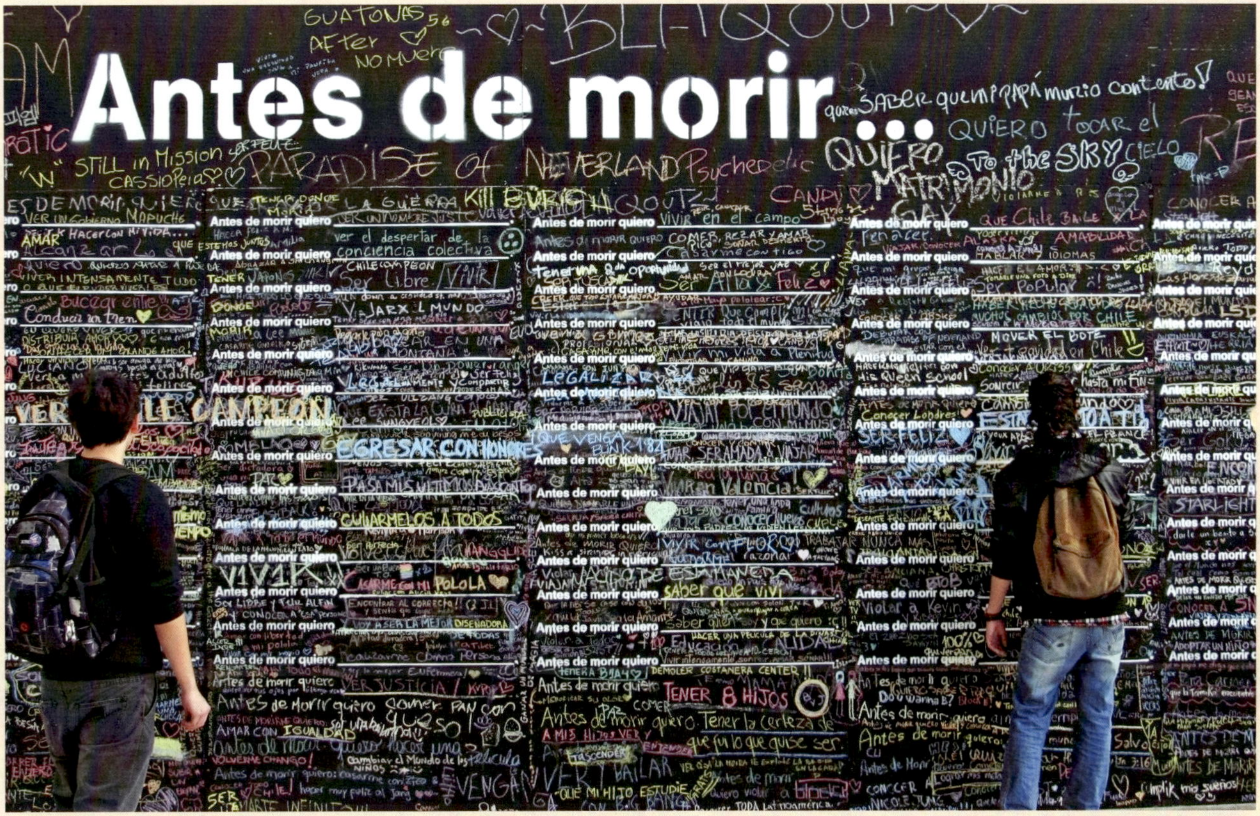

CANDY CHANG, *Before I Die*, Santiago, Chile. | Photo: Bernd Biedermann

When I made a Before I Die installation with students in Virginia, someone wrote, "Before I die, I want to overcome depression." We immediately let down our guards and began sharing ways that depression had affected us or our loved ones and the things that helped. Experiences like that made me passionate about creating more spaces for emotional communion. Loneliness, stress, and anxiety have been called the health epidemics of our time. Society feels increasingly tribal. These are alarming trends, but I believe our shared spaces can help. Our environment shapes the human spirit. It can divide us, or it can connect us. It can minimize us, or it can enlarge us. As social isolation and polarization continue to grow, local infrastructure for the soul is more important than ever.

LEANNE: Do you think there are any misconceptions about participatory work?

CANDY: I can't think of any misconceptions, but participatory work is often treading into new territory that can cause anxiety in communities. It's helpful to address them. When I proposed Before I Die on an abandoned house in my neighborhood in New Orleans, I got support from the property owner and most of my neighborhood association. Still, some residents feared people would write on other properties nearby. I understood their concern and promised to take care of the area, and if it became a problem, I would paint over the whole thing. Then they had nothing to lose. In the end, the installation was up for almost a year, and no one ever wrote beyond the wall.

LEANNE: You are known for your collaborations, both with communities and with individual artists, such as James A. Reeves, with whom you have the collection Ritual Fields. What qualities does a good collaborator possess?

CANDY: It's fun to get wrapped up in ideas with someone else. My mom says we're as harmonious as two fish in the water. We studied design together in college. A friend once called us Short Attention Span Theater because we always made so many things, from music to books to stop-motion animation. We enjoy conceptualizing work together. One of our favorite activities is going to art museums and talking through possibilities for our projects. We can be completely ourselves with one another. Nothing is too dark or absurd. We share similar struggles and desires. We make each other laugh. We improve each other's ideas. We respect each other's perspectives. We are each other's biggest fans.

CANDY CHANG, *Looking for Love Again*, 2011, Fairbanks, Alaska. | Photo: Candy Chang. Looking for Love Again renewed attention to an abandoned high-rise in downtown Fairbanks by transforming it into an emotional beacon pleading for love and inviting people to come in for a closer look. A four-story sign and chalkboards at the street level invited people to share their memories of the building and their hopes for its future.

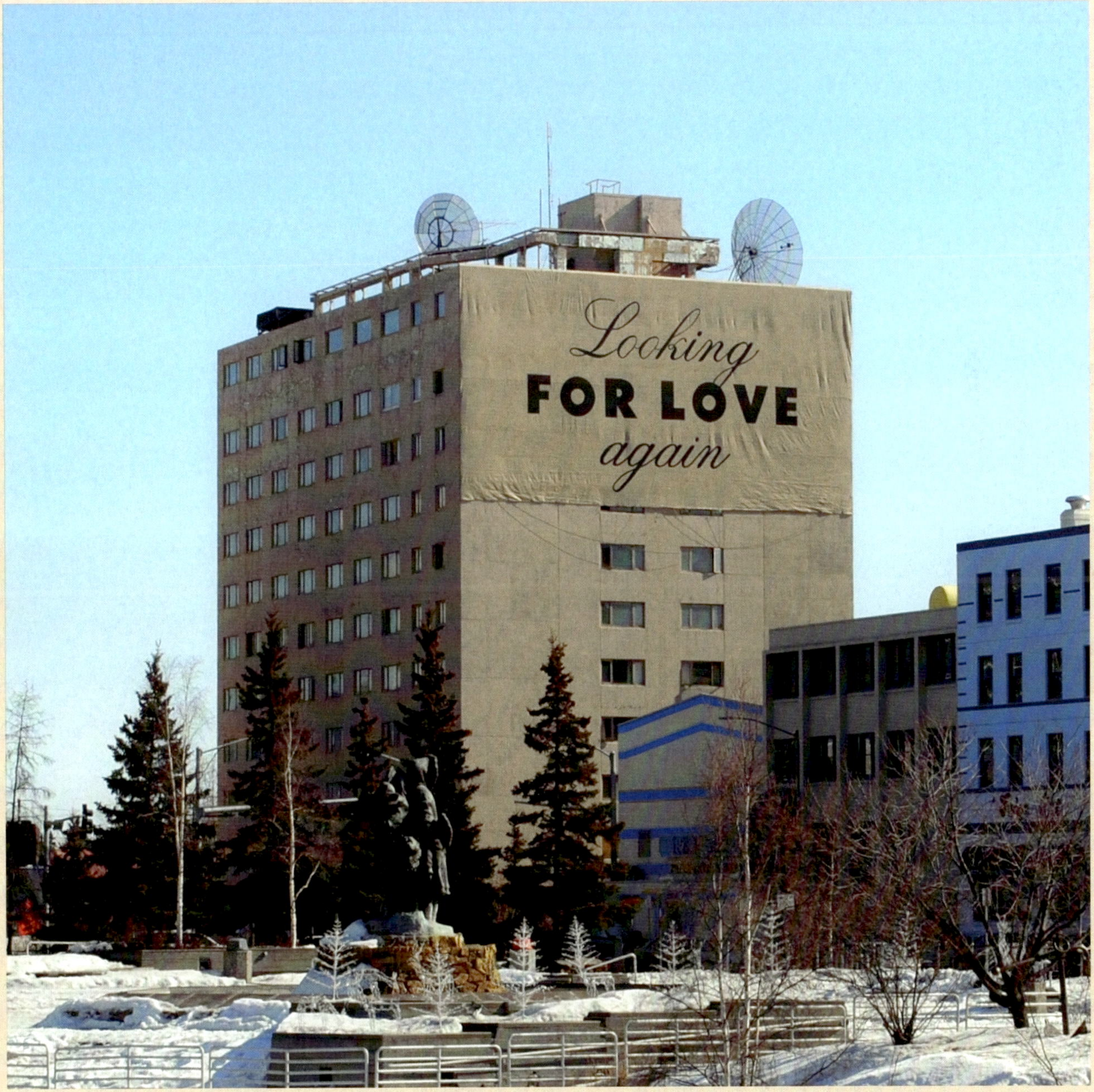
Looking
FOR LOVE
again

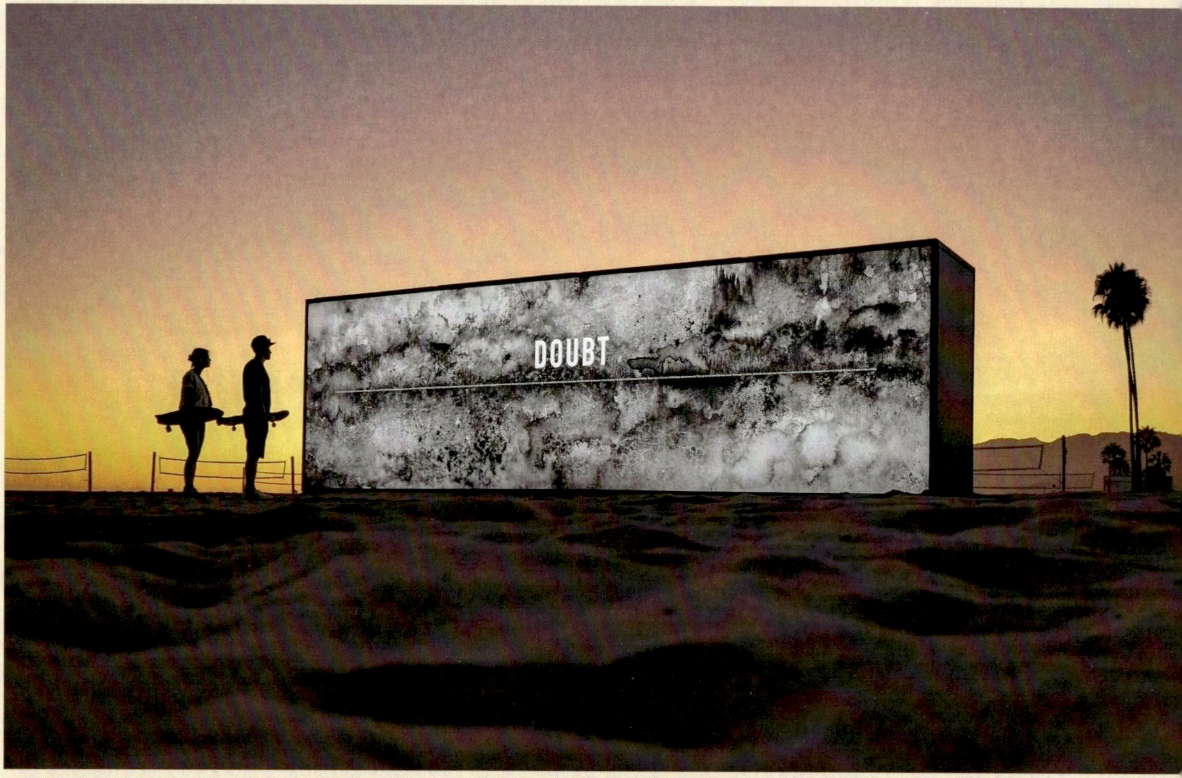

LEANNE: How do you stay inspired to continue projects, and how you know when it is time to pivot to something else?

CANDY: I keep following my curiosity. Each project comes from my questions at the moment, and my questions continue to evolve as I evolve. One work will often inform the next work. I stay inspired by looking at art, watching movies, and reading books. I keep lists called "What if" and "What next" so that when my distracted self becomes untethered, I can refer to the moments of clarity from my brighter self.

I've never had a five-year plan, let alone a one-year plan. I've had a few-months plan, and it's worked out for me because I've stumbled onto so many things that have changed the course of my life. It's good to have goals, but it might be even greater to keep an open mind. We can only have new insight into our life and work when we are receptive to the unexpected.

CANDY CHANG AND JAMES A. REEVES, *Light the Barricades*, 2019, Ritual Fields, Los Angeles. | Photo: James A. Reeves. By reconfiguring the traditions of Chinese landscape painting, light boxes, and silent contemplation, Light the Barricades offers a modern ritual for these distracting times that draws upon the *I Ching*'s advice to pause and reckon with our inner obstructions during times of uncertainty and flux.

CANDY CHANG *is trained in architecture, design, and urban planning. She first created participatory art to reflect with her neighbors on their neighborhood. After struggling with grief and depression, she used this medium to reflect on the psyche. She has created a monument of over 50,000 anxieties and hopes, transformed a building into a device for philosophical reflection, and created electric shrines on inner obstructions. She has worked with organizations including Mural Arts Philadelphia, Art Production Fund, the Rubin Museum of Art, and the Annenberg Foundation. She often collaborates with James A. Reeves, and their work can be found at Ritual Fields (ritualfields.com). Candy is a TED Senior Fellow, an Urban Innovation Fellow, and a World Economic Forum Young Global Leader. She is a recipient of the Tony Goldman Visionary Artist Award and was named a "Live Your Best Life" Local Hero by O, The Oprah Magazine, as well as one of the Top 100 Leaders in Public Interest Design. Her work has been exhibited in the Venice Architecture Biennale; the Cooper Hewitt, Smithsonian Design Museum; the Ogden Museum of Southern Art; and the Smithsonian American Art Museum.* **candychang.com | beforeidieproject.com**

PREPARE YOURSELF FOR THE DAY

One of the best things you can do for yourself on the day you execute your project is to take care of yourself. Eat breakfast. Stretch. Meditate, if that's your thing. The last thing you want to do is to show up at your project site frazzled and hangry. Do whatever you typically do in the morning to ensure that you have a good day and fully show up, physically and mentally.

Give some thought to your wardrobe. If you know that you will be on your feet for a full day, wear your most comfortable shoes, or pack a second pair. If your project requires a bit of sparkle, then dress up—but don't wear anything you don't want to sacrifice to messy art materials.

DUCT TAPE IS ALWAYS HELPFUL: A CHECKLIST FOR YOUR BIG DAY

Whenever you are working in a new place, you are bound to need something that you don't have. Here are a few things that I like to keep in my kit:

- A large bottle of water. There's nothing worse than losing your energy because you are dehydrated.
- Pre-packed snacks and fruit. Don't get hangry; eat snacks.
- Scissors. Even if you think you will have nothing to cut, trust me, you will.
- Clear packing tape and Scotch tape. Even if you think you have nothing to stick, trust me, you will.
- A few pieces of cardstock and large felt markers for making signs and marking territory.
- Business cards with your contact info.
- Bulldog clips.
- A sweater and/or scarf in case it gets cold; sunblock and a hat in case it gets hot.
- Liquid soap and hand sanitizer, paper towels or reusable cloths—sometimes the site will be dirty and need a wipe down. Sometimes you'll need to clean up a mess in the middle of things.

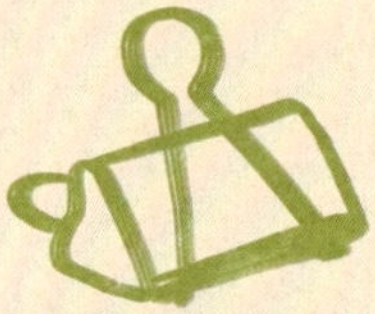

- A clean bedsheet or some nice-looking fabric (for projects that do not create a lot of mess) or a cheap plastic drop sheet or two (for covering surfaces when you do plan to make a mess). I have been using my grandmother's vintage linens as tablecloths for years, and I often find cheap but colorful drop sheets in the tablecloths section of dollar stores.
- Small cotton pouches or Ziploc bags. I can't say enough about having extra bags on hand. Want to save half of your lunch? Need to clean up in a hurry but don't know what to do with 200 loose googly eyes in a busted package? Put them in Ziploc bags, fire them in your carrying case, and move on.
- A container to take projects home with you. Sometimes projects will become larger than they started once participants have worked on them. Remember, it is up to you to pack it in and pack it out.

Don't leave the house without doing a complete inventory of your art supplies. Nothing is worse than showing up to a place confident that you are ready to go, only to find something missing. I often treat getting ready for workshops as I would packing for a long trip. I write out a list of supplies and gather them in a place where I can see them all together. By grouping materials, it usually becomes obvious to me what could be missing.

PARTICIPATORY PROJECTS

Community projects can take a lot of time and energy. If they are successful, you will always hear from people who regret having missed it or are asking you to keep it open indefinitely. If you haven't considered your project's duration, consider setting a firm start and end time for your participation. Determining your project's duration in advance is an act of self-care that will support you, your coconspirators, and any external partners.

For community projects that will be on-site, I recommend a window of two to eight hours, depending on the number of people available to execute the project. If you are going solo, you'll likely need someone to relieve you for a break after an hour or two. If you are in a group, you'll want to plan your work in two- to four-hour shifts, with shorter shifts for the introverts among us. Don't forget setup and takedown, as each can take an hour or two outside of your project hours. If you are working with a festival or another event, plan to be there for the hours you committed to. Don't disappoint the person who ran over to see your work at the end of the day, only to find that you packed up early.

"I love creating participatory, socially engaged projects; there's always something the public does that surprises me, that adds so much more to the project."

—ARAM HAN SIFUENTES

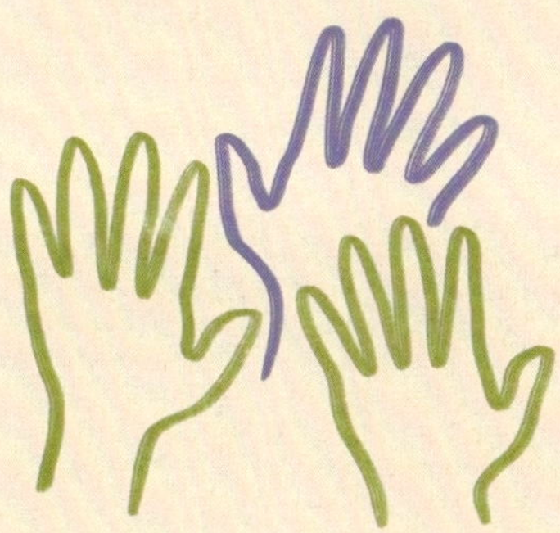

CASE STUDY

CREATIVITY IS NOT ENOUGH

A CONVERSATION WITH

The Center for Artistic Activism

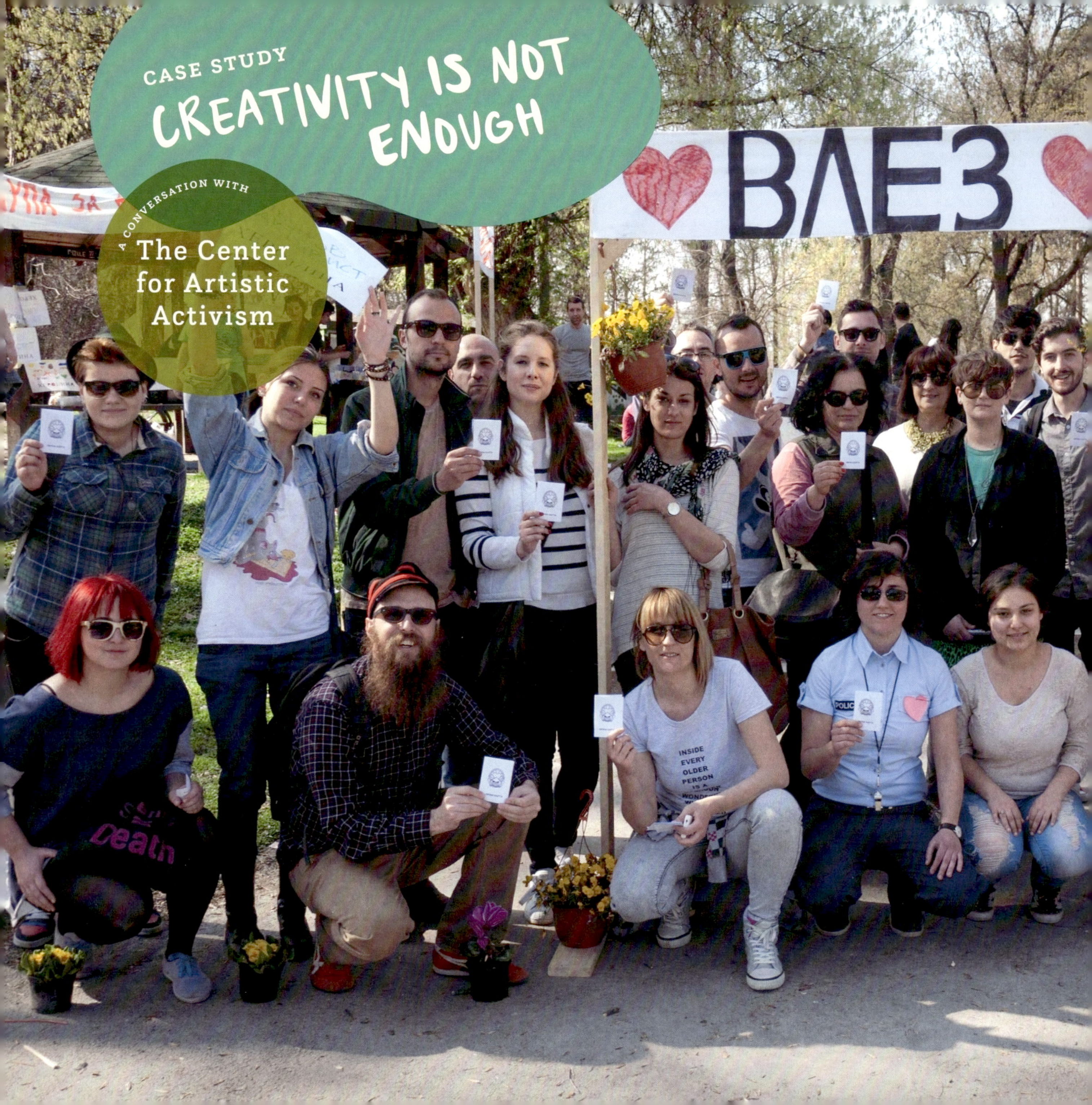

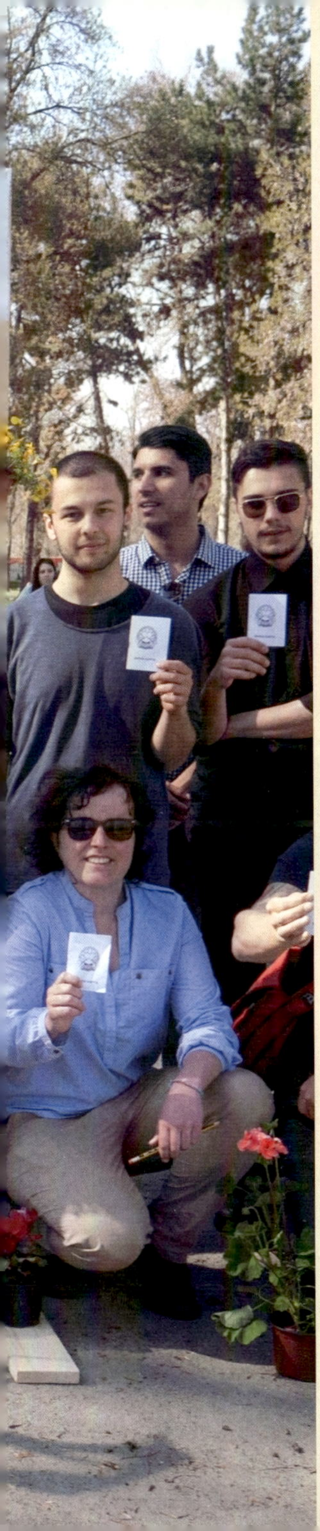

The Center for Artistic Activism in New York, New York, is on a mission to support artists and activists who want to exchange skills. Since 2009, they have trained and mentored over 1,500 people around the world on a range of issues. They offer training and organization to artists struggling to create change and to frustrated activists working to engage people. The remarkable research out of the Center combines learnings from the fields of culture, art, and creativity to propel social justice work, creating opportunities for marginalized people to use their own unique perspectives to gain power, representation, and political change.

I spoke with Rebecca Bray, director, artist, and interaction designer; Stephen Duncombe, research director, cofounder, educator, author, and activist; and Steve Lambert, director, cofounder, and artist about their work and the opportunities for artists and activists to work together to make meaningful change.

LEANNE: How did the Center for Artistic Activism come about?

STEPHEN: I was working as a community organizer in the Lower East Side in the '90s, and I was getting increasingly frustrated with the sort of activism that represented a lot of the scene. It's tragic when you organize a demonstration that you don't really want to go to. At the same time, I met a lot of artists who brought their sensibilities to my organizing. I got the sense that the merging of arts and activism was a powerful combination. And then I ran into Steve.

STEVE: I was in San Francisco for art school during the first dot-com boom, and I had to fight two different residential evictions in the courts, one at the beginning of my studies and one at the end. This bookended my fine arts training and put me in a high-stakes legal battle with the city involving economics and gentrification and local elections. In contrast, I would go up the hill to

2014. | Photo courtesy of the Center for Artistic Activism. A twenty-four-hour creative action in Skopje, Macedonia, by LGBTQ2S+ and Roma rights organizers.

this art school that was designed to look like a monastery and be around all these painters who were only talking about their work. And I was like, "What is this?" It was hard to make sense of that and to understand how making art was relevant when I was trying not to be homeless. I started to figure out how to bring these two worlds together. I wanted to know that I could make an actual difference. When I found Stephen Duncombe, I was like, "This guy might know."

REBECCA: When Steve and Stephen got to know each other, one of the first things that they did before formally founding the Center for Artistic Activism was to host a workshop with artists working on different social change issues at Eyebeam Art and Technology Center in New York. I was an artist-in-residence working on environmental issues, and I attended their workshop. It was an exploration on how to think: how does this work and how does it not work? And that workshop became a kind of seed for the organization: artistry and activism, and how you could bring the best of both worlds together.

STEPHEN: We always use these terms, "affect" and "effect." Activists are very good at thinking about how something is going to effect social change. Artists think about expression and how to move people with emotion. When you put those two skills together, it's a powerful combination. One of the things we often say is when you look back in history at successful social movements, you always find that they have this combination of both affect and effect.

REBECCA: One of the things that we like to remind people is that to do this work, you don't have to be a trained artist with a capital A. This work is about finding people's creativity and empowering them to use it in the course of their work. When we talk about artistic activism, we remind people that it is about the activism. It's about making it more powerful, not just through art, but through recognizing who your audience is and making stuff that engages them and moves them to action.

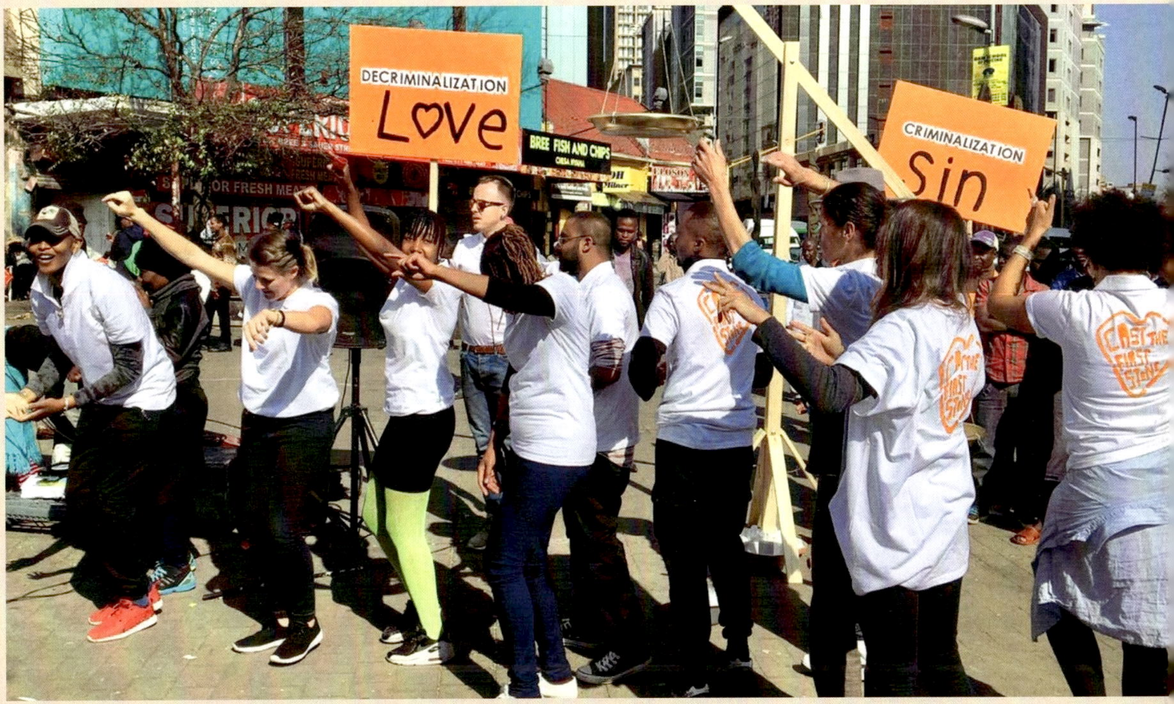

2017. | Photo courtesy of the Center for Artistic Activism. A creative action in the form of a play performed by sex workers in the middle of a busy space in Johannesburg, South Africa.

The artistry is not just frosting. It's not making some nice posters or a beautiful song. Those expressions might be part of the project, but it is about embedding creativity through the whole process. A lot of our training helps artists, activists, and all kinds of people to get on the same page using the language of creativity.

LEANNE: You've worked with artists throughout the world on a variety of issues that are meaningful to them. When you are training or coaching people through creative actions, how do you ensure they are sensitive to viewpoints that might not be their own?

STEVE: I think that situation is more common when you're working alone. In our workshops, there's a perception of who we are when we arrive in the room, such as, we all have advanced degrees or are coming from the United States.

FREE THE VACCINE
FOR COVID-19

Since 2020, the Center for Artistic Activism has been working with its network to free the COVID-19 vaccine and place it in the hands of everyone around the world. | Logo design: Nancy Nowacek.

Stephen and I are professors in New York. When we're working with people in a place like Kenya, a bunch of baggage comes with those things.

Part of winning trust with people is showing them where expertise lies and where it doesn't. We don't live in these places. We are not experts there. We can provide a framework, but we don't know any of the details of these places. We're very forthcoming about that concept early on: we're going to help provide the framework, and you're going to build on it, and then adapt and change it. We do not tell them what to do; we ask, "What are you working on? What would success look like? Okay, let's refine that together."

STEPHEN: Effective artistic activism requires you to reverse the "expert model." The actual people we work with in our workshops are the real experts. They understand the cultural terrain, the signs and symbols, and the stories that we're going to work with. When we provide a framework, we can give many examples of things that have worked in other places, but we're very suspicious of that model of "Yeah, you should do a flash mob."

LEANNE: It sounds like your framework creates a situation where participants have to draw on their own experience to figure out what change they are seeking to make around topics that are close to them.

STEPHEN: Very much so. We start out with an exercise where we ask people how they became what they are now, which is someone who's engaged in society. Invariably, participants share very personal, emotional stories around their own experiences. We ask that question because we want to demonstrate quite literally that social change and activism is something which is about affect as much as it is about effect. We also do it to honor the fact that people are coming out of their own individual experiences. That's important because they have to think about themselves, but when they work with other people, they need to imagine that idea for their audiences.

LEANNE: Could you tell me about the workshop experience?

REBECCA: A typical workshop is five days long. First, we talk about what is artistic activism and what is not. We consider what's outside of this, which is activist art—art that's about activism or about social change. What we're talking about is activism using art and culture to have more impactful results.

We also invite people who are in the workshop to come up and talk about examples of artistic activity. In doing this, we're often talking about their own cultural history of this kind of work. And then we talk about the history of artistic activism.

We talk about culture with a big C, too. It's important to understand popular culture to truly understand what can engage audiences. One thing we usually do in the workshop is to go on an outing and do something that the artists and activists attending the workshop would not normally do themselves. We choose something very popular in that place, such as a big Hollywood movie or a baseball game in Yankee Stadium, with people who have never been to such an event before.

The next day we talk, analyze, and take the experience apart. We ask, "Why do people love doing that thing, and what is it that attracts them to it? What feels good about that experience, and what can we learn about it for our practice?" It helps to give them a methodology for doing research on their audiences and deeply understanding what they love.

STEVE: Often the activists and artists we work with are very liberal and have a hard time understanding why other people would not want things like better public education. They tend to assume people are not on board because they are ignorant or don't care.

It can easily slip into blaming the audience that you're trying to help. Instead, we try to help them understand that everyone is smart, and they all have reasons for doing what they do, so it's our job to learn and understand so we can address it. We help our participants figure out how to be persuasive with people who don't believe or do what they do. It's not like you just provide the truth and put it in front of them and they have a revelation, like,

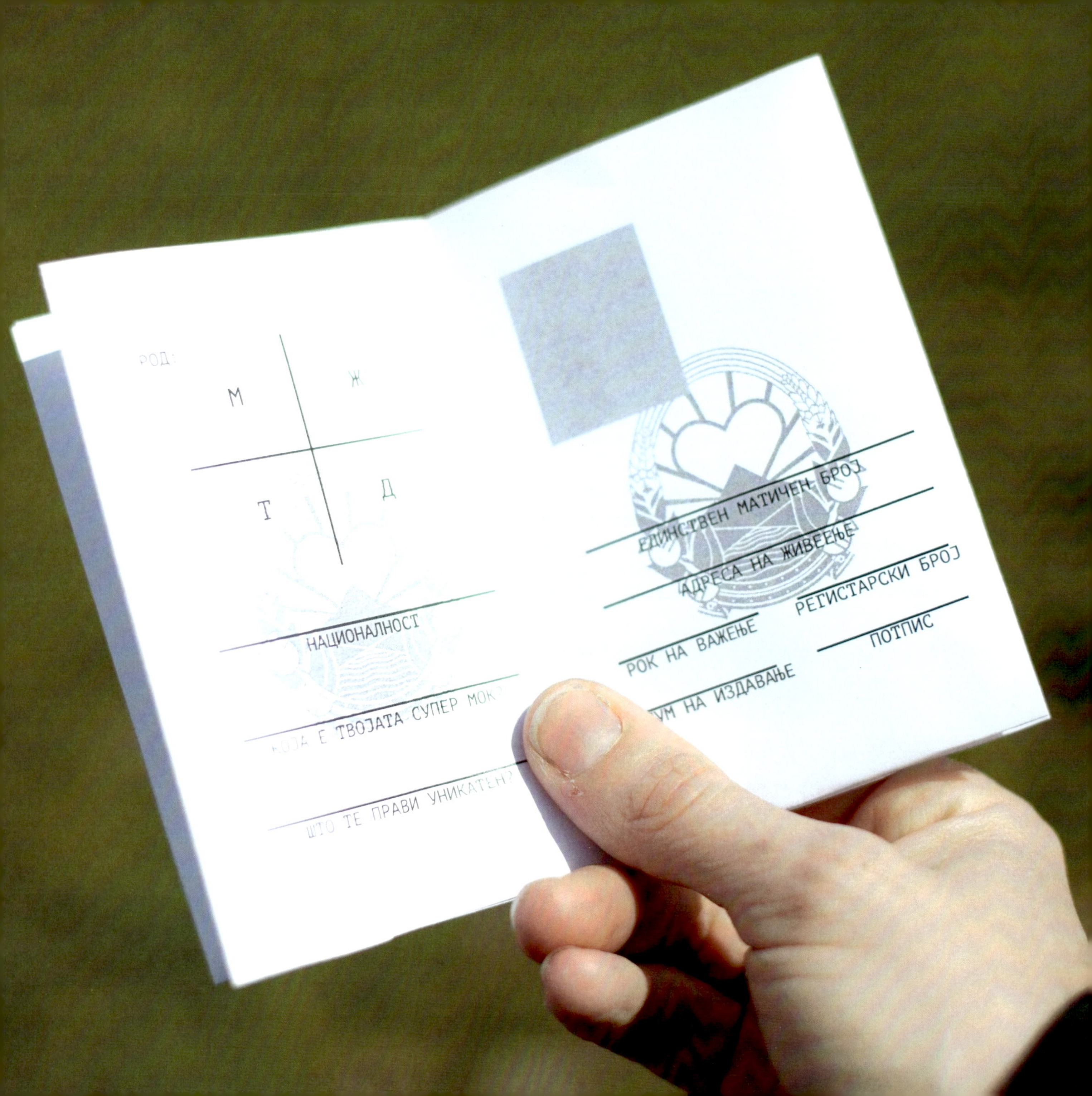
РОД:
М
Ж
Т
Д
НАЦИОНАЛНОСТ
ОЈА Е ТВОЈАТА СУПЕР МО
ШТО ТЕ ПРАВИ УНИКАТЕН?
ЕДИНСТВЕН МАТИЧЕН БРОЈ
АДРЕСА НА ЖИВЕЕЊЕ
РЕГИСТАРСКИ БРОЈ
РОК НА ВАЖЕЊЕ
ПОТПИС
УМ НА ИЗДАВАЊЕ

2014. | Photo courtesy of the Center for Artistic Activism. A twenty-four-hour creative action in Skopje, Macedonia, by LGBTQ2S+ and Roma rights organizers.

"Oh, I was a fool before, and now I understand this better." That is not the process that people go through when they change their minds.

REBECCA: We also have a section of each workshop where we talk about the idea of utopia. One thing that happens in the activism and the advocacy world is being reactionary and thinking about the worst possible thing that can happen if we don't take action right now. We think it's critical to spend time imagining the place that we want to get to—utopia. We might not get to that state, but we need to collectively share that vision to be able to start on the same path. We have them think about very traditional advocacy methods that are often used to get to a goal, such as getting everyone to vote in this country. We ask, "Okay, how do you do that?" We give people fact sheets or white papers or other traditional tools to think about, but then we start to imagine crazy, impossible things. Magical things, like involving aliens or things that involve spending a lot of money. This [sort of thinking] frees people up to the possibilities of surprising and innovative tactics.

In the last twenty-four hours of the workshop, they're actually choosing a specific objective and brainstorming tactics around that, then working together to implement an actual artistic action to occur in public. An important part of our work is reflection and self-evaluation.

STEVE: The other thing about the quick action is that it forces the timeline. Most activists would plan an action six weeks ahead. If we say, "We're going to do it tomorrow," they're just like, "No, we can't. It's impossible!" Together artists and activists can make something pretty good very fast, and then learn from the process. It doesn't have to be perfect the first time. You can rehearse, then build on it.

LEANNE: Do you have any favorite projects or moments from over the years?

STEPHEN: My all-time favorite project was the first time we worked in North Macedonia with LGBTQ2S+ organizers and Roma rights organizers. At that time Macedonia was run by a right-wing nationalist government, and it was ranked the second-worst place to be queer in all of Europe, Russia being number one. These were people whose center was literally firebombed the year before. Roma were treated like the absolute bottom of society, and their government was complicit.

We decided to do our twenty-four-hour action. The first ideas they came up with were understandably ne'er-do-well, along the lines of "People have been saying f*ck you to us, so we're going to say f*ck you back to them, right?" It's pretty natural to react that way, but in many ways, that reaction played straight into the narrative of the right-wing nationalists about these people, which is that they're not Macedonians, they're outsiders.

We asked them to think about a different way to approach this problem, and they came up with this idea: instead of protesting against what they didn't like about Macedonia, they would create a utopian Macedonia for a couple of hours in the middle of a popular public park. And at that time Macedonia was not allowed to call itself Macedonia—it had to be called the Former Yugoslav Republic of Macedonia—and so [the workshop participants] came up with the name "The Future Republic of the Former Republic of Macedonia."

We created a border guard and frontier gate. We had flowers for all of these crazy nationalist statues, and we built our own pedestal for our own statue, where people stood on it and held up signs that read "everyday hero" or "heroine." They would write "teacher" or "lover" or their own name, and they would hold it up to get the Instagram moment. For a couple of hours, there was this incredibly joyful experience. And it was the most well-attended protest that these groups had held in over a decade, partly because people didn't quite understand what they were joining. It just looked like a lot of fun, but they would get a little passport. In that passport, it would have little things like a different seal of Macedonia, altered with a heart in it. When you got to the box on gender, instead of the choices of only male or female, it had a scatter plot. It was a beautiful, playful way of imagining the world that we want to inhabit, as opposed to concentrating on the world that we want to reject.

REBECCA: One of my favorite projects was in Johannesburg in 2017. We were working with a group that was interested in sex workers' rights. There is a lot of violence around sex workers and against women in general in that country, and they wanted to find ways to work against that. After our training session was finished, they identified that there was an opportunity to talk to churchgoers about sex workers' rights because they could talk about the morality of helping less fortunate people, and these are such vulnerable people. Ultimately, they decided to do an action at the most popular bus stop in the middle of Johannesburg. This was a place where people would be coming from church on a Sunday, and they would perform a play.

They didn't just plan a play, they did this wonderfully culturally specific action incorporating dance, and they acted in five languages. There was a theme in the play about casting stones, and at the end of the play, they gave people in the audience their own stones. They had built this beautiful big working scale, and they asked people to put the stones on one of two sides. Do you think that the sex worker in this play should be forgiven?

They created a moment of tension that worked so beautifully. It was astounding; hundreds of people—men, women, and children—had these stones and very solemnly went up and put them all in the "We forgive the sex worker" side of the scale. It went beyond the typical "we're just going to put on a play and raise awareness about the issue" action. They wanted to engage people in a public dialogue around a thing that nobody would talk about. People had to consider the issue in a deep way and publicly proclaim how they felt about it.

LEANNE: What advice would you give someone who has many creative, ambitious ideas, but might not know where to start?

STEVE: One, have a clear, specific outcome in mind. What does it look like? Are you trying to pass a law or change a policy? Are you trying to get a certain amount of press mentions by a certain time? What will move your goal the furthest?

Two, you don't have to do it all on your own. There are people who can work with you. You will be good at some things, and not at others. Our culture has mythologized art as a solo practice, making individual artists into heroes instead of being part of a group of collaborators, influencing each other. You can't do it all on your own, but you can do it all with other people over a longer period of time.

THE CENTER FOR ARTISTIC ACTIVISM *continues to conduct innovative research and training. They share this work broadly through case studies, podcasts, video trainings, papers, and research. Discover a wealth of resources to support your work at* **c4aa.org**.

GUERRILLA PROJECTS

Guerrilla projects have their own rhythm. If your project is going to break the rules, only you can accurately assess how far you will go to make your project a success. A few tips:

- Do you need to be covert? If so, you may need to set up or stage your work under the cover of darkness or in the early hours of dawn.
- Do you care if someone catches you in the act, or is it vital to remain anonymous? Disguises may be in order.
- How long do you need to set up without being detected? You may need a couple of extra hands to help you set up quickly.
- Is your setup elaborate? How can your installation happen stealthily over a couple of days? For example, can you paint a wall ahead of time and stencil over it later?
- Do things need to be installed quickly? Can you create your whole work on something like a flatbed truck, then quickly place it where it needs to be? Or can you make it somewhere nearby, like a garage, and bring it over carefully?
- If you get discovered, what is your plan? Are you going to pack it all in, or will you continue?

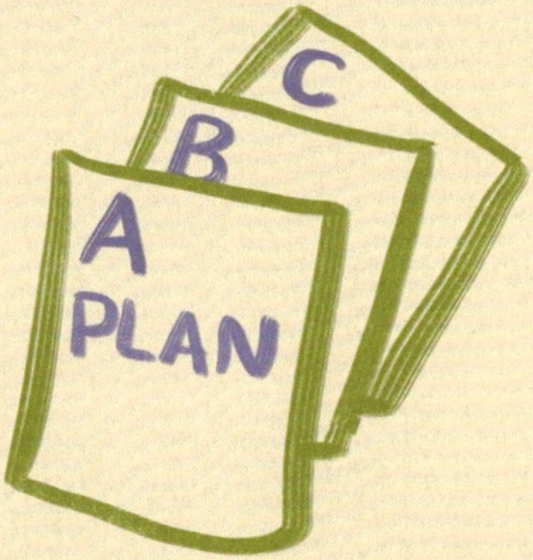

In the early days of the yarn bombing movement in my city of Vancouver, British Columbia, I could install work in the city proper quite easily. Most people saw that it was yarn and either ignored me or stopped to chat. I received positive emails in response to blog posts on the topic from city councillors and even urban graffiti removal services, so I never worried about my identity or safety. On the flip side, another yarn bomber that I knew in Berkeley, California, which has a reputation of being a liberal bastion, received warnings about fines and needed to conceal her identity. Only you can make a proper risk assessment about the customs, rules, and attitudes where you live and how you will navigate them.

One of the added challenges of unsanctioned art is, of course, that you may end up dealing with authorities whether in the form of law enforcement, security guards, nosy neighbors, lifeguards, or parking attendants. It is up to you and your coconspirators to plan what you want to do if caught. Ensure that there is a consensus among your group about what you will do. Will you continue and risk legal action or restraint, or will you quickly accept any feedback and pack up and go? I'm not going to advise whether you should go so far as to get a criminal record for your creative statements. Still, I ask you to go into all projects with full awareness of any long-term consequences.

Authorities do not treat everyone equally. If you have never thought about this before, take the time to learn that you cannot assume one group member's experience will be the same as another's, or that everyone can afford to take a risk. Have a frank conversation about everyone's expectations. Ask: Is this unsafe for you? Do you have bail money? Do you need to arrange childcare if detained? Does anyone have a criminal record already and therefore need to avoid further charges? Does anyone have a recognizable name that they'd prefer to keep out of the news? Do you know how to contact each other's families or roommates? The more you know about each other, the more you'll be prepared if anything should happen.

Creepers Suck

While I hope that everyone participating in your project is there to be part of your designed experience, unfortunately, we live in a world with creeps. If someone is making you or anyone else uncomfortable, you don't need to interact with them. Tell them to leave. Never hesitate to follow your gut and do whatever you need to in order to keep yourself and your coconspirators safe, even if it means temporarily shutting down your project. Call for reinforcements if you need them.

LAUNCH IT ONLINE

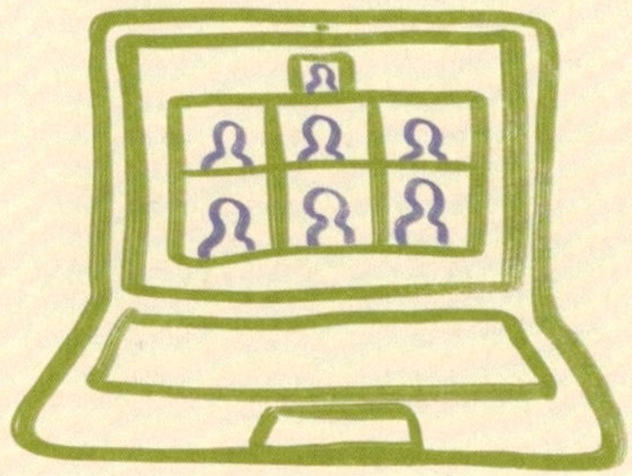

Launching creative projects online poses a different set of challenges. During the beginning of the 2020 global pandemic, artists of all kinds learned quickly to pivot their work online. It was not seamless. Technical difficulties were the norm. Audiences got used to twenty-minute delays while hosts trouble-shooted their microphones and lighting. Zoombombing could mar an innocent event with hate speech, and procedures had to be put into place to protect attendees.

Despite these challenges, the pandemic created new ways for us to connect. Although participatory projects like online art swaps, virtual galleries, and make-alongs have been part of the internet since its origins in the 1990s, the pandemic removed the divide between what could happen on or offline. Virtual presentations of poetry readings, puppet shows, dance performances, and live-action art presentations became normalized in a short time. Social media, particularly video, has added another way to engage with others worldwide, from live video conversations to behind-the-scenes tours.

There is a certain level of polish we've come to expect from the virtual world. Professional social media influencers and marketing companies have mastered glorious lighting, sophisticated filters, and fancy video cameras. If this is your aesthetic and you have the means to execute it, all power to you. If you don't have access to these resources, do the best you can with what you have. The work that you've put into your content will engage people. Things do not need to be perfect to be effective.

There are a few things that you can do to make your online work launch seamlessly:

- If the technology you are using allows you to project a countdown clock for your audience, consider doing so. YouTube and Instagram Live both offer this feature.
- Check your audio. The number one complaint about online media is poor audio quality. You don't want to lose your audience before you even begin!
- Use social media accounts to talk to and engage with your audience.
- Remember, from the moment you turn on the camera, viewers can see you. Be ready to go live.
- Showing up on time matters. Don't make people wait.
- Have everything that you need within arm's reach.
- If things go wrong, don't try to cover it. Be honest; your audience will appreciate it.
- Provide captioning for those who need it. Many video technologies have settings that you can choose to make captioning easy.
- Design ways for your audience to interact with your work. Ask them to participate through comments and questions, using chat functions.
- Remember that online events can be more fatiguing than in-person events. Keep it brief.
- Give your audience somewhere to post their impressions afterwards.

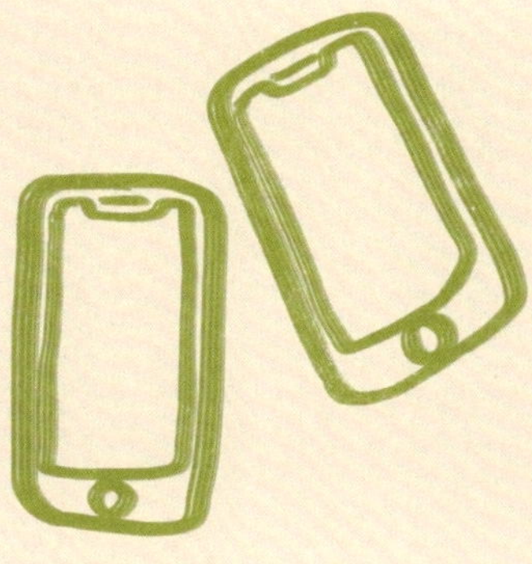

SERVING YOUR AUDIENCE

Often, public projects provide a container for others to present their creative selves to the world. As you interact with the public, you will find that their voices surface in delightful and unexpected ways.

In my early twenties, I worked at a community arts council directed by a dynamic woman named Linda Feil. One of Linda's favorite things to say to her young staff when we took on new responsibilities was "fill your boots," meaning take it all, do it all, do what you need to do. As a public facilitator, that's your role. You have to allow every participant to fill their boots creatively.

With every participatory community project that I've created, there's been someone who goes against the grain. If I've asked for pink crochet, there's been someone who provided purple knitting. If I've asked people to stitch within a two-inch area using a template, someone has gone free-form. If my coconspirator has written a poem on the outside of a cup, someone has written a poem inside the cup. These changes made the project different from what I'd anticipated, but those were the ways that the participants wanted to contribute. Their contributions transformed the works into community projects, and as an organizer, I had to accept that.

WORKING WITH THE PUBLIC

As a creative facilitator who is interacting with the public, there are several things that you will need to do to support those who are creatively participating in your work:

TEACH. As the creative facilitator, you will need to explain how specific tools work (e.g., how to thread a needle, which paintbrush will yield specific results) and demonstrate how they work. Don't assume that everyone will come to your project with the same experience that you have.

DEMONSTRATE. Encourage participants by giving them a few examples of how they might get started. You can show them a few things that you've made in advance, or you can create a live demo for them on the spot.

COACH. As a creative instigator, it is imperative to remember that many who interact with your project are likely not as confident with their skills as you are. They may be apprehensive about participating, or they may experience a crisis of faith while they participate. Remember, anything you say to them can impact their creative confidence. Speak to others as you would wish to be spoken to. Catherine West of the Quarantine Quilt Project (see page 158) loves to uncover hidden talent in her participants. She said, "Invariably when we do a project like this, we find quite a lot of people who have a lot of hidden skills. Sometimes they know they have those skills, and sometimes they don't appreciate how talented they are."

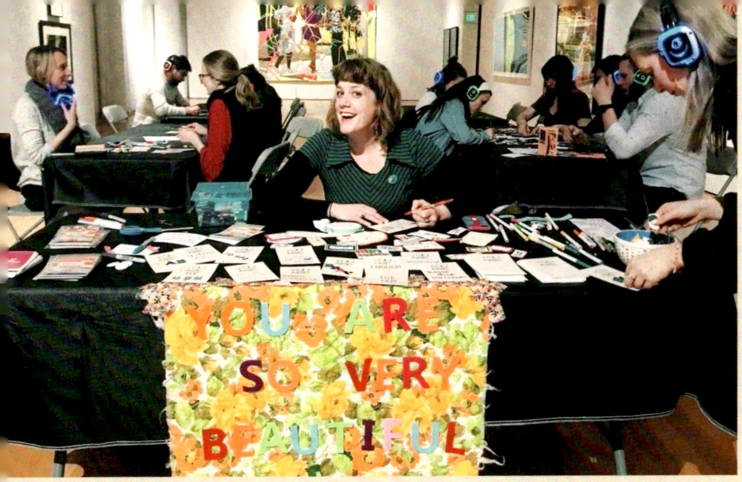

BETSY GREER. | Photo: Rachel Berbic. Replicating You Are So Very Beautiful with postcards at the North Carolina Museum of Art, Raleigh, North Carolina.

RALLY. Once someone has participated in your project, it is a chance to applaud their participation. For on-site projects, find a spot to display the item they have created, read their words aloud, or offer to take a photo of them and their finished work. Acknowledge what they have contributed. Whatever it is, be sure to celebrate the moment and thank them for participating. Everyone, be they young children, seniors, teenagers, or adults, likes to have their work acknowledged.

MANAGE. While I believe that people should be free to play with the materials and ideas that you've provided them, keep an eye out for issues. Some parents can see community artists as free babysitting and will try to leave their children alone with you—tell them that all children must be supervised. Others may add offensive words to your project or see it as an opportunity to grab a handful of free supplies. If you feel that someone is not acting in the project's interests, take a deep breath and explain the project's intent and rules. If their behavior does not change, you are in your rights to ask them to leave. Remember, you are not obligated to take abuse, and as the project host, you set the rules—not only of play, but of engagement.

WHO OWNS WHAT?

One of the more challenging aspects of participatory projects is the concept of ownership. Depending on the scope of your project, you may find that those who have made something want to take it home with them. If you've designed your project for takeaways, fantastic! But if the whole point is to contribute something to a greater piece, this situation can be tricky. There's no one way to handle this issue, but here are a few ways that I've dealt with it in the past:

- Gently remind them of the rules of engagement. Empower participants to tell you where they would like you to place their contribution to the project.
- If you are struggling to get them to see the participatory aspect of your project, allow participants to take their part of the project home. In the case of young children, let it go.
- Create a "take one, leave one" policy. If you have enough supplies, ask participants to make a second piece to gift to the community in addition the one that they're taking home.
- Create a secondary element like a photograph of their contribution or a congratulatory sticker that celebrates their participation. Invent new and novel ways to satisfy participants' need to "own" what they've made.

Big Feelings and Big Attitudes: Am I Still an Artist If I Am Facilitating Other People?

Sometimes when you work with the public, your patience can be tried. You've put a lot of work into developing a gift for people, but maybe not all of them are dazzled. Maybe someone has told you that the idea is bizarre, or maybe you feel like a de facto babysitter. If you've racked up huge student loans getting an art degree or put countless hours into planning this project, then sometimes the work can feel a little defeatist. Expect big feelings to come up sometimes. Yes, you are still an artist when you are facilitating the work of others. The work of participatory or social art is not so well known in society, but it is a skilled discipline in which you are now a practitioner. If you are getting frustrated, take some time out, but remember that you and your work matter.

INTERRUPTIONS ARE TO BE EXPECTED

When you work in public, sometimes you will be informally elected to the role of the community information booth. There's nothing more disconcerting than having someone interrupt you with an unrelated question while you're in the middle of staging your project, holding ten feet of purple fun fur. I've been in this situation countless times, and really, all I can do is slap on a patient grin, help them with what I know, and move on. While there will probably be an underlying irksome feeling of "Can't you see I'm busy here?" ultimately, I choose to recognize that they see me as someone that should be here, a working part of my community. There's something magical in knowing that art can integrate with regular day-to-day life and that your amazing installation is as much as a part of a community as a gas station, grocery store, or beauty salon.

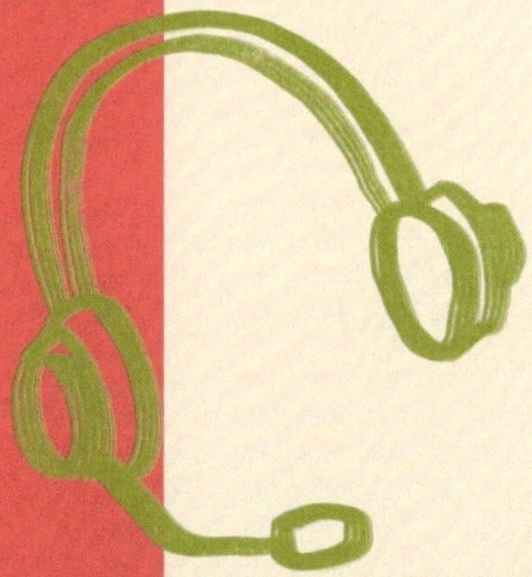

IS IT FREE?

One of the most common questions that I get when working on participatory projects is, "Is it free?" We live in a society where almost everything is monetized to some degree; public art often stands alone in this respect. Your relationship to fees is a personal one that you will need to explore with your coconspirators as you figure out how to make things viable.

If money is keeping you from executing the project, then you've got to ask yourself, "What can I scale back? What can I minimize? What can I let go of to be able to stage this project?"

For many creative people, money is a hard thing to think about. Event and project budgets are plans for any costs associated with your project. A budget allows you to figure out how much money you will need and how you might recoup your costs.

Things that you may need a budget for include:

- art supplies
- space rental
- lighting and/or a lighting artist
- music licensing fees
- font or software licensing fees
- transportation (parking, parking tickets, taxis, public transit)
- electronic equipment (projectors, screens, extensions cords)
- Wi-Fi access and data usage
- refreshments for volunteers or participants
- marketing materials (flyers, digital ads, business cards, takeaways)
- event licenses
- postage costs
- after-party expenses
- thank-you cards or gifts for hosts and volunteers
- honorariums for yourself and your coconspirators

If you are staging your creative project as part of a community festival or neighborhood event, I recommend looking into community grants or other funding from those entities to cover supply costs and artist fees. The lower you can make the barrier to entry for participants, the more likely they are to participate.

If you want to offer the public some options to help you fund your project, you can sell merchandise such as limited-edition project T-shirts or buttons. For both in-person and online projects, implement a donation box or optional paid ticketing. See if your supporters will give a small donation to be part of a patrons list on your website.

You don't have to be a genius to make a budget; think of it as a jar into which an equal amount of money needs to go back in if money goes out. A budget will help you figure out whether an item you want to purchase truly is essential, and you'll know if you need to move on or trim your costs in other areas.

PROMPT

Find the Joiners

Sometimes you do a ton of work to make a participatory project happen, but no one wants to participate. Passersby just skirt your table, one after another, avoiding eye contact. Did you forget to brush your teeth? Is something seriously wrong with the project? No, it is just human nature to be shy about what we don't know or understand.

Some people will be instantly excited, but others will hang back or even pretend they don't see you. I once stitched twenty-three feet of hot-pink eyelash yarn onto a lamppost in the middle of a city street while dozens of people looked the other way.

As the instigator, it is up to you to open the conversation with those who seem interested in participating. Don't forget, you are the host, and it is up to you to make them welcome. Always have a few opening lines, such as:

- "This is a free community art project. We invite you to join us ..."
- "Can I tell you about what we're doing? It's a creative project ..."
- "Do you want to know more? This project is made up of (x amount of materials) and took us (x amount of time) to make."
- Or, if you don't know what else to say, "Can I answer any questions?"

DON'T FORGET TO ENJOY IT

A creative launch can be somewhat like a wedding. Everyone shows up and looks to the smiling hosts for clues about what to do while they wait for the big event to take place. It is a lot of pressure on the host.

One of the pieces of standard advice that wedding planners give couples is to have enough support on hand to enjoy the day and to take some time out for themselves. The same thing should apply to you and your creative projects—if you don't take a moment to pause and reflect on where you are, what you are doing, and who you are impacting, the magic of your project might elude you. Don't let this happen. You deserve a moment (or more!) of joy. Stop and soak it all in. Remember why you started this project in the first place. Making it all come together is a cause for reflection and celebration. You did it!

CHAPTER 9

THE PIVOT: HOW TO DEAL WHEN THE LOVE IS GONE

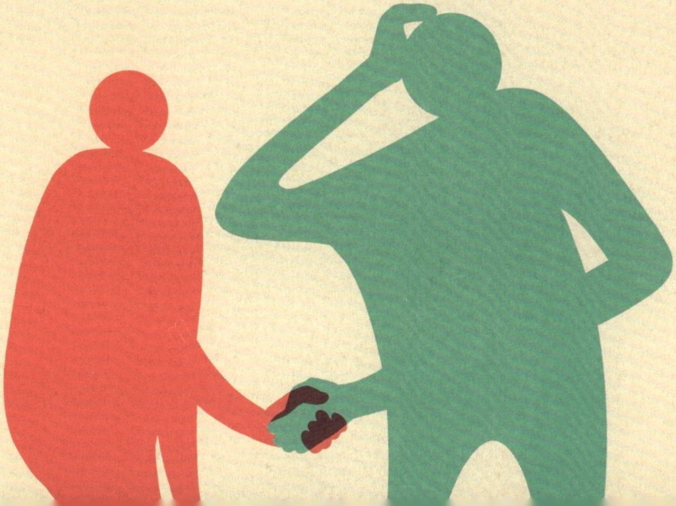

Have you ever had a day when everything went exactly the way that you planned? If so, I'd love to know your secret. No matter how much we prepare, the universe will pitch curveballs at us. Life is not perfect, and neither is art-making. Human beings are not perfect. We get annoyed, hangry, dismissive, heartbroken. Our coconspirators have bad days. Art spaces get sold to developers. Packages of necessary materials get lost. Reality rarely matches our ideal plan.

The hardest part of creative work is that no matter how well you plan, you still don't have complete control. Having strong expectations about the outcome of a project can set you up for disappointment. Instead, I encourage you to think about how you can guide, rather than lead. Think of all your planning as a road map, not the final destination.

As a project leader, you have to be able to navigate challenges. Coconspirators move away. Tools get broken. Funds fall through. The weather doesn't cooperate. Making community-focused work is challenging. You might get tired or sick or disenfranchised, but if you believe in your inherent ability to work through challenges, you'll have all the tools you need.

IF I COULD TURN BACK TIME

If you are struggling to find time to work on your project, you and your collaborators need to steal some time from your obligations. When can you create spare moments in your existing schedule for creative thinking? Use the time you spend waiting in line at the grocery store to text ideas to your coconspirators. Tackle a small goal like a single phone call or one Google search over your lunch break. If you and your coconspirators can't meet face-to-face, set up a video chat. If a video chat isn't convenient, set up a shared Google Doc to trade ideas. Making a constant effort to reconnect with your project several times a week will provide the momentum that you need to keep going.

PROMPT

Check Your Head

When things change beyond your control, here are some questions that will help you clarify your intentions:

- What am I making now?
- Why am I making it?
- Who is this work for?
- Is it still possible to achieve my original goals under the current circumstances, even if the end project does not turn out the way that I anticipated?
- If this doesn't happen, who will I disappoint?

In my experience, if you can honestly answer, "Why are you still making it?" you'll know pretty quickly if your current project still aligns with your values and goals.

When I was a young child, I took painting classes at my local community center. My teacher explained that a "happy accident" (a term coined by landscape painter Bob Ross) is when you make a mistake, such as spilling some paint onto a canvas, that makes the art better by happenstance. Who knows? In the face of frustration, you may find your own happy accident. Work created under challenging circumstances is an opportunity to examine what elements make your project meaningful.

How to Deal With the Things You Can't Control

- Received mean feedback? Go home and scream into a pillow.
- Waiting to hear back from someone? Start a thousand-piece puzzle. Add a few pieces every time you get frustrated.
- Funding disappeared? Play loud cathartic music.
- Broke your favorite tool? Allow yourself a few hours for a serious pity party.
- Your collaborator ghosting you? Wear a sheet over your head and start moaning loudly.
- Venue canceled? Take a tip from the Poetry Society of New York and host a dance party on their doorstep.

If you are truly overwhelmed, don't feel that you have to spend every moment working on your project. Maybe your exhaustion is a sign that your project needs a longer timeline. Perhaps you need to meet with your coconspirators a little less often. As we all learned in 2020–21, sometimes it is completely acceptable to put things on hiatus until everyone is less frazzled.

WHEN MIGHT WE PART WAYS?

Nothing in life lasts forever, and as much as we would like to be lifelong partners in creativity, an exit plan helps things go more smoothly when it is time to leave.

Sometimes the unforeseeable happens—a new baby, a death, a move. Other times, it may be that one or more people feel stagnant and want to try something new, or perhaps greater creative horizons are calling. If it feels like things are headed that way, ask whether the project is just on hold or it has reached a natural conclusion. Someone who's just had a baby may need a hiatus. Someone who is burned out from working on the project may need a permanent end.

BEFORE YOU PART WAYS, GET CLEAR ON A FEW THINGS

- Do the remaining collaborators have the right to continue with the work?
- Who owns the work and the right to use it?
- If future money is earned by the project, how will it be shared or divided?
- Who will maintain, pay for, and own any social media and website domains associated with the project?
- Do the leaving collaborators still want their name on new works?
- Who holds the rental title to shared spaces or music licenses, insurance, or bank accounts? Who has signing authority?

A CONVERSATION ON

The Brooklyn Art Library

CASE STUDY

COLLECTING STORIES

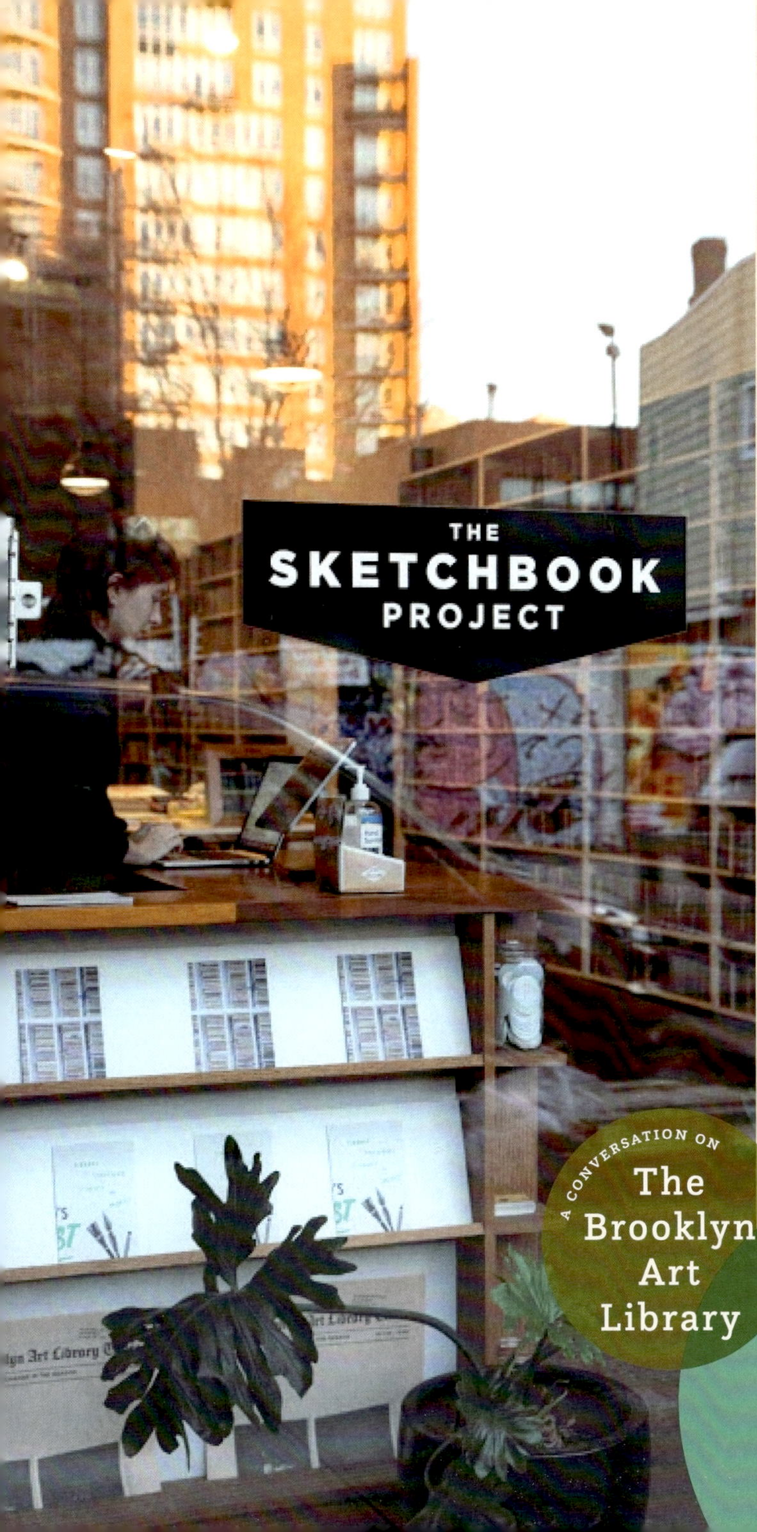

The Sketchbook Project was one of my favorite online participatory projects in the early 2000s. Artists would purchase a sketchbook with the intention of filling it up and sending it back to the project in order to enter a global art exchange. While my intentions to finish a sketchbook did not end up being realized, there is a special place in my creative heart for what the project has grown into. Now called the Brooklyn Art Library, the collection houses the world's largest library of artist sketchbooks. Filled with comics, stories, poems, scrapbooks, ephemera, and other materials, the library documents the international exchange of 50,000 handmade artist journals and art books and now serves as a repository, education space, and storytelling hub. I was inspired to talk to project founder and managing director Steven Peterman about how his project has evolved over fifteen years and about the realities of turning a complex project into a lasting one.

Photo courtesy of the Brooklyn Art Library. The Brooklyn Art Library contains 50,000 sketchbooks made by artists.

LEANNE: I understand that the Sketchbook Project started over a dinner conversation with friends in Chicago. How did you transform that idea into a real project, with over 50,000 sketchbooks from 30,000 contributors and a space, the Brooklyn Art Library?

STEVEN: In 2006, we had an art space, but we were wondering how we could keep our doors open, so we started coming up with different projects. We had the idea of an object, like a canvas or a disposable camera, that could be sent in alone to become part of a bigger project. Eventually, we landed on sketchbooks, and for the first project, we sent out 500 little Moleskine journals, which people would send back to us.

While we were in Chicago for an exhibition, we were brainstorming what would come next. We thought it would be interesting if we could find a way to keep the books in a collection, rather than just to send them back to the artists, where they would sit in a closet. People were putting so much of their lives onto the pages, and we knew that we had something more than just the creation of an object. That's when we started to specifically focus on growing the Sketchbook Project into something bigger.

LEANNE: You've recently launched a podcast of stories from those in your community.

STEVEN: Yes, my favorite part is that this project is a conceptual idea that I've spent my entire adult life doing, but for participants, the Sketchbook Project was like something they discovered in their path, where we met. It's like we walked by each other on the street one day, and then I kept going and kept going. The most gratifying thing for me is to talk to these artists who had an interesting experience in the project and then moved on.

For our podcast, we interviewed this artist, Linda Serrone Rolon, for a Mother's Day blog, because she is a mom and an artist. We showed up at her house in Brooklyn, and she handed us this sketchbook she had never submitted. It was created a few weeks before Hurricane Sandy. She had just bought the house where her grandfather was living. He was really sick, and she was taking care of him, and literally three weeks after they had closed on the house, the entire basement flooded. The flood was one step away from reaching the first floor. All her art that was in her studio was underwater, and she used her sketchbook to record her anger at what was happening. When we randomly reached out to her, she was, like "All right, I finally have to give this sketchbook up." When we showed up to interview her, it was a huge moment for her to just hand the sketchbook over. She had gotten her first book when her son was born, and she wasn't making her art like she used to. She'd realized that she could use the Sketchbook Project every night when she was sitting with her son, waiting for him to fall asleep. Every time we talk to her, she just feels so connected to the project. We're so grateful that we could give someone that outlet, and there are 50,000 different stories like hers.

In 2013, we were sent to Australia for a three-week exhibition at the University of Melbourne. This older woman came up to us and said she had never made artwork in her entire life, but someone had bought her the Sketchbook Project. She did it, and then she was inspired to apply to art school in her sixties. There are so many stories like these that we've heard over the years, and that really is my favorite aspect of the mature part of this project.

I want to share with the world how big the project is. We have so many people, even professional artists, who use the project as the one nonprofessional thing that they create each year. They need an outlet that's just for them, and that's what we provide.

LEANNE: I imagine that you never really know what you're going to get. Unlike social media, with sketchbooks, nothing is driven by an algorithm; you just have this spontaneous collection of intimate stories from around the world.

STEVEN: It may seem kind of silly now, in the world context, but ten years ago when we were getting books, some were from these schoolkids drawing the elephants outside their classroom. It was crazy. We were sitting here in New York, and there were these people in Malaysia recording their everyday lives for us to see. We're obviously so much more globally connected now, but at the time it felt insane.

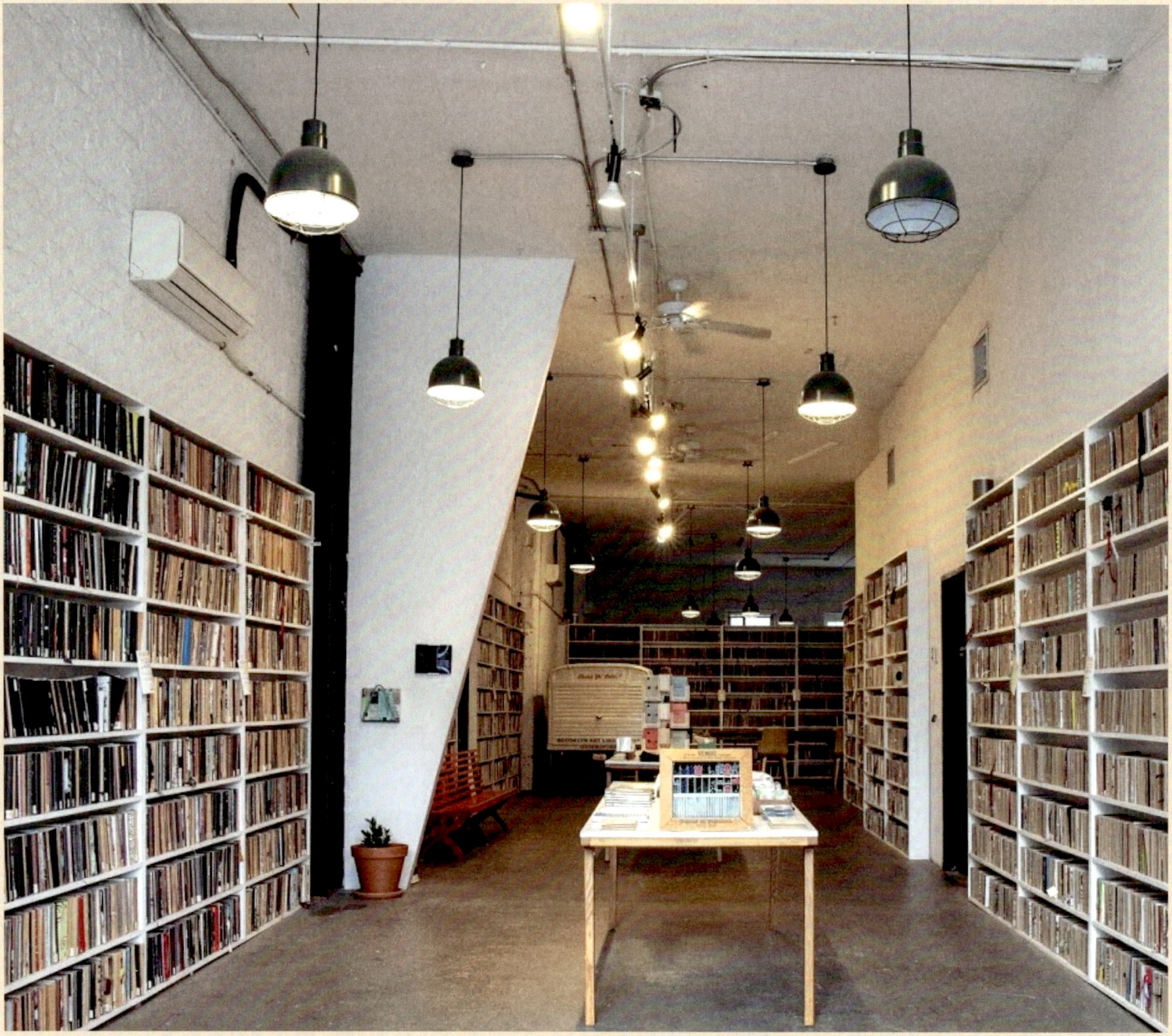

Photo courtesy of the Brooklyn Art Library. The Brooklyn Art Library contains 50,000 sketchbooks made by artists.

LEANNE: In terms of artist-made books and collections, there isn't a ton of digitization of these items in artist-run spaces. Despite the challenges, I imagine you're still very far ahead of many other organizations.

STEVEN: People are so used to how perfect Instagram photos can look that we feel we're visually behind. With advancements in smartphone technology, people can easily see that something doesn't look like the high-definition screens they're used to looking at.

A small fee to support a digitized book becoming part of our website and part of a resource library forever is reasonable. We are really proud that that part of our mission is to ensure you still have that place to help you do that.

LEANNE: You've recently become a nonprofit—can you tell me about that?

STEVEN: Obviously, the project wasn't a profitable business model, but we wanted to maintain our sort of stamp on it, and we needed to find a team that understood where we wanted to go next with programming and podcasting. We want unique things to come out of the nonprofit, rather than just funding art programs. We have given ten different inner-city schools the means to do the Sketchbook Project in our traditional program, but we also want to show that this project is a global one that allows anyone to be creative, and we are making a new podcast to be part of that programming. It took years to find the right people to help us become a nonprofit, and it took years to find the right moment to create the nonprofit.

LEANNE: What do you hope the legacy of the Sketchbook Project and the Brooklyn Art Library will be? You said you'd like the library to last "forever"?

STEVEN: We were the Sketchbook Project for fifteen years, and now we're the Brooklyn Art Library. We have 2 million spreads of artworks. We like to joke that we have just as much artwork as the Metropolitan Museum of Art, so we want to become a viewing platform. After collecting all of these sketchbooks, how do we now share that work? We were always so focused on traveling exhibitions, but that's almost become outdated with the global community and technology. We are now focusing on the online experience—podcasts and storytelling and larger residencies where we partner with museums and send the books there.

LEANNE: You and your wife have truly lived your project for fifteen years. What advice can you give people who want to start their own ambitious projects?

STEVEN: It was a struggle for a long time. Five years ago, things were intense. The project was all on our shoulders, and I didn't have the tools or the people to help me move things forward. It was definitely a struggle, but now we've really found a way to exist in sort of a bigger way than we have been in the past. When I became a father last year, I had to learn to bring other people into the project who loved it as much as I did. We've been lucky to have great staff members over the years. They're like, "We're in this for the rest of our lives."

During the start of the COVID-19 pandemic, we were in survival mode, but now we're at the point where we can be whoever we want. I'm really trying to focus on thinking, "Okay, forget about everything we've done. If someone just handed me this collection of sketchbooks, what would I do with it?" So that's what I'm doing now, and it's really fun. If you believe in what you're doing, you just have to keep adapting.

STEVEN PETERMAN *is the founder and managing director of the Brooklyn Art Library. Founded in 2006, the Brooklyn Art Library is a 501(c)(3) nonprofit organization that has been completely funded by participants since its inception. The organization's mission is to encourage creative storytelling within a global community by keeping a physical library space free and open to the public, as well as a digital library accessible worldwide. It also works to make the collection as accessible as possible to people of all ages and skill levels through robust education programming.* **brooklynartlibrary.org**

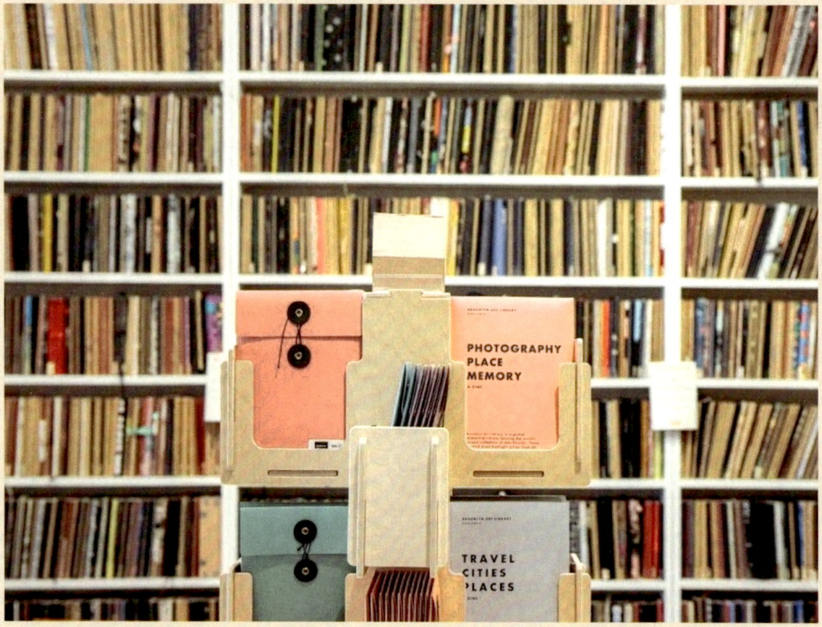

Photo courtesy of the Brooklyn Art Library. The Brooklyn Art Library contains 50,000 sketchbooks made by artists.

TRUST FALLS: NAME THAT FRUSTRATION

Creative collaboration is a relationship, and all relationships have their twists and turns. If things stop feeling good, take a hard look at what might be going on. Even when things get weird, you should be able to have conversations with your coconspirators. The more transparent you can be about your needs, the easier it will be to navigate challenges together. You can stew and resent them, or you can ask, "What the heck is going on?" Often this is enough to realign the project's goals; otherwise it will be a chance for you to cut ties and start anew with other coconspirators.

While I hope that every creative relationship you have is an amazing one, it's true that sometimes things fizzle out. If things don't feel right, look at what might be going on with your collaborators. It could be one of the following issues:

A ONE-SIDED RELATIONSHIP. You might have started this collaboration as a partnership, but it has become pretty apparent that you are the only one doing the work. Often this scenario starts with one person taking on a little bit more, and then more, until they realize that they are the only one who is contributing. If this is your situation, get curious. Is a collaborator struggling with a significant life event? Do they think that you should be doing more at this stage because you have specific talents in a given area?

SCENESTERS. Creative projects can be sexy. Everyone wants to be involved in a cool mural or an amazing art party and be part of the scene, but if their motivation is to be involved in the optics only, the project will not last. Cut ties as soon as you can. You want to work with people who are invested in the impact that your project can create.

GIMME ATTENTION. When the media comes calling, things can get weird. If you are working in a group or a partnership, you may start to notice that some people like to be in the spotlight, while others shy away from it. Even if media attention is not your goal, if you are doing something that impacts your community, you will likely be contacted by the media. Have these conversations up front and elect who will step up to the mic. Don't let one person take all of the credit. If you have a spokesperson, everything they say should be reflective of your whole team.

DIFFERENT POLITICS. You might get into the thick of a project and realize that while you are rallying around the same cause, you and your collaborators have radically different viewpoints, visions, or even personal politics. While art is a space for healthy conversation, I would encourage you to go back to your original mission for the project and determine whether you can still achieve your objectives.

WHO IS PAYING FOR ALL THIS? Money can destroy relationships. There's nothing worse than discovering that you can't access a bank account or that your coconspirator didn't reimburse you for the supplies that you bought before they took half of the artist fee. Make sure that you have conversations about money and reimbursements before finances become an issue.

CHANGING SCOPE. In the thick of a project, demands can change. External partners may invite you to bring your project to a festival. You might be asked to tour. A new venue might present itself. Before your project attracts outside attention, there should be a mutual understanding of what each group member can handle. If there is an opportunity to grow, are all coconspirators comfortable with supporting a more extensive project? Who will drop out, and who will continue? When will you say no? Nobody wants more in their life than they can handle.

THE EGO HAS LANDED. Creative people love to brainstorm, but ultimately, ideas must be executed. In group settings, leadership is usually assumed by the person who exceeds at setting big-picture goals for the team. Leadership should provide support and direction when things get tough. Be directive and encouraging, never dismissive, abusive, or belittling. If your leader is not acting in the best interests of the group's long-term health, revolt against the dictator or bring in someone to help facilitate a conversation.

Artist and designer Courtney Dailey described how the Projet Mobilivre-Bookmobile Project collective handled group challenges. She said, "A lot of us had activist backgrounds, so the notion of a nonhierarchical collaborative project was something that we were invested in. Consensus and collective decision making were important to hold up, and doing so was rarely pretty. When we faced bigger disagreements, we would facilitate conversations and sometimes even bring in an outside facilitator for those conversations that faced an impasse. It was helpful to realize that we needed help when we couldn't figure things out as a group. We knew the value of having someone who could be impartial in those conversations to help us move forward."

ALL THE FEELS: COMMENTARY VERSUS CRITIQUE

When your work gains an audience, you will receive feedback (or critique), and you will need to sort out what is constructive critique versus commentary. As creatives, we desire compliments that validate our objectives, but it is essential to remember that not all commentary is critique. You get to decide how to receive feedback and whether doing so has merit for your project.

Here are some examples of commentary:

- I don't like blue because it reminds me of rain.
- Your hair is dumb.
- This is so pretty!
- I had so much fun today.

Separate from commentary, critique is the act of examining something to determine and suggest what may make it more effective. Critique aims to point out our blind spots and serves to place work within an artistic conversation. A strong critique may ask you to examine the weak points of your project. Here are some examples:

- Did you choose the most effective way to reach your audience?
- Does your project exclude people? Why?
- Does this project speak to this current moment in time and to current politics?
- Have your misappropriated[3] something that you should not have? What can you learn about appropriation so you don't do it again? How can you right this wrong?
- How could you do this in a different setting that would encourage more people to interact with your project?

Even if you have experienced critiques in classroom settings and developed a thick skin for receiving feedback, a critique can still be challenging to hear. You've worked hard on your project, but the person who is giving the critique has not seen all the invisible work you've put in. They do not see your struggles or your triumphs. They see only the result.

Critique is something that all creative people should practice giving and receiving. At a certain point, you will want to invite trusted people to critique your work. A good critique will help you grow and refine your skills. If you work in the public realm, formal critiques may not occur; you will need to seek them out from trusted allies and experts.

When you work with the public, it helps to develop the ability to hold space for each participant. Listen deeply to the information that they share with you. Ask yourself, "What is their goal with this feedback? Can I learn something here? Is this feedback rooted in making my project even better in a realistic way?" If you repeatedly hear the same feedback from public participants or notice an unexpected pattern of behavior in participants, it is time to pay attention. Evaluate what this information says about your project. Do you need to make changes?

3 Appropriation is the act of taking something that doesn't belong to you. Cultural appropriation is adopting an element of a culture or identity that is not your own, and it is an act that disrespects, fetishizes, or desecrates that culture. Cultural appropriation can happen when a more dominant culture uses the artifacts, dances, clothing, signs and symbols, languages, music, food, or religious symbols of a minority culture. Cultural appropriation can negatively impact the collective intellectual property rights of minority cultures and the cultural preservation of oral cultures. The guide *Think before You Appropriate: Things to Know and Questions to Ask in Order to Avoid Misappropriating Indigenous Cultures* (Intellectual Property Issues in Cultural Heritage Project, Simon Fraser University, 2015) is an excellent primer on cultural appropriation for artists and designers. I recommend that all artists read it before engaging in work that may intersect with cultures that are not their own. *sfu.ca/ipinch/resources/teaching-resources/think-before-you-appropriate/*

If your project has a large number of collaborators, each of you may be experiencing these reactions in different ways. Some of us have greater creative self-confidence than others. Cover for each other, listen to each other, and be each other's champions.

BE KIND, REWIND: TAKE A BREAK IF YOU NEED TO

As hard as we work to make things happen, sometimes we do need to take a break. When your heart and mind are exhausted, or if you feel like you're working far harder than you should have to, you likely need to put things on pause. A break is not a failure. A break is a choice to stop doing what is not working and focus on finding a way forward. There will be projects where you know that the only right thing to do is to walk away.

If you have come to a point where you know you are better off stepping away from your project than continuing it, it is time to reconnect with your coconspirators and have the following discussions:

1. Is the feeling mutual among all parties? Do a few folks want to drop out while everyone else keeps on going? Is it okay for others to keep going after some of the original cast and crew have dropped out?
2. How will you communicate changes to your external partners and friends?
3. Will you be putting things on hold indefinitely?
4. If the break is for a defined amount of time, when will you revisit this decision? I recommend choosing a date for everyone to come back and check in with one another.
5. Who owns the assets that belong to the project, and what is the plan for these materials?

No matter what decision you come to, make sure you feel comfortable with it. If one person asks for a break, others will likely want the same thing. Don't take it personally; as time goes on, needs can change. If you are the last person standing, explore whether you want to keep it going with new coconspirators or it's time to retire the project.

If you choose to walk away, don't forget that you will have many new ideas and projects in your future. Don't forget to keep the lines of communication open with your collaborators. You might not reconnect on this project, but you've likely built some great memories and friendships. Often the time we spend producing one creative project is but a single moment in a lifetime of incredible collaborations.

A CONVERSATION ON

The Heidelberg Project

CASE STUDY

FINDING THE BEAUTY IN THE BROKEN

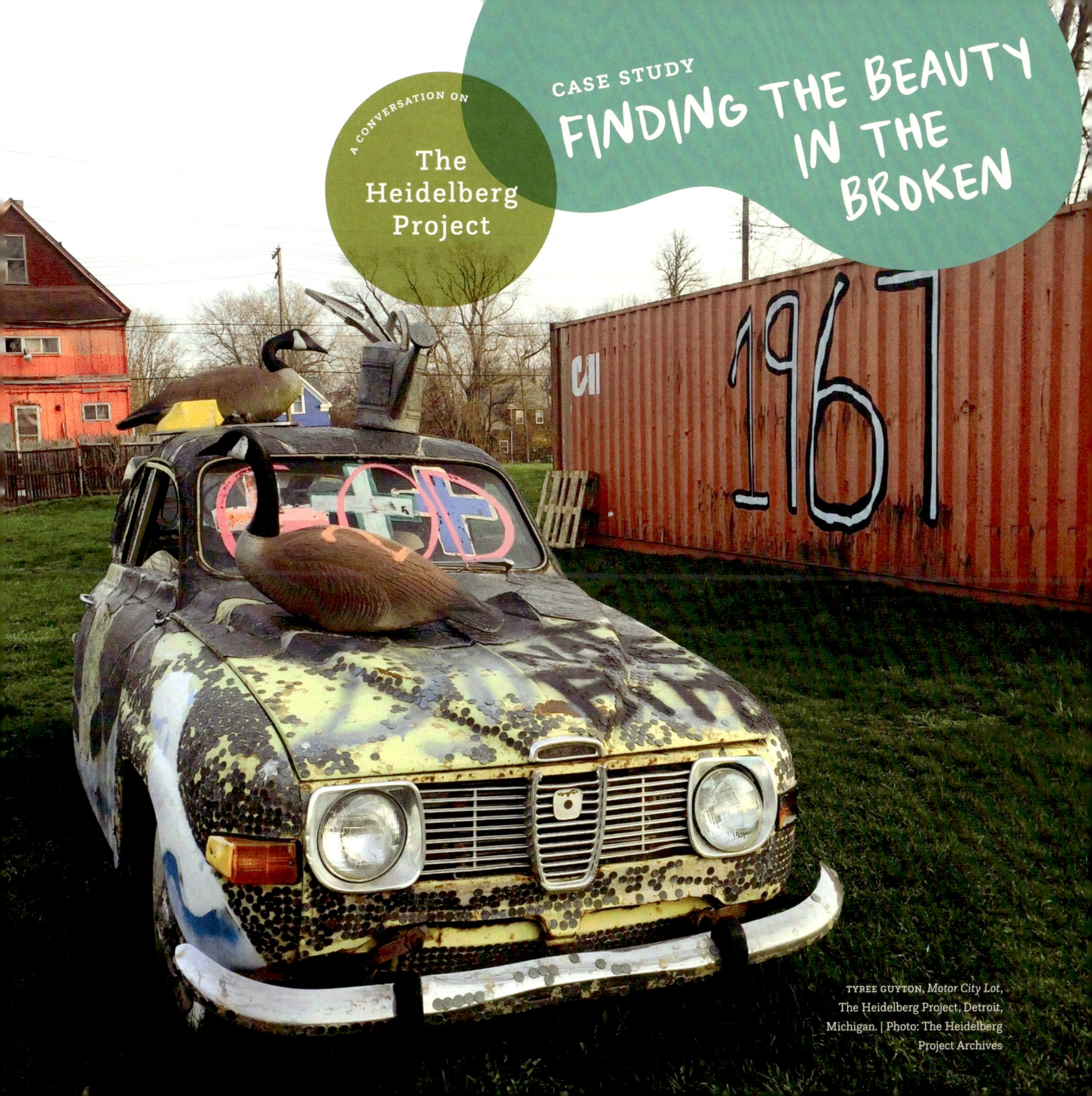

TYREE GUYTON, *Motor City Lot*, The Heidelberg Project, Detroit, Michigan. | Photo: The Heidelberg Project Archives

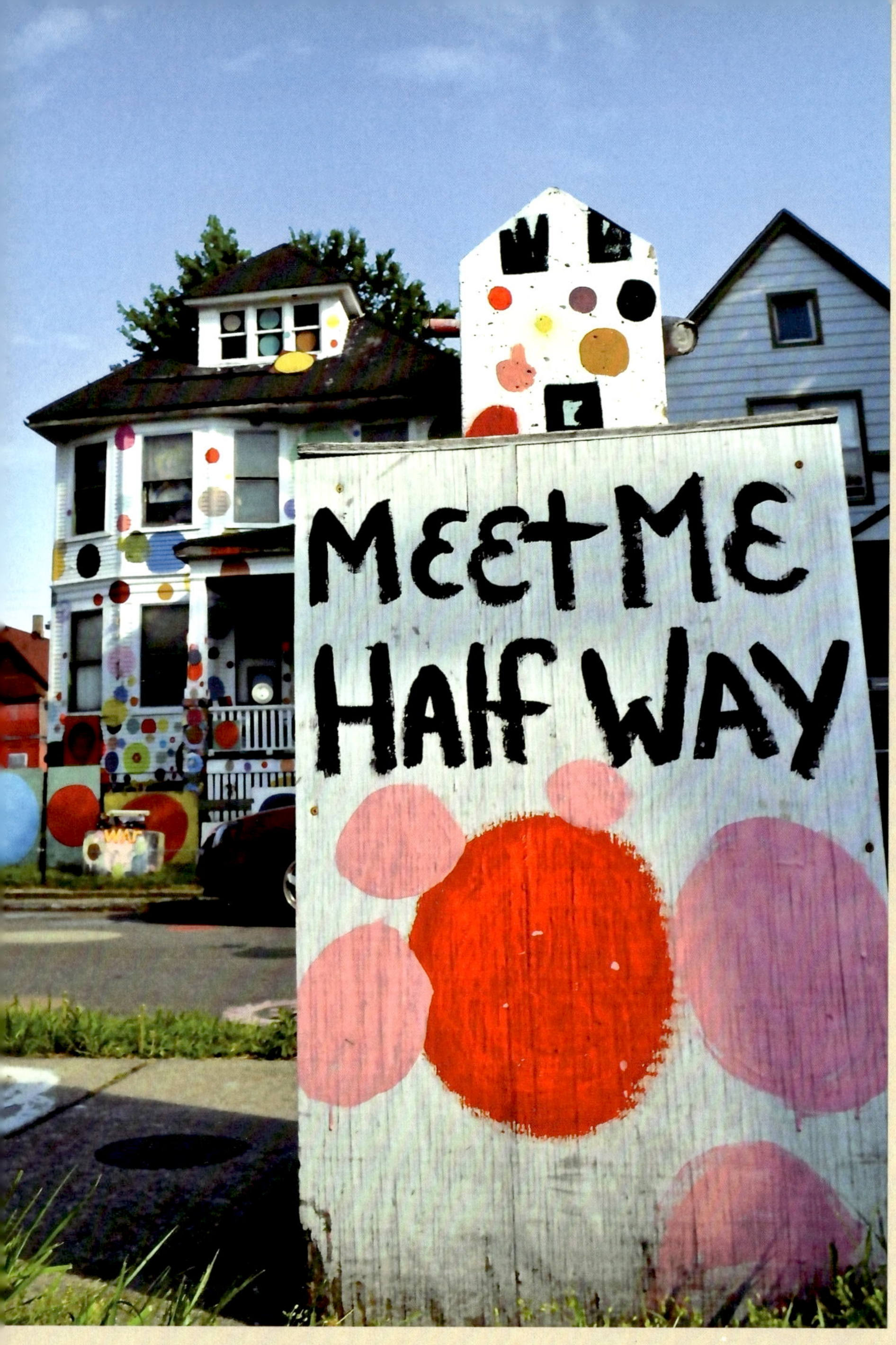

TYREE GUYTON, *Meet Me Halfway*, The Heidelberg Project, Detroit, Michigan. | Photo: The Heidelberg Project Archives

The first time I saw an image of a wood-trimmed house festooned with enormous polka dots as part of the Heidelberg Project, I thought, "I want to do that." For over thirty-five years, the world-renowned project has lived in the heart of Detroit's east side. Recognized as one of the most impactful outdoor art environments in the world, the Heidelberg Project connects local citizens through art while inviting the admiration of visitors from around the world. Created by artist Tyree Guyton, this delightful and continually evolving artistic streetscape sustains his neighborhood as a living art gallery. The following is an interview between Tyree and Jenenne Whitfield, president and CEO of the Heidelberg Project.

JENENNE: Can you tell me a little bit about your journey as an artist?

TYREE: By the age of nine I knew I wanted to be an artist. My grandfather gave me a paintbrush, and it was like magic. My hand felt like it was on fire. I went to art school, but I was told that I didn't fit in. Looking back, it was the best thing that institution could have done for me. After getting over the shock of being told I didn't fit in, I had to find a true magic that was inside of me. That same institution, the College for Creative Studies, gave me an honorary Doctor of Fine Arts in 2009.

JENENNE: Why do you use found objects in your work?

TYREE: Most people say that ugly is as bad as broken, but I see the beauty in the brokenness. I came up in a neighborhood that, even today, is still broken. In a sense, the neighborhood is a reflection of the people. You get broken people in a broken neighborhood. You've got a broken world, but at the same time, it's perfect. It came to me that I could give the broken new life. When I was a kid, I would walk up and down the alleys collecting things. There was something about taking those broken pieces and gluing them together and painting on them to make them say something else. There was something very magical about broken Popsicle sticks. What people would call trash became treasures to me.

I live in a section of the city of Detroit that is considered a very dangerous place. But in my case, I was able to see the beauty, and that's why I created the Heidelberg Project. The neighborhood was broken, and I said, "I'm going to come here and do something." The whole world comes here to see my art, and they have to drive through the brokenness to see the Heidelberg Project.

JENENNE: I think this is natural for you, because you've been doing it for a very long time, and you're very prolific. You're always creating. You create on toilet paper. You create on napkins. You create on Post-it notes. You create

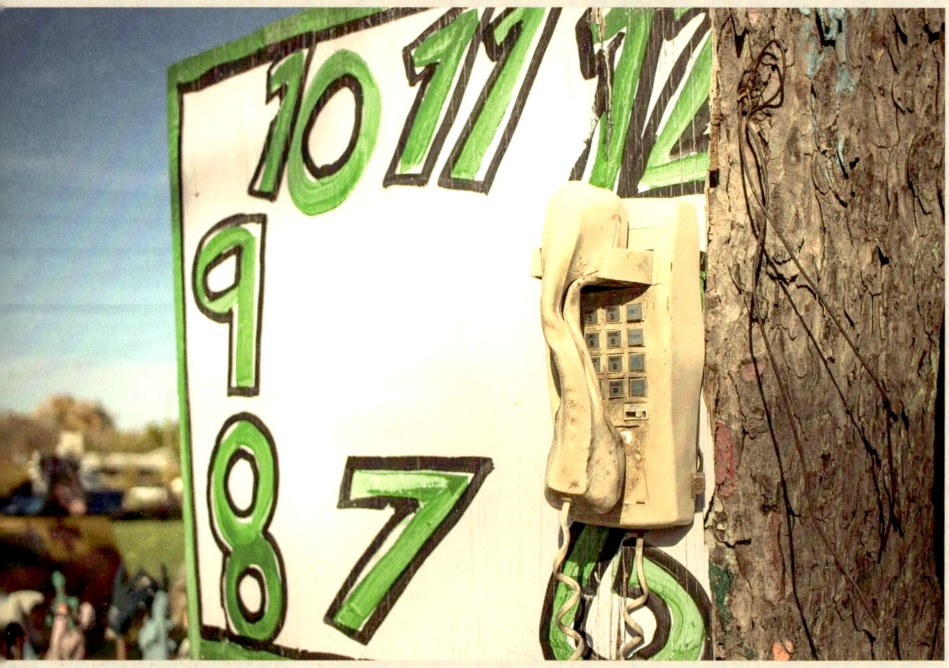

LEFT: TYREE GUYTON, *Detail of Clock Series*, The Heidelberg Project, Detroit, Michigan. | Photo: The Heidelberg Project Archives

RIGHT: TYREE GUYTON, *The Holy Place*, The Heidelberg Project, Detroit, Michigan. | Photo: The Heidelberg Project Archives

everywhere, and that has become part of your process. I've seen projects on pieces of paper that become large works or installations. Art is almost like eating for you.

During the life of the Heidelberg Project, you've had to fight for its survival many times, and you've dealt with huge challenges such as arson and obstruction by the city of Detroit. How do you maintain your creativity while dealing with those who don't understand your work or your intentions?

TYREE: In your mind and your intellect, when life knocks you down, you have two choices: stay there or get up. In my case, every time I have dealt with something like fires or vandalism or city government, a voice inside of me said, "Make it greater every time." In neighborhoods like the one the Heidelberg Project is in, and around this country, our African American neighborhoods—they're broken. For the most part, people are broken, and they are looking for something. When people are in the ups and downs of life, bureaucratic systems come and knock you down. You have to have something you can trust that's going to pick you up.

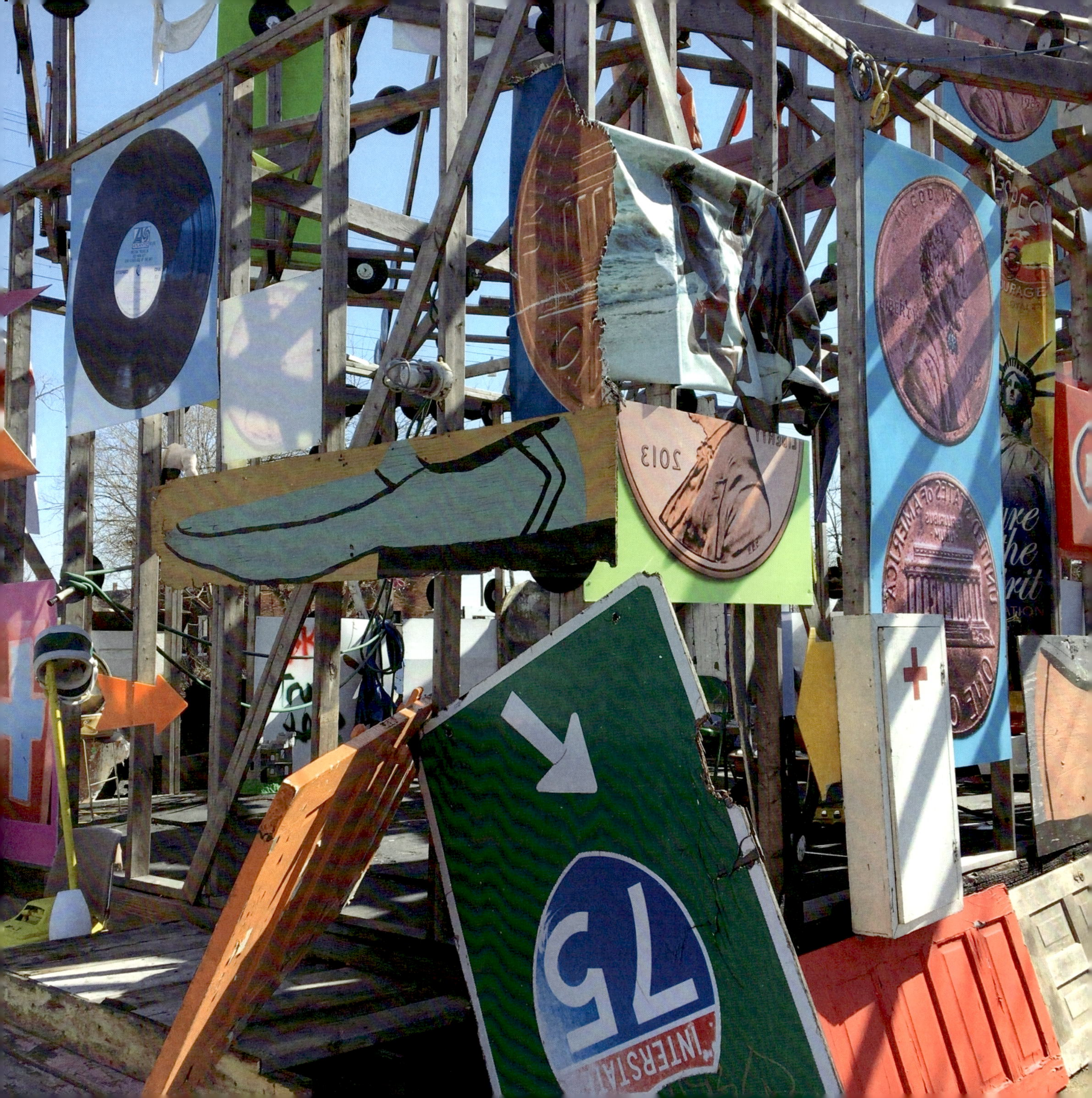

BELOW: TYREE GUYTON, *Noah's Ark*, The Heidelberg Project, Detroit, Michigan. | Photo: The Heidelberg Project Archives

RIGHT: Photo: Geronimo Patton. Tyree Guyton at work.

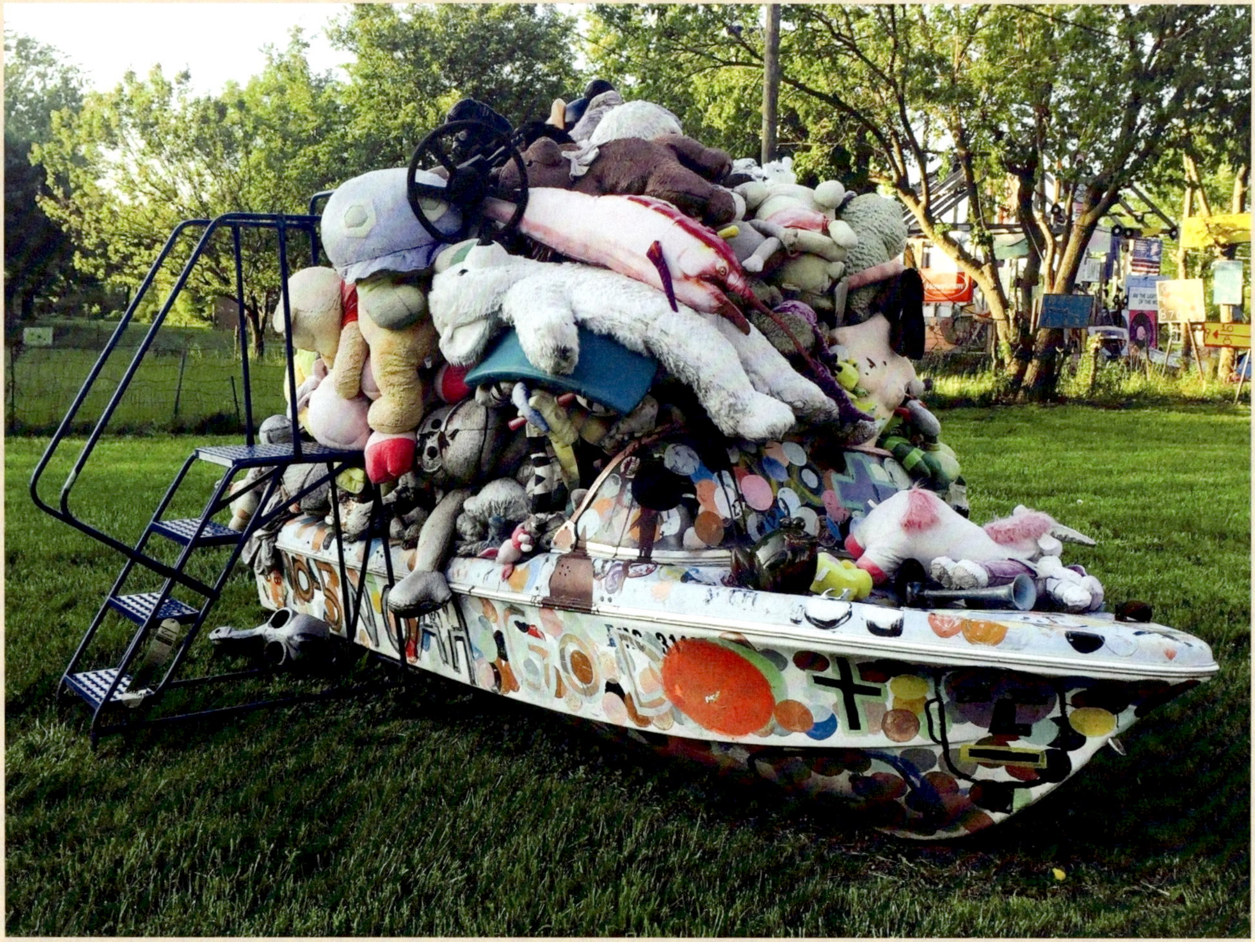

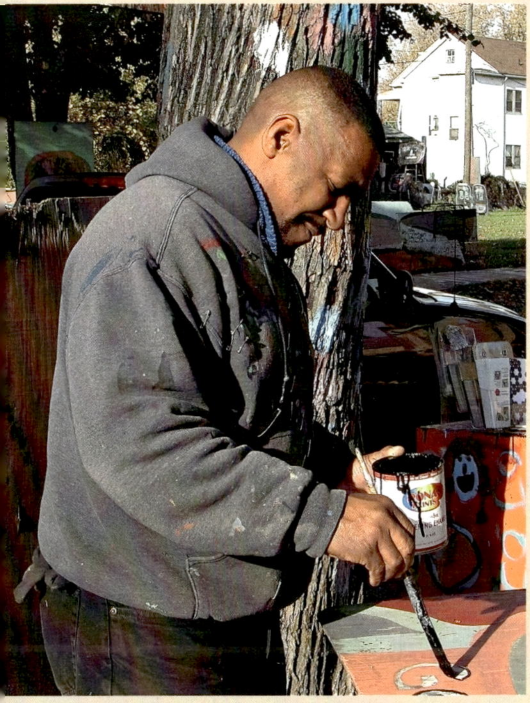

JENENNE: What would you say to other artists who find their work misunderstood?

TYREE: I would say that they have to flip the script and understand: when people say that something is no good, know inside that it is good. You need some opposition. You've first got to know what's good to you. I'm at a point where I don't need somebody to validate my work. I trust me. It takes time to love your work. It takes time to know bad stuff. And it takes time to reach a point where you know how to push the fear aside. The process is like a roller coaster taking you all around and upside down, and you're screaming like a girl, but you have a good time.

JENENNE: Is there a favorite memory from the thirty-plus-year legacy of the Heidelberg Project that stands out for you?

TYREE: I have so many stories. Every day is like a new story. Three years ago, it was a beautiful day—the weather was just right. I was working on the Heidelberg Project, and a white station wagon drove down the street. I noticed it because it was old, like a 1965, but clean and beautiful.

After the lady driving parked the vehicle, she went around to the passenger side and opened the door. She grabbed the hand of a young man to assist him in getting out of the vehicle. I noticed the accent glasses, and then a cane. It came to me that he was blind. They went westbound down the street, crossed over at the end of the block, and came down back down the other side of the street to where I was standing. I noticed that as she was taking him down the street, she was talking in his ear. I met them. And that young man said to me, "I can see it."

JENENNE: Beautiful. The city of Detroit has been through many changes over the last thirty years, and the Heidelberg project has evolved with it. What is your hope for the future of the project?

TYREE: Change is inevitable. I'm taking part of the Heidelberg Project apart. I've received an honorary doctorate for the work I've done on the project, and it has been a case study of everything I wanted to learn. After thirty-five years, I'm so excited about life, to the point that I'm turning the Heidelberg Project over to [Jenenne Whitfield] and a new group of folks under [her] leadership.

If some catastrophe came in and took the project away, the legacy would live on in the minds of visitors and people all around the world. The legacy of institutions and scholars that have followed this project is incredible. The ups and downs of fighting with city government but hanging in there because I see something—this was worth fighting for. If I had to do it over again, would I change anything? No. Everything that I've gone through over these last thirty-five years has been worth it.

Primarily a painter and sculptor, **TYREE GUYTON** *has also been described as an urban environmental artist. Tyree studied at the College for Creative Studies in Detroit, and in 2009 was awarded an honorary Doctor of Fine Arts. He exhibits his work extensively throughout the United States and the world. Tyree's art is featured in the Detroit Institute of Arts, the University of Michigan Museum of Art, the Studio Museum in Harlem, and many others. His work as an artist has earned him over eighteen awards locally and nationally. Tyree has also been featured in major publications, books, and television (including* The Oprah Winfrey Show*) and was the subject of the Emmy Award–winning documentary* Come Unto Me: The Faces of Tyree Guyton *and the book* Connecting the Dots: Tyree Guyton's Heidelberg Project *(WSU Press, 2007), a 2008 Michigan Notable Book.* **tyreeguyton.com**

JENENNE WHITFIELD *is the president and CEO of the Heidelberg Project. Since assuming the role, she has written her first children's book,* Yeret Nutyog, *inspired by the real adventures of Tyree Guyton. In her role at the Heidelberg Project, she supports site-specific tours, arts camps, virtual programming, and arts initiatives such as the Heidelberg Arts Leadership Academy (HALA), which is a free arts education program designed to empower students with the tools they need to become active change agents in their community.* **heidelberg.org**

CHAPTER 10

CELEBRATE IT! MEMORIALIZE YOUR PROJECT

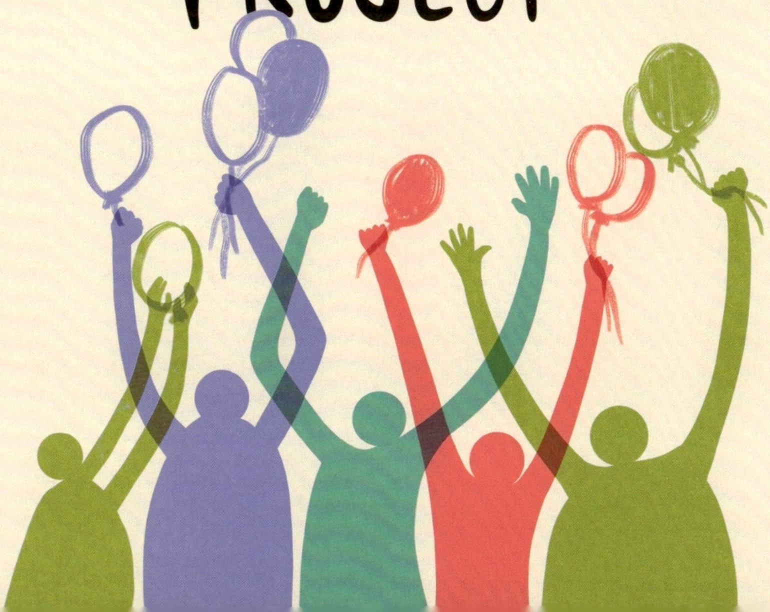

Art shows. Book launches. Opening night. Cast parties. Members-only salons. Curtain calls. A standing ovation! We need to celebrate our creative projects. As author Loretta LaRoche once quipped, “Life is short—wear your party pants!”

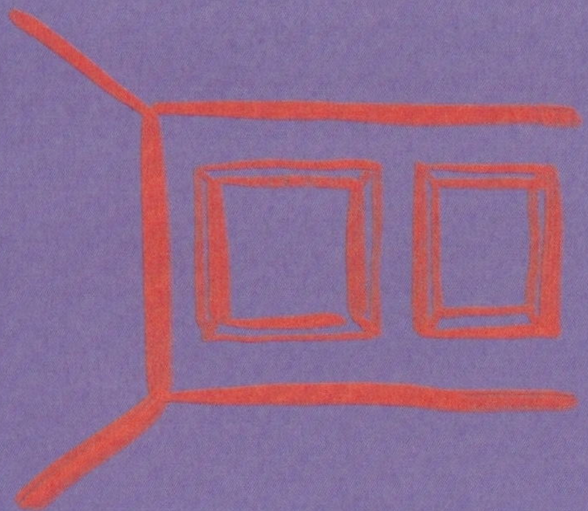

There is no right or wrong way to celebrate your project, as long as you do take the time to celebrate. Don't miss this critical milestone. Recognize the hard work that you've put into executing what once seemed impossible. We tend to be constantly moving on to the next thing in life, but I believe an artistic act is not complete until you've taken a few steps back to savor it. It might not be exactly what you had expected, but it is yours, in whatever incarnation it appears. You deserve to share your accomplishments with those who have been there with you along the way.

While cake and balloons are always enjoyable, why not celebrate in a way that reflects your project? For example, if you are a graffiti artist who works covertly, the best celebration might be a drawing party in a kitchen. If you are a community organizer who created a large quilt with a global community of contributors, a virtual thank-you party might be the best way to reach out to all those who helped make the project a success. Find a celebration that reflects you and what you have achieved.

NINETY-NINE RED BALLOONS

Find a meaningful way to celebrate the finale of your project. Here are some suggestions:

- Engage a musical friend to sing a song about the trials and tribulations of the project.
- Create an online gallery of photos, quotes, videos.
- Host a public dance party or a sing-along at the site of your participatory project.
- Make party hats out of leftover project materials.
- Order a cake decorated with an edible laser print of a photo of your project. Serve cake to your coconspirators and/or the public.
- Gather people for a revelatory parade.
- Host a "write-in" party with your fellow organizers to send thank-you cards to everyone who helped out.

TRY THIS

Picture This

Plan the most outlandish, ruckus-filled celebration that you can think of. Close your eyes and picture it:

- What are you wearing?
- Who is in the room?
- What's on the menu?
- Where are you?

If you can dream it, you can make it happen. Sketch and write down your ideal celebration. The very act of putting it down on paper will bring you closer to making it happen.

- Hang images of your project from a lamppost or a tree.
- Take inspiration from Burning Man and host a public bonfire of your temporary installation.
- Make a podcast celebrating the different voices of contributors.
- Make a plaque (order a fancy one, or make one out of bristol board, or sketch it on a child's blackboard) including the names of all the people who supported you and install it at the scene of the crime.
- Host a public gifting and present various parts of your artwork to the public.
- Write about your artistic process on the walls of the party space.
- Buy some strange knickknacks from a thrift store, paint them all one uniform color, and gift them to your coconspirators as "awards of artistic excellence" for work well done.
- Make a piñata in a shape that reflects your project, then fill it with items that mean something to those who contributed.
- Host a potluck at your project site.
- Plan a treasure hunt.
- Find a new vantage point to view your project from—a hill, bridge, or rooftop—and toast it from afar.

LOVE YOU, MEAN IT: SHOW PEOPLE THAT YOU VALUE THEM

Show your coconspirators how important they are to you. Those who support your creative ambitions deserve special praise, and they also deserve your equal support in the things they make. What can you do to give back to them?

PRAISE. Give your coconspirators praise—publicly, loudly, and even when they are not asking for it.

REFERRALS. When you can, always take a minute to recommend and refer your coconspirators, contributors, and other volunteers for opportunities. Help them to find their own dream projects.

PATRONAGE. Go out and experience the work that your coconspirators make with other people. Buy tickets to their presentations. Attend their opening nights. Be loud and enthusiastic in your reviews.

LEND A HAND. If you genuinely want to give back to those who have helped you, ask them what you can do on their next creative project. Can you pick up a paintbrush or deliver some supplies? Can you help them write a grant application or a mission statement? Offer help where you can.

Building and maintaining bonds with the people you create work with is vital. You may even develop lifelong partnerships.

CASE STUDY

ART ON THE MOVE

A CONVERSATION ON

The Projet Mobilivre-Bookmobile Project

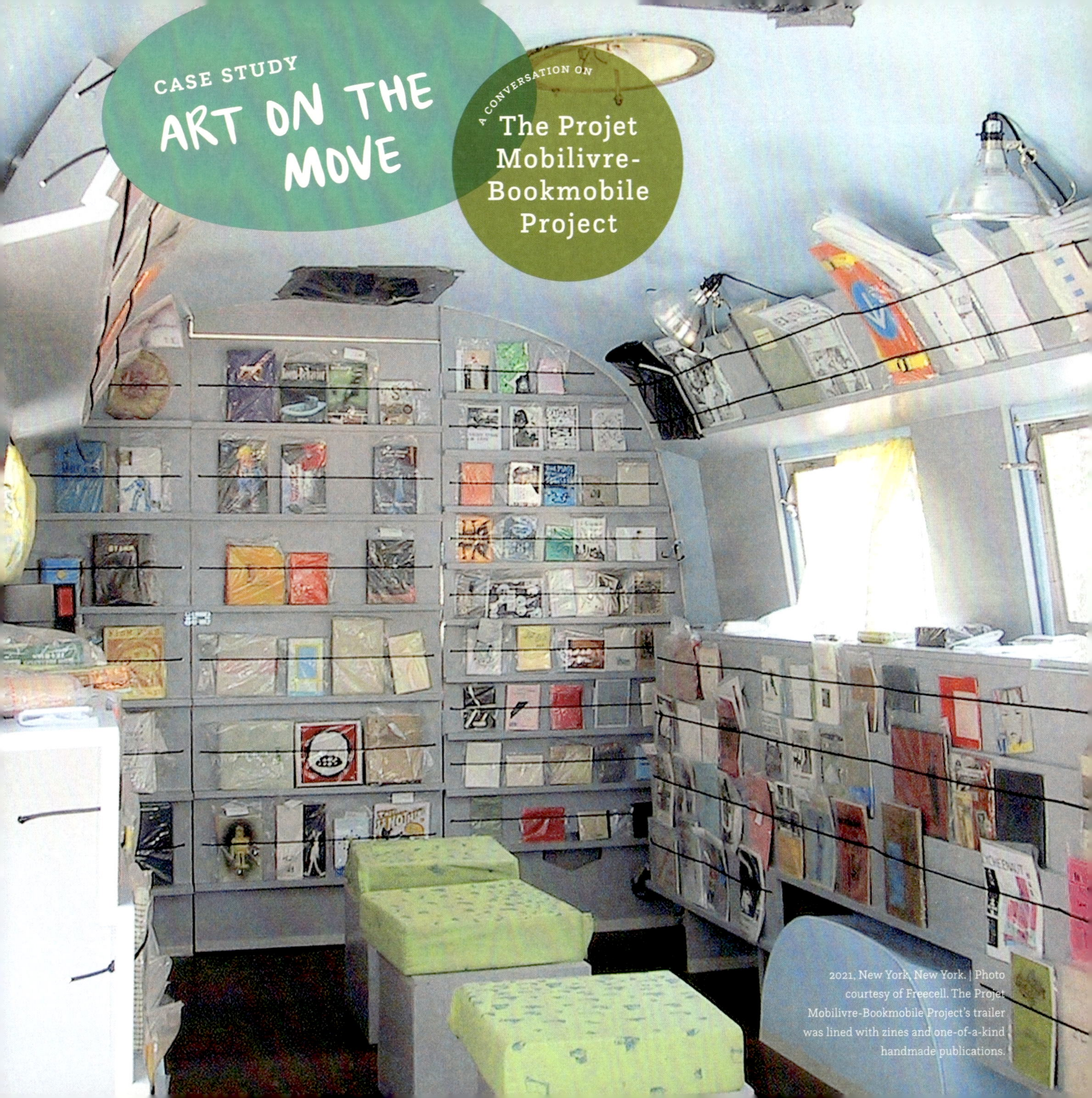

2021, New York, New York. | Photo courtesy of Freecell. The Projet Mobilivre-Bookmobile Project's trailer was lined with zines and one-of-a-kind handmade publications.

Between 2000 and 2005, a shiny Airstream trailer containing a mobile library of zines, books, and indie publications traversed North America. My friend Janet and I were among the lucky visitors who waited in line at their Vancouver stop at the Emily Carr University of Art + Design. This groundbreaking traveling exhibition dazzled us with its collection of one-of-a-kind handmade books and zines from across North America. I spoke to two of its cofounders, Courtney Dailey and Onya Hogan-Finlay, about how the Projet Mobilivre-Bookmobile Project was a consensus-driven collaborative project. Remarkable in the number of volunteers involved and the distances that they were able to travel, the project inspired curious people in Montreal, Philadelphia, Vancouver, Toronto, Halifax, Pittsburgh, New York, and beyond. This grassroots initiative not only crossed borders and over 48,337 miles, it continued to build capacity by offering public workshops in bookbinding, zine-making, and media literacy designed to empower people to share their stories. The project is a truly successful study in consensus-based decision making and combining the best talents of a group to make something incredible come together.

2003, Banff, Alberta. | Photo courtesy of the Projet Mobilivre-Bookmobile Project. Project attendants take a rest in lawn chairs while parked at the Banff Centre.

LEANNE: Can you tell me a bit about the Bookmobile and how the two of you became involved with it?

COURTNEY: Onya and I went to high school together in Ottawa. We've known each other for probably thirty years. When we went to university, we lived together and had a business together. When we started the Bookmobile Project, I was living in Philadelphia with cofounder Ginger Brooks Takahashi, and Onya and cofounder Leila Pourtavaf were living in Montreal, so the project was international from the beginning. One of the core beliefs of the project was to build connections between ideas and people across the US and Canada; we knew that books and zines could help bring diverse groups of people together.

LEANNE: In 2000, when the Bookmobile began, we communicated differently; the internet was still new, and social media didn't exist yet. Zines were something that you learned about through word of mouth. Why were zines and art books so important to you back then?

COURTNEY: After attending university, I moved to Chicago around 1996–97. I became aware that there was this huge world of letterpress printing that had started to happen, and Onya and I started making books together. We were interested in creating artist multiples, and multiples make you think about distribution and serial storytelling.

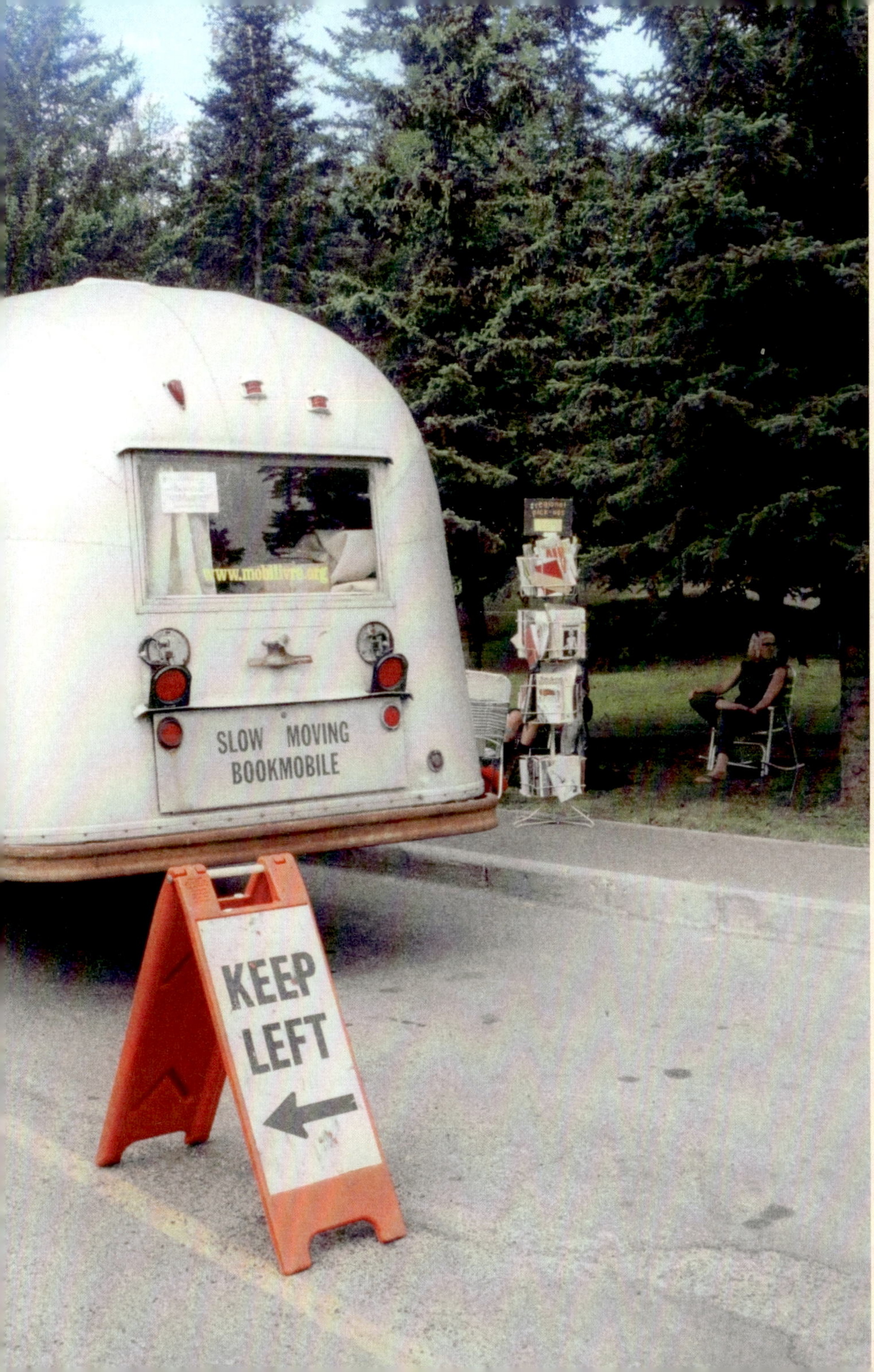

Cofounders of the Projet Mobilivre-Bookmobile Project:

Ginger Brooks Takahashi

Courtney Dailey

Onya Hogan-Finlay

Leila Pourtavaf

Rebecca Watt

We had also come to it from DIY activist backgrounds. Those values stood in pretty sharp contrast to this new-to-us rarefied artist-book world. We were interested in challenging the preciousness of artist books that were in the special collections of libraries. Limited-edition and one-of-a-kind artist books were not mass-distributed objects, like zines or comic books. Zines were communication devices; they were accessible. We were motivated to make printed multiples to address issues and subject matter that no one else was talking about.

LEANNE: How did you go from making books and zines to filling an Airstream trailer with art books and zines and touring across North America?

ONYA: We exhibited a collection of 300 to 400 zines, artist books, and indie publications that would change from year to year. In the first year of the project, Courtney, Ginger, and I started the initial conversation about touring with the collection of artist books and zines for one summer, planning a route to take us through Québec and potentially into the States. We tried to imagine what that would look like, how we would fund the tour, and where we would go. We plotted out our potential route by looking at who we knew at artist-run centers and began making a lot of cold calls. We began by looking within our social circles and networks to find those who might have a connection to venues that would host a visit. All of us were immersed in community-minded collective punk houses, and planning for the first tour evolved around our network and through individual connections.

I remember Leila and I initially saying, "Well, since we're going to do this tour just for one summer, let's just rent a U-Haul trailer and set up some bookshelves." Courtney and Ginger brought up the idea that we needed to create a welcoming, immersive space that would stand out. We decided that an Airstream trailer would be an excellent vehicle. There were many people who helped us get the tour on the road. In our core collective, we would have at least twenty-two people working together over a given year to share in the planning of seasonal tours.

LEANNE: The Airstream trailer looked incredible. How did you come to collaborate with Freecell Architecture on the interior?

COURTNEY: Ginger and I had seen a one-page article in a magazine about an architectural firm called Freecell who had made a book cave at Soft Skull Press's bookstore in New York's Lower East Side. The cave was formed from an awning support and was a really cheap and clever way to make a functional bookshelf. Freecell was a small company—only three people who had just finished graduate school. They always say that they responded because I had neat handwriting.

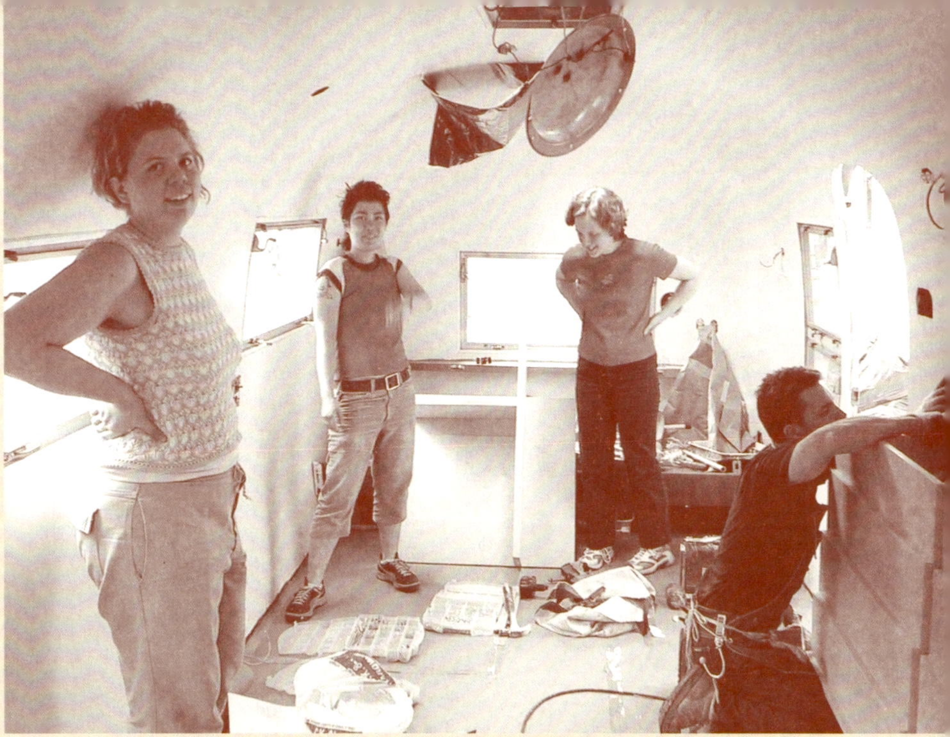

2001, Philadelphia, Pennsylvania. | Photo courtesy of Freecell. Courtney Dailey, Ginger Brooks Takahashi, Lauren Crahan, and Troy Ostrander in the Airstream trailer retrofitted to be a mobile library on wheels by Lauren Crahan and John Hartmann of Freecell.

Airstreams are ubiquitous now, but at the time they didn't have a lot of mainstream visibility. We bought the Bookmobile for $3,000, which is unheard of now. We drove the Airstream from Philadelphia to New York City for a weekend, and we worked with the architects in their studio—running extension cords across the sidewalk in the Lower East Side. We thought we were going to finish the retrofit in a weekend, but then the Freecell team came to Philadelphia so we could finish it there, with many more days of work.

ONYA: The focus of the crew in Montreal was to look at the cultural structures across Canada of artist-run centers and comb through the index of members listed in the RAAV [Regroupement des artistes en arts visuels au Québec] directory. We came up with a list of places to visit and tried to figure out how we would be able to potentially secure a small chunk of funding through grant writing.

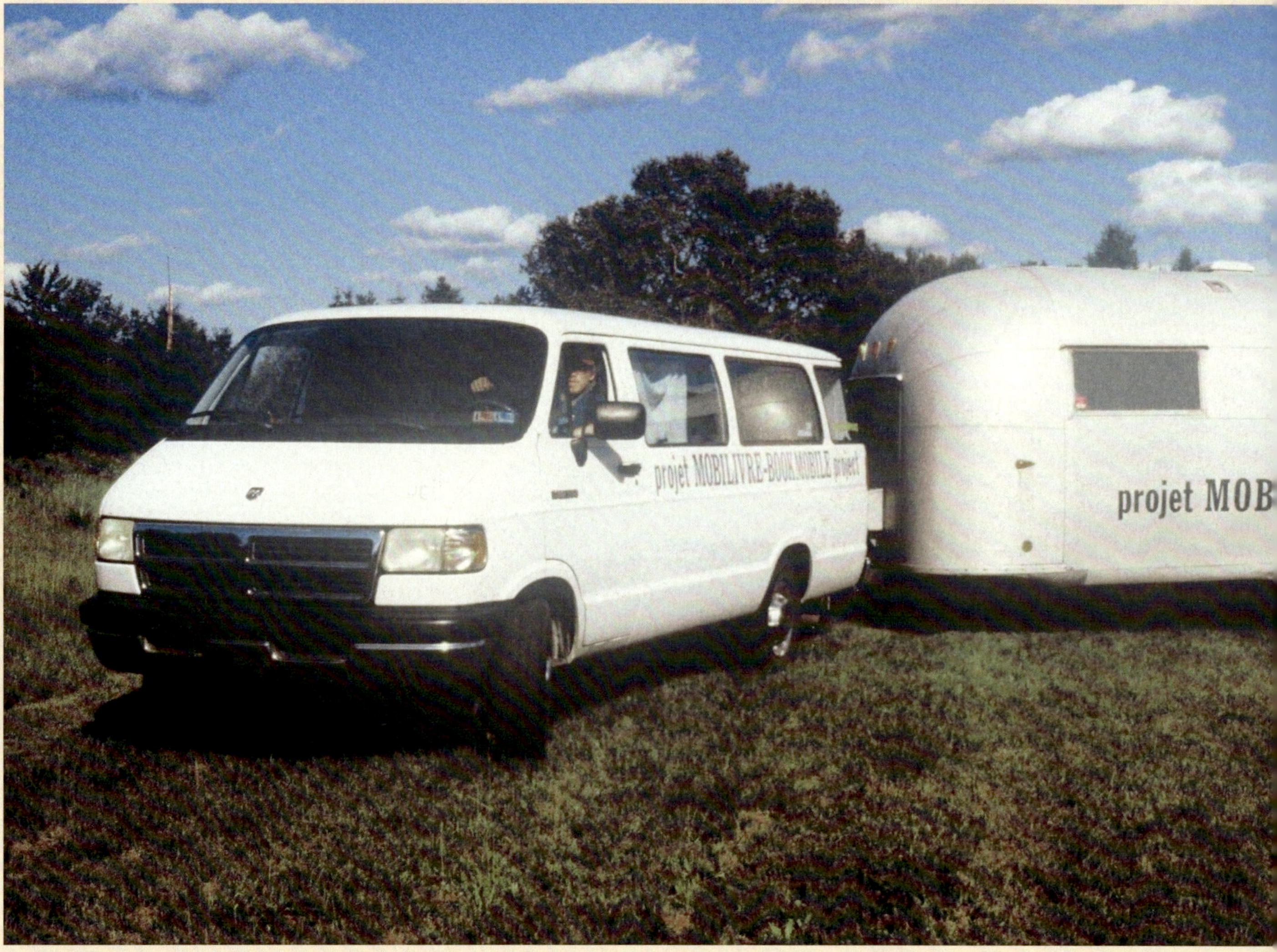

2004, Tuscaloosa, Alabama. | Photo courtesy of the Projet Mobilivre-Bookmobile Project. The Bookmobile on the road.

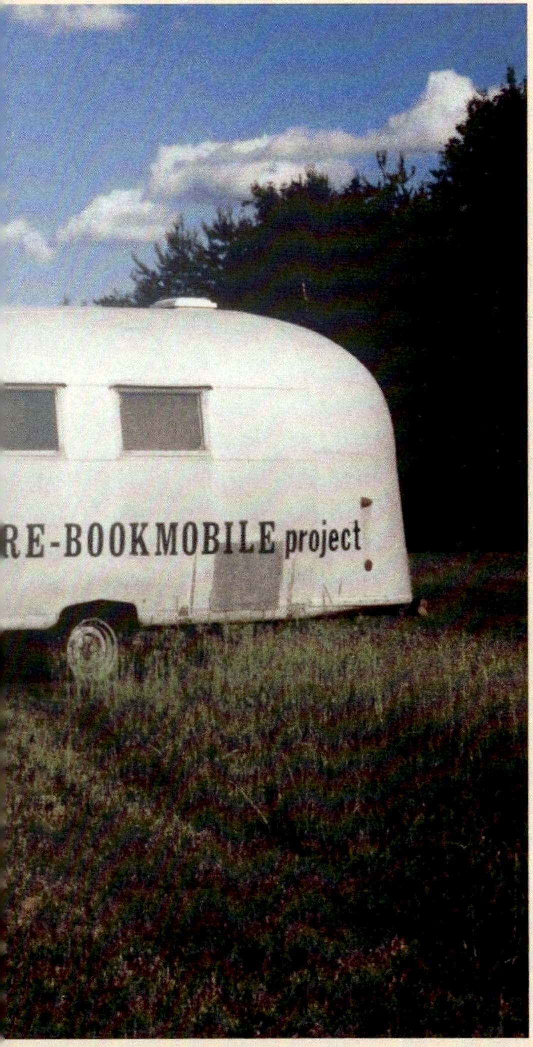

The Bookmobile was a bi-national project, and we had to figure out what that meant in terms of logistics and fundraising. Given that we maintained two headquarters in Montreal and Philly, there were definitely constraints and considerations, but we were so driven to make it work. We would hop on the Greyhound bus to New York to just grab a paintbrush and work around the clock to help prepare the trailer for its first voyage. Each of us was willing to drop everything and show up for the Bookmobile, whether this meant getting ready for the tour, setting up the jury, or raising the rent money to maintain two satellite headquarters.

COURTNEY: We learned a lot by figuring it out as we went along. For instance, fundraising involved collective learning. In Canada, government support for [the] arts is more readily accessible. Comparatively, in the US, there's very little government support, but a much deeper personal philanthropy culture. The institutional structures are very different. We had to navigate through this complexity and figure out what kind of balance we needed to make the project possible.

We were really lucky—cultural production and social practice in the art world was entering the conversation at the time. The Bookmobile wasn't a familiar art form to schools or museums because it didn't fall into the familiar disciplines of painting or dance. It was this other thing. In that moment, we were part of the community of artists who were figuring it out and navigating this world alongside and within institutions.

We were also in our mid- to late twenties, and during the years of the project, our networks of supportive people began to take on more responsibility in their careers at the institutions that we were working with. Our hosts were friends or friends of friends who took a chance on us and helped organize a one- to three-day-long visit.

ONYA: We solicited invitations, and I'm sure that we were refused many times, but as the project grew and started getting recognition, we became more confident. And as it became more established from year to year, we were able to build on funding we were awarded and venues that hosted us. We used the resources that were available to us and just kept asking, you know, with the idea that it can't hurt to ask.

A significant component of the project was teaching people how to make books and zines and producing media literacy workshops. Every once in a while, we would get a book or a zine from someone who had taken a workshop the year before. It was fulfilling for us because they were often someone who may not have thought this medium was accessible to them prior to encountering the Bookmobile. This integration of educational programming with artistic programming plus media literacy was new, even in schools, museums, and artist-run centers.

LEANNE: Was there a natural end to the project?

COURTNEY: We intuitively came to a conclusion when we stopped touring in 2005. We said, "Let's take a pause." We were getting more connected to our careers and to projects that we had going on outside of the Bookmobile.

A lot of people stop doing projects when it's gotten to the point where you're like, "Oh my god, I don't wanna do this." Stopping it when we all still felt some love for the project was an incredible lesson. I think that was part of the reason we could come back ten years later and make a book about the experience [*The Bookmobile Book* (Justseeds, 2014)].

ONYA: As each tour had wrapped up, the artist books that were exhibited in the trailer would either be sent back to the folks who made them, or they would be retained in the Bookmobile collection, which was a bunch of boxes in Courtney and Ginger's Philadelphia studio or in some people's closets in Montreal.

When each of us had had enough space and time away from the project, we knew that we needed to centralize these narratives and to make a lasting document before it was lost. It was a fun reunion where we were able to reconnect with many of the folks who had contributed over the years. We had received multiple requests from authors to write a book about the Bookmobile, and it felt really important to write our own story.

THE PROJET MOBILIVRE-BOOKMOBILE PROJECT *wrapped up in 2006, but a limited number of books that were in the Bookmobile's annual collections are now housed in a public archive at Artexte, an artist-run center in Montreal. The Airstream trailer has been retired; it now exists as a physical space used at the Black Fly Sustainable Living Education Co-operative on unceded Algonquin Nation territory near Lake St. Peter, Ontario.* **mobilivre.org**

CLOCKWISE FROM TOP LEFT: Publications in the Bookmobile's roaming library. DAN WU, *Oriental Whatever #7, #8, #9*, 1999–2000; MATTATHIAS SCHWARTZ, *The Philadelphia Independent*, Vol. 1, #1, 2002; LAURIE COUGHLIN, *Ice Cream Sandwich*, 2000; RICK LINES, *Des pros pour les détenus: Un guide pour créer et réussir des actions communautaires contres VIH/sida*, 2002. | Photos: Léa Trudel.

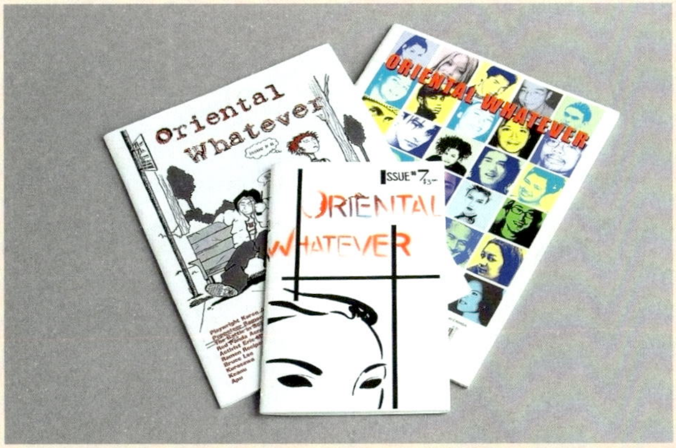

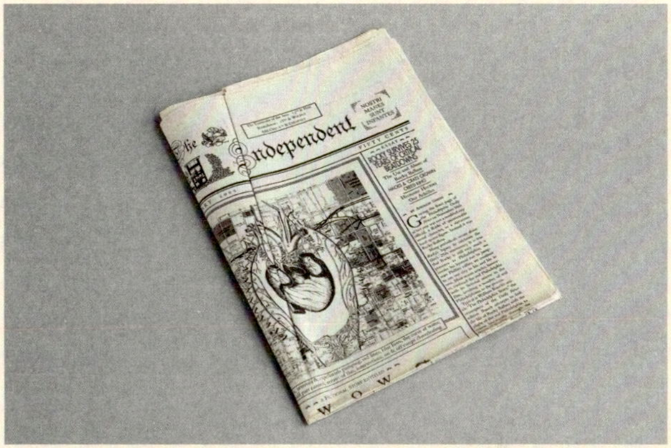

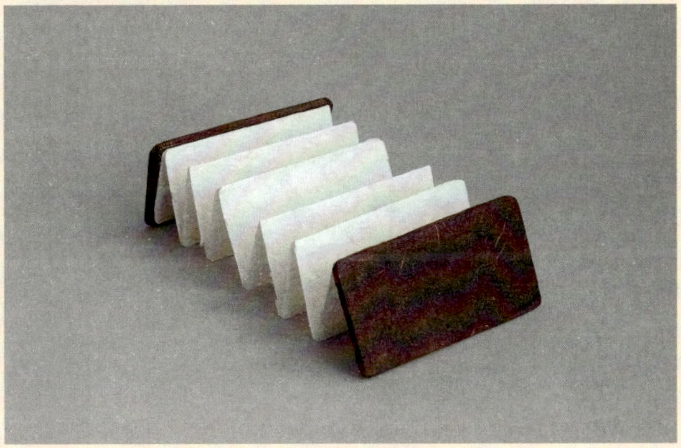

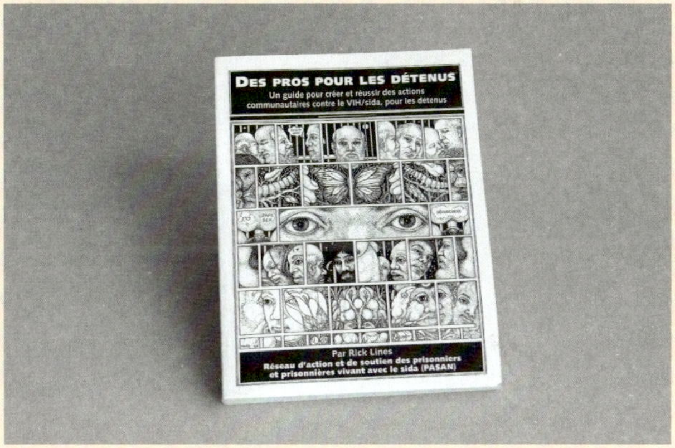

COURTNEY DAILEY *is a collaborator and organizer of projects both large and small, currently living in her home base of Portland, Oregon, where she is a creative director by day. She is a cofounder of the Projet Mobilivre-Bookmobile Project. Prior to moving west, she lived in Philadelphia and was a member of Space 1026, a collective gallery and studio space, for seven years. Courtney graduated from California College of the Arts in 2010 with an* MA *in curatorial practice, and she also holds a* BFA *from Concordia University.*

ONYA HOGAN-FINLAY *is a Canadian artist with a* BFA *from Concordia University and an* MFA *from the University of Southern California. Her interdisciplinary practice uses humor to look at gender and marginalized subjects through installation, drawing, and public interventions. She is a cofounder of the Projet Mobilivre-Bookmobile Project. Previously based in* LA*, she now lives in rural Nova Scotia.* **onyahoganfinlay.com**

WHAT GOES AROUND COMES AROUND

What's next? If your creative project has a definitive end, you may choose to quietly move on to your next idea. Alternatively, you may find that you have a sustained interest in your project as you continue to meet audiences who want to keep it going. Institutions such as libraries, art galleries, nonprofits, and schools and independent artists can offer an extended life to many types of projects.

To facilitate a project over a long period of time, an artist may choose to go on the road and work with public institutions in different cities far from home. Some may be lucky to have commissions to pay for ongoing work, but for most of us, this likely means your project becoming the thing that fills your nights and weekends alongside day jobs, school, or your own entrepreneurial work.

While it is a dream to do creative work on an ongoing basis, it is not always possible for everyone. If you don't want to travel or to continue the work, that doesn't mean that the project has to end. There are many other ways that you can extend a project's life through other people. Here are a few examples of how some of the artists in this book have given their projects longevity.

NEAR AND FAR, EXPAND WITH LOCAL HOSTS

The Poetry Society of New York (see interview on page 172) has extended its reach into other countries with their popular NYC-based Poetry Brothel series in cities as diverse as Madrid, Bogotá, Mexico City, Edmonton, Reykjavík, London, and Valparaiso. Rather than organizing these events herself, organizer Stephanie Berger carefully vetted local hosts to organize and run Poetry Brothel events in their home cities. The Poetry Society of New York remains the umbrella organization that supports and encourages this network of trusted hosts.

EXPAND YOUR REACH

Terrence Kelleman of the BE MIGHTY Project (see interview on page 43) found that other people wanted to put his tags up in their own cities. For this reason, he worked with others to translate his original tags into other languages. He also created an online store to allow participants to either download digital pages that they could print and post themselves or buy pre-printed labels for a nominal fee.

SPIRITED AWAY

Artist Candy Chang (see page 187) has made an online resource kit for anyone who wants to replicate her Before I Die project independently. People in over seventy-five countries have completed over 5,000 Before I Die walls using this digital kit.

On the Before I Die website, she provides detailed instructions for prospective project leaders. The site includes a checklist of materials, a step-by-step instructional guide, an option to buy ready-made stencils, and templates. Not only does Candy provide instructions for how to physically make the work, she also outlines her intentions for those who want to replicate the project. She asks participants to read through the FAQs and a page called "The Spirit of the Project" before using her downloadable resources. "The Spirit of the Project" advises that the project be open and accessible to anyone, that it focus on communication (rather than persuasion or sales techniques), and that the title, Before I Die, remain as intended, as acknowledgment of mortality is key to the project. This generous and intelligent offering provides future participants with everything they need while offering some governance around the intended impact of Candy's work.

Before I Die has been released under a Creative Commons[4] Attribution-NonCommercial-NoDerivatives 4.0 International License, which means that creators have the right to copy and redistribute Candy's work in any medium or format as long as they use it for noncommercial purposes, do not distribute modified versions of the work, and give appropriate credit to the original creator.

4 Creative Commons is a global nonprofit organization that enables sharing and reuse of knowledge and creativity through the provision of free legal tools. Among their projects, they provide Creative Commons licenses to give any person a free, simple way to grant copyright permissions for their creative work. To learn more about how to apply Creative Commons licenses to your work, visit *creativecommons.org*.

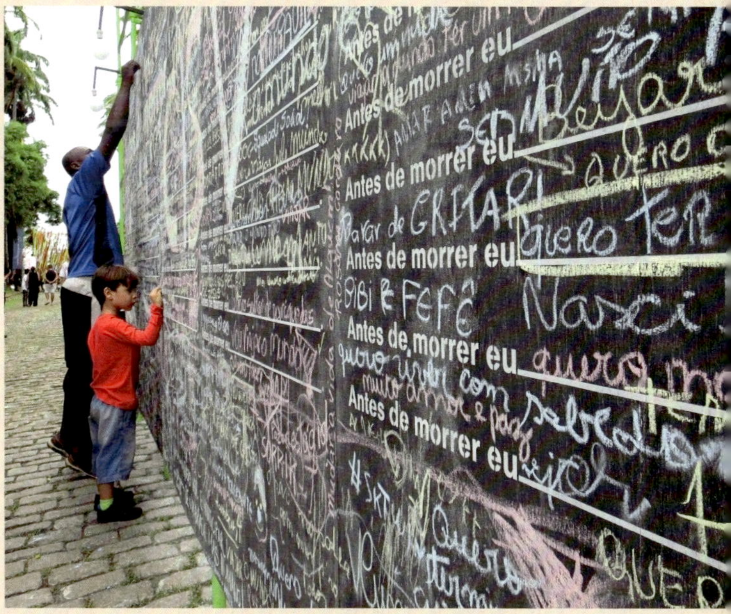

CANDY CHANG, *Before I Die*, Brazil. | Photo: Candy Chang

GIVE IT AWAY, GIVE IT AWAY, GIVE IT AWAY NOW

What can you do to make your project scalable for others? Why not try the following:

- Make a video documenting your process.
- Consider gifting instructional materials through digital downloads.
- Train other artists who would be good representatives of your methods and allow them to create "franchises" of your project.
- Create a book or zine that reflects on your experience and all that you learned in doing your project.
- Mentor another artist to take over your project and make it their own.
- Create a manifesto for others who want to become part of the project.
- Create a website, blog, or social media gallery to share images from participants.
- Tell the story of your project through a film.

THE JOURNEY, NOT THE DESTINATION

They say that all good things must come to an end, but really, good things evolve. Your project may not seem to change much day by day, but as time passes, you will find that the world around you has changed. There will be new things that you need to consider about your processes or your project. Major life changes, technological developments, social justice movements, artistic passions, relationships, global pandemics, financial issues, health concerns—each of these can shape how we engage with our creative work over time.

What works today may not work tomorrow. In the past ten years, we've gone from the web being a place of blog updates and Flickr photo galleries to a place of live-streaming creators, massive debates on social media, and the selling of just about everything. We've been through a global pandemic, during which many of the traditional means for delivering art (theaters, bookstores, gallery spaces) were put on hold. People have had to reinvent themselves and their creative practices. No matter what happens, you will likely need to alter your project over time. You might change your tools, your tech, or your perspective. Change is constant.

PROMPT

Write It Down before You Forget

What stands out for you about the project? Can you respond to these questions?

- How many places was the project or event staged in?
- How many participants did you host?
- How many visitors came to the website?
- How many people did you teach, share stories with, or amplify?
- How many hours did the team spend developing the project?
- How many tons of materials were used, shared, or saved?
- How many places did you visit?
- What were your favorite memories?
- How did you know that the project had reached people?

Every element that you collect about your story adds to the nuance of your project's history, including what you achieved and who you touched. Take the time to compile this information and share it alongside your project and any materials you produce. You might keep it for your personal use, or it may come in handy for a website, exhibit, or book in the future.

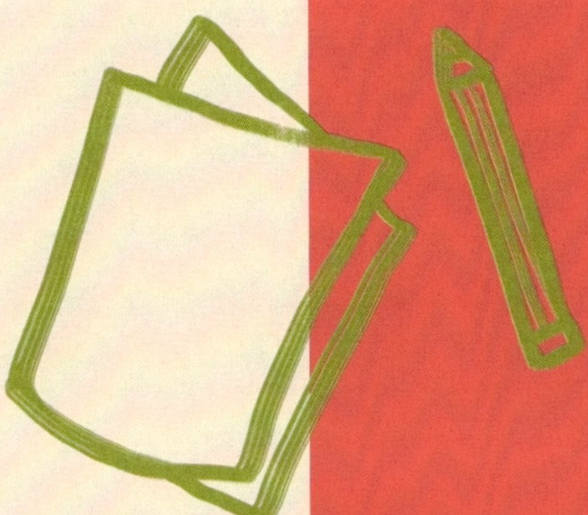

What does change in an artistic project look like? Here are some examples:

- Training others to carry on the project for you
- Dismantling or destroying the project
- Filing for nonprofit status
- Changing artistic direction
- Gifting a project to a school, museum, gallery, or artist-run center
- Creating new streams of programming
- Expanding into new creative forms
- Creating a board of directors
- Taking on a mentor or a coach
- Running educational programs
- Monetizing
- Duplicating in other cities
- Creating new partnerships with outside institutions
- Tool kit building
- Donating or repurposing your materials
- Making a commemorative book or film
- Archiving digital materials
- Quietly fading away
- Consciously calling an end to the project

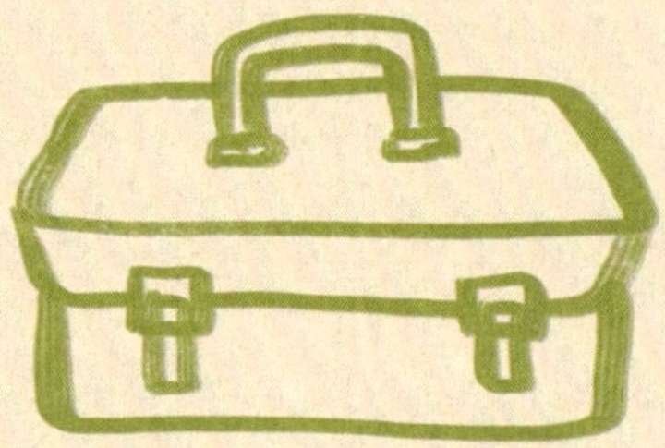

Life brings us many surprises; you never know what new opportunities will present themselves. The artist you are today will inform the artist that you become tomorrow, whether you choose to keep your project going over days or decades.

CAPTURE THE FLEETING MOMENT

Over the life span of your project, I recommend that you document as much as you can. Take photos of early experiments, meetings, swatches, journal entries, photos, and prototypes. As your memory fades, this ephemera will help you remember your journey and allow you to share the story of your project with others.

IN THE VAULT

Before you completely wrap up the project, take some time to do some deep thinking about the experience that you've had. Whether you journal or host a conversation or tape yourself talking about it, don't forget to capture your thoughts on this project. Time is tricky and can change our hearts. Memory can prove unreliable. When you revisit the project in the future, you may one day find yourself surprised looking back at these materials and discovering what you have romanticized or forgotten.

Dig deep into your experience and be honest. What do you remember most about the project? What impacted you? What was hard? What would you have changed? What do you regret? What would you keep the same?

Being a public artist is a constant balance of internal trust and external exchange, where you continually learn from those around you. How did the project impact others? What criticism did you hear? What feedback did you receive? Most importantly, what did you learn?

Your post-project recollections will inform your next creative endeavor. Making a creative workplace puts you in dialogue with many people—yourself, the creator that you were, and creator that you will eventually be. Don't miss the opportunity to listen to your inner voice.

We are each part of a long historical line of creativity, and each artistic act builds upon the legacy of work that came before it. Making things with friends and strangers is an extraordinary act of hope and faith, but I know that you are up for the challenge. Don't wait another moment—the only way to know what comes next is to begin.

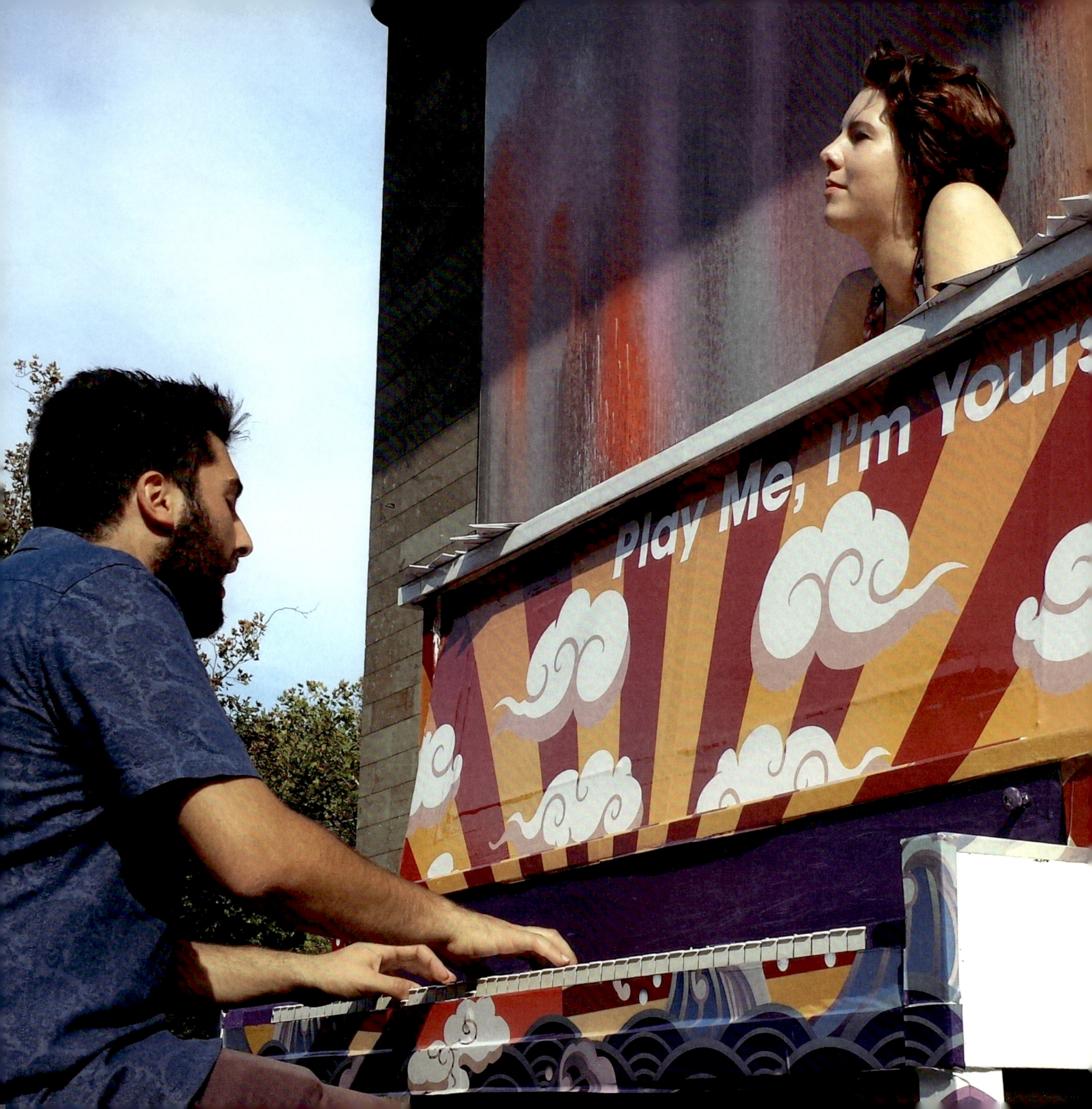
Play Me, I'm Yours

ACKNOWLEDGMENTS

Thank you to the team at Arsenal Pulp Press. I truly value the long-standing relationship that we've had, and I still cannot believe that I have the good fortune to work with such an incredible publisher. Brian, Robert, Cynara, Shirarose, Catharine, Jaiden, and Jazmin: thank you for everything that you do. I'm honored to work with you.

Even when self-isolating, one does not write alone. I'm eternally grateful for the wisdom of The Clarence scribblers—much love to Laura Farina, Erin Ashenhurst, and Rachel Burns. I would also like to acknowledge the wonderful folks of Just Write Tuesday Night, especially Noel Coloma, for cohosting all of those weird pandemic nights, and to Shannon Stange, for providing a virtual platform for writers.

This book would not have been possible without the artists who entrusted their voices, images, and time to me. Thank you to Chris Bentzen, Stephanie Berger, Rebecca Bray, Minahil Bukhari, Mark Busse, Candy Chang, Sara Clugage, Courtney Dailey, Thomas Dambo, Stephen Duncombe, Dave Eggers, Lee Everson, Betsy Greer, Tyree Guyton, Aram Han Sifuentes, Melissa Higgs, Jim Hoehnle, Onya Hogan-Finlay, Luke Jerram, Jacob Keinicke, Terrence Kelleman, Erin Kruczek, Steve Lambert, Meg Lewis, Juan Martinez, Colette Miller, Troels Nielsen, Steven Peterman, Mustaali Raj, Katherine Soucie, Kevin Spenst, Amanda Uhle, Catherine West, Diana Weymar, and Jenenne Whitfield. You made it meaningful.

LUKE JERRAM. | Photo: The Great Imposter. A Play Me, I'm Yours street piano in Melbourne, Australia, 2014.

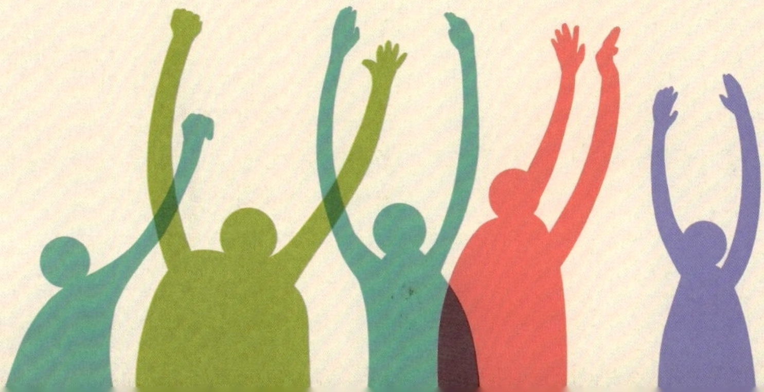

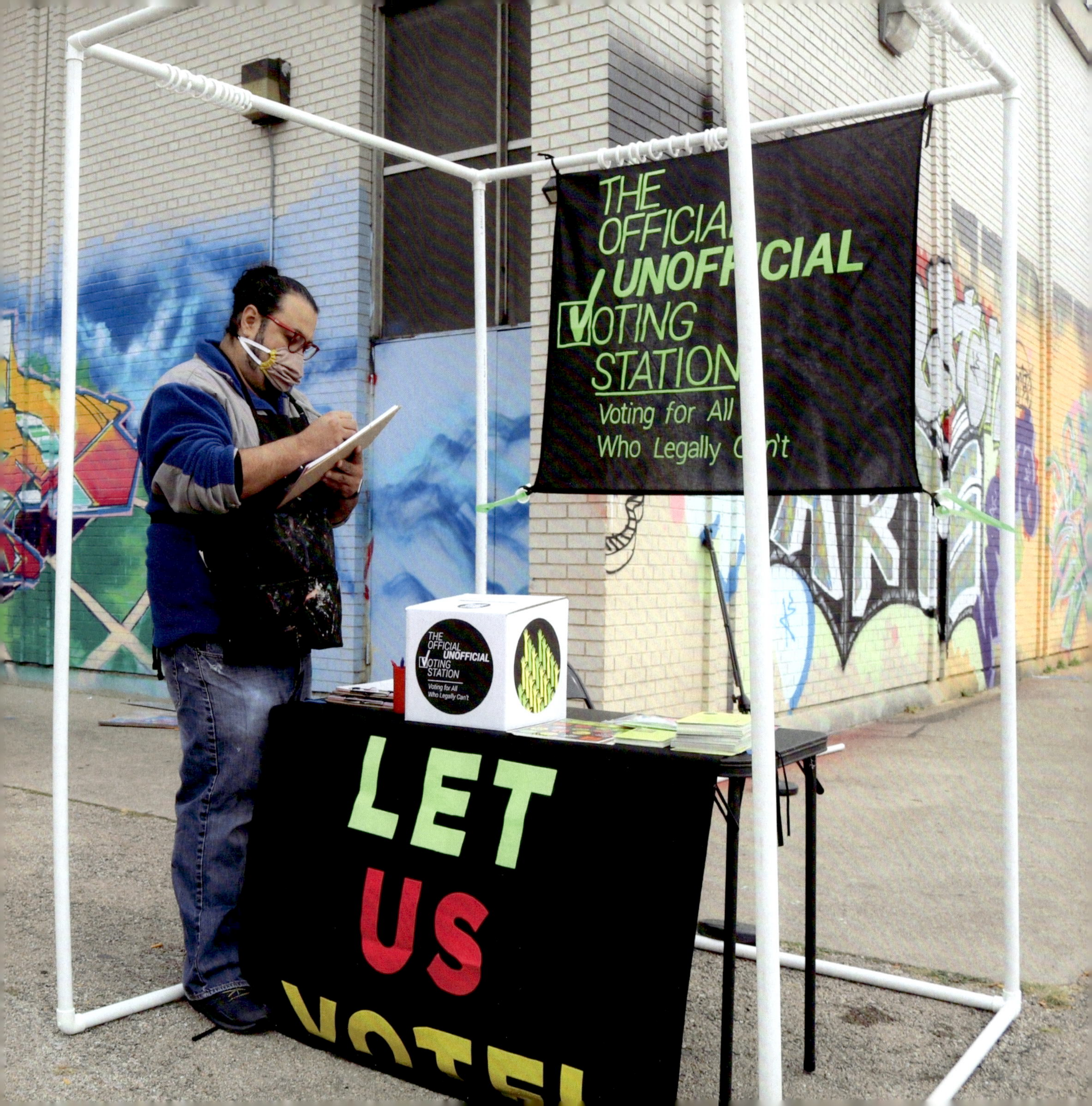
THE OFFICIAL UNOFFICIAL VOTING STATION
Voting for All Who Legally Can't
LET
US

INDEX

ARAM HAN SIFUENTES, *Official Unofficial Voting Station*, 2020, Chicago, Illinois. | Photo: Aram Han Sifuentes. Wide Awakes Chicago: Family Affair.